T0311205

The Colony of New Netherland

THE COLONY OF NEW NETHERLAND

A Dutch Settlement in Seventeenth-Century America

JAAP JACOBS

Cornell University Press
ITHACA AND LONDON

Copyright © 2009 by Cornell University

All rights reserved. Except for brief quotations in a review, this book, or parts thereof, must not be reproduced in any form without permission in writing from the publisher. For information, address Cornell University Press, Sage House, 512 East State Street, Ithaca, New York 14850.

First published 2009 by Cornell University Press
First printing, Cornell Paperbacks, 2009

Printed in the United States of America

Library of Congress Cataloging-in-Publication Data

Jacobs, Jaap, 1963–
    [Zegenrijk gewest. English]
    The colony of New Netherland : a Dutch settlement in seventeenth-century
America / Jaap Jacobs.
        p. cm.
    Includes bibliographical references and index.
    ISBN 978-0-8014-7516-0 (pbk. : alk. paper)
    1. New Netherland—History.   2. New York (State)—History—Colonial period,
ca. 1600–1775.   3. Dutch—New York (State)—History—17th century.   I. Title.

    F122.1.J33   2009
    974.7'02—dc22   2009019266

Cornell University Press strives to use environmentally responsible suppliers and materials to the fullest extent possible in the publishing of its books. Such materials include vegetable-based, low-VOC inks and acid-free papers that are recycled, totally chlorine-free, or partly composed of nonwood fibers. For further information, visit our website at www.cornellpress.cornell.edu.

Paperback printing   10 9 8 7 6 5 4 3 2 1

To Charly

Contents

Preface

The year 2009 marks the four-hundredth anniversary of Dutch-American relations, commemorating the first voyage, in 1609, by Henry Hudson, an Englishman in Dutch service, up the river that now bears his name. The news of his "discovery" provided the impetus for Dutch merchants to equip fur-trading expeditions to the area, resulting in the eventual colonization. New Netherland became the only Dutch colony in mainland North America; it gradually changed from a small trading post into a settlement colony with distinctive Dutch features. Yet nowadays, visitors to New York City can walk the streets without being aware of its origins. New Amsterdam has disappeared under the towering skyscrapers and the asphalt of the streets and avenues of the modern city. Signs of the old Dutch colony can still be found, but only if you know where to look, for instance in the landmarks and place names along the Hudson: Claverack, Tappan Zee, Kinderhook, and Watervliet. Along the Atlantic coast, other names, sometimes Anglicized, show Dutch origins: Coney Island, Sandy Hook, Barnegat Bay, Cape May. Further south, the Dutch pronunciation [sxœylkɪl] of the Schuylkill River provides the ultimate tongue twister to modern Philadelphians, who settle for [sku:kəl].

New Netherland also lives on in numerous documents on both sides of the Atlantic. Ever since the early nineteenth century, translators have worked on these documents, producing translations of varying quality. The early translations are defective in many places, whereas the modern translations by Charles Gehring, director of the New Netherland Project, are of an outstanding quality. Yet true historical scholarship can come only through direct contact with original sources; for me, a Dutchman used to reading seventeenth-century Dutch documents, relying solely on translations was never an option. However good a translation may be, it still imposes a screen of varying transparency between the researcher and his sources.

Also, I prefer to make my own mistakes and not to be accountable for those of others. I have therefore checked the original Dutch documents every time, during which process I also found much material that has not been translated and in some cases discovered documents that were completely unknown. For untranslated materials, a full reference is provided, but for documents available in published translations, short references will suffice. These consist of abbreviations followed by a page number. A list of abbreviations precedes the endnotes. Anyone tracing the original manuscripts will find complete information in previous editions of this book.

This book is organized into seven chapters, preceded by an introduction that charts the lay of the land and the indigenous inhabitants. The chapters are thematic, rather than chronological, which allows the unique character of New Netherland as the only seventeenth-century Dutch colony in the Atlantic that developed from a trading post into a settlement colony to take center stage. For each theme—immigration, government, economy, religion, status and mentality—a comparison with the Dutch Republic is made. Within David Armitage's triad of Cis-, Trans-, and Circum-Atlantic historiography, this book is first and predominantly Trans-Atlantic, with the comparison between New Netherland and the Dutch Republic as its backbone. It is Cis-Atlantic ("the history of the people who crossed the Atlantic, who lived on its shores and who participated in the communities it made possible") second, and Circum-Atlantic (the study of "particular places as unique locations within an Atlantic world") only third, but I have tried where relevant to position it in the general framework of the Dutch Atlantic in the seventeenth century.[1]

All the quotations have been translated by me, and they often differ from published translations. Translating the seventeenth-century Dutch into modern English brings along some specific problems. For instance, in nineteenth- and twentieth-century publications the Dutch words *wilden* (plural), *wilt* (masculine singular), and *wildinne* (feminine singular) are usually translated into either the neutral "Indians" or into "savages," rather too strong to the modern ear. In both cases some of the nuance of the original is lost, especially as several other terms are also used. I have used *Indians* in the main text and left the original in the quotations in italics. For a number of other words, I have chosen to use an italicized Dutch word rather than an English equivalent that may evoke a divergent meaning in the reader's mind. For personal names, I followed the method outlined by Charles Gehring: "Professional and craft names as well as nicknames and places of origins associated with individuals are kept in the Dutch."[2] Seventeenth-century Dutch patronymics usually end in various abbreviations, such as *ss, sen,* or *szen,* for *zoon* (son). These variations have all been standardized in my own text and are indicated by *sz.* In quotations I have left the spelling unaltered. Amounts of money are designated by three numbers, indicating guldens, stuivers, and penningen (guilders, stivers, and pennies) and written with an

f symbol and colons, for example, f23:2:10. Last, in New Netherland the Gregorian calendar style ("new style") was used, which differed from the Julian calendar ("old style"), used in England and its colonies, by ten days.

The origins of this edition go back to September 2006, when I was the Quinn Foundation Visiting Professor at the Department of History of Cornell University. Alison Kalett, then acquisitions editor, stopped by to ask me whether I had anything that Cornell University Press might want to publish. This book is the result. In preparing it, I have received support and suggestions on where to cut from Martha Shattuck and Firth Fabend, to whom many thanks are due. David Voorhees, Joel Grossman, and Paul Otto pointed out some errors, which have been corrected. The support of Michael McGandy of Cornell University Press was of high professional quality. Of course, all remaining errors are mine.

The opportunity to spend a semester at Cornell, as well as a semester at the McNeil Center for Early American Studies at the University of Pennsylvania during the spring of 2007, was made possible by the Quinn Foundation, for which I am very grateful. Mary Beth Norton, Jon Parmenter, and Dan Richter were instrumental in making my stay at their respective universities a success, while Charles Gehring initiated the idea of a visiting professorship. The importance of Charly to New Netherland studies is inestimable. He took upon himself the task of translating the New York Dutch manuscripts in 1974, after a gap of many decades. His work, through translations, articles, and talks, has put New Netherland and the continuation of Dutch culture on the historical map. Ever since I first contacted the New Netherland Project in 1992, Charly has been very generous and supportive. He has shown me great friendship over the years. Therefore, this book is dedicated to Charly.

Introduction

"A Blessèd Country, Where Milk and Honey Flow"

O fruitful land, heaped up with blessings kind,
Whoe'er your several virtues brings to mind,
Its proper value to each gift assigned,
                                    Will soon discover,
If ever land perfection have attained,
That you in all things have that glory gained;
Ungrateful mortal, who, your worth disdained,
                                    Would pass you over.

In his "Praise of New Netherland," Jacob Steendam depicts the colony as a land of milk and honey. He praises the form in which the four elements manifest themselves in the colony: its air, clear, sharp, and moderate; its fire—the sun—warm and pure; its water, clear, fresh, and sweet; and its earth, varied and yielding rich harvests. He extols its geology, the fish in its rivers, its animals, its plants. It is "a happy land," "a very Eden." Steendam appears to have been genuinely impressed by the natural beauty and the plentiful resources of New Netherland.[1]

European Eyes

Describing the New World with biblical comparisons is perhaps the ultimate way for a European to represent the unfamiliar in familiar terms. The encounter with what to them was a New World posed numerous problems for Europeans, who struggled to make sense of it and found it difficult to incorporate it into their worldview. In this gradual process the descriptions of travelers played a crucial role. After attempting to wrap their minds around everything new they had experienced, the second step was to describe it to their audience back in the Old World in an understandable way. This applied even more to Adriaen van der Donck, who in 1655 published his *Beschryvinge van Nieuw-Nederlant* (*Description of New Netherland*). His motives included enticing more people to come over. Like others, he tried to connect with what was familiar to his readers and emphasized similarities in an attempt to bridge the two worlds.

A Newfound Netherland

Why was it named New Netherland? Adriaen van der Donck provides two explanations. New Netherland was

> fertile and situated in a moderate climate, possessing good opportunities for trade, harbors, waters, fisheries, weather, and wind and many other worthy appurtenances corresponding with the Netherlands, or in truth and more accurately exceeding the same. So it is for good reasons named New Netherland, being as much as to say, another or a newfound Netherland.[2]

More important than the similarities between old and new Netherlands was his second explanation: Dutch sailors had been the first to visit and populate the area. In the same way, Van der Donck wrote, the French named their colony in Canada New France, although its climate displayed considerable differences from that of France. The same was true for New Sweden on the South River, where the climate was rather warmer than that of Sweden. As was common practice in European expansion around the globe, in naming first discovery took precedence over similarities between the old world and the new.[3]

In the seventeenth century the primacy of water transportation limited the presence of Dutch colonists to the areas accessible by boat along the coast and along the banks of the colony's main rivers. The descriptions of the colony, of which Van der Donck's is the most extensive and most important, therefore generally begin with the coast and then proceed inland via the rivers. Contemporaries knew little about the interior. Van der Donck reports that several Dutchmen had traveled inland as far as seventy or eighty miles from the sea, but no one knew how large the continent was. They traded with Indians living twenty or more days' journey inland, but from the Indians' reaction when asked about the size of the continent, Van der Donck surmised that they did not know. Other indications, such as the large number of beavers the Indians trapped in the interior and the climatic features, led Van der Donck to conclude that the continent must be several hundreds of miles wide, but its exact size remained unknown to him.[4]

Coasts and Rivers

The first part of New Netherland that an immigrant arriving from the Dutch Republic saw was, of course, the coastline, which is why Van der Donck

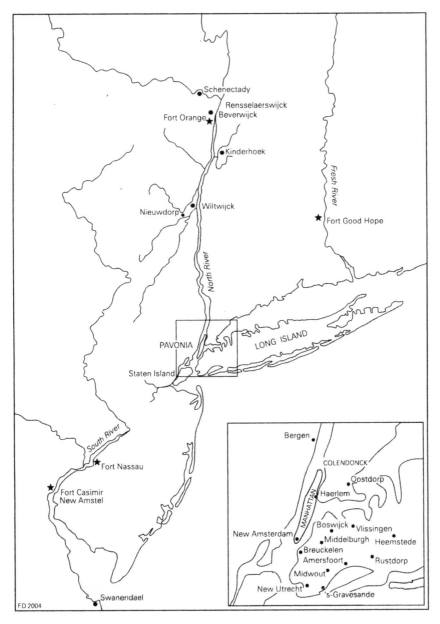

1. New Netherland, ca. 1664. By permission of Brill.

opens his *Beschryvinge* with it. He describes it as clean and sandy, with good anchorage, due to the sandy soil and the lack of severe gales from the sea. In some places the foreshore was broken up into islands, which were useful for keeping cattle, as they could not stray away. The creeks inland were navigable, and therein lay the primary usefulness of the rivers, channels, and creeks of New Netherland.[5]

Van der Donck provides little detail on the navigability of the bays and rivers, but he could afford to be brief, since the coast of New Netherland had been described extensively in 1625 by Johannes de Laet in his book *Nieuwe wereldt* (*New World*). De Laet, a *bewindhebber* (director) of the Amsterdam chamber of the West India Company, compiled this work to provide the other directors of the recently founded Company with sound information about America. His main intention was to describe the geography, and the work is filled with descriptions of the coasts, with copious details about distances, sandbanks, and the depths and navigability of the rivers. De Laet, who never went to America in person, based his work on the journals and reports of Henry Hudson (now lost) and Cornelis Jacobsz May, among others.[6]

Both De Laet and Van der Donck indicate two large rivers as the most important, today's Delaware and Hudson Rivers. The most southerly river in New Netherland, the Delaware River, was named the "Zuydtrivier" (South River). According to Van der Donck, some compared the South River to the Amazon, not so much in size as in other attributes. Fertile stretches of land along the South River made this area highly suitable for colonization. Van der Donck regarded the bay and the river, despite the sandbanks, as reasonably navigable, but thirty years earlier De Laet had thought differently: "The bay within is full of sandbars and shoals, and even though there are numerous kills and channels, one should not come in unless he is familiar with the bay, for it is a dangerous bay."[7] The difference may reflect the increase in geographical knowledge. In the thirty years between De Laet and Van der Donck, Dutch ships had sailed the South River regularly, and the sandbanks had been charted. On the other hand, Van der Donck, in his efforts to promote the colonization of the area, had a tendency to portray New Netherland in a rosy tint.[8]

The second river was the "Noort-Rivier" (North River), "the most famous and most populated of New Netherland."[9] Various names were used for this river: "Rio de Montaigne," the "Manhattes rieviere," the "Groote Rivier," and "de grootte Mouritse reviere," after Prince Maurits.[10] The name most frequently used was "Noort-Rivier." According to Van der Donck, the bay into which the North River flows was large enough to accommodate over a thousand large ships. It was easy to sail into this bay between the "Hamelshoofden" (the Narrows), he wrote, and with a favorable tide ships could sail through to New Amsterdam in one stretch.[11] On the west bank of the North River, opposite Manhattan, lay the area called Achter Kol, with "a great deal of waste reedy land."[12] The North River was a tidal river for many miles. Even beyond the colony of Kiliaen van Rensselaer, Rensselaerswijck, in the north of New Netherland near Fort Orange (present-day Albany), the influence of the tides was noticeable. Slightly to the north of Rensselaerswijck lay the confluence of the North River with the Mohawk River coming from the west, where the Cohoes Falls were. Van der Donck was clearly impressed by this waterfall: it was "very pleasant to behold. If there were any ancient poets there, they could conjure up wondrous and pleasant tales of this place, as being very suitable for that."[13] The other branch of the river came from the north and was navigable for small boats. According to the Indians, the river rose in a large lake, from which the "river of Canada" (St. Lawrence River) also sprang. It was named "het lack der Iracoysen" (the lake of the Iroquois, today Lake Ontario). The Indians correctly reported that it was possible to sail in a small boat from the North River to the St. Lawrence River, but Van der Donck doubted this.[14]

Of much less importance was the "Varsche rivier" (Fresh River, Connecticut River), called "Fresh" because its waters were less saline than the South River and the North River, as it was less affected by tidal flow. In his *Nieuwe wereldt,* De Laet paid little attention to the Fresh River, which in some places was quite shallow and not easily navigable. Van der Donck, on the other hand, praised the Fresh River for its navigability, its good fertile soil, and its good opportunities for the fur trade. It was all academic, however, for by 1655, when he published his *Beschryvinge,* the English were in firm possession of the Fresh River, and Van der Donck did not find it worthwhile to devote much attention to it.[15]

Van der Donck describes the other waterways in a manner that shows his utilitarian perspective: water mills could be erected on the many small streams, and the lakes were well furnished with fish. He considered the waterways useful for transport and for powering water mills of great importance, but he also noticed the beauty of the natural surroundings, for instance of the waterfall at Cohoes. In placing primary importance on the usefulness of nature's gifts, Van der Donck was typical of his time, in which the world was seen as having been created to serve mankind.[16]

Land and Soil

The same emphasis on the potential utility of nature can be found in other descriptions of New Netherland's waters and land. Quoth Johannes Megapolensis:

> The country here is in general like that in Germany. The land is good, and very rich in every one of those provisions that the human body needs, except clothes, linen, woolen stockings, shoes etc., which are all dear here. The country is very mountainous, partly soil, partly rocks, and so exceedingly high that they [the mountains] seem almost to touch the clouds.[17]

The soil in the mountains was of a reddish type of sand or stone, but near the rivers it was mostly clay, described by Megapolensis as very fertile. Van der Donck was rather more specific in his description of the types of soil. Along the coast the soil was mostly sandy but always mixed with some clay. The soil along the rivers was generally black, mixed with clay, a foot or more deep. He spoke highly of the plains of hundreds or even thousands of *morgens* (a measure of land equal to about two acres) along the rivers, regarding them as fit sites for future villages. Some of these plains were flooded in the springtime, as were the river forelands in Holland, but, he wrote, they could be diked, drained, and cultivated, thus bringing New Netherland within the mental framework of his Dutch readership in *patria*.[18]

Van der Donck opined that the pleasant vistas in the hills and mountains would provide delight for lovers of landscape paintings or hunting. More important, he presumed that minerals could be found in the hills. In 1625 Willem Verhulst, one of the early directors of the colony, was explicitly instructed to explore this possibility. Like other Europeans, for instance Columbus at the end of the fifteenth century, the Dutch colonists were obsessed with precious metals. The possible presence of gold ore in the vicinity of Rensselaerswijck raised hopes when one of the Indians visiting the area appeared to have decorated his face with it. The location where he had found the ore was examined, and samples were dispatched to the Dutch Republic in two ships. Both ships sank, and it was only after replacement samples had been sent that it turned out that the material was not gold but probably pyrite. However, copper and mercury were found in New Netherland. Of less value, but nonetheless useful, was the clay, which was suitable for use in pottery and brick making. Also found were a type of stone suitable for making millstones, and quartz, alabaster, and marble, although little use was made of them at the time Van der Donck published his *Beschryvinge*. Again Van der Donck emphasized the opportunities awaiting new settlers.[19]

Climate and Seasons

The first accounts of New Netherland settlers, experiencing the heat of New York summers, sparked the mistaken idea that the colony had a tropical climate. In his *Historisch Verhael*, Nicolaes van Wassenaer reported in 1624 that the land enjoyed a warm climate with hot summers. His information was secondhand, but he even asserted that one could hardly speak of winter weather in the area of the South River. It soon became clear in the Dutch Republic that New Netherland was not tropical, despite the fact that it lay considerably further south than the Dutch Republic. In 1625, Johannes de Laet wrote that, although the climate and seasons agreed with that in *patria*, it was colder in New Netherland than the latitude suggested. Yet De Laet concluded that it was "a country well adapted for our people to inhabit, on account of the similarity of the climate and the weather to our own."[20]

But the similarities were not so great as De Laet had presumed. New Netherland clearly had a continental climate, with colder winters and warmer summers than the colonists were used to. According to Van der Donck, describing the area around New Amsterdam, spring generally began at about the end of February, after which frost was rare. Nature then began to come to life again. In the spring the easterly winds sometimes brought thunderstorms with them, he wrote, although these were not long-lived. The cows could be put out into the fields in March, and April was the time for sowing. Wild strawberries were to be found as early as mid-May.[21]

The summers, which began in May or June, were warmer than the colonists were used to and generally drier. Often a refreshingly cool breeze came in from the sea. Van der Donck waxed lyrical about the summers in New Netherland. He noticed that in the summer the days were not so long as in the Netherlands, nor so short in the winter. He was also aware of a time difference between New Netherland and the Netherlands, and accurately estimated it at six hours.[22]

Autumn in New Netherland was generally mild and even more pleasant and agreeable than summer in the Dutch Republic. It lasted quite long. In the vicinity of New Amsterdam it could be Christmas before winter set in, although to the north the cold weather and frost arrived earlier. Autumn was the time for hunting and slaughtering. Surprisingly, Van der Donck did not mention the colorful fall foliage.[23]

The nature of winter in the colony varied according to the northerly position and proximity to the sea. Near the sea the winters were relatively mild, but in Rensselaerswijck, in the north, the temperature fell so low that the North River was frozen over by the end of November, cutting off this section of New Netherland from the south. Of course, temperature was much dependent on the wind. The cold northwesterly wind could be strong and penetrating. At sea, these winds rarely caused problems, as they were offshore, but on land they took down many trees in the forests, Van der Donck noted. In the north, the snow could lie for months on end, while in the south it would quickly melt when the wind shifted to the south. Van der Donck was surprised that New Netherland experienced such cold winters, despite lying at the same latitude as Italy and Spain. The cold was much drier than in the Netherlands. Van der Donck suggested that the northwesterly winds swept over a frozen sea before reaching the colony. Inland, the snow often lay longer between the mountains, keeping the weather cold even late in the winter. The cold "clears the land of various kinds of vermin, and takes away all sharp and evil humors."[24]

All in all, New Netherland had a favorable climate, and for colonists from the Netherlands it was healthier than West Africa or the West Indies. The air in New Netherland was good, without "heavy fumes or stinking mists." Those who had fallen ill in the West Indies, Virginia, or elsewhere could be cured swiftly by the healthy air of New Netherland, according to

Van der Donck. In warm weather, the air was further purified by thunder and lightning.[25]

Flora

Although New Netherland and Europe lay roughly at the same latitude and had to some extent a similar climate, both flora and fauna were different from what the colonists were used to in their mother country.[26] When Dutch colonists arrived in New Netherland it was almost completely forested. According to Johannes Megapolensis, they found the

> finest fir trees the eye ever saw. There are also in this country oaks, alders, beeches, elms, willows, etc. In the forests, and here and there along the water-side, and on the islands, there grows an abundance of chestnuts, plums, hazel-nuts, large walnuts of several sorts, and of as good a taste as in the Netherlands, but they have a somewhat harder shell. The ground on the hills is covered with bushes of bilberries or blueberries.[27]

Van der Donck was more utilitarian than Megapolensis in his attitude to the trees to be found in the colony. For him, the proximity of the forests meant a good supply of fuel. The hard walnut, particularly suitable for burning, could be used for making flails and mill components. Other trees were utilized in the construction of ships and houses. Some colonists were afraid that the profligate manner in which the colonists used wood could result in shortage, but Van der Donck considered these worries unfounded. He believed that the abundance of wood was such that it would never be lacking.[28]

The great variety of species of plants and trees in the forests of New Netherland did not come about solely through natural causes. Where the Indian had farmed, America was no natural wilderness, untouched by human hand. The Indian method of farming, whereby areas of forest were burnt down and the land planted for several years with maize and other crops, resulted in a mosaic of afforestation at different stages of development, with a wealth of species as a consequence. Van der Donck recounts that, when colonists put into culture a parcel of land, an Indian told him that it was very good land. It had been planted on by the Indians only twenty-five or twenty-six years previously, and it had now become forest again. Van der Donck found this quick reversion to forest difficult to believe, but other Indians confirmed the story. Walnut and oak trees covered the land and some trees were a *vadem* (fathom, ca. 1.70 meters) wide, growing so thickly that it was virtually impossible to pass through the wood on horseback.[29]

The sedentary farming carried out by the colonists differed from the way the Indians used the land, with the result that the appearance of New Netherland changed considerably. Van der Donck considered farming in New

Netherland to be less arduous and difficult than back in Holland, mainly because there was no need to dig drainage ditches. The colonists could easily erect fences, as plentiful wood was available. For winter wheat or rye, the land was plowed twice, while this was necessary only once in the summer. The land was regularly left fallow or planted with peas, but in many instances the soil was so rich that this was not necessary. Megapolensis reported that one particular farmer had had good crops of barley for eleven years in succession without having to leave the land fallow. The grains most cultivated by the colonists were wheat and rye. Barley and buckwheat were less common, as the finches and other birds were fond of these. In his description, Van der Donck devoted much attention to "Turkish wheat,"—maize—which the Indians sowed at intervals of approximately six feet, alternating with pumpkins or beans. This Indian custom was quickly adopted. Maize was frequently used as the first crop in newly cultivated soil.[30]

The colonists brought a number of different fruit trees to the colony, such as apple, pear, and cherry. The trees sometimes bore so much fruit that branches would break off under the burden. Peaches and apricots flourished in New Netherland, and Van der Donck continues with a summing-up of all the fruits that were to be found there: plums, almonds, medlars, cornelian cherries, figs, several sorts of currant, gooseberries, and thorn apples. He also saw opportunities for olive-growing.[31]

Vegetables and herbs were imported as well, including lettuces, salads, cabbages, parsnips, carrots, beets, endive, succory, sorrel, dill, spinach, radishes, Spanish radishes, parsley, chervil, cresses, onions, leeks, and the like. Enumeration seems to have been Van der Donck's main strategy for convincing potential colonists of New Netherland's possibilities. Vegetables and herbs generally grew better in the colony than in the Dutch Republic. This also applied to pumpkins, the cultivation of which required little attention. These were stewed in water and vinegar. In *patria* the pumpkin was generally despised as an article of food, but in New Netherland pumpkins were so good that they were a favorite food. The English colonists in the New World used pumpkins in pie fillings and also produced a type of drink from them. The Indians had their own kind of pumpkins, presumably a variety of squash, which they called *quaesiens* or *cascoeten,* names which the colonists adopted. Also grown were watermelons, cucumbers, peas, turnips, and many kinds of beans.[32]

Grapes grew in the colony in such abundance that Van der Donck thought it almost unbelievable. With a little human intervention, the vines could produce wine as good as was produced in Germany or France, as the Swedes had shown on the South River. But not all types of grape were suitable. Some were rather fleshy and were therefore called *spekdruiven* ("fat" or "lard" grapes). These produced a thick sap called *draeckenbloet* (dragon's blood). Few Dutch colonists possessed any knowledge of viniculture, reason to bring over a German viniculturist from Heidelberg. Van der Donck remarked that, as a result, an abundance of wine could be expected within a couple of years.[33] However, no evidence exists that this actually came to pass during the Dutch colonial period.

Apart from edible plants, the colonists also brought to the New World ornamental plants, such as roses and tulips. Imported medicinal herbs, of which Van der Donck provides an extensive list of Latin names, flourished in New Netherland. A surgeon, whose name Van der Donck does not mention, had established an excellent herb garden, which unfortunately was not maintained after his departure. Colonists in Rensselaerswijck also attempted to cultivate indigo plants from seeds sent over by Kiliaen van Rensselaer to produce dyestuff. As this was not carried out properly, the attempts proved unsuccessful. Later Augustijn Heermans met with some success, as he tried it further south, in the vicinity of New Amsterdam. The soil in New Netherland was suitable for the cultivation of tobacco, but the tobacco from New Netherland was not as good as that from Virginia. Van der Donck expected that, with the increase in population, more tobacco would be grown and that the quality would improve. As with maize, tobacco was used to make newly cultivated land suitable for the cultivation of other agricultural crops.[34]

Fauna

The fauna in New Netherland was as varied as the flora. Van der Donck, and others too, reported the presence of lions, bears, moose, deer, wolves, and many kinds of birds and fish.[35] According to him, lions were never glimpsed by Dutch colonists but were known through pelts bought from the Indians. It is likely that these were lynxes (*Lynx canadensis*) or bobcats (*Lynx rufus*), which can still be found in the Adirondack and Catskill Mountains. Every so often bears were spotted, but these were not dangerous, as they took flight as soon as they smelled humans. Some bear hunting was carried out, for bear skin was suitable for muffs. Van der Donck advised the bear hunter to make sure he could escape up a nearby tree before shooting, since the chances of putting a bear out of action with a single shot were small. The Indians savored bear meat. Van der Donck, who had never tasted it himself, had heard it said that it was as good as pork. The Indians sometimes took the animals alive in order to fatten them up. Bear hunting was usually carried out in the winter, as the bears were drowsy and slow due to their winter hibernation. The colonists valued moose for their meat more than deer. Van der Donck asserted that moose were easy to tame, and so could be used both as working animals as well as for slaughter, which must be considered a flight of fancy.[36] Large numbers of deer featured in New Netherland, and venison figured heavily in the Dutch diet. Van der Donck was of the opinion that the wolves in New Netherland were not too much of a nuisance, since their main prey was deer. Occasionally they would take a calf, sheep, goat, or pig, although pigs were no easy prey if they were in a group. Many snakes inhabited New Netherland, most of which were not dangerous, with the important exception of the rattlesnake, described by Megapolensis at length with some fear.[37]

New Netherland's waterways were rich in fish, both in quantity and in diversity. Salmon and sturgeon were plentiful, but the colonists did not bother to process the sturgeon's roe to make caviar, to Van der Donck's surprise. In spring the perch were so prolific that in one hour Megapolensis's sons caught fifty perch, each a foot long. The colonists also caught *elft* (shad), a fish already known to the colonists, not unlike the herring. Unfamiliar were the *twalift* (striped bass) and the *dertien* (drum-fish). These two were discovered after the capture of considerable numbers of *elft* ("eleventh," in Dutch) during the first years of the Dutch presence in the colony, and their names were the Dutch words for "twelfth" and "thirteenth," respectively.[38] In the inland waters carp, pike, trout, and eels abounded. Haddock, herring, mackerel, ray, flounder, and plaice were caught in the bays. Also lobsters, crabs, oysters, mussels, shrimps, and turtles were there for the taking. Other sorts of sea animals were available that were unknown in the Dutch Republic, but Van der Donck found them to be of small importance, as they were of little use to the colonists.[39]

A less usual phenomenon in New Netherland was the presence of whales. In his *Beschryvinge,* Van der Donck devoted ample attention to the two whales that swam quite some distance up the river in 1647. The *commies* (a subaltern administrative official) of the patroonship Rensselaerswijck, Anthony de Hooges, witnessed it:

> The 29th of March in the year 1647 there appeared before us in the colony [patroonship] a certain fish, which, as far as we could see, was of extraordinary size. It came from downstream and swam a certain length past us upstream up to the fords and returned downstream past us again by evening. It was as white as snow, without any fins, round of body and blew out water from his head, like the whales or tuna.[40]

The inhabitants observed it with great wonder. The other whale was stranded close to the Cohoes Falls, and the colonists got a large quantity of train oil from it. Whales were also to be found in the South River, and Van der Donck foresaw lucrative opportunities for whaling there.[41]

Far more important than whales were the fur-bearing animals. The beaver (*Castor canadensis*) was the most valued of these, although raccoons, mink, and bobcats were also hunted, as were otters and foxes, the fur of which was sold into in Germany via Amsterdam and Hamburg. Van der Donck devoted no fewer than eight pages to the beaver, more than any other subject, with the exception of the Indians. Beaver pelts had drawn Dutch merchants to New Netherland. The animal was hunted by the

Indians both for its meat and its fur during a hunting season that lasted from December through to the end of May. Beaver meat was a delicacy, which the Indians rarely sold to the colonists. The tastiest part of the beaver was the tail, but its prime possession was its pelt, which was covered with a soft ashen fur, verging on pale blue, used to make felt hats and to trim garments. The winter coat of the beaver was thick and brown, and contained long, shining protective hairs of no use in the production of felt. If the protective hair had not been removed, the pelt was called *castor sec*. This type of pelt was highly valued in Muscovy, where a major proportion of the beaver pelts ultimately ended up. Another type was called *castor gras* and was greatly prized, because use by the Indians had worn away the winter hair and had given the pelts an oiliness necessary for producing felt. These pelts were shipped via Amsterdam to France, where they were further processed.[42]

Of the birds of prey, Van der Donck paid the most attention to the eagle, which he thought very pleasant to behold.[43] But he also mentions other birds of prey, such as falcons and hawks. At the time, little use was made of these birds for hunting. In 1651, Jan Baptist van Rensselaer used a hawk for hunting, which he described as "keen and alert and...king of all New Netherland."[44] However, this bird had been sent over to him from *patria*. Many of the birds were familiar to the colonists, although the large numbers astonished them. The colonists regularly consumed turkeys, partridges, pheasants, grouse, and pigeons. Some fowl, particularly the migratory birds, were present in such numbers that, according to Van der Donck, they hung as clouds in the sky and projected shadows on the earth. Their large numbers made them easy to hunt. Megapolensis reports that in the spring and autumn each morning and evening every man stood in front of his house with a shotgun ready to shoot them as they flew by. Among the other birds mentioned by Van der Donck was a strange one, dubbed the West Indian bee, because it used its beak to suck honey from the flowers—the humming-bird. Hummingbirds could be caught by first spraying them with water, and then enfolding them in paper and drying them in the sun, after which they were given as a present to friends, sometimes with a cage to keep them in. Among the waterfowl, many were edible, such as geese and ducks, both of which were represented in different varieties and in large numbers. Also, swans, widgeon, cormorants, and even pelicans inhabited New Nether-land's waterways.[45]

Native People

Among all the new and remarkable phenomena to be found in the New World, the Indians occupied a special position. Both Van der Donck and Megapolensis devoted more attention to the Indians than to any other aspect of New Netherland. The interest in unknown and exotic peoples was large among their readers in the Dutch Republic.

Wilden

The colonists called the Indians *wilden,* not only in New Netherland but also in other parts of America. Van der Donck provides a three-part explanation for this. The Indians were considered wild "on account of the religion, because they have none or so little as to be virtually wild in this." Second, Indian customs regarding marriage and the ownership of land were far removed from the European general laws that Van der Donck implicitly used as the norm. Third, the names "heathens" or "blacks," customarily used for Turks and blacks, were too general. It was for this reason that the term *wilden* was used, the first word that came to them, "since the first opinion or notion of women and the uneducated who do not know much is best."[46] Although the term was widely used, other words were also employed. Megapolensis uses *Indianen* (Indians) considerably more frequently than *wilden.* In other sources, the term *naturellen* (aboriginals) is found. On the whole, the first argument supplied by Van der Donck in defense of using the designation *wilden* was shared by most of the colonists: religion, rather than race, was the defining factor.[47]

Iroquois, Mahicans, and Susquehannocks

In Dutch descriptions of the Indians, much attention is paid to the Mohawks. This group in the area to the west of Fort Orange was the most easterly of the five Iroquois nations and was called "Maquas" or "Mahakobaasen" by the colonists. The other Iroquois groups, the Oneidas, the Onondaga, the Cayuga, and the Seneca nations lived to the west of the Mohawks and were given the collective name of "Sinnekens." The colonists had less contact with the western groups, although distinctions among the Iroquois groups were recognized by them.[48] The Mohawks were the most important, but certainly not the only, suppliers of beaver pelts to the Dutch colonists. On the east bank of the North River, opposite Fort Orange, lived the Mahicans, referred to by the colonists as "Mahikanders." Although at the beginning of the seventeenth century they lived on both banks of the North River, in about 1628 the Mahicans were driven off the west bank by the Mohawks, thus leaving Fort Orange lying between the two Indian communities.[49] To the south of the Iroquois, around the Susquehanna River, which has its source west of that of the South River and runs south to flow into the Chesapeake Bay, lived the Susquehannocks, whom the colonists named "Minquas." Along the North River and in the vicinity of Manhattan a variety of small groups lived, such as Esopus Indians, Wappinger, Tappan, Manhatan, Raritan, and Canarsee Indians. These groups formed a branch of the Delaware Indians known as the Lenapes. They spoke Munsee, an eastern Algonquian language. Another branch, which was principally to be found around the South River, spoke Unami, a related language. The colonists were aware that the languages and dialects of the Indians were diverse, but when it came to describing the lifestyle and appearance of the Indians, most made little distinction among them.[50]

Body and Clothing

All Dutch observers noticed the physical appearance of the Indians. Their stature was comparable to that of Europeans, according to Van der Donck. Their skin was not as white, but yellowish. They had dark brown eyes and snow-white teeth, and their hair was jet black. The women wore their hair in long plaits, but the men shaved their heads, leaving a cockscomb over the middle of the head. Here and there they left wisps of hair on the shaven areas, "such as are in sweeping-brushes, and then they are in fine array." It was the custom of the men to paint their faces, making them look like devils, according to Megapolensis. The Indians had little or no facial hair and looked on hair other than on the head as ugly. Van der Donck reports that such hair was pulled out at the roots.[51] The Indians were not particularly clean, as Megapolensis writes with obvious disgust. They smeared their heads with bear fat to prevent lice, and they never washed themselves: "They are very slovenly and dirty; they wash neither their face, nor hands, but let all remain upon their yellow skin, and look like hogs."[52] The Indians suffered few physical disabilities; cripples and hunchbacks were rare, according to Van der Donck. He had, however, come across an Indian who had become blind as a result of smallpox. As with smallpox, the Indians had little or no resistance to such infectious diseases as measles and influenza, which European colonists had brought with them. Van der Donck's 1655 estimate that the size of the Indian population had diminished to about 10 percent of that prior to the arrival of Europeans is impossible to corroborate with other evidence. Yet the scanty evidence available suggests that by about 1660, the five Iroquois groups had been reduced to about twenty-five thousand people. Among the Mohawks, with whom the colonists had the most contact, the mortality rate was much higher, but they still numbered 4,500.[53]

In the summer the Indian men clad themselves in a loincloth, by the colonists dubbed a *clootlap*. Van der Donck apologizes for the use of this word, which might appear unseemly to his Dutch audience, but which in New Netherland was so normal "that it does not offend the delicate ear of women or maids."[54] During the winter the Indians wore animal skins, with shoes made of deerskin. In many instances, their clothing was decorated with *sewant* or *zeewant*, the Narragansett name for polished shell, threaded like beads. The colonists in New England adopted a different Algonquian word, *wampum*. It was made from two types of whelk (*Busycon carica* and *Busycon canaliculatum*) for the white beads, and a clam, the northern quahog (*Mercenaria mercenaria*), for the black beads, which were actually dark purple. As the trading relations with the colonists increased, instead of animal skins the Indians began to wear more duffel and other woolen cloth and also adopted the use of stockings, shoes, and shirts. Van der Donck remarked that the Indians wore these garments without laundering them, until they were completely worn out.[55]

Eating and Housing

The Indians provided for their needs by hunting, fishing, and farming. Invariably, the Dutch descriptions point to a rigorous division of labor. Hunting and fishing were the responsibility of the men. Fishing was carried out in the spring and early summer, with the use of fykes or bag-type nets.[56] The catch was cooked as it was, neither gutted nor skinned. Nor, according to Van der Donck, was it preserved with salt. The Indians did, however, dry fish, "which they pound half stinking into meal, to use in the winter (as has been heard) in their porridge."[57] In the autumn and winter they hunted bears, otters, beavers, and deer, among other animals, for which they utilized traps, bows and arrows, and later also guns. During the hunting season, the men were often away for months. The women carried out the farm work, to the indignation of the colonists, who considered this division of responsibilities inappropriate: "The women are obliged to prepare the land, to mow, to plant, and do everything; the men do nothing but hunt, fish, and make war upon their enemies."[58] The principal crop was maize, from which a porridge or mush, called *sappaen,* was made, which was the main diet. Some of the maize harvested was also stored in pits in the ground for the winter.[59] Beans were an important part of the Indian diet, and were, together with fresh meat, used in stews that were regarded as a delicacy. The eating habits of the Indians surprised Van der Donck: "They have tremendous control over their appetite, stomachs, and bodies, so that they can get by with very little for two, three, or four days. When supplies are ample again they will quickly make up for the loss or the delay, without upsetting their stomachs or making themselves ill."[60] The Indians lived in villages, the larger of which were encircled by palisades and called *casteelen* (castles) by the colonists. Generally, the large settlements were situated on top of hills, in the vicinity of water. Their houses were approximately seven meters wide and, according to Van der Donck, who might be referring to the Iroquois longhouses here, could be as long as some hundred feet. They constructed them by placing walnut stakes in the ground and then bending and binding these together to create a canopy or tilt. The sides and roof were covered with wood and bark. Holes were made in the roof to allow the egress of smoke. The hearths were situated in the middle of the houses, with the sleeping areas along the sides. In these houses, twenty to thirty of which stood in a *casteel,* lived a number of families in extremely close proximity, sometimes up to one hundred and fifty people, according to Van der Donck, who was amazed by the large numbers living under one roof.[61]

Government and the Exchange of Gifts

Although a degree of kinship and cooperation existed among the peoples of the Iroquois, this did not result in any form of central authority. Each village was, in principle, autonomous. Within the village a form of governance existed, which in the eyes of the colonists carried little authority: "The government among them consists of the oldest, the most intelligent, the most eloquent and most warlike men. They commonly make the decisions, which are then executed by the young men and the warriors. But if the common men do not like the decision, the matter is laid before the mob."[62] The Indian leaders were called *oversten* (headmen) by the colonists, although the Indian word *sachem,* and its variations *sackimas* or *sackemackers,* were also used. This word was also used in dealings with the Indians as the title of the colonists' leaders. Van der Donck opined that leadership was hereditary among the Indians. Although he was correct, it might have amazed him, had he known it, that in this matrilineal society it was the female heads of the families who selected the male leaders.[63]

The authority of the *sachems,* relatively limited in Dutch eyes, was based on their capacity to maintain mutual peace and consensus by means of persuasion and the ritual exchange of gifts. Megapolensis believed that the *sachems* were the poorest among the Indian peoples, as they had to give rather than receive, in contrast with European societies, in which one of the powers of people in authority was to levy taxes. Megapolensis did not grasp that the *sachems'* authority was founded on the ritual exchange of gifts, a custom soon transferred to diplomatic negotiations between the colonists and the Indians. After each point that the Indians brought up, they presented some *sewant* or a few beavers. The colonists were quick to learn that reciprocation kept relations with the Indians from deteriorating.[64]

Language

Interaction between the Indians and the colonists was hampered by the linguistic situation. Most of them were capable of communicating with the Indians to carry out trade, but their mastery of the language rarely went beyond that. The Reformed *predikant* Jonas Michaëlius, who was on Manhattan in 1628, stated that "even those who can best of all speak with the *Wilden* and get along well in trade, are nevertheless altogether blind and bewildered, when they hear the *Wilden* talking among themselves alone."[65] Neither did the traders at Fort Orange understand much of the Indian languages. Johannes Megapolensis tried to learn the language of the Mohawks but experienced several problems. In attempting to compile a vocabulary, he failed to make them understand his goal. Also the variety of tenses, declinations, and conjugations confused him, as it did not conform to his knowledge of Latin and Greek.[66] Colonists who had been living in New Netherland for a longer period could not give him much assistance. When he requested the help of the *commies* of Fort Orange, Harmen Meyndertsz van den Bogaert, the latter replied that he was of the opinion that the Indians changed their language every two or three years. Megapolensis considered this highly unlikely. Despite the linguistic problems, some of the colonists had sufficient mastery of an Indian language to function as interpreters during negotiations. In a few cases Indians could speak French or English. The observations of Van der Donck and Megapolensis on the religious perceptions of the Indians indicate that the language barrier was not so great that abstract questions could not be discussed.[67]

Religion and Character

"They are totally estranged of any religiosity," stated Megapolensis. The Indians had a "genius" whom they treated as a god, but whom they did not worship. On the other hand, according to Megapolensis, they worshiped the devil, for example by making libations, or by the slaughtering of bears as a peace offering in the event of setbacks in battle. Van der Donck reports that on the swearing of an oath, the all-seeing sun was invoked, although the Indians were not actually worshippers of the sun. In the same way, the moon and the planets were assigned powers.[68] Neither Megapolensis nor Van der Donck had any affinity with the animistic spiritual world of the Indians so alien to the monotheistic European religions. With a mixture of astonishment and repugnance, the colonists describe the Indian rituals through which, for example, evil spirits were driven out of a sick man. This was accompanied by "such *apen spel* [antics] that it was a wonder to see."[69]

Astonishment and repugnance characterize the early Dutch descriptions of the Indians. However, in a few instances a tinge of admiration can be detected in the accounts of Megapolensis, for example as he describes how Indian women get back to work immediately after having given birth. This example deserved imitation: "We sometimes try to persuade our wives to lie-in likewise, and that the way of lying-in in Holland is mere *ticktackelerij* [fiddle-faddle]."[70] But generally the character of the Indians was described in negative terms: Johannes de Laet, for example, found an Indian group to be "not at all industrious"; they were "very evil thieves and wicked people."[71] This is, of course, secondhand information, which De Laet, who had never been to the New World himself, may have gleaned from the reports of returning captains. Comments of a similar nature were made by people who had actually had personal contact with the Indians, and the implicit assumption of European superiority and Indian inferiority is evident. Most of the Indians were, according to Van der Donck, "simple and ignorant," "most vengeful and headstrong."[72] Isaac de Rasière described them as "very inveterate against those whom they hate; cruel by nature; so inclined to freedom that they cannot by any means be brought to work."[73] Again, the utilitarianism is evident. Van der Donck, too, reports that the Indians were not suitable as slaves: "To heavy sustained labor which may seem slavish, they, especially the men, are quite averse."[74]

That did not prevent observers in the seventeenth century from considering New Netherland a land of considerable potential. All that was needed was the right people to make use of it. Again Johannes de Laet: "It is a beautiful and pleasant land, full of very beautiful forests and also vineyards, and nothing is wanting but the labor and industry of people to be one of the most beautiful and fruitful lands of that region."[75]

1   *Reconnaissance and Exploration*

In early 1609, Henry Hudson was commissioned by the Dutch East India Company to explore the Northeast Passage to Asia. This route north of Novaya Zemlya had been tried before, but all attempts had faltered and failed as low temperatures and frozen seas proved a formidable barrier. Hudson did not succeed either. Driven back by a northeastern storm, faced, not for the last time, with a mutinous crew, and unconvinced that the Northeast Passage was a viable option, he quickly turned his ship *Halve Maen* to pursue another dream: discovering the Northwest Passage. Again he was unsuccessful, but his reports sparked some interest among the merchants back in the Dutch Republic. They sent out ships to engage in trading furs with the local Indians, thus starting the Dutch involvement with the North American continent.

An unsuccessful voyage of exploration by an English mariner may seem an unlikely starting point for a history of a Dutch colony. It might be argued that better alternatives are available, such as 1624, supposedly the first Dutch settlement in the area, or 1625, when Manhattan may first have been settled. New York State and New York City have proclaimed these respective years as their official year of founding, thus using the criterion of "first permanent settlement" as touchstone, similar to other colonies along the eastern seaboard. Yet this criterion emphasizes permanency and settlement and reveals its implicit teleological desire to link the present with the past and locate "origins" and "birth places." As such it favors one specific form of colonial involvement—that is, settlement—to the disadvantage of, for instance, nonterritorially based trade. Another objection sometimes voiced against 1609 is that Hudson was not a Dutchman but an Englishman. Yet this objection is anachronistic. Nationality had a different meaning in the seventeenth century, and the practice of seeking employment abroad was widespread among aspiring explorers, the Italian Columbus being the prime example.

Early Voyages

The most important argument in favor of 1609 is the immediate effect of Hudson's voyage. His reports made Dutch merchants aware of commercial opportunities and thus triggered the first direct involvement between the largely unknown North American continent and a small, new European country bordering on the North Sea.

The Dutch Republic

The Dutch Republic was one of the last of the states of Western Europe to enter the colonial competition. Until 1572 the Netherlands were under the control of the Spanish crown, which prohibited direct contact with overseas colonies. The success of the Dutch Revolt in the last quarter of the sixteenth century made it possible for Dutch merchants to send their ships out across the oceans. Initially, Dutch merchants focused on Asia, where valuable spices could be obtained. Here, they encountered relatively powerful indigenous states, in which the economies were well developed and the density of the population usually was high. Partly because of these factors, the trading posts in the East remained small. Territorial expansion with the objective of establishing colonial settlements was difficult in the East, and it was rarely the intention, at least initially.[1]

On the other hand, there were opportunities for expansion in the Atlantic. Here, resistance was not so much to be expected from the indigenous populations, whose numbers declined due to the European diseases previously unfamiliar to them, but from other European nations, who had established colonies earlier. The objectives of the two great Dutch trading companies expressed this difference. Trade was the main objective of the *Verenigde Oost-Indische Compagnie* (East India Company, or VOC), and gaining a foothold was a means to this. The principal objective of the *Geoctroyeerde West-Indische Compagnie* (West India Company, or WIC) on the other hand was to inflict damage on the colonial resources of the Iberian enemies. In pursuit of this objective, the WIC tried its hand at the conquest of enemy colonies and privateering on its shipping. In the first half of the seventeenth century some successes were achieved, such as the occupation of parts of Brazil and the capture of a Spanish fleet carrying a large treasure of silver off the northern coast of Cuba in 1628. But the combination of business enterprise and instrument of war ultimately proved unsuccessful. Gradually, the WIC was compelled to relinquish parts of its shipping and trading monopoly to private merchants.[2]

Hudson's Voyage

Few Spaniards or Portuguese were to be found in North America, where the English were the main opponents. English colonists had started settling in

Virginia in 1607, and Hudson was well aware of that. He had been informed by John Smith that the unexplored lands between the Chesapeake and Cape Cod could be of potential interest to Europeans. Taking the northern route across the Atlantic, he arrived at Nova Scotia in mid-July. After touching the coast of Maine and Cape Cod, he left the coast and sailed south to the entrance of the Chesapeake Bay. From there he began exploring the coast to the north. On August 28, the *Halve Maen* entered the Delaware Bay, only to find its passage blocked by shoals. Continuing north, Hudson reached Sandy Hook five days later. Hudson's first mate, Robert Juet, considered it "a very good Land to fall with, and a pleasant Land to see."[3]

After entering the Lower Bay, Hudson and his crew had their first encounter with the local Indians. When Hudson came on shore, he was greeted by a line of "blacks singing in their fashion." As Juet described it, the natives seemed glad of their coming and brought tobacco in exchange for knives and beads. Juet considered them "very civill," but Hudson was a bit more wary: they were much inclined to stealing and adroit at carrying off anything they fancied. The exact location of this first encounter is not specified, but Gravesend Bay, between Fort Hamilton and Coney Island, is the most likely candidate. Although the first contact was friendly, other Indian groups were more hostile. Hudson sent out crewmember John Colman and four other men in a sloop to take soundings in the Upper Bay. On their return, they were attacked by twenty-six Indians in two canoes, and Colman was killed by an arrow into his throat. The next day he was buried on a point the crew named Colman's Point, probably the tip of Coney Island, now called Nortons Point. After the incident, the crew of the *Halve Maen* became even more cautious.[4]

On 11 September 1609, the wind turned south-southwest, enabling the *Halve Maen* to sail through the Narrows and enter the Upper Bay. Again the crew encountered Indians, who presented tobacco and maize. They were even allowed on board, but the next day, when no less than twenty-eight canoes turned up, the risk was too great to repeat such friendliness. Weighing anchor in the early morning of 13 September, and using the tide, the ship made good progress up the river, passing by Manhattan without any reference to it. Over the next days, the *Halve Maen* sailed up to the latitude of present-day Albany, where it was stopped by shoals. Again the sloop was sent out, only to discover that further on, the river became too shallow for oceangoing ships. And so Hudson decided to head downriver and return to Europe.[5]

During a month in the area, Hudson had a number of meetings with different groups of Indians, mostly Munsee, Catskill, and Mahican bands. If he had arrived two or three months later, he might not have seen any Indians at all. During the summer, many small groups of Indians stayed in camps near the river and engaged in fishing, hunting waterfowl, and gathering various plants. With the arrival of fall, they retreated to larger villages inland.

Most of the meetings between the crew of the *Halve Maen* and the Indians took place in a friendly atmosphere. Gifts were offered, leading to exchanges which the Europeans strictly interpreted as trade, thus misreading the Indians' primary emphasis on the importance of social reciprocity. On one occasion, when at the highest point up the river, Hudson sailed ashore in an Indian canoe and visited a small village. He was offered food, maize and fresh meat and poultry. When the Indians noticed that he was afraid of their bows, they broke their arrows into pieces and threw them into the fire. Some of the remarks by Juet indicate that the Indians treated Hudson with great respect, showing him "all the Countrey there about, as though it were at his command."[6]

Other sources confirm this attitude of respect and awe. Decades later, Adriaen van der Donck reported that the Indians, upon first seeing a European ship, considered it a strange fish or a sea monster. The people on board were regarded as "devils" rather than human beings. To make sense of these strange-looking new arrivals, the existence of the Europeans had to be incorporated into the animistic worldview of the Indians, in which maintaining good relations with the spirit world was paramount.[7]

For Hudson, commercial relations were far more important than spiritual relations, and in that sense his voyage of exploration had yielded useful information. Yet when he departed from North America in early October and set course for Europe, he may have dreaded returning to Amsterdam. He had after all ignored his instructions and potentially faced accusations of disobedience and even treason. Neither would his crew have been eager, as their threat of mutiny had played a role in the decision to go west. Hudson therefore decided to put in to an English port. Upon his arrival at Dartmouth he was arrested by the English authorities, for in making his voyage of discovery, Hudson had contravened a charter that the King of England had issued in 1606, by which a major portion of the North American continent had been allocated to two English trading companies. Although the *Halve Maen* was handed back to the East India Company and Hudson's and Juet's journal also found their way to Amsterdam, Hudson himself remained in England. A year later he made a final attempt to discover the Northwest Passage. This time it proved fatal: part of the crew mutinied, and he and eight other members of the ship's company, including his son, were set adrift in a shallop in the icy James Bay, never to be seen again.[8]

Christiaensz and Block

The journal of Robert Juet, one of the members of the crew, is a good source on Hudson's 1609 journey, but far less is known about subsequent voyages from Amsterdam to the area which by 1614 was called New Netherland. It is not even known for certain when the first voyage after Hudson's took place. Possibly a ship under the command of Hendrick Christiaensz entered the North River from a southerly direction as early as 1610. A little more is known about the second voyage. After reports of Hudson's trip reached Amsterdam, a group of Lutheran merchants quickly showed interest. This group, under the name of the Van Tweenhuysen Company, consisted of Aernout Vogels, Hans Hunger, Lambert van Tweenhuysen, and the brothers Franchoy, Leonard, Paulus, and Steffen Pelgrom. In 1611, the Van Tweenhuysen Company dispatched the ship *St. Pieter,* under its captain Cornelis Rijser. It is probable that Hendrick Christiaensz and Adriaen Block sailed with this voyage as supercargoes.[9]

The following year, Block made a second trip for the Van Tweenhuysen Company, this time as captain of the *Fortuyn.* It is believed that during this journey a fortification, Fort Nassau, was built on what was later to be called Castle Island, near Albany, where some of the crew remained to continue trade during the ship's absence. During Block's voyage, in the winter of 1612–1613, it became clear that the Van Tweenhuysen Company was no longer the only party interested in the fur trade on the North River. While Block's ship was lying in the bay, the ship *Jonge Tobias* arrived, captained by Thijs Volckertsz Mossel. He had been dispatched by the Hans Claesz Company of Amsterdam, which consisted of Hans Claesz, Barent Sweers, Arnout van Liebergen, Wessel Schenck, Jan Holscher, and Jacob Bontenos. Because Hans Jorisz Hontom, the supercargo on Mossel's ship, offered the Indians twice as much for their beaver pelts as Block, a disagreement ensued. Obviously, such practices would reduce profit margins considerably. The traders managed to avoid further difficulties by reaching a temporary compromise in which, presumably, they agreed upon a predetermined price per beaver. In addition, they probably agreed that Block would receive two-thirds and Mossel one-third of the profit from beavers.[10]

After both ships had returned to the Dutch Republic, the companies of Van Tweenhuysen and Hans Claesz started negotiations to avoid the costly consequences of too much competition. When it became apparent that no agreement could be reached, the Van Tweenhuysen Company dispatched two ships: the *Fortuyn,* this time under Hendrick Christiaensz, and the *Tijger* under the command of Adriaen Block. The Hans Claesz Company sent out a single ship, the *Nachtegael,* of which Mossel was the captain. Continuation of the conflict in America was inevitable. Only after Block, who had sailed a month later than Christiaensz and Mossel, arrived in the North River was a compromise reached: Mossel was to receive two-fifths and Block and Christiaensz three-fifths of the beaver trade. Block promised not to trade on the North River, but elsewhere on the American coast. However, floating ice delayed his departure, and he was still in the bay of the North River at the end of January 1614 when fire accidentally destroyed his ship.[11] Mossel was not above taking advantage of Block's unfortunate situation. He and his supercargo Hontom offered Block their help in exchange for a change in the previously agreed ratio of the allocation of the beaver trade.

Block refused, and ordered his ship's carpenter to build a small yacht that, significantly, was named the *Onrust* ("unrest" or "restless"). This is the first ship known to have been built in New Netherland. Unfortunately, the fire was not the end of Block's misfortunes. A month later part of his crew mutinied. A number of them boarded Mossel's ship *Nachtegael*, while supercargo Hontom and several of his crew members were away engaged in trade. After several skirmishes the mutineers sailed away to carry out piracy in West Indian waters.[12]

The situation was exacerbated when, shortly afterwards, two new ships appeared in the bay. The first of these, also called the *Fortuyn,* was commanded by Cornelis Jacobsz May, who was in the employ of a company of Hoorn. The other ship was the *Vosje,* which almost a year earlier had sailed from Amsterdam to explore the Northwest Passage. The *Vosje,* captained by Pieter Fransz, had been dispatched by Jonas Witsen, Simon Willemsz Nooms, and the Admiralty of Amsterdam. The arrival of these ships made it necessary to revise the earlier allocation ratio. Each of the four companies now was to receive one-quarter of the beaver pelts, a change to the disadvantage of the Van Tweenhuysen Company. In June 1614, after several months of trading, the three ships left for home. A number of the crew of Block and Christiaensz stayed behind with the *Onrust* at the Fort Nassau trading post.[13]

New Netherland Company

Back in *patria,* the four companies swiftly reached an agreement, leading to the founding of the Compagnie van Nieuwnederlant (New Netherland Company), the first time that name is used. Some of the merchants had already combined their efforts in the Noordse Compagnie (Northern Company), which was set up for whaling near Spitsbergen and Jan Mayen Island. The competition on the North River had made them realize that it was also necessary to work together in the fur trade. The investments in transatlantic voyages could yield profits only if the buying price for the beaver pelts was kept low. But even the cooperation among the four companies could not ensure that no other competitors would appear on the horizon. The only way to achieve this was by securing a governmental charter. On 27 March 1614, the States General issued an ordinance that paved the way for granting monopolies for trade with a newly discovered area. Seven months later, with effect from 1 January 1615, the States General granted such a patent to the New Netherland Company, allowing it to undertake four voyages in three years. The area to which this patent applied lay between the fortieth and forty-fifth parallels, so it did not include the South River.[14]

Immediately after having been granted this patent, the New Netherland Company was compelled to defend its monopoly. An Amsterdam company, for which Albert Gerritsz Ruijl acted as factor, was involved in equipping

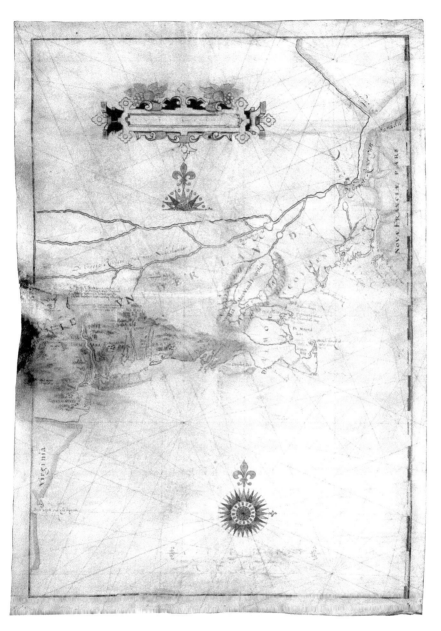

2. Map of New Netherland, 1614. Nationaal Archief, The Netherlands, Inv. no. 4. VEL 520.

a ship, yet another one bearing the name *Fortuyn*. Under the command of Erasmus Pietersz, this ship intended to sail to the area reserved for the New Netherland Company. When the New Netherland Company attempted to forbid the voyage, Ruijl countered by saying that his company had been the first, or perhaps the second, in the area and had already sailed there a number of times. Although nothing is known about any voyages that Ruijl and Pietersz may have made, the possibility cannot be ruled out, if not to the North River, then to another river. Ruijl and the New Netherland Company probably came to some agreement whereby ship, equipment, and goods were taken over by the New Netherland Company.[15]

Little is known about the voyages commissioned by the New Netherland Company. One report states that Hendrick Christiaensz undertook ten voyages for the Company, but that would be an extraordinarily large number in four years.[16] Between 1614 and 1616 Cornelis Hendricksz van Monnickendam explored the coast around the South River as captain of the *Onrust*. Another small ship built in New Netherland, the *IJseren Vercken*, was used for reconnaissance and trade, making the first trip up the South River in 1616 and interacting with the local Indians. On the basis of these explorations, in August 1616 Gerrit and Jonas Witsen, Lambert van Tweenhuysen, and Paulus Pelgrom on behalf of the Company requested a separate patent for this area, which lay below the fortieth parallel. The States General first requested more written information, subsequently postponing the decision three times, after which no patent was granted. By this time the States General were already considering the establishment of a West India Company.[17]

Free Trade

In October 1618, ten months after its patent had officially expired, the New Netherland Company applied for a new monopoly. The States General wanted first to reconsider its ordinance of 1614 and decided to reject the application for the time being. As in 1616, the latent plans for the establishment of a West India Company played a role in their decision. The decision meant that the monopoly enjoyed by the New Netherland Company came to an end, opening the trade to all. As a consequence, the New Netherland Company disintegrated. Two merchants, Hendrick Eelkens and Adriaen Jansz Engel, who had joined the Company later, on the expiration of the patent and on their own initiative immediately dispatched the ship *Schildpad* to America. The captain, Jacob Jacobsz Eelkens, who had earlier visited the North River as supercargo under Christiaensz, was Hendrick's nephew. The principal actors of the New Netherland Company, including Van Tweenhuysen, Witsen, and Samuel Godijn, who had joined later, sent the ship *Swarte Beer* under the command of Hendrick Christiaensz to New Netherland in October 1618. Christiaensz had been warned by Eelkens and

Engel not to hinder their trading activities, but nonetheless his conduct led to dissension among the Dutch traders in America. Furthermore, Christiaensz had problems with the Indians. Early in 1619 Indians attacked the *Swarte Beer* in the vicinity of "Nooten Eylandt" (Governors Island) and killed him and most of his crew.[18] The five survivors believed their problems to be over when a ship from Vlissingen arrived in the bay. This ship, the name of which is unknown, sailed under captain Adriaen Jorisz Thienpont for a company in Zeeland. For the crew of the *Swarte Beer,* the arrival of Thienpont meant that they would be able to return home safely, but it also meant problems for the ship's owners, because Thienpont seized part of the ship's cargo, consisting of goods for trade with the Indians such as kettles, knives, and adzes, and took the ship to Zeeland. This compelled the *Swarte Beer*'s Amsterdam owners to take up legal proceedings to regain their property.[19]

Up to 1623, both Eelkens's company and the New Netherland Company regularly sent ships to the North River. Situations of conflict still occurred but, in contrast to 1614, this did not lead to any real form of cooperation. Although the competition probably resulted in a reduction in profit margins, the ongoing dispatch of ships to the North River shows that the merchants still believed a profit could be made. Not all the voyages were successful, even so. For example, in 1620 the Indians refused to trade with Willem Jorisz Hontom and Jacob Jacobsz Eelkens.[20]

The formation in 1621 of the West India Company had a considerable impact on the enterprises of the private merchants. Because the WIC, for some time after the granting of the charter on 3 June 1621, was unable to develop activities, the States General granted dispensation. In September 1621 the New Netherland Company received permission to send out two ships, on the condition that these would be back in the Dutch Republic before 1 July 1622. When on 18 June 1622 the ships had not yet returned, their owners decided to apply to the States General for a six-months' extension. Eelkens's company also rounded off its activities. The *Witte Duyf* left the North River in September 1623, and the yachts and sloops that remained were sold to the WIC after some haggling over the costs. The New Netherland Company had fewer problems with the new Company, probably because Witsen and Godijn became directors of the Amsterdam chamber.[21]

The West India Company

For a number of years in the period prior to 1621, Dutch merchants had been sailing to areas of the Atlantic other than New Netherland. To *patria* they carried sugar from Brazil, the Canary Islands, São Tomé, and Madeira, and salt from the Cape Verde Islands, the coast of Venezuela, and islands in the Caribbean. Salt was essential to the Dutch fishing industry. Dutch ships also sailed to the coast of West Africa to obtain pepper, ivory, and gold.

Even before the Twelve Years' Truce (1609–1621) there had been plans to amalgamate the separate ventures into a single chartered company, in the same way as had been done in the East India trade.

Willem Usselincx, one of the many merchants who had moved to the northern Netherlands after the fall of Antwerp, was a particularly firm believer in a West India Company and published many pamphlets promulgating his ideas. In his eyes, a West India Company could provide a valuable contribution in the continuing war against Spain, but the colonization of overseas lands and the spread of the Reformed religion were equally important to him. Usselincx believed that agricultural colonies could provide *patria* with a variety of products, at the same time becoming markets for manufactured products from the Dutch Republic. Considerable emigration would be necessary to achieve this objective, and it remained to be seen whether merchants would be eager to undertake the risks inherent in such a venture. The States General remained unconvinced by the economic aspects of Usselincx's plans, although the need for consolidation was acknowledged. Yet the formation of the WIC was hindered by the prospect of a truce with Spain, to which such an organization would be an immediate threat to its American colonies. The abandonment of plans for the formation of a trading company for the Atlantic areas was one of the concessions made by the States General.[22]

Charter

Almost immediately when hostilities with Spain were resumed after the end of the Twelve Years' Truce, the States General issued the patent for the West India Company. The newborn Company was considerably different from the one Usselincx had envisioned. Colonization scarcely played a role in the patent, whereas privateering and trade, which in the eyes of the merchants offered better opportunities for profit, were principal objectives. The political situation in the Atlantic demanded a belligerent company. But financiers in the Dutch Republic were not particularly enthusiastic, most likely because they perceived the West India Company, to a far greater extent than the East India Company, to be a privately financed weapon in the fight against Spain. The most lucrative areas, which did not include New Netherland, had already been in the hands of Spain and Portugal since the beginning of the sixteenth century. To create an Atlantic empire, the Dutch Republic would have to wage war. So trade and war were allies in the formation of the West India Company. It remained to be seen, however, whether it would be a particularly fortunate combination. As long as the Company's activities were limited to privateering and carrying out attacks on Spanish colonies, private and state interests coincided to a great extent. But the establishment of Dutch colonies, especially settlement colonies, was another matter.[23]

In its organization, the Company was subdivided into five chambers: Amsterdam, Zeeland, Maze, Noorderkwartier, and Stad en Lande. Its central administration, which was in charge of general policy, consisted of the *Heren XIX* (Lords Nineteen), in which Amsterdam had eight votes, Zeeland four, and each of the other chambers two. One vote was reserved for the States General, ensuring that the government's interests were represented at the highest level within the Company.[24] The presidency of the *Heren XIX* rotated between the chambers of Amsterdam and Zeeland. In principle, meetings were held in the place where the presiding chamber was established, but sometimes the States General called meetings of the *Heren XIX* in The Hague.[25] Since most of the voyages to New Netherland had been organized by Amsterdam merchants, New Netherland was supervised by the Amsterdam chamber, which had twenty directors. These were elected with a tenure of six years from the *hoofdparticipanten* (large shareholders), each of whom had to invest a minimum of six thousand guilders. Committees within each chamber were charged with specific executive duties, such as the management of the wharves, the equipping of the ships, and the sales of the cargoes brought in.[26]

A Slow Start

The first problem for the new Company was to raise startup capital. This took considerably longer than had been the case for the VOC twenty years earlier. It was almost two years before the Company had collected approximately seven million guilders and could start its activities. Most of the initial capital came from cities with little or no experience of trading outside of Europe and which were inspired by religious motives, such as Utrecht, Deventer, Haarlem, and Leiden. Leiden was able to amass 269,800 guilders, of which most came from Johannes de Laet, who personally invested 54,000 guilders. This significant investment from Leiden allowed it to appoint two directors in the Amsterdam chamber. Other cities that produced investments of more than one hundred thousand guilders also gained the right to appoint directors.[27]

A second problem for the WIC was the inclusion of the salt trade with Punta de Araya in the area covered by the patent. Initially, this part of the coast of Venezuela, where a large natural salt pan produced sufficient volume to fill many ships each year, had been excluded from the monopoly. Merchants from Hoorn, Enkhuizen, and other cities in the Noorderkwartier had been involved in this trade, and they were keen to keep it out of the hands of the WIC. But in 1622, the sluggish rate of applications for shares in the WIC forced the States General to include Punta de Araya in the monopoly after all. This, of course, caused considerable anger in the Noorderkwartier, the part of Holland north of the river IJ, where the city governments refused to promulgate the new patent. In the beginning of 1624 the *Heren XIX* therefore sent a delegation to the Noorderkwartier, commissioned to attempt to reconcile Hoorn and Enkhuizen with the amendment.

As a result of the conflict over the salt trade and the slow rate of investment, the WIC got off to a slow start. It was not until 1623 that the private merchants brought back their last ships and their personnel from New Netherland or transferred them to the WIC. The first Company ship to reach the colony was the yacht *Mackreel*. It sailed on 16 July 1623, together with the *Duyf*, which was to found a colony on the coast of Guyana. The *Mackreel* traded all winter on the North River and returned home in the summer of 1624.[28]

Although this first voyage under the auspices of the WIC was exclusively aimed at carrying out trading activities, the Company's attitude to New Netherland quickly changed. On 3 November 1623, the *Heren XIX* decided to establish a small trading colony in the area. No grandiose ideas for large-scale colonization underlay this decision. The principal reason was to establish a firmer basis for the fur trade and to strengthen the Dutch claim on the territory. In 1622 the English ambassador in The Hague, Sir Dudley Carleton, had protested to the States General about the Dutch activities, referring to prior English claims to North America. When the States General requested information from the *Heren XIX*, the WIC reacted by sending a memorandum elucidating their opinion about claims on newly discovered territories. For the WIC, the discovery of the area or the allocation thereof by a government were insufficient legal bases for possession. Only a claim supported by actually occupying an area by populating it with at least fifty colonists was valid. This line of reasoning made it necessary for the WIC to send a number of colonists to New Netherland.[29]

Owing to lack of data, the exact start of settlement is uncertain. There are some indications that the first colonists arrived in 1623, but the evidence is incomplete and unreliable, so 1624 is a better choice. In January of that year a small vanguard departed from Texel with the ship *Eendracht* under the captaincy of Adriaen Jorisz Thienpont, who had visited New Netherland earlier. The number of colonists on board the *Eendracht* is unknown, but it cannot have been more than a few dozen. Presumably, these colonists were divided over four locations: the mouth of the Fresh River (probably Kievits Hoeck (Saybroeck Point) on the western bank), Fort Wilhelmus on the Hooghe eylant (Burlington Island) on the South River, *Nooten Eylandt* near Manhattan, and the upper reaches of the North River, where Fort Orange was founded. The reason for the dispersion of the colonists was to lay claim to the whole area.[30]

A little more is known about the voyage of the ship *Nieu Nederlandt*, on which thirty Walloon families sailed to the colony in March 1624. The captain was Cornelis Jacobsz May, another man with experience sailing the New Netherland route. When May returned to *patria* in October 1624, he was able to report to the directors that Fort Wilhelmus on the South River had been established. A month earlier, on 23 September 1624, the WIC had decided to strengthen the colony by sending more colonists and a number of horses and cows. The Company dispatched a number of ships at the end of 1624 and in the first few months of 1625. A director of the colony was also appointed: Willem Verhulst, who had probably sailed to New Netherland earlier as supercargo on May's ship.[31]

Trade Faction and Colonization Faction

The decision to strengthen the colony was made despite serious differences of opinion within the Amsterdam chamber. One faction within the committee for New Netherland saw good opportunities for an agricultural colony. Among the members of this colonization faction were Kiliaen van Rensselaer, Samuel Godijn, and, possibly, Johannes de Laet. Other directors—the trade faction—thought that the investment needed to establish an agricultural colony would be far too great. They preferred establishing only a small colony sufficient to protect the trading interests. The decision of 23 September 1624 was a victory for the colonization faction, which would, however, soon have to make concessions. New instructions to Verhulst in April 1625 emphasized trade. The Amsterdam directors also ordered him to concentrate the colonists in a single settlement. This measure was probably inspired by the desire both to limit expenses and strengthen the defense. Choosing the exact location of the settlement was left to Verhulst, but two locations were suggested: the southern tip of Manhattan and Fort Wilhelmus. With these new instructions, the engineer and surveyor Krijn Fredericksz was sent to the colony to build a fort there.[32]

The instructions reached the colony in the summer of 1625, and efforts were presumably made to carry them out in the months that followed. However, it quickly became apparent in the colony that Verhulst had insufficient capacities to lead the budding settlement. Early in 1626 he was replaced by Pieter Minuit who, with the help of Secretary Isaac de Rasière, tried to sort matters out. In the course of 1626, Minuit bought the island of Manhattan from the Indians for the sum of sixty guilders, presumably in the form of trading commodities. The ship *Wapen van Amsterdam* arrived with this news in Amsterdam in early November 1626. The meeting of the *Heren XIX* was being held in Amsterdam at the time, and all the news from New Netherland was relayed to the assembly. Pieter Jansz Schagen, a delegate to the States General and present in Amsterdam as its representative, reported the news of the purchase to The Hague. In the nineteenth century his letter, the now-famous Schagen letter, was discovered in the archives of the States General. The Schagen letter is neither the deed nor the "birth certificate" of New York, although it has been called both. At the exchange rate of the 1840s, the sum paid to the Indians was converted to twenty-four dollars, starting one of the most persistent misconceptions in the history of New Netherland. Much more appropriate to assess the purchase price of 60 guilders for Manhattan is the value of the cargo of furs that the *Wapen van Amsterdam* carried: about 45,000 guilders.[33]

2   *Population and Immigration*

In 1659, New Amsterdam merchant Cornelis Steenwijck, back in Amsterdam for a short visit, took Geertgen Dirx into service as a maidservant, giving her an advance of sixty guilders. On reflection, Geertgen regretted her decision and refused to accompany him to New Netherland. Via a notary Steenwijck warned her to bring her goods to the lighter that lay ready to depart from the West India Company warehouse. From there, her goods would be taken to Texel, where they were to be put on board ship. As a precautionary measure, Steenwijck authorized a relative, Abraham Grevenraet, to take legal steps on his behalf if Geertgen disobeyed. The next day, Geertgen, accompanied by her two sisters, appeared in front of the house on the Nieuwendijk where Steenwijck and his wife were staying, cursing and swearing that attempts were being made to transport her to New Netherland against her will. This tactic, bringing the dispute into the public domain, so upset Steenwijck's wife, Margaretha de Riemer, who was in an advanced stage of pregnancy, that she was literally unable to speak, according to a deposition. It is likely that Steenwijck had to be satisfied by Geertgen's repayment of her advance to avoid further commotion.[1]

Steenwijck failed to persuade Geertgen Dirx to become a colonist, but many others made the voyage. Over the course of its existence New Netherland grew from a small trading post of a few hundred inhabitants into what was, by Dutch standards, a considerable settlement colony of seven thousand to eight thousand colonists. The increase in numbers was not gradual but took place mainly in between 1649 and 1664, when the economic growth in *patria* had slowed. By 1664 the colony consisted of two major settlements, the city of New Amsterdam, with approximately twenty-five hundred inhabitants, and Beverwijck, with about a thousand. The other colonists were spread out over two patroonships (Rensselaerswijck on the North River and the city-colony Nieuwer-Amstel [New Amstel]) on the

South River; fifteen towns with a court of justice (Heemstede, Vlissingen, 's-Gravesande, Breuckelen, Middelburgh, Amersfoort, Midwout, Oostdorp, Rustdorp, Haerlem, Boswijck, Wiltwijck, Bergen, New Utrecht, Staten Island); and several smaller settlements, such as Schenectady, Kinderhoek, Hurley, Claverack, Arnhem, Coxsackie, and Catskill.[2] New Netherland's population growth raises the question why the colonists made the voyage, in particular why they chose New Netherland. Viable alternatives existed, such as the East Indies, or Brazil where for a time the cultivation of sugar offered profitable opportunities.

Leaving the Dutch Republic

Why did people undertake the long and risky voyage to New Netherland, when they could have stayed safely at home instead? They had many reasons not to leave the Netherlands. In the first half of the seventeenth century, the economy was booming, which drew many immigrants to Holland, for example from the German states that had been ravaged by the Thirty Years' War, and from the southern Netherlands, where Catholicism was becoming the dominant religion. The Dutch Republic was relatively tolerant in matters of religion in comparison with the rest of Europe, which meant that, in contrast with England, religious persecution was rarely a motive to move to a colony. As early as 1633, the West India Company was aware that the economic situation in the Netherlands was not conducive to emigration, because, as its directors put it: "The peopling of such empty and unfurnished lands, demands more people than our lands can supply; not so much for want of population, with which our provinces swarm, as because all those who will labor in any way here, can easily obtain support, and therefore, are disinclined to go far from home on an uncertain outcome."[3]

Adriaen van der Donck in 1655 expressed a slightly different view. He admitted that there had been many immigrants to the Dutch Republic from other countries for whom previously work had been available, for example in the army. But now little work could be found because of the recently concluded peace with Spain. It would therefore be useful, he argued, if a new Netherland could be founded abroad that could be populated by those unemployed in the Netherlands. Van der Donck was correct: the economic situation had changed, and this no doubt contributed to the extent of emigration to New Netherland in the 1650s. Another important factor was that the colonization of nontropical countries was not very profitable. The WIC's policy in the first decades was oriented toward a minimum of colonization, sufficient to substantiate its claim on New Netherland. In the 1650s the Company tried to make immigration more attractive, but by that time its scope was limited. In 1649 it was already burdened by a debt of some thirty-six million guilders.[4]

3. Dutch Republic, ca. 1648. By permission of Brill.

Individual Decisions

Motives for emigration to New Netherland are difficult to discover. In some instances, though, the sources throw some light on individual motives for emigration. First, Daniël van Gelder. In 1635, he asked the directors of the West India Company to be sent to New Netherland. He had heard from many people who had been there that "the thorn-bush flowers in abundance and the strawberries are fertile for as long as six weeks." He wanted to produce honey and knew how to prepare beaver pelts. Daniël van Gelder clearly saw opportunities to prosper in New Netherland. However, whether he ever arrived in the New World is unknown.[5]

In the second example, there is also a direct link with people who had personal experience of New Netherland. Jannetje Blockx and her fiancé Lieven van Coppenol, a well-known Amsterdam calligrapher, had been in a relationship for a year and a half and were betrothed. Jannetje's sister, Harmtje Blockx, had gone to New Netherland with her husband. The reports Jannetje had received from her sister were apparently so positive that she had considered emigrating herself. Her fiancé, who was considerably older than she, did not share her enthusiasm. The disagreement contributed to their breakup. It is unlikely that Jannetje traveled to New Netherland alone.[6]

In the third set of circumstances, it is certain that those involved actually made the crossing to the New World. In April 1660, a young man, Boudewijn van Nieuwlandt, had promised to marry Maria Besems, but he tried to get out of his obligations by fleeing to New Netherland. As Maria was pregnant, she did not let matters rest. She followed Boudewijn to New Netherland and asked the New Amsterdam city court to place him under bail, to prevent him from leaving New Netherland. Boudewijn was not particularly willing to fulfill the conditions of bail, and in the autumn of 1660 left in secret for Virginia, in the company of yet another young woman. Maria had in the meantime had given birth to a son to whom she pointedly gave his father's name. She recovered part of the costs of the child's maintenance by auctioning off some of the possessions that Boudewijn had left behind and subsequently returned to the Netherlands.[7]

These three situations demonstrate how individual the reasons could be for going, or not going, to New Netherland. In many cases the immigrants had a link of some kind with New Netherland, often a family connection. For many, employment was the prime motivation. On this basis, the stream of immigrants can be subdivided into a number of job categories: West India Company employees, in which there is a distinction between the military, the sailors, and the higher-ranking officials; merchants, either self-employed or as agents of trading houses; farmers and artisans, who traveled independently; and contract laborers, who were in the service of others. Some made the journey for other reasons, and these warrant separate attention: orphans sent over from Amsterdam and those for whom religious grounds may have played a role, for example the earlier-mentioned Walloons and the followers of Plockhoy and De Labadie. These categories overlapped to some extent: soldiers sometimes became farmers, sailors became craftsmen, and so on. Totally different of course was the influx of enslaved people. Although their number was low in comparison to Virginia, Maryland, or the Caribbean islands, enslaved blacks were a distinct feature of the New Netherland population.

Crossing the Atlantic

Once a decision to depart had been taken, prospective colonists awaited an arduous sea voyage. The ships, which mostly departed from Amsterdam in April or May, were at sea for two to three months on average. Most would-be colonists were unused to voyages at sea, and life on the ship was anything but pleasurable for them. It was also expensive. In 1638 the West India Company, which then still held the monopoly on shipping, set a price of one guilder per day in the *kajuit* (luxury cabin), twelve stivers per day in the *hut* (regular cabin), and eight stivers for accommodation between decks. In a society in which the common worker on average earned a guilder per day, such travel expenses could be prohibitive. To promote the colonization of New Netherland, the Company from the 1650s advanced the cost of the voyage to some passengers who went over as freemen. Sometimes a fixed price was determined instead of a daily rate. In 1652, poet Jacob Steendam paid 120 guilders for accommodation for himself and his wife in the *kajuit* of the ship *Hoff van Cleeff,* but for this sum captain Adriaen Bloemmaert undertook to furnish them with food and drink, which suggests that in other cases the passengers had to provide their own rations. Those who could not afford the *kajuit* accommodation did not fare as well. Most of the passengers had to spend weeks in a confined space between decks, with little privacy or ventilation. If the weather was against them, extending the length of the voyage, shortages of water and food might worsen the already meager daily supplies.[8]

Ships destined for New Netherland generally sailed via the Caribbean, which was easier because of the prevailing winds and currents. The voyages, which on average lasted three months, were less risky than those to the East Indies, as the duration of the voyage and the length of time spent in the tropics were shorter. Even so, deaths occurred regularly. On the ship *Meulen,* heading for New Netherland in 1658, ten or eleven of the 108 passengers and crew died for lack of water. A further three died on arrival in New Amsterdam. It is impossible to assess the death rates on ships that sailed to New Netherland, as in many cases it is unknown how many people they carried. The danger that the ship would be lost at sea was everpresent, although the chance of this on a voyage to New Netherland was not great. Only a few ships perished on this route, and rarely was the result as dramatic as in the case of the ship *Prinses Amelia,* which during the return journey in 1647 ran ashore on the coast of Wales. Of the 107 passengers and crew, only twenty-one survived the disaster.[9]

Hardship and danger were unavoidable companions on a transatlantic trip. Yet the main factors that kept Dutch migration to New Netherland down were the relative tolerance and prosperity of the Dutch Republic.

Soldiers with Unknown Destination

Many of the men who joined the WIC as soldier or as *adelborst* (cadet), two of the lowest ranks within the military branch of the Company, were recruited via *zielverkopers* (literally: "sellers of souls"), who provided them with food and a place to sleep until the appointed day of recruitment arrived. The *zielverkopers,* also called *volkhouders* (literally, "keepers of people") or *gasterijhouders* (keepers of a hostel), were the most important suppliers of low-level personnel to both the large companies and the Admiralties. When these employers required sailors or soldiers, the guests of a *zielverkoper* were taken into service. The new recruits generally received two months' pay on signing up, which they had to hand over immediately to the *zielverkoper* to clear outstanding debts for board and lodging. Usually the amount was not sufficient, and a *transportbrief* (note of assignment) had to be signed. This document gave the *zielverkoper* authority to collect part of the employee's future pay from the Company or the Admiralty. A *transportbrief* was referred to as a *transportceel,* and the Dutch word *ceel* (warrant) was corrupted to *ziel* (soul). As the tavern-keepers often sold these documents to third parties at lower than their nominal value, they came to be known as *zielverkopers.*[10]

As a result of the practices of *zielverkopers,* many of their hapless guests had little chance of actually choosing their destination. Rather, they had to take the first opportunity for work that presented itself, irrespective of whether the ship sailed to the East or to the West. In 1642, for example, Laurens Ackerman, a German soldier originating from Hamburg, departed for Brazil on the ship *Utrecht* in the service of the WIC. In 1644 he was sent to Curaçao; he eventually ended up in New Netherland. In 1647, he embarked for *patria* on the ill-fated *Prinses Amelia.* Laurens survived the shipwreck and returned to Amsterdam in November, where he authorized tavern-keeper Willem Watson to collect his pay from the Company. With the *Prinses Amelia,* however, the copies of the books of monthly wages from Curaçao and New Netherland also went down, and it was the policy of the WIC only to pay wages after receiving confirmation from the colonies of the dutiful conduct of their employees. As a result, Laurens was once more compelled to go into debt, and when he departed at the end of 1647 as a sergeant for the East India Company, he again had to sign a *transportbrief.*[11] So, after stints in Brazil, Curaçao, and New Netherland, Laurens sailed to the East. He had little opportunity to choose his destination. However, he was fortunate in that he had survived and, because of his experience, even gained promotion. Many others were not so lucky.

The *transportbrieven* of soldiers who signed up with the Amsterdam chamber of the WIC were usually recorded by notaries in the city. Many of these, including those of Laurens Ackerman, were dealt with by notary Hendrick Schaeff, who was also bookkeeper of the WIC and often held session at the West India Company House on recruitment days. The amounts of money involved were tens of guilders, consisting of debts owed to *zielverkopers* resulting from victuals consumed, monies advanced, as well as for equipment for the journey. These were considerable sums of money for a soldier with a monthly pay of eight or nine guilders or for an *adelborst* who received ten guilders per month. Director General Stuyvesant acknowledged that the soldiers' pay was low, even though they had guard duty only one day out of three and could spend the rest of their time pursuing other vocations. In a letter to the Amsterdam directors, he wrote that it was difficult for them to "stay afloat, especially for those who are burdened with wife and children," which was not uncommon.[12]

A Foreign Garrison

The nationalities of the soldiers who arrived in New Netherland were varied. A third of them originated in the seven provinces that formed the Dutch Republic. As far as the other nationalities were concerned, the majority came from Germany. Numerous German men, either refugees or adventurers, emigrated to Amsterdam, the largest city of the Netherlands. However, good jobs were not easy to find there, especially for unskilled foreign laborers. Many soldiers originated from Scandinavia, France, and England. In many cases Frenchmen and Englishmen joined the WIC via French and English *zielverkopers* who lived in Amsterdam. For German and Scandinavian soldiers the route is more difficult to establish, but the pattern suggests international recruiting networks ensured that new arrivals in Amsterdam quickly found a place to sleep. The countries of origin of the West India Company soldiers were no different from those of the East India Company, of which until about 1660 some 68 percent came from outside the Dutch Republic.[13]

The defense of the colony, both against the Indians and the European powers, required a sizable garrison. As early as 1627, the colonists requested forty soldiers to defend New Netherland against the English. In 1643 the garrison of Fort Amsterdam consisted of only fifty to sixty soldiers, which some colonists believed to be far too few in these years of war with the Indians. A year later the garrison of the fort consisted of fifty-four men: forty soldiers, a gunner, a provost-marshal, three corporals, a commander, an ensign, two sergeants, a drummer, and four *adelborsten*. With the growth of the colony, the number of soldiers also increased. In the beginning of the 1650s, the Company employed 250 soldiers in New Netherland. The strength at Fort Casimir on the South River was in 1656 planned to be sixty men. The number of soldiers in the colony was continuously supplemented. In 1660 alone, a total of forty-six soldiers and *adelborsten* sailed to the colony on three ships, far fewer than Director General Petrus Stuyvesant would have liked. In January 1664 he requested, in vain, the Amsterdam directors to provide him with 300 to 400 soldiers. When New Netherland was taken later that year, 180 soldiers were stationed in New Amsterdam. With the garrisons at Fort Orange, on the South River, and in Wiltwijck, which in 1660 had a garrison of seventy men, a total of some 250 to 300 soldiers guarded New Netherland in 1664, which represented 3 to 5 percent of the total population. The number of soldiers in New Netherland may have increased gradually in absolute terms, but their proportion in terms of the total population decreased. In comparison with the garrison at the Cape of Good Hope, the number of soldiers in New Netherland was low, for which the WIC's financial situation was to blame.[14]

Some of the WIC soldiers stayed in New Netherland after completing their terms of service. Jacob Leisler, born in Frankfurt, was one of them. In 1660 he stayed at the premises of Hendrick Hendricksz Loen in Amsterdam. He went to New Netherland as *adelborst* and, partly as the result of family connections, moved up to be one of the most important merchants of New York. He played a major role in the upheaval in New York after the Glorious Revolution in 1688. Another example is Gijsbert Cornelisz van Weesp, who in 1636 joined the service of the WIC as a soldier. He was first sent to Brazil. In 1638 he went to Curaçao, and a year later he turned up in New Netherland, where he left the service of the Company to be a freeman. He probably stayed on Manhattan for a few years, after which he became an innkeeper in Rensselaerswijck in about 1644. Here he married Lijsbeth, the daughter of Cornelis Segersz van Voorhout, a tenant on a farm on Castle Island. Gijsbert himself was also interested in farming and tried to run a farm. Unfortunately, shortly after hiring a farmhand in Amsterdam, he died.[15]

Colonizing via Soldiers

For many prospective colonists, a few years of serving as a soldier guaranteed a free passage to New Netherland. The West India Company directors reported explicitly that some of the soldiers intended to stay in the colony on completion of their service and take up their previous occupation. From the early 1650s, the WIC instituted a deliberate policy to encourage colonization by enlisting soldiers who would subsequently become colonists. The soldiers who went to New Netherland in the 1650s and 1660s were thus of a different kind than those of the 1630s and 1640s, as is also indicated by the fact that some brought over their wives and children. The soldiers of the 1630s and 1640s had considerably less choice as to their destination and could just as easily end up in West Africa or Brazil as in New Netherland. The later soldiers knew for certain that their destination was New Netherland.[16]

Many soldiers who found themselves in New Netherland decided to settle there and take up another trade. However, it is not clear how many of them repatriated after a number of years' service. Efforts of the West India Company to persuade them to remain were not always successful. In 1661 the Amsterdam directors gave director general and council, the highest governmental authority in New Netherland, specific instructions to turn soldiers who were no longer needed in the colony after the end of the First Esopus War into colonists. They were to grant them a suitable parcel of land without holding them there against their will. But the soldiers were not enthusiastic, as the provincial government had to report to Amsterdam. The reaction of most of them was: "Trades nor farming have we learned, the sword must provide our living, if not here, then we must seek our fortune elsewhere."[17]

Soldiers initially arrived more or less by chance in New Netherland, by way of Brazil or Curaçao. Later on, using soldiers as prospective colonists became Company policy, but it could not prevent repatriation. In geographic origin, the soldiers were the most heterogeneous group among the immigrants into New Netherland.

Seafarers

As with the soldiers, it is unknown how many sailors remained in New Netherland. From the 1640s onwards the majority of the sailors were no longer in the service of the Company. The WIC had started a system of recognition fees, through which it granted permission to the captains of privately owned ships to undertake a voyage to New Netherland. Partly because of the relatively short crossing, in comparison with the length of the voyages to the East, the types of ships used in transatlantic shipping were similar to those used within Europe. The procedures of recruiting the crews were also the same.[18] This means that a distinction should be made between the seamen in the service of the West India Company and those in the service of the captains of privately owned ships.

First, the Company's seamen. For the early period, until about 1640 when the shipping activities of the WIC began to decrease, WIC seamen probably remained in the colony for some months, occasionally years.[19] But this is only partly true for the more specific maritime trades, such as able seaman, boatswain, and sailmaker. Although a number of small yachts and sloops in New Netherland required crews, the majority of the sailors that remained in the colony served as carpenters, coopers, surgeons, and the like. These were trades that could be exercised both on ships and on land in a newly founded colony. Consequently, the categories of sailors and other Company employees are difficult to distinguish from one another, and the sources often provide insufficient information to determine whether a particular crewmember practiced his trade mainly at sea or on land in New Netherland.

Second, the crews of privately owned ships. Although some research has been carried out on the crews of VOC and Admiralty ships, relatively little is known about the seamen of the mercantile fleet in the seventeenth century. In many instances, the captain signed on the crewmembers, sometimes via an intermediary, for a single voyage. This often took place in Amsterdam, which in the seventeenth century boasted a good supply of seafaring folk, originating largely from the Noorderkwartier. Charles Boxer conjectures that two classes of sailors existed in the Netherlands, on the one hand the crews of VOC, WIC, and naval ships, and on the other hand the better-paid crews on the shipping along the coasts of Europe. This distinction also existed in the shipping to New Netherland after private shipping was allowed, but little is known about the wages of the seamen who sailed on the New Netherland run. All in all, little material can be found on the crews of the ships sailing to New Netherland. However, a number of depositions by sailors of occurrences during the voyage are available, for instance on the behavior of passengers, on storms resulting in damage, and on smuggling. Only occasionally does specific information place them in New Netherland as colonists.[20] Nevertheless, some of the sailors remained in the colony, both from Company vessels and from privately owned ships. For example, Abraham Willemsz van Amsterdam in 1643 sailed out as able seaman on the Company ship *Swoll*. In 1647 he asked director general and council in New Netherland for permission to leave the service of the WIC, since he had in the meantime married Aechtje Jans van Norden. He worked for a short period in New Amsterdam as a carpenter. On 12 November 1649 he was seriously injured in a duel; he died the next day.[21]

Captains

Of the highest in rank, the captains, some stayed in New Netherland, like Paulus Leendertsz van der Grift, who originated from Amsterdam. He was captain of the WIC ship *Groote Gerrit* and in 1647 was appointed *equipagemeester* (equipage master) in New Amsterdam, where, after leaving the service of the Company, he climbed to the rank of *burgemeester*.[22] Other captains who settled in the colony were Adriaen Bloemmaert and David Pietersz de Vries. Bloemmaert, born in Maassluis, was in the service of the WIC as captain and as *equipagemeester* at Fort Elmina in West Africa. From the middle of the 1640s he started sailing the New Amsterdam run, where in about 1651 he and his wife Helena Jacobs Swanevelt went to live. In the 1650s he made a number of voyages to Amsterdam as a captain and was also active as a merchant. In 1657 he was appointed *schepen* (member of the municipal court of justice) of New Amsterdam but did not remain in office for long. In 1660 he returned to *patria* and settled in Breukelen near Utrecht, where he died several years later.[23]

David Pietersz de Vries was born in La Rochelle, France, where his father was a merchant. He sailed as captain from his hometown of Hoorn to the Mediterranean and Newfoundland, among other places. In 1624 he crossed swords with the West India Company, which considered his proposed voyage to Virginia to be in breach of their charter. De Vries subsequently joined the service of the East India Company, for which he sailed to Batavia. After his return in 1630 he became involved in the plans of an

Amsterdam consortium of merchants for a patroonship on the South River, to which he made a journey in 1632 and 1633. After the failure of this attempt at colonization, he withdrew from the collaboration, but he continued to be interested in colonization. In 1634 he made a journey to Guyana in an unsuccessful attempt to found a colony on the Oyapock River. During his return De Vries once more called in at New Netherland, where he laid a claim on Staten Island as a patroonship. From 1638 to 1643 he tried to establish an agricultural colony there, in partnership with Frederick de Vries, secretary of the city of Amsterdam and director of the WIC, but problems with the Indians caused this project to fail. Disappointed, De Vries returned to Hoorn, where he arranged for the publication of his travel accounts in 1655. He died later that year.[24]

David Pietersz de Vries is less typical of the captains than Adriaen Bloemmaert. As patroon of Staten Island, De Vries was directly concerned with colonization, and he virtually ceased to exercise his skills as a captain. In contrast, Adriaen Bloemmaert continued his voyages after settling in New Amsterdam, and he differed from other regular captains on the New Netherland run, such as Jan Jansz Bestevaer and Jan Bergen, both from Graft, Pieter Jansz Æmilius, and Jan Reyersz van der Beest, in that they continued to live in the Dutch Republic.

Men such as these captains are noticeable in the sources both because of their recognizable names and the many times they occur. They are easier to trace than sailors with unremarkable names, who swiftly disappear from the records. Some of them preferred the life of a colonist to that of a sailor. As the Company's sailors were paid less than the crews of the privately owned ships, they may have been more inclined to become colonists. But after the abolition of the Company's shipping monopoly, most of the ships were privately owned, and as a consequence fewer colonists originated from the sailors than from the soldiers.

Servants of the Company

Besides the soldiers and sailors in the service of the WIC, the Company was master of many others in New Netherland. An overview from 1650 mentions those employed by the Company in that year: a director, a vice director, a *fiscael* (high official, charged with upholding the rights of the WIC), a councilor, a secretary, three *commiezen,* a supercargo, a barber, a foreman, a *gerechtsbode* (court usher), a slave-master, a midwife, two ministers, and finally, a *voorlezer* (reader of the church lessons) who also performed the duties of schoolmaster.[25] Other officials include clerks; surgeons; *commies* of the merchandise, of the victuals, or of the store; receivers of the recognition fees; and *equipagemeesters*. The Company also employed artisans, such as carpenters and masons.

Within the heterogeneous group of Company employees, a distinction can be made between higher and lower officials, a distinction that corresponds with the difference between administrative and executive duties. The lowest positions were those in which manual work was carried out by workers with special skills, such as carpenters and masons. When the function required the ability to read and write, a higher salary was paid. For the highest functions, commercial and legal insight and administrative experience were required. However, little is known about the criteria the West India Company directors applied in the selection of their personnel. In some instances the words of the directors make clear what they thought of the men they sent to New Netherland. For instance, of Johan de Deckere, who went to the colony in 1655 as supercargo on the ship *Swarte Arent,* they wrote that his "good qualities merit a higher and more powerful position, as besides the fact that he leads a good life and is well trained and experienced by practice, as he has faithfully served several years as attorney and notary in Schiedam [a city in the south of Holland, near Rotterdam], he is also a young man of sound judgment and has a capable and neat style of writing."[26] For these reasons the directors were of the opinion that the director general would be able to employ him in some position. In the case of De Deckere, an exemplary life, good judgment, and tidy handwriting were not the only reasons that secured the high position of councilor and supervisor of finances for him. His uncle, Abraham de Deckere, was receiver general of the WIC, and it is probable that he exercised some influence in the appointment of his nephew.[27] It is also safe to assume that Dirck Looten, who in 1659 was sent to New Netherland as a Company clerk and who later became a *commies* there, to some extent had his family connections to thank for his position. This "person of good family" was very likely related to Company director Charles Looten.[28] Johannes Dijckman, who in 1651 went to New Netherland as a bookkeeper and was subsequently *commies* at Fort Orange, started out as a clerk at the West India Company. In the case of Dijckman, the fact that he had been declared bankrupt in Amsterdam may have played a role in his departure for the colony.[29] Although Dijckman is an exception, lower administrative functions in the WIC were often used to allow the sons or sons-in-law of directors to gain experience overseas.

Family relations also played a role in appointments for functions in the patroonships. Arent van Curler, who went to Rensselaerswijck as *commies,* was a relative of patroon Kiliaen van Rensselaer. Dirck van Hamel, secretary of Rensselaerswijck from 1655 to 1660, was a brother of Maria van Hamel, who was married to Jeremias de Laet, son of Johannes de Laet, director of the WIC and shareholder in Rensselaerswijck. Also, a number of Van Hamels served the company in Brazil. Anthony de Hooges, secretary of Rensselaerswijck from 1648 to 1655, was a son of Johan de Hooges, bookkeeper of the WIC. These relations all confirm the existence of extensive transatlantic networks.[30]

Directors

In some cases employees climbed in the ranks of the Company because of their abilities rather than their family. For example, Petrus Stuyvesant, born in Peperga in Friesland in 1611 or 1612, started out as *commies* on the island of Fernando de Noronha off the coast of Brazil, and served in the same capacity on Curaçao, where he was promoted to director. After losing his right leg while leading an attack on the Spanish-held island of Sint Maarten, he returned to the Dutch Republic to recuperate. He was subsequently appointed director general of New Netherland.[31] Neither of his predecessors, Wouter van Twiller and Willem Kieft, had any experience in the administration of colonies when they were appointed. Van Twiller, a nephew of Kiliaen van Rensselaer, had been a clerk at the WIC in Amsterdam.

Kieft, who had worked as a merchant in France prior to his appointment as director of New Netherland also had family connections in the West India Company.[32] Family connections indeed were more important than colonial experience in the appointment of New Netherland directors. However, at the time of Van Twiller and Kieft, New Netherland was a small trading post, of minor importance when compared with other activities of the WIC. An appointment as director of a small trading post was not an unusual early step in the career of a man from a merchant background.[33]

The officials with the highest positions stayed in the service of the WIC for a long time. On the other hand, lower officials at the level of *commies* and clerk often left the WIC to make their living as freemen in the colony. Claes van Elslandt, born in Haarlem about 1601, was in the 1630s *commies* of the victuals and inspector of tobacco. In 1640 or 1641 he went back to *patria,* but he soon returned to the colony. In the years that followed, he earned his living through a variety of jobs and owned a house in New Amsterdam and land on Manhattan Island and Long Island.[34] It was not unusual for the WIC to promote sailors or soldiers to the position of *equipagemeester* or *commies*. Oloff Stevensz van Cortlandt, born in Wijk bij Duurstede in about 1615, came to New Netherland in 1637 as a soldier, and made rapid promotion to *commies* of the Company store. After leaving the service of the Company he worked his way up to become one of the wealthiest merchants in New Amsterdam and served three times as *burgemeester.*[35]

Staying or Leaving?

The higher Company employees remained faithful to the Company and became attached to living in New Netherland. Some of them stayed in the colony after it passed into English hands, in some cases holding senior administrative positions. Cornelis van Ruyven was secretary of the colony from 1653 through 1664. He had come to the colony in the company of his brother Levinus, who became a clerk. In 1668, Governor Nicolls appointed him to the post of "collector of the customes."[36] Shortly after Johannes La Montagne arrived with his family in New Netherland in 1636 "to settle himself there for life," he was appointed council member in New Amsterdam, until in 1656 he became vice director at Fort Orange. In 1664 he pledged his allegiance to the English administration, but it is believed that he subsequently returned to the Dutch Republic, where he probably died in 1670. As his family had remained in New Netherland, his return to *patria* was presumably intended to be temporary.[37]

Petrus Stuyvesant also settled permanently in New Netherland. Four years after his arrival in New Netherland, he bought a farm on Manhattan from the Company, known as the Director's Bowery. After the surrender of the colony to the English, Stuyvesant went back to the Netherlands to defend himself against a number of charges, but he returned after a couple of years to New York (as it had been called since 1664), where he died in 1672.[38] Things turned out differently for Johan de Deckere. Shortly after the surrender, the new English administration caught him in the act of smuggling powder and slaves, a misdemeanor to which a hint of rebellion was attached. He was immediately expelled from the colony and went to the Caribbean island of St. Kitts. De Deckere, his wife Margriet van Belcamp, and their children reached the Dutch Republic in 1665 on the ship of Admiral Michiel de Ruyter. In 1670 he was back in New Amsterdam to arrange some business, but whether he stayed or not is unclear.[39]

Employees of the Company who went to the colony to fulfill administrative positions stayed longer than the soldiers and sailors. A number of them arrived in the colony via family connections, to gain experience in lower positions such as clerk or *commies*. The higher officials remained in the service of the WIC for a longer time and developed roots in the New World to such an extent that they were not inclined to return to the Netherlands after the English takeover.

Factors and Merchants

At the end of the 1630s, the States General put increasing pressure on the West India Company to give up parts of its commercial position in New Netherland. First to go was the monopoly on the fur trade. Whereas previously it had been prohibited for private individuals to buy beaver pelts from the Indians and ship them to the Dutch Republic, this was now permitted, albeit after payment of the required imposts. The shipping was also privatized; as a consequence, privately owned ships, on payment of a recognition fee and with a supervisory supercargo from the WIC, sailed the New Netherland run. These changes offered valuable opportunities to private merchants, who eagerly took advantage of the new circumstances.[40]

Many minor merchants went independently to New Netherland with small consignments of merchandise, returning to the Netherlands within a short space of time. During their stay in the colony, usually lasting through the summer, they rented rooms in New Amsterdam or Beverwijck. These itinerant merchants were known as *schotse* ("Scotch") merchants.[41] Because they had no permanent place of residence, they are often difficult to trace. One of the few ways of doing so is via the financing of their merchandise. Many of them made use of *bodemerijen* (bottomry bonds), drawn up in the presence of notaries in Amsterdam. In this system, money was borrowed from a bottomry bond financier, with the ship or merchandise as security. The risk of the ship's sinking, the *avontuur van de zee* (adventure of the sea), was borne by the financial backer. After the expiration of the bottomry, which could be either after a specified number of months or on the return to Amsterdam, the beneficiary of the bond had to repay the amount of the loan and interest. For New Netherland the interest varied between 3 and 4 percent per month, with higher rates during the First Anglo-Dutch War.[42]

A bottomry bond not only provided the smaller merchants with an easy, albeit expensive, method of financing their ventures; ships' crews also took advantage of the system, as did colonists departing for New Netherland. The amount owed was sent back to Amsterdam in the form of goods, usually beaver pelts. This transaction did not always happen within the agreed period of time, and the backer was then compelled to give power of attorney to someone going to New Netherland to collect the money. An example is Claes Bordingh, a minor merchant from Bloemendaal. Before sailing to New Netherland in 1647, he, together with Seger Theunisz van Enkhuizen, had acquired six hundred guilders on bottomry from the Amsterdam merchant Olphert Dircksz Claes. Bordingh sent a number of beaver pelts back to Amsterdam, and Olphert Dircksz gave power of attorney to Govert Loockermans to collect the remainder. Apparently Loockermans was successful, since there is no indication that Bordingh was taken to court. Claes Bordingh settled permanently in New Netherland, where he became captain of a yacht and continued to trade. Although he became involved in several instances of arms smuggling, he was a respected and prosperous citizen. In 1653 he owned a house on *Paerlestraat* (Pearl Street) in New Amsterdam, he was in the same year mentioned as one of the most eminent inhabitants of the city, and in 1657 he obtained small burgher right.[43]

Major Merchants

Merchants who acted as agents for the large Amsterdam trading houses and who lived semi-permanently in the colony often worked their way up to becoming prominent, independent merchants and, as the result of their experience as factors, had good commercial contacts. Govert Loockermans, earlier an assistant cook and clerk in the service of the WIC, was

taken on by Seth and Gillis Verbrugge on behalf of their company, probably on account of his previous experience in the colony. His marriage to
a member of the Verbrugge family also played a role. In 1641 he returned
to the Dutch Republic and married Adriaentje Jans in Amsterdam. Shortly
afterwards he returned with his wife to New Netherland, where he acted as
senior factor for the Verbrugges. In the 1640s and 1650s, the Verbrugges'
trading company had a number of other agents in New Netherland, such as
Johannes Pietersz van Brugh, Johannes de Peijster, Joseph da Costa, François
van Hooglant, and Storm Albertsz van der Zee.[44] Most of the people sent
as factors to New Netherland originated from Amsterdam or Haarlem.

The Verbrugges' trading house was by far the most important in New
Netherland. Besides this company, three other large trading houses played a
role in the New Netherland trade. Gillis van Hoornbeeck and his associates
employed Cornelis Steenwijck, Abraham Jansz van Coesant, and Nicolaes
Gouverneur as agents in the colony. Dirck and Abel de Wolff employed Gerrit Bancker and Harmen Vedder as factors. The third large trading house
consisted of the Van Rensselaers, Van Twillers, Van Welys, and Mommas.
They sent, in succession, Gerrit Vastrick, Jan van Twiller, and Jan Bastiaensz
van Gutsenhoven to the colony, while Kiliaen van Rensselaer's three sons,
Jeremias, Jan Baptist, and Rijckert, also represented the family's interests
there.[45]

Family ties linked most of these factors to their masters in Amsterdam.
Johannes de Peijster, dispatched by the Verbrugges to New Netherland to
assist Govert Loockermans, was described by Seth Verbrugge as "my wife's
uncle's sister's son, of good background." He was "a good faithful servant"
and would be a valuable assistant in the store, as he had worked for a long
time in a silk shop. The custom of the merchants that traded in New Netherland was no different from normal seventeenth-century practice, in which
business relations often coincided with family connections.[46] Many of the
merchants did not intend to spend the rest of their lives in New Amsterdam.
At the end of the 1640s Loockermans lived in the colony while his wife was
still in the Netherlands. When he complained about this to the Verbrugges,
the answer was: "There is many a good man who, to gain further advancement, is absent from his wife for two, three, or even more years, one must
strike while the iron is hot. Also, the time will pass quickly there and will
soon be over."[47] Although some factors ultimately returned to the Dutch
Republic, quite a few remained in New Netherland. They started to trade
for their own account and gradually formed in New Amsterdam a class of
merchants independent of Amsterdam, which maintained intensive business
contacts with their counterparts in Holland. This group formed the core of
burgemeesters and *schepenen* of New Amsterdam.[48]

The rise of independent merchants permanently living in New Amsterdam created tension with the minor, itinerant merchants. Because the minor
merchants' stay in New Netherland was short, their costs in the colony were

relatively low, enabling them to offer their goods at lower prices. Other trading practices also caused irritation. In 1648 Govert Loockermans reported to Gillis Verbrugge that the "small traders and 'Scotch'...go inland with their goods, and so make themselves the slaves of the *wilden,* which is entirely contrary to nature."[49] He expected Stuyvesant to put an end to this swiftly. A couple of months later, director general and council issued an ordinance in which the itinerant traders, described as "spoilers of the trade," were required to remain in the colony for a minimum period of three years.[50] The directors in Amsterdam thought this measure unjust and reacted with a remark from which their abhorrence of using compulsory measures to gain colonists is clear:

> In such tender beginnings of a slowly growing state, whose growth must be sought and furthered rather by encouraging and unlimited freedoms than by forced regulations, because to constrain people (who thereto have neither opportunity nor inclination) to own houses or land, is too repugnant, and to compel them to stay, is too servile and slavish.[51]

Instead, they suggested that the merchants in New Amsterdam be required to keep open store. Protests from Stuyvesant and the council were to no avail, but several years later another way was found to counter the activities of the itinerant traders. In 1657, in a petition to director general and council, *burgemeesters* and *schepenen* of New Amsterdam, including in that year Govert Loockermans and Johannes de Peijster, asked for the introduction of a system of burgher right. One of the motives put forward was that the itinerant merchants brought nothing but harm to the community. Small burgher right was a requirement for carrying on a business while in the colony; it would expire after an absence from the colony of four months. This condition excluded the itinerant, "Scotch," merchants from small burgher right, as it prohibited their practice of limiting their stay in New Amsterdam to the summer months. In 1664, director general and council introduced similar measures against merchants who left Manhattan in the summer for Beverwijck.[52]

The abolition of the Company's fur trade monopoly opened the door for private merchants. Minor merchants, usually originating from the Noorderkwartier, engaged in activities of an itinerant nature, whereas large Amsterdam merchant houses sent permanent factors to New Amsterdam. These gradually developed into an elite merchant class and tried to protect their own interest by advocating a burgher right system.

Farmers and Craftsmen

Some colonists made the choice, usually on the basis of a deliberate decision, to leave the Dutch Republic with their families to settle in New Netherland for life and take up the trade or profession they had practiced in Europe. In the last eight years of New Netherland, family immigration formed the largest part of the new colonists. In the types of immigrants dealt with earlier, a number of the colonists came to New Netherland more or less by chance, and in many instances eventually returned to the Netherlands. However, it is likely that farmers who immigrated to New Netherland often intended to stay.[53]

The most important distinction between the farmers and artisans and other types of immigrants is that the former were to a great extent neither in the service of the Company nor of a private individual, something they had in common with the minor merchants.[54] It may be assumed that, because of the availability of agricultural land, New Netherland attracted more farmers than other types of immigrants. Prior to the decision of the WIC to relinquish parts of its monopoly, only few *vrijburgers* (freemen) lived in New Netherland. The term is used occasionally in the sources prior to 1645 to indicate people who were not in the employ of the Company. Later, when Company employees were only a small minority of the total population, the term lost its distinctive meaning and went out of use. Of the early *vrijburgers,* most were farmers. Most of them had not gone to the colony as freemen but had stayed there after leaving the service of the Company. More exceptions occur after 1639. Jonas Bronck, a captain who was probably born in Sweden in 1600, married Teuntje Jeuriaens in 1638 in Amsterdam. A year later he had a one-quarter share to the value of 4,830 guilders in the equipage of the ship *Brant van Troyen,* which carried cattle and colonists to New Netherland. Bronck took a number of laborers and a female servant with him to the colony. In New Netherland he leased a maize and tobacco plantation on Manhattan to Pieter Andriesz and Laurens Duyts. Bronck himself lived on the farm called Emmaus to the north of Manhattan in the area that was to be named after him, the Bronx. He died a few years later, in 1643.[55]

Investing in a New Start

The most important precondition for successful immigration was to have sufficient funds, for the costs of the passage for family and personnel could amount to several hundred guilders. Then, land had to be obtained in New Netherland. Although new colonists could sometimes acquire existing farms by means of lease or purchase, most of them, without much expense, would have obtained land that had not yet been developed. Even in the case of potentially rich agricultural land, the colonists would have to take into account the fact that during the first few years, when the land had to be cleared of trees and undergrowth and a house built, their income would be meager. Adriaen van der Donck, who tried to stimulate immigration, optimistically claimed that as early as the second year the income would be sufficient to make the venture self-supporting. The third year would already yield profits. To set up his own establishment in New Netherland, the prospective farmer needed to have a minimum of two thousand guilders before making the crossing.[56]

Because few emigrants had such capital at their disposal, the directors of the Amsterdam chamber tried to lower the financial barrier in a number of ways. In 1650 Adriaen van der Donck, Jacob Wolphertsz van Couwenhoven, and Jan Evertsz Bout, with the financial support of the directors, planned to equip a flute ship of two hundred *last* (approximately four hundred tons) for two hundred passengers, of which half were free farmers and farm laborers.[57] In early 1656 the WIC decided to provide free passage to "all artisans and farmers who can show that they will be able to provide there for themselves, their wives, and their children."[58] In announcing this decision to Stuyvesant and the council, the directors reported that they were trying "to promote the population and cultivation of New Netherland." The provincial government had to make sure that if these people returned to *patria,* they would pay for the double passage.[59] Stuyvesant was pleased to see more colonists coming, as it strengthened the colony against English infiltration. However, he remarked that it was not always the most suitable people who came to New Netherland. According to him, the majority were

> people without a trade and therefore without work, of which some will later become a charge of the deaconry.... It would be better and more secure for the Company to recover her advances and more useful for the country, instead of such poor people, to send over farmers and farmhands, foreigners and refugees, who are used to labor and poverty.[60]

Origins and Group Migration

Many of the immigrants originated from outside the Dutch Republic.[61] However, this does not apply in the same way to the farmers. A considerable number came from the less prosperous inland provinces of the Dutch Republic, Gelderland, Drenthe, and Overijssel, often in groups. In 1661 the Amsterdam directors wrote to Stuyvesant and the council about "a certain Huijch Barensen de Kleijn van Bets [Beesd] in Gelderland, baker, grocer, and farmer who by his enthusiasm had drawn from there about thirty-six souls and it appears [more] will follow." They recommended that the provincial government help this man to the greatest possible extent.[62]

Group immigration may have occurred more often, but it is not easily recognizable, so that extensive research will be necessary to uncover it. Some emigration took place from the southwestern corner of Drenthe. In 1660 a group of thirty-nine emigrants made the crossing on the ship *Bonte Koe,* followed two years later by a group of twenty-three from the same area. They had been preceded some ten years earlier by Gerrit Jacobsz and Jan Strijcker, who went with their families from Ruinen in Drenthe to New Netherland. It is likely that the later groups had gained their information about the opportunities in the New World from them. Most of the families from Drenthe settled in Midwout on Long Island. From 1654 on, the minister for Midwout, New Amersfoort, and Breuckelen was Johannes Polhemius, who had earlier served the WIC in Brazil. He had been *predikant* in Gieten and Meppel in Drenthe until 1634, and it is conceivable that a number of the colonists from southwest Drenthe were already acquainted with him.[63]

For emigrating farmers, family and group connections played an important role in their choice of New Netherland, even if during the mid-1650s, the time at which the emigration into the colony was in full swing, they had few alternatives. Brazil was no longer in Dutch hands, and colonization of the Cape of Good Hope had just begun. The increasing pressure of taxation and the problem of the division of smaller farms between numbers of sons played a role as push factors. The problem of increasing taxation is mentioned in the petition of a number of Utrecht farmers to the West India Company in 1639: they requested permission to go to New Netherland "seeing that the taxes on the lands are becoming higher and higher and that the farmer finds it hard to earn a living."[64]

The number of farmers who repatriated after 1664 may have been smaller than among other types of immigrants, for whom the ownership of land was less of a tie to the colony. In many ways, the emigrating behavior of independent farmers conforms to the classic type of family colonization. This was different for contract laborers.

Farmhands and Servant Girls

A number of colonists in New Netherland arrived as a result of a contract signed in the Dutch Republic. These were unskilled, wage-earning laborers, such as general hands, farmhands, and maidservants. In a few cases contract laborers were hired for higher positions, such as foreman on a farm, surgeon, or blacksmith, but these form only a small minority. The majority of the contract laborers took up their employment by signing a contract of service before a notary in Amsterdam. These contracts provide insight into the terms under which the contract laborers went to New Netherland and their characteristics.[65]

Of the contract laborers, almost 80 percent were male, a figure consistent with the nature of their employment. Of the fifty-one women or girls, twenty-three were taken into service as maidservants. The majority of the males were farmhands. Other tradesmen, such as tailors, shoemakers, bakers' or brewers' hands, or carpenters, are less numerous. The lengths of the contract periods varied between three and six years, with three to four years being the most common. The younger the laborer, the longer the contract period. On 20 March 1651, Johannes van Rensselaer took into service twelve males for Rensselaerswijck who sailed on the *Gelderse Blom*. In age they ranged between fourteen and forty years. Five youths between fourteen and nineteen years old had contracts for six years, four men aged between twenty-one and thirty-four years had contracts for three years. Their wages also depended on their age. Of the twelve males, the five youngest had initial rates of pay of 30 to 40 guilders per year, while the older males received 120 to 125 guilders.[66] The wages of skilled artisans' assistants were generally higher than those of unskilled farmhands, and they were subject to more rapid increases. An annual pay rise was included in the majority of the contracts. Workers were provided with board and lodging and in most cases also with clothing. Their masters paid the passage money, but the contracts for maidservants specified that the girls had to repay the cost of their voyage if they married during the period of their contract.

Recruitment

Employers had many ways to find laborers prepared to go to New Netherland. A number of the contract laborers were foreigners who had been attracted by the prosperity of Amsterdam and who subsequently were taken into service for the colonies, thus becoming in effect transmigrants. However, other recruitment patterns also existed. A considerable number of the contract laborers who went to New Netherland in the service of the Van Rensselaer and Van Twiller families originated in the neighborhood of Hilversum and Nijkerk, where these families had estates.[67] In particular the Van Rensselaers used their local contacts to recruit farmhands, although no details about the actual method are available. Besides these, Kiliaen van Rensselaer took into service a few people with previous experience of New Netherland, such as Jan Fransz van Hoesem, who had served the WIC as able seaman, and Hendrick Albertsz, who had worked in the colony as a baker. Another patroon, Adriaen van der Donck, largely passed over the region from which he himself originated. For his patroonship of Colendonck, the present Yonkers to the north of New York City, he recruited at least eighteen colonists between the years 1651 and 1653, and only three of these originated from the area of Breda, where he himself was born.[68]

If a colonist in New Netherland needed a laborer, he could request a family member in *patria* as an intermediary to make arrangements. On four occasions during the 1650s, Coenraet ten Eijck, master shoemaker in New Amsterdam, asked his brother-in-law Engel Uijlenberg, a knife seller in Amsterdam, to sign up a shoemaker's assistant on his behalf. It was also possible to entrust recruitment to the ships' captains who sailed the New Netherland run. In 1652, Adriaen Bloemmaert signed up three farmhands from Gelderland for Petrus Stuyvesant, who could make good use of their services on his newly acquired Director's Bowery. Captain Willem Thomasz, who made several journeys to the colony in the 1650s, also recruited a number of farmhands on behalf of others. Their contracts included the passage on his ship.[69]

The signing of a contract in Amsterdam did not always mean that the contract laborer actually ended up in New Netherland. Jan Baptist van Rensselaer wrote to his brother Jeremias in New Netherland on 12 April 1663 that he had hired eight servants. But only three turned up on the appointed day.[70] The others had second thoughts after contemplating the prospect of an arduous voyage and a hard life in the colony.

Labor Relations

Problems between servants and their masters occurred not only prior to their departure from the Netherlands but also after their arrival in New Netherland. On 28 April 1639, in Amsterdam, Jonas Bronck took Clara Matthijs into service as maid for five years. Together with board and lodging, her contract stated that she would receive forty guilders per year. Before three months had passed, Bronck had to appear before the court in New Amsterdam with Gerrit Jansz van Oldenburg, who wanted to marry Clara. Bronck demanded either that the contract be fulfilled or that he be awarded damages. The court ruled in Bronck's favor, and he received an indemnity of 100 guilders.[71]

Contract laborers attempted to avoid fulfilling their obligations in other situations as well. Complaints about ill treatment by the master were usually sufficient reason for the court to annul a contract, although often one of the parties, usually the servant, had to pay. Disobedience of a farmhand was rarely rewarded by the court with the annulment of his contract. In September 1651 the court at Rensselaerswijck sentenced the forty-two-year-old Adriaen Dircksz van Bil to fourteen days' imprisonment because he refused to serve out his contract. The Rensselaerswijck court viewed such behavior of servants as a serious problem. Adriaen Dircksz was punished to ensure "the maintenance of good order and justice and to curb the refractory spirit and intolerable insolence of the contracted servants."[72] Cornelis Melijn took a much more accommodating standpoint when he declared void the contracts made in Amsterdam with two of his employees. Their wives were too afraid to live on Staten Island with their husbands because of the recent Indian attacks.[73]

Relations between servant and master were considerably better in the Dutch Republic than in England. In many ways the servant was the master of his own labor, and he could not be sold off against his will into the service of another master. In America a corresponding difference existed between New Netherland and the English colonies. Nonetheless, it was also necessary in the Dutch colony to take measures against servants who walked out on their masters. Ordinances against this were promulgated in 1640, 1642, and 1643. The fine for harboring a runaway was initially 50 guilders, but it was raised to 150 guilders in 1648. Director general and council promulgated these ordinances with the approval of the Amsterdam directors, who agreed that they were necessary. However, in 1653 they urged director general and council to implement the measures in such a way as to give offense neither to masters nor to their servants.[74]

Similar ordinances in the English colonies have been linked with servants' motivations for running away. An abundance of land and a shortage of workers drove up the price of free labor. This made it attractive for indentured servants in the English colonies to run away from their masters and offer themselves for employment elsewhere as free agents, thus increasing their income. This was not the case in New Netherland. The Dutch hands mostly had contracts of shorter duration than their English counterparts, enabling them to obtain a higher price for their labor when signing a new contract. Besides, they had adequate opportunities for obtaining the annulment of their contracts if they were ill treated by their masters. As a consequence, running away was a less obvious option for Dutch employees in New Netherland than for English colonial servants.[75]

As with other types of immigrants, how many contract laborers remained in the colony after the fulfillment of their contracts is not clear. If a farmhand saved assiduously, he could over time either become a tenant farmer, as did some of Kiliaen van Rensselaer's contract laborers, set up his own farm on land provided by the government, or follow another trade. In 1639, Aert Willemsz van Garderbroek was contracted as farm foreman by former director Wouter van Twiller, who had just returned to the Dutch Republic, for his farm, the *Commandeursbouwerij* (Commander's Bowery) on Manhattan. Aert Willemsz and his wife received the considerable sum of two hundred guilders per year for overseeing the farm. After five or six years Aert abandoned farming to become a brewer, as in 1645 he owned his own house in New Amsterdam, and in 1655 he was identified as a brewer and was charged twenty guilders as a contribution towards the costs of the construction of defensive works around New Amsterdam. He probably died in 1659.[76] Aert Willemsz had already begun his career in the colony with a good salary and, after going into business on his own, managed to better his position to an even greater extent. Occasionally even farmhands after the expiration of their contract period established themselves as free farmers and were able to carve out a reasonable existence for themselves.

Contract laborers were mostly young farmhands and servant girls, recruited in Amsterdam for three to six years. Occasionally colonists contracted their servants through the use of intermediaries in the Dutch Republic. Migration from the Dutch Republic to New Netherland could only take place on a voluntary basis and could not be sold to other masters, a contrast with the English indenture system. A result was that labor relations were better under Dutch law, and runaways were less common.

Enslaved Blacks

New Netherland was not a plantation colony like the English colonies Virginia and Maryland or the colonies in the Caribbean. Partly because of this, the number of blacks, most of them enslaved, remained relatively small. In 1639 about one hundred blacks worked in the colony, a number that grew to approximately 250 in 1664 and was doubled by the arrival of 291 slaves on the ship *Gideon* in August. In that year, blacks, both free and enslaved, made up between 6 and 8 percent of the total population, with a concentration in New Amsterdam, where it may have been 10 to 17 percent. With this, the proportion of slaves in the population of New Netherland was considerably lower than in Batavia, where in 1632 approximately 30 percent of the population consisted of enslaved people. Subsequently it grew to 52 percent in 1679. In the eighteenth century more than half the population on the Cape consisted of slaves.[77]

The slaves that were imported into New Netherland usually did not come directly from Africa but originated from Iberian ships seized in the Caribbean. In only a few cases, such as that of the journey of the *Witte Paert* in 1654–1655, were slaves imported directly from Africa. After 1658 Curaçao developed into a transit post in the Dutch slave trade, and as a result the importation of slaves into New Netherland became more common. Most of the time, the number of slaves per shipment was small, with a maximum of a few dozen blacks. The arrival of the ship *Gideon* was a rare exception. Once in New Netherland, some of the slaves were sold, sometimes by public auction. The prices paid for them were considerably lower than those paid for slaves that had been sold from Curaçao to the Spanish colonies, which suggest that at least part of slave import in New Netherland consisted of mancarons (slaves with a physical handicap). In New Netherland the price varied from 140 to 375 guilders in the 1650s. Later the prices rose, even reaching 600 guilders in 1664. Given the increasing demand for slaves in the colony, director general and council tried to prevent exports of slaves by introducing substantial export fees in 1655.[78]

Initially all enslaved blacks were owned by the West India Company. Although the WIC remained the largest slaveowner in the colony, a number of wealthy private individuals could afford to purchase slaves. In 1665 thirty of the 254 people named on a New York taxation list, only 12 percent, were the owners of slaves. Roughly half of their number belonged to the two highest categories in the list, those assessed for three or four guilders. The remaining half is spread throughout the other categories, with the exception of the lowest category, those who were exempt from paying tax. After the

Dutch period ownership of slaves gradually became more general and the slave regime hardened. By 1703 41 percent of the households in New York City owned slaves and New York developed the toughest slave laws of the thirteen colonies.[79]

Orphans

In 1628, the directors of the East India Company sent twenty orphans, thirteen boys and seven girls, from the orphanage in Delft to Asia, in an attempt to promote the growth of the European population there. Twenty-two years later the West India Company, with the same goal in mind, developed similar plans for New Netherland. In 1650 the Amsterdam directors proposed to the *burgemeesters* of Amsterdam that three hundred to four hundred boys and girls from ten to fifteen years of age be sent from the orphanages of the city to the colony. Of primary importance in this plan, as in later plans, was the children's free will. If they did not wish to go, they did not have to. If they would go, they were to be quartered with people in New Netherland as apprentices or maids. The maximum period of service was to be six to seven years. After the expiration of their contract, the orphans had the choice of going into service once more or becoming free settlers in the colony. In the latter case, the director general would make land available to them free of charge, and they would receive a ten years' exemption from the *tienden* (tenths), the 10 percent tax on produce of the land which had biblical origins (for instance Genesis 14:20). The plan, in fact, had a twofold goal: by sending orphans to the colony, the settlement of New Netherland would be advanced and the coffers of the city of Amsterdam would be relieved of the considerable cost of their maintenance. But the WIC directors also had an ulterior motive for their proposal. The correspondence between the directors and the *burgemeesters* of Amsterdam shows that the former regarded the plan as a service in return for the *burgemeesters*' support in defeating the proposals for changes in the administrative structure of New Netherland under review by the States General.[80]

The orphan plan was not put into action at this time. The Amsterdam directors informed director general and council at the beginning of 1651 that it would cause too many problems, without stating the exact nature of these problems. However, the Amsterdam city government had already adopted these ideas. At the end of 1651 the *vroedschap* (city council) requested the *burgemeesters* to investigate whether the boys and girls, who were a burden on the *aalmoezeniers* (almoners or supervisors of poor relief) and also "other useless persons, who here are a burden and there are worth their fare," could be sent to New Netherland. The *vroedschap*'s concern was to lower the *aalmoezeniers*' expenses. The orphans of city burghers were taken into the *burgerweeshuis*, but foundlings and the orphans of the poor were boarded out to so-called *houmoeders* (surrogate mothers) at the expense of the *aalmoezeniers*. A separate orphanage for children in the care of the *aalmoezeniers* was not founded until the 1660s. If some of these children could be placed with masters in New Netherland instead of with *houmoeders* in Amsterdam, the *aalmoezeniers* would no longer have to bear the cost of their upkeep.[81]

Selection

With this in mind, all the children living at the expense of the *aalmoezeniers* were examined early in 1652 both as to their suitability to make the journey to New Netherland and their willingness to do so. The suitability referred to their age. The children had to be at least eight years old. Their health also played a role. Naturally, strong and healthy children were considered more eligible than weak and sickly children. The sources give the impression that the *aalmoezeniers* visited all the children at their places of residence and asked each child if he or she was prepared to go to New Netherland. This immediately raises the question what the children were told about the colony, a question to which, unfortunately, the sources provide no answers. If some of the children intimated that they were "very willing" to go, it may be assumed that they were in possession of at least some information of a positive nature. However, if they based their reply only on information provided by the *aalmoezeniers,* one might ask how objective such information was.

The type of education the children had received was of little importance. Most of the girls could sew, as in the case of the eighteen-year-old Stijntje Thomas, or could be of help in housekeeping, as with Aeltje Jans, who was seventeen. However, some of the boys were apprenticed to gold-wire drawers, such as Robert Gordon, who was fourteen, or to letter founders, such as sixteen-year-old Isaac Gerritsz, trades hardly in demand in the colony, although both boys were inclined to go to New Netherland. As it turned out, most of the children were not eligible: they were too young, did not want to go, still attended school, still had to serve out a number of years with a master, or preferred the trade they had already chosen. Of the hundreds of children that might have been sent, only a few dozen were deemed suitable.

After the first round of visits in January 1652, the *aalmoezeniers* invited the selected children to come to their office and asked them whether they were really sure about their decision. A few had changed their minds, and the *aalmoezeniers* had to report to the *burgemeesters* that most children were unwilling to leave the Netherlands. Displeased with the whole plan, they added that dispatching the children to the colony would not be advantageous after all, since the directors wanted only children over fourteen years of age, which would make little difference to their expenses. The *aalmoezeniers* drew up a list of twelve boys and eleven girls, aged between thirteen and twenty-one, who were not learning their chosen trade well and who met all the requirements.[82]

For reasons not clear, the Amsterdam directors reported shortly afterwards to Stuyvesant and his council that the *burgemeesters* had offered to send one hundred and fifty boys and girls to the colony. Such a number is more likely to have originated from the financial aspirations of the Amsterdam city government than from a realistic assessment of the willingness on the part of the children to emigrate. Arrangements for transport were made with a number of ships' captains, and the amount of land that would be made available to each child at the end of his or her service was also announced: twenty-five *morgens*. However, the plans now hit another snag. In the months before the outbreak of the First Anglo-Dutch War in the middle of 1652, the English had captured a number of Dutch ships, and the directors did not want to put the children in harm's way.[83]

In 1654, after the conclusion of this war, the Amsterdam directors renewed their attempts to carry out the orphan plan. They mentioned a figure of fifty children, for whom they were also to send over provisions. The task of placing the children with good masters was entrusted to the provincial government. The *burgemeesters* of Amsterdam came up with a lower number, however, twenty-seven or twenty-eight. The precise number of orphans who actually made the crossing on the ship *Peereboom* is not known, but as a house was rented to provide them with temporary accommodation in New Amsterdam, it must have been more than just a handful of children. A matron was employed to accompany the children on the voyage and to look after them in the early days of their stay in the colony.[84]

Boarding Out

The name of only one of these orphans is known, the sixteen-year-old boy Hendrick Claesz. On 16 November 1654 *predikant* Johannes Megapolensis, *schepen* Paulus Leendertsz van der Grift, and elder and *schepen* Oloff Stevensz van Cortlandt placed Hendrick in the service of Lodewijck Jongh, farmer at the deacons' bowery in New Amsterdam. The contract stipulated that Jongh must give his new hand the opportunity to attend church on Sundays and, if Hendrick should so wish, to learn to read and write. If Hendrick behaved improperly, Jongh was not entitled to discharge him without the permission of his supervisors, nor could he let him go if he became ill. Jongh was not permitted to transfer the boy, without permission, into the service of another: He was to be treated as "a free-born Dutchman." Every three months, Jongh, accompanied by Hendrick, had to report to the supervisors to check his situation. Lodewijck Jongh was to provide Hendrick with good board and clothing and at the end of his four-year period of service give him a final payment of at least sixty guilders. That amount was sufficient to pay for the return passage to the Dutch Republic, if he so desired.[85]

Although the contracts for the boarding out of the other children are not available, it may be assumed that theirs did not differ much from that of Hendrick Claesz. In any event, the WIC directors were satisfied with the efforts to find suitable placements for the children, and in 1655 another number of children was dispatched: nine girls varying between thirteen and twenty-three years of age, and seven boys from twelve to seventeen. In 1659 another small group of six children followed. An unknown number of children were sent in 1658 to New Amstel, the city-colony of Amsterdam on the South River. Director Jacob Alrichs of New Amstel reported to the commissioners of the city-colony in Amsterdam that the orphans had arrived safely and had all been placed with good masters, the oldest for two years, the majority for three, and the youngest for four years. They were to earn twenty guilders per year. Alrichs added that he would be pleased when more children came over, but only if they were older than fifteen years and strong enough to work well. In 1662, the Amsterdam *burgemeesters* even contemplated establishing an almshouse in New Amstel for children from Amsterdam.[86]

The *aalmoezeniers* dispatched all these children to New Netherland. Only a few orphans reached New Netherland in a different way. Jan Reijndertsz Spits from the Amsterdam *burgerweeshuis* was in the service of the WIC as a gunner in New Amsterdam in 1659 and 1660. Because his contract was drawn up in Amsterdam, his salary had also to be paid out there. In 1660 he requested the regents of the *burgerweeshuis* to collect his salary and deposit it with the orphan masters as provision for his old age.[87] In other cases, orphans went to New Netherland on the same basis as regular contract laborers. In this way Metge Davits, an eighteen-year-old girl in the care of the *aalmoezeniers,* entered into the service of Johannes La Montagne for three years as a maidservant. She received a considerably higher salary than other orphans, no fewer than forty-eight guilders per year. Marritge Jochems, who had been recruited in Amsterdam for five years as a maidservant, found a position with Anna Hendricks, the wife of surgeon Jacob de Hinse at Fort Orange. For her first year Marritge received fifty guilders and for the following years sixty guilders per year.[88]

New Netherland was a more suitable place for orphans than the East Indies, if only because of the climate. The plans to utilize orphans to populate the colony were launched only after the colonial society had become sufficiently well established, so the orphans were not confronted with the trials of a pioneer settlement. Financial considerations in Amsterdam played an important role in the orphan plan, but the welfare of the children was not disregarded. Only children of good health and suitable age were sent over, and only those who wished to go of their own free will. The optimism of the Amsterdam directors and *burgemeesters* for the success of the plan was grossly exaggerated. In all, no more than one hundred orphans actually ended up in the colony. How many remained after their service ended is unknown, as in the case of many of the other types of immigrants.

Religious Migration

Compared with emigration to New England, the emigration to New Netherland was rarely inspired by religious motives. It may have played a role in the case of the Walloon families who went over in 1624. The same is true of the English families from Leiden and England who in 1620 volunteered as colonists (and were rejected) and who the following year settled Plymouth Plantation.[89] For those New Englanders who wished to leave the "City upon a Hill," New Netherland was an option, "both to have freedom of conscience and to escape from the unbearable government of New England."[90] Yet after the early 1620s, no signs of religiously inspired transatlantic group immigration for New Netherland are evident for many years. Religion may have been important in the case of individual colonists, especially for Protestant refugees from the southern Netherlands, who subsequently emigrated to New Netherland. But it does not seem to have been of major importance.

Only in 1662 did religion begin to manifest itself as a motive for immigration, with the publication of two pamphlets: *Kort Verhael van Nieuw-Nederlants Gelegenheit* (Short Account of New Netherland's Situation) and *Kort en klaer ontwerp* (Concise and Clear Design).[91] Franciscus van den Enden wrote the first treatise, a work describing New Netherland, based to a large extent on Van der Donck's *Beschryvinge*. Van den Enden in this pamphlet unfolded the utopian model of a democratic and egalitarian society that he thought should be founded in New Netherland. The pamphlet gives a report of Van den Enden's negotiations with the Amsterdam city government to establish such a colony on the South River, but the anticlerical tenor of Van den Enden's ideas, of which his suggestion of banning ministers from the colony is an extreme example, made the plan unacceptable to the magistrates of Amsterdam. Van den Enden's ideas for New Netherland never went beyond the drawing board.[92]

In contrast, the ideas of pamphleteer Pieter Cornelisz Plockhoy did become reality. Plockhoy's ideas, as laid down in the *Kort Verhael,* were Baptist-inspired, but he was at least as democratic and egalitarian in tone as Van den Enden. He had already made a vain attempt in 1657 to interest the English Protector Oliver Cromwell in his plans, and he put them forward again later in Amsterdam. In May 1663 he left with a number of colonists for the South River where, under the authority of the city of Amsterdam, he established a small colony. During the English conquest of New Netherland a year later, Plockhoy's colony was destroyed, and the colonists were sold to Virginia as slaves.[93]

A later instance of religious immigration, in which New York appears in the margins, concerned the followers of Jean de Labadie. At the end of the 1670s this pietist group, which at that time formed a small commune in Wieuwerd in Friesland, sent Jaspar Danckaerts and Peter Sluyter to New York to investigate the opportunities of settling there. They searched the area around New York and along the Delaware River to find a suitable location for a settlement. Although a number of the Labadists ultimately emigrated to North America, albeit not to New York but to Maryland, the journal of the travels of Danckaerts and Sluyter provides an interesting account of how the Dutch colonists lived under the administration of the English. Interesting as this may be, the immigration of the Labadists remained as marginal a phenomenon as the earlier religious immigration.[94]

The geographic origins of the colonists were diverse, and there is a clear link between the colonists' occupations and their geographical origins. The soldiers originated in the German states, although after 1650 soldiers from the Netherlands were more numerous. A number of the sailors employed by the West India Company came from Scandinavia, while the majority of those on privately owned ships probably came from the Noorderkwartier. To a major extent, the lower-ranking Company employees did not come from the Dutch Republic, but their higher-ranking counterparts did originate principally from Holland. The minor merchants mainly came from the Noorderkwartier, while most of the major merchants were from Amsterdam and Haarlem. The farmers came mainly from the less prosperous eastern provinces of the Netherlands. The contract laborers were mostly recruited via Amsterdam's international labor market. Finally, the orphans came from Amsterdam. The population of New Netherland was indeed, as director general and council wrote in exasperation, "a motley collection (few excepted) of various countries."[95] Yet they had in common that they were under Dutch rule.

3   *Authority, Government, and Justice*

At seven in the morning on Saturday, 30 December 1656, three members of the New Netherland council, Brian Newton, Cornelis van Ruyven, and Carel van Bruggen, departed from New Amsterdam in a small boat, rowed by the captain of the Company's yacht and a sailor. Their destination was Oostdorp, a town recently founded by the English in what was later to be called Westchester, where new magistrates had to be installed. As the result of a miscalculation of the high and low tides, the expedition was compelled to land on Long Island, close to Vlissingen. There they found the remains of the house of William Hallett, which the Indians had burned down a year before. The men made a fire and fried oysters while they waited for a favorable tide to continue their journey. When they finally arrived in Oostdorp, they met John Lard, one of those due to be appointed as a magistrate. They asked him to call the inhabitants together the following morning for the announcement of the appointments, but John Lard told them that the population would not be prepared to meet on a Sunday. So, on the morning of Monday, 1 January 1657, the inhabitants were literally drummed up and the announcement was made which three of the six nominees were appointed. Although one of the inhabitants objected to one of the appointments, the new magistrates were sworn in. The assembled folk then voiced a number of complaints to Newton, Van Ruyven, and Van Bruggen, who promised to lay all the points before director general and council. When all business had been conducted, they took their leave, departing after breakfast for New Amsterdam, where they arrived at three in the afternoon. The presence of council members at the installation of magistrates, reminded the community that director general and council had the last word over the affairs of New Netherland.[1]

In the early years of New Netherland, the creation of local authorities for the exercise of justice and government was not required. The crews of the ships that frequented the area remained under the authority of the captain, and his powers to dispense retribution continued ashore. But the founding of the West India Company changed this situation. The States General, which held sovereignty over the Dutch colonies, had granted the Company extensive rights in its 1621 charter. Its directors could appoint and replace governors and officers of justice and send out soldiers, all for the defense of the conquests, the maintenance of order, and the furtherance of trade.[2] Some restrictions applied. If the WIC wished to appoint a governor general, the highest rank in the Dutch colonial system, his appointment and the description of his duties had to be approved by the States General. The higher-ranking Company officials, directors general, directors, commanders, and *fiscaels* usually received a letter of commission from the States General. Just as with the VOC, the higher officials of the WIC had to pledge their loyalty not only to the Company but also to the States General. Moreover, the States General had a seat in the highest governing body of the West India Company, the *Heren XIX*. As the poor financial situation of the Company made it dependent on government subsidies, the States General could exert considerable influence on the affairs of the WIC.[3]

In New Netherland, the sovereignty of the States General was recognized in the opening words of ordinances and in the oath that the local magistrates had to take. In practice, however, the States General intervened in the day-to-day running of the colony only in exceptional circumstances. The WIC had been entrusted with laying down colonial policy in the Dutch Atlantic, establishing a situation that displays similarities with that of the Generality Lands, the southern part of the Dutch Republic that had been conquered in the course of the Eighty Years' War. Within the Company the Amsterdam chamber was charged with the administration of New Netherland, a result of the fact that the merchants who had traded to the area prior to 1621 mainly came from Amsterdam. The other chambers of the WIC were involved with New Netherland only when the colony was discussed in meetings of the *Heren XIX*. A small number of directors in the Amsterdam chamber formed a committee for New Netherland and corresponded with the colony. In the same way, small groups of directors were responsible for other colonies, such as Curaçao, and for other matters such as equipage or recruitment. These committees prepared the decisions that were subsequently officially taken by the whole board of the chamber. In the early years the committee for New Netherland included Albert Coenraetsz Burgh, Johannes de Laet, Samuel Godijn, and Kiliaen van Rensselaer. In later years many directors signed the letters to director general and council. Appearing most frequently are the names Isaack van Beeck, Jacob Pergens, Eduard de Man, David van Baerle, Abraham Wilmerdonck, and Hans Bontemantel, all prominent Amsterdam regents with close contacts to the Amsterdam city government.[4]

In the colony itself, the highest authority was the body of director general and council, as it was called after 1647. In the early years, the title commander, lower than that of director, was used for the highest official in New Netherland. Subsequently the highest official of the WIC in the colony had the rank of director. Only after Stuyvesant took over in 1647 was the title director general put into regular use, reflecting the fact that he was also in charge of Curaçao and the other Dutch Caribbean islands. Although the title governor also occurs in some sources, the rank of director general was lower than that of governor general, which was held for instance by Count Johan Maurits van Nassau-Siegen in Dutch Brazil. The difference in rank reflects the lesser importance of New Netherland.

Governing a Trading Post

The dispatch of thirty Walloon families to New Netherland in 1624 prompted the WIC to design a system of administration and justice for the colony. The conditions under which the first colonists went to the colony were laid down in the *Provisional Regulations,* a remarkable contract between colonists and Company. Eager to substantiate its claim on New Netherland by taking actual possession, the West India Company decided to employ the Walloons to be settlers for six years, albeit without salary. The colonists obtained many other benefits. They received free passage, free victuals, and other necessities for two years. The Company promised to provide them with land and the required seeds and animals to start farms, and they were allowed to trade with the Indians. In return, the WIC expected them to be obedient, settle where they were ordered to, use the Dutch language in all public matters, and not to engage in any handicrafts that could compete with produce made in the Dutch Republic, a measure that reflects the contemporary thinking on the economic role of colonies. Also, they were sworn to secrecy on Company affairs. After six years, the Walloon colonists would be free to sell their farms or retain them, as they desired. The conditions laid down in the *Provisional Regulations* were liberal, although the fate of the Walloons would rest with the ability of the Company to fulfill its side of the agreement. Also, it was uncertain whether two years of free victuals would give the colonists enough time to become self-sufficient. With the *Provisional Regulations* the Company's model for the colonization of New Netherland was closer to the Jamestown model than to the New Plymouth model.[5]

Director and Council

The first leaders of New Netherland were ship captains Adriaen Jorisz Thienpont and Cornelis Jacobsz May. Subsequently, Willem Verhulst was sent in 1625 as provisional director to New Netherland. Verhulst chaired the council, which consisted of two officials of the WIC and two Walloon colonists. Verhulst was supposed to "deliberate and act upon all matters of importance" with his councilors.[6] With this stipulation the governmental responsibility was made collective, as was usual in the Dutch Republic and its overseas territories. It meant that the director could not act on his own authority or make important decisions without consulting the council, although as chief executive officer he had substantial influence. Even a strong leader like Director General Stuyvesant was on occasion outvoted by the council.[7]

Director and council were responsible for all the administrative affairs of the colony, but they had to follow orders from the Dutch Republic. Only "after mature deliberation, and not without great and important reasons" were they permitted to vary from the orders.[8] Although the directors were often inclined to listen to the opinion of their servants, they always had the final say. They wanted to be kept informed of what happened in New Netherland, down to the last detail. The directors in Amsterdam usually obtained oral information from the captains of ships and others in the Company's service on their return home, but the main source was direct correspondence.[9]

Nevertheless, the Amsterdam directors could only exercise control retroactively, so the authorities in New Netherland often had to deal with matters as they saw fit, especially where relations with the Indians were concerned. The director in New Netherland had the authority to negotiate and make treaties with "foreign princes and potentates in that country."[10] Relations with the Indians were of the utmost importance; efforts were to be made to prevent giving any form of offense. Individual colonists committing felonies against the Indians were to be punished in a suitable manner "in order that the *Indianen* may see that both in civil and criminal cases we do justice without regard to persons." In its early years, when the colony contained only a few hundred inhabitants, such a degree of caution was necessary for its survival.[11]

An important administrative task of director and council was the allocation of land. Land had to be obtained peacefully from the Indians and subsequently granted to colonists, giving "each family as much land as they can properly cultivate."[12] Later on, private individuals were permitted to purchase land from the Indians, but this always had to be approved by director and council. Apart from the wish of the colonial government to maintain an overview of the exact ownership of land, such control could prevent the same plot of land being sold several times over, which happened when the different conceptions of land ownership led to misunderstandings and conflicts.[13]

The Exercise of Justice

In the early period, director and council exclusively exercised justice in the colony. It is unlikely that the situation in the WIC was different from that in the VOC. The punishment for offenses was usually entrusted to the *scheepsraad* (ship's council) or the *brede raad* (broad council). The ship's council was empowered to punish minor infringements, and it had the powers to deal with more serious cases if the ship was sailing alone. When ships sailed in convoy, the broad council would try cases of a more serious nature. The ship's council and the broad council were composed of the captain and other officers as well as commercial officials, such as the *opperkoopman* (senior merchant). Such a combination of positions is also evident in the council in New Netherland.[14]

Jurisprudence in the colony was based on the laws in force in the Dutch Republic. Already in 1625 the customary practices in civil law in the Netherlands were established for New Netherland, as well as the regulations concerning matrimony and inheritance. Printed copies of relevant ordinances were sent to the colony.[15]

In addition to civil law, the administration of parts of criminal law also fell under the duties of director and council. In some criminal cases, the council could be expanded to include several colonists. Just as in the promulgation of new laws, the authorities in the colony were subordinate to their masters. "All adulterers and adulteresses, thieves, false witnesses, and useless persons" had to be sent back to *patria*.[16] Any pardon granted by director and council in New Netherland was subject to the approval of the authorities in *patria*. Not until 1629 were the authorities in the colony vested with high jurisdiction (that is, the power to impose capital punishment), nor were they empowered to order corporal punishment. The system of justice in force in the colony in the early period was thus a mixture of regular maritime law and the practice current in the Dutch Republic. Gradually, the latter prevailed. The only exception was the military law, which retained its own characteristics, such as the nature of punishments.[17]

Administrative Staff

To carry out its tasks, the West India Company employed a number of officials in New Netherland. The most important of these were the director, the secretary (who also acted as notary), and the *fiscael*, positions that had existed from the colony's early years. Other positions, such as that of bookkeeper or receiver of the recognition fees, were created only after several years when, with the growth of the colony, the Company's personnel was expanded.[18]

The *fiscael* was also one of the councilors, and his task was to uphold the rights of the West India Company. These can be divided into two parts. First, he had to defend the rights of the Company both as an employer and as a commercial entity. In the case of improper behavior of Company employees, such as contraventions of the *artikelbrief* or dereliction of duty, the *fiscael* investigated and acted as prosecutor. The WIC's commercial monopoly allowed it to try cases of smuggling, for instance. Second, the Company had rights deriving from its role as a governmental institution, which it exercised through the promulgation of ordinances and the collection of taxes, such as the *tienden*. Director and council could try any contravention of these governmental ordinances. The *fiscael* acted as public prosecutor both in cases of the infringement of the ordinances and in criminal cases.[19] In trials before director general and council, the *fiscael* had to collect evidence and demand a sentence reflecting the seriousness of the crime. After the council had pronounced a verdict, the *fiscael* executed the sentence. In the Netherlands, the duties of the public prosecutor in criminal cases were generally carried out by a *schout* (local officer in charge of investigation and prosecution) or, in rural areas, by a *baljuw* (district magistrate). For part of the 1650s, the *fiscael* of New Netherland was also *schout* of New Amsterdam, thus combining in one official two positions of different levels, with different jurisdictions.[20]

The secretary and *fiscael* belonged to the group of council members who, like the director general and vice director or first councilor, had executive tasks. Other councilors had no specific tasks, apart from giving their advice in meetings of the council, although they could be assigned ad hoc tasks. The secretary usually had no voting rights, nor did the *fiscael* when acting as public prosecutor in criminal cases.[21] Other officials could also be members of the council, although this was more common in the early period than later. With the growth of the administrative staff, a distinction was introduced between the council duties on policy on the one hand, and lower administrative and executive tasks such as those carried out by the *commiezen*, on the other hand.[22]

Although the administration of the colony was set up adequately by means of the instructions for Verhulst, problems soon arose, as a letter from Isaac de Rasière to the Amsterdam directors shows. De Rasière had arrived in New Netherland in July 1626 and discovered that the council had appointed Pieter Minuit as director instead of Verhulst, who was suspected of mismanagement. Under his rule, "the people here have become quite lawless, owing to the bad government hitherto prevailing." They had, according to De Rasière, "heretofore been very harshly ruled by Verhulst, and that without any form of justice, but merely upon his own authority," which had caused discontent among the employees of the WIC and the colonists.

Ambiguities and Conflicts

De Rasière's letter also touched upon the way decisions were made in the council. He felt that he, as secretary, should not have the right to vote in trials, "since it is a secretary's duty to impartially take notes of all things and to be neutral in such matters." On the other hand, he believed that "in matters of legislation and administration my vote and seat should come next to those of Minuyt," making him in effect vice commander. But the council withheld this position from him, which was even more galling for De Rasière because the position of secretary, which he combined with that of *commies* of the merchandise, cost him more time than he had anticipated, while receiving scarcely any extra payment.[23]

Such conflicts about the rights and responsibilities of officials were to be expected in an administrative structure that still suffered a degree of ambiguity. An extra problem for New Netherland was that the directors in Amsterdam could not act swiftly when anything went wrong in their overseas colony. In such a situation, much depended on the leadership of a few prominent men on the spot, but the capabilities of the early directors of New Netherland left a great deal to be desired. Like Verhulst, Minuit had difficulties in maintaining his authority. When the situation got out of hand, the directors decided to replace the entire secular and ecclesiastical administration of New Netherland. In 1632 Director Minuit, Secretary Van Remunde, and Minister Michaëlius were recalled. Wouter van Twiller, who succeeded Minuit, also lacked the qualities necessary to gain the united backing of the colonists and Company employees.[24]

Wouter van Twiller's reputation has suffered great damage at the hands of David Pietersz de Vries, in whose *Korte Historiael* the director is spared little criticism. Yet it is obvious that De Vries blackened the reputation of others to improve his own. The incompetence of which he accused the Directors Van Twiller and Kieft was a convenient excuse for the failure of De Vries's own projects. Thwarted ambition also played a role. De Vries applied to the Amsterdam directors to take over Van Twiller's position as director himself but was turned down. Because few sources are available for the 1630s, the image created by De Vries has rooted itself firmly in the historiography. Other information indicates that Van Twiller was not a particularly strong director, and he also drank rather more than was good for him.[25]

In the early period, three aspects of the administrative history of New Netherland clearly come to the fore. First, the administrative apparatus displayed similarities with the way authority was exercised both on ships and on trading posts of the East India Company, following a general Dutch pattern. As the administrative staff expanded, the demarcation between different administrative functions improved. Second, the judicial system of the Dutch Republic was adopted right from the earliest beginnings of the colonization of New Netherland. And third, neither experienced administrators nor the WIC directors themselves were inclined to spend a number of years in self-imposed colonial exile. None of the early directors of the colony possessed sufficient character and independence to keep a cool head and steer a steady course in a far-off place to which a ship bearing instructions from *patria* sailed only a few times per year. As a result, they resorted to authoritarian methods, which did not sit well with the colonists. One of the consequences was that a number of the original Walloon settlers, having served out their time in the colony, returned to Europe. The conflicts between directors and colonists did not contribute to the construction of a well-balanced administration in New Netherland in its early years.

The Compromise between Colonization and Commerce

More important than the incompetence of early officials was the conflict between a trade faction and a colonization faction within the Amsterdam chamber. Unanticipated high costs had made several WIC directors doubt the profitability of the early attempts at colonization. The income from the fur trade was insufficient to cover the costs of colonization, and some of the directors came to the conclusion that it would be better to invest sparingly in New Netherland, carrying on the fur trade at the lowest possible cost with the goal of maximizing short-term profits. Protecting the Company's monopoly on the fur trade was therefore necessary. Of course, the drawback would be that the colony would not be strong enough to defend itself against attacks by the Indians or by European nations, especially England. On the other hand, any financial losses would be small, whereas profits from the fur trade would continue to come in during the years that the colony was in Dutch hands.

The colonization faction in the Amsterdam chamber took a different view. Attempts at colonization and the establishment of agriculture in New Netherland would indeed imply making major investments. But once the colony became self-sufficient, the need for investments would diminish and profits would then roll in. This policy would yield strategic benefits to the Dutch Republic, for New Netherland could take over the role of Scandinavia and the area around the Baltic Sea as a producer of grain and timber, thus eliminating the Dutch dependence on those resources. Within the Dutch Atlantic world, grain from New Netherland could be exported to other colonies within the area of the Company's charter, such as Curaçao and Brazil, taking away the need for expensive shipments of provisions from *patria*. But, the colonization faction warned, this policy would require a large number of colonists, and only by abolishing the Company monopoly on the fur trade would colonists be attracted to emigrate in sufficient numbers.[26]

A compromise was reached when the two factions in the Amsterdam chamber agreed on a set of *Vryheden ende Exemptien* (Freedoms and Exemptions), which were approved by the *Heren XIX* on 7 June 1629. In this compromise, the trade faction achieved its goal of retaining the WIC's monopoly on the fur trade, and the colonization faction obtained the opportunity to try its hand at colonization, at its own expense. The *Freedoms and Exemptions* thus mark the introduction of the patroonship system to New Netherland. The New Netherland patroons, all directors of the Amsterdam chamber, obtained the right to

> own and possess and hold from the Company as a perpetual fief of inheritance, all the land lying within the aforesaid limits, together with the fruits, plants, minerals, rivers, and springs thereof, and the high, middle, and low jurisdiction, rights of fishing, fowling, and grinding, to the exclusion of all others.[27]

The patroonship system has been labeled feudal, but in fact patroons were given privileges similar to holders of *heerlijke rechten* (manorial rights) in the Dutch Republic, receiving jurisdiction and administration over parts of New Netherland on loan from the overlord, in this case the West India Company. The jurisdiction in civil cases was limited: judgments of the patroons' courts with fines exceeding fifty guilders could be appealed to the commander and council. The patroons were also given the right to sail and trade along the entire coast of North America, although the Company retained its monopoly on the fur trade in New Netherland, except in areas where it did not have a trading post. There they could freely trade in pelts, although they had to pay an impost of one guilder on each pelt obtained in addition to imposts on other imported or exported goods.[28]

In retrospect, the introduction of the patroonship system in 1629 was an isolated victory for the colonization faction. Over the course of the next years, most of its adherents lost their seats in the Amsterdam chamber, failing to win reappointment when their six-year terms ended. Consequently, the influence of the colonization faction diminished. But in 1629 there was little sign of imminent decline. Several members of the colonization faction set up patroonships. Michiel Pauw, son of the influential Amsterdam *burgemeester* Reinier Pauw and younger brother of *Raadpensionaris* (Grand Pensionary) Adriaen Pauw, reserved two parcels of land, the first on the Fresh River and the second on the west side of the North River, opposite Manhattan, where he planned to establish the colony of Pavonia. Samuel Godijn registered an area on the west bank of the South River, where he envisioned founding the colony Swanendael. Albert Coenraetsz Burgh was also interested in the South River, but he chose the east bank. Samuel Blommaert preferred the Fresh River, while Kiliaen van Rensselaer sought to establish the colony Rensselaerswijck near Fort Orange along both banks of the North River.[29]

Fortune did not smile on the patroonships. Neither Burgh nor Blommaert brought their plans to fruition. Godijn's Swanendael attracted several shareholders, including David Pietersz de Vries. A colony was founded in 1630, with a small fort and a few dozen colonists who, among other activities, were to engage in whaling. Within a year the fort was overrun by the Indians and none of the colonists survived.[30] Michiel Pauw seems to have established Pavonia without outside investors. Although this patroonship, managed by Cornelis van Vorst, existed longer than some of the other ventures, it was not a success. In 1635 Pauw sold his patroonship rights back to the West India Company.[31]

Rensselaerswijck

Only Rensselaerswijck was to be blessed with a longer existence. Kiliaen van Rensselaer was the only patroon who persevered, despite the high initial costs and meager yields. Although he experienced opposition from the Amsterdam chamber, where in the early 1630s the trade faction had gained the upper hand, he gradually built up his colony, buying land from the Indians, sending cattle over, and hiring contract laborers. He also established administrative and judicial systems in the patroonship.

The *Freedoms and Exemptions* had provided Van Rensselaer with the power to appoint magistrates in his territory and to establish a *kleine bank van justitie* (small bench of justice), set up in the same way as in the Dutch Republic. Van Rensselaer made use of this prerogative in 1632 by appointing a *schout,* also known as *officier* (officer of justice), who was instructed to swear in the five *schepenen* of the small bench of justice. The *schout,* as director of the patroonship, was in charge of the day-to-day management of Rensselaerswijck. In his capacity as representative of the patroon, he had the duty of ensuring that the colonists in Rensselaerswijck adhered to the conditions of the *Freedoms and Exemptions,* six printed copies of which were sent to the colony. Although the patroon had the right to engage in the fur trade in places where the West India Company did not have a *commies,* Van Rensselaer forbade most of his colonists to do the same.[32] A succession of officials held the position of *schout* and director of the patroonship until the arrival in 1648 of Brant Aertsz van Slichtenhorst, a native of Nijkerk. From 1652 until the abolition of the patroonship's court by the English administration in 1665, the position of *schout* was in the hands of Gerrit Swart, while sons of Kiliaen van Rensselaer took charge of the management of Rensselaerswijck: Jan Baptist (1651–1658), Jeremias (1654–1655, 1656–1674), Rijckert (1664–1670), and Nicolaes (1674–1678). The eldest son Johannes, who inherited the title of patroon, occupied himself with the family's properties in the Nijkerk area and like his father never went to America. Neither did any of Kiliaen's four daughters.[33]

Conflicts

During its entire existence, Rensselaerswijck was bedeviled by conflicts. First, disagreement arose over the shareholders' authority over the administration. The foundering of the colonies of the other three participants in the combination resulted in Burgh, Blommaert, and Godijn retaining only their one-fifth share in Rensselaerswijck. The participants, led by Johannes de Laet, who had taken over Burgh's share, opined that the directorship and the manorial rights were not the sole prerogative of Van Rensselaer but of them all, as in an *ambachtsheerlijkheid* (manor) in the Dutch Republic. In their opinion the patroonship was registered in the name of Van Rensselaer just for the purposes of the inheritance of the manorial rights. Van Rensselaer disagreed, and the conflict dragged on from 1640 until 1650, when the States General decided in favor of the other three participants.[34]

The second conflict, with the West India Company, Van Rensselaer initially did not fight alone but in collaboration with the other patroons. Soon after the approval of the *Freedoms and Exemptions,* the trade faction had taken over power in the Amsterdam chamber and tried to hamper the patroons in many ways. Its most important weapon was the interpretation of the clause of the *Freedoms and Exemptions* that concerned the fur trade. According to article fifteen, the patroons were allowed to carry out trade "all along the coast of New Netherland and places circumjacent," except for the fur trade, "which trade the Company reserves to itself alone. But the same is allowed to happen where the Company has no *commies.*" A recognition fee of one guilder per skin had to be paid for the peltries obtained there.[35] The conflict rested on two aspects of this article. First, according to the patroons, "the coast of New Netherland and places circumjacent" did not apply to the trade in the hinterlands or in the areas that belonged to a patroonship. In the patroons' opinion, no recognition fee should be paid on the beaver pelts obtained in these places. The second point concerned the places where the WIC did not have a *commies* in charge of the fur trade. In the view of the patroons, this should be interpreted as the places where the WIC did not have a *commies* at the time of the promulgation of the *Freedoms and Exemptions* in 1629. The Company had positioned *commiezen* at several places afterwards, but that did not negate the patroons' right to trade in beaver pelt there.[36]

This interpretation was, of course, unacceptable to the West India Company, which issued ordinances stipulating that no private colonist was allowed to trade in furs. It did not improve relations between the Company and the patroons when the Company dispatched *commiezen* to areas that fell under the auspices of the patroons. The matter was brought before the *Heren XIX* at the end of 1633 with little success, whereupon it was decided to resort to the States General for arbitration.[37]

An obvious solution was for the WIC to buy out the patroons. On 21 July 1634 Kiliaen van Rensselaer reported this to Johannes de Laet and added that the combined patroons would be prepared to accept such a course of action if they were to receive a reasonable price. He would ask six thousand Flemish pounds (thirty-six thousand guilders) for Rensselaerswijck, quite a large sum. The West India Company probably thought it excessive and refused to pay. Pavonia and Swanendael were sold to the WIC, but Rensselaerswijck remained a patroonship and went on to experience a number of further conflicts with the WIC.[38]

New Freedoms and Exemptions

After the other patroonships had been bought out, the relation between the Company and Van Rensselaer enjoyed a few peaceful years. The two parties even worked together on occasion, although such collaboration was not always carried out in the most cordial spirit. Tension flared up again when new plans were initiated for the creation of patroonships. When Van Rensselaer became aware that a set of new *Freedoms and Exemptions* was considerably less liberal than those of 1629, he managed to have most of his rights assured. An initial concept of the new *Freedoms and Exemptions* from the pen of Johannes de Laet was rejected in 1638, not because it encroached upon Van Rensselaer's rights but because it provided too little stimulus for the growth of the colony's population.[39] A subsequent proposal met with the approval of the States General in 1640, principally because the WIC was now prepared to make the important concession of relinquishing its monopoly on the fur trade and replacing it with a system through which private merchants received permission to trade after payment of a recognition fee.[40]

The new *Freedoms and Exemptions* attracted several new patroons, such as Godard van Reede, *heer van* Nederhorst (lord of Nederhorst). In 1641, in cooperation with Cornelis Melijn, he began a patroonship on Staten Island. Van Reede acted as financier, while Melijn took care of business matters in New Netherland. After the death of Van Reede, the patroonship was continued by another representative to the States General, Hendrick van der Capellen tot Rijssel, a nobleman from Gelderland. Under the local supervision of Adriaen Post, the colony on Staten Island expanded to a total of about ninety souls and eleven farms, until attacks by Indians in 1655 ruined it. Fifteen colonists were killed, and the rest fled to Manhattan. Attempts to build up the colony again were not successful.[41]

Other gentlemen of less noble birth were also interested in patroonships. Adriaen van der Donck in 1646 began a small colony in present-day Yonkers, which he named Colendonck, after himself. After his premature death in 1655 the patroonship was not continued. In 1641, another patroon, Meyndert Meyndertsz van Keeren selected the area known as Achter Kol, between the North River and the Hackensack River. Here a small colony was established, which was destroyed by the Indians in 1643. The Utrecht magistrate Cornelis van Werckhoven in 1651 reserved parcels of land near the Nevesinck Creek and the Tappan Zee in his name. He later changed his mind and bought land on Long Island, where New Utrecht was to be established. After Van Werckhoven's death in 1655 his heirs dispatched surveyor Jacques Corteljou to New Netherland to look after matters on their behalf.[42]

The patroonship of Van Reede and Van der Capellen on Staten Island was the only one of the second-generation patroonships that lasted more than a couple of years. Partly as the result of the conflicts about Rensselaerswijck, the West India Company had had enough of this sort of experiment. After the death of Van der Capellen in 1659, his heirs decided to sell back the patroonship to the WIC for three thousand guilders. The same year the Company decided not to grant any further rights for patroonships.[43]

Van Slichtenhorst versus Stuyvesant

Despite all the attempts inspired by the new *Freedoms and Exemptions,* only Rensselaerswijck remained, and its relations with the Company were not good. In 1647 Brant Aertsz van Slichtenhorst was appointed to the directorship of Rensselaerswijck. He was soon to encounter problems with Director General Stuyvesant, who arrived the same year. In April 1648 Stuyvesant proclaimed a day of prayer and sent a copy of the proclamation to Van Slichtenhorst, who considered its promulgation in Rensselaerswijck an encroachment on the authority of the patroon. This was the overture to a conflict that was to last for several years and acquired a bitter and violent nature.[44]

Van Slichtenhorst displayed a high degree of inflexibility in protecting the rights of the patroonship. In Stuyvesant he found an opponent who was equally intractable. Early in 1652 the director general resorted to tougher measures, after ensuring he had the support of the directors in Amsterdam. In two ordinances he permitted the Company employees and the free burghers of Fort Orange to gather firewood in the forests around the fort and declared the area within two hundred and fifty Rijnland rods of the fort (941.85 meters or about 3090 feet) under the jurisdiction of the WIC.[45] Johannes Dijckman, the new Company *commies* at Fort Orange, arrested Van Slichtenhorst and had him transported to New Amsterdam, where he was jailed for sixteen months. In his absence, the court of Fort Orange and Beverwijck, as the town under the jurisdiction of the West India Company was named, was installed in the WIC fort. In this way Rensselaerswijck lost its most important settlement. Years of fruitless litigation ensued in the Dutch Republic, but events were mooted by the English takeover of the colony in 1664.[46]

New Amstel

Most patroonships were in the hands of private individuals, but the city of Amsterdam also founded a colony within New Netherland. In 1655 the West India Company conquered the Swedish colony on the South River was conquered. The warship *Waegh,* which had been hired from the city of Amsterdam, took part in this operation. To protect the conquered area both from renewed attempts at colonization by the Swedes and from the English in Maryland, it was necessary to provide it with settlers quickly. The Amsterdam chamber once again turned for help to the city of Amsterdam, which recognized the advantages of establishing its own colony. It anticipated importing grains and timber for masts, for example, to make it less dependent on imports from the Baltic area. The outbreak of war between Sweden and Denmark in 1655, which threatened the passage of Dutch ships through the Sound, the narrow strait between Denmark and Sweden, also played a role in the city's colonization plans. As the Swedes had their hands full with this war, they were unlikely to send a relief force to their American colony. An incentive for the Company in this venture was that, in this way, its debt for the hiring of the *Waegh* could be repaid.[47]

The enterprise was dogged with setbacks from the outset. In March 1657 the *Prins Maurits* ran aground near Long Island. Although no casualties occurred and the cargo was saved, the accident made the task of transporting all the colonists and equipment from New Amsterdam to the South River more difficult. In the winter of 1657–1658 New Amstel had to import additional provisions from New Amsterdam since its own stocks were insufficient. In the summer of 1658 an epidemic broke out among the colonists, with a toll of more than one hundred victims. Then winter set in early with extreme severity. It seemed that the summer of 1659 was going to be kinder to New Amstel, but before long new problems surfaced. Because the promised supplies arrived either too late or not at all, the colonists began to get uneasy and the fears of an attack by the English from Virginia increased. Many of the colonists, deciding that they had had enough, left.[48]

After all these misfortunes, the *vroedschap* in Amsterdam concluded that the costs of the colony outweighed the revenue it produced. No further benefits could be expected, and it was decided to revert the colony to the WIC. But Amsterdam quickly found that it could not dispose of New Amstel easily, as the WIC was not inclined to dig into its depleted coffers to relieve the city of its burden. Negotiations with the Company followed in which the city voiced major objections to the earlier arrangements.[49]

The Company acquiesced quickly, because it realized that the South River would otherwise become depopulated, opening the area for intrusions by the English from Virginia and Maryland. The city once more embarked upon a program of major investments and contracted numerous colonists, including the group of followers of Pieter Cornelisz Plockhoy. Although the population of New Amstel now increased, these measures came too late to prevent the English takeover. Yet New Amstel was the only place in New Netherland where in 1664 any resistance to the English was offered.[50]

The system of patroonships was not the infallible method of populating the colony envisaged by the colonization faction. The friction between the Company's monopoly on the fur trade and the rights of the patroons created a conflict that was not conducive to the colonization of New Netherland. Some of the patroonships were plagued by attacks by the Indians, as in the case of Swanendael. The Indians were also a major cause of the foundering of the second generation of patroonships. Rensselaerswijck was spared thanks to its good relations with the Indians and to the efforts of Kiliaen van Rensselaer to invest in the future of Rensselaerswijck by furnishing it with people and cattle. He established an administration that resembled that of manors in the rural areas of the Netherlands. In New Amstel the proposed form of administration displayed similarities to the practices customary in the Dutch Republic, although in this case with more similarity to those of the urban areas, with Amsterdam as the main model.

A Paradigm Shift for the WIC

The administrative and judicial system of New Netherland in its early years displayed many similarities to that of the Dutch colonies in the East Indies and to that followed aboard ships. The power was in the hands of the West India Company, usually regarded as a commercial entity. The new *Freedoms and Exemptions* of 1640 changed this. The WIC lost its fur trade monopoly, and commercial matters subsequently played only a marginal role in its activities. After 1640 the Company became an administrative institution, fulfilling the role of government.[51]

The directors and their local employees had difficulty in adapting to the new role of the WIC, especially as the number of colonists with a material interest in the colony grew. After the abolition of the WIC monopoly on the fur trade, many WIC employees resolved to make a permanent living in New Netherland rather than just spend the contracted number of years there, as Company employees usually did. They became free colonists and formed a group that, as it grew, began to develop a local community and identity. This development was strengthened by the conflicts with the Indians that had been brought about by Director Kieft and that threatened the interests of the colonists. The resulting antithesis between Company and some of the colonists was a constant factor in the existence of New Netherland, and it played a key role in the administrative development of the colony, particularly in the 1640s and early 1650s.

Kieft's War

The problems with the Indians began in 1639. On 15 September 1639, director and council agreed to a resolution that would prove disastrous:

> As the Company has to bear great expenses, both in building fortifications and in the upkeep of soldiers and sailors, we have therefore resolved to demand from the *Indianen* around here (whom we have until now protected from their enemies) some *contributie* [contribution], like pelts, maize, and *sewan,* and if there is any nation which is unwilling to agree in friendship to contribute, [we] will seek to bring them to this by the most justified means.[52]

The WIC incurred major expenses in the construction of forts and the maintenance of a military presence, but as Kieft and his council argued, the Indians enjoyed the benefits thereof through the protection provided against neighboring groups, and therefore it was reasonable that they should contribute. Subsequently it became painfully clear that it was a completely incorrect assessment, both of the willingness of the Indians to pay and of the balance of power between the Indians and colonists. The refusal of Indian groups to pay was one of the causes of the deteriorating relations, which eventually led to war. The first military action of Kieft and his council was directed against the Raritan Indians, who had attacked a sloop and were blamed for killing pigs on Staten Island. The Raritans refused to make reparations, so fifty soldiers and twenty sailors under the command of Secretary Van Tienhoven were sent out in July 1640 to attack them, destroy their harvest, and take as many prisoners as they could, unless the Raritans were prepared to agree to a settlement and pay damages. The expedition turned into a bloodbath.[53]

The Twelve Men

As the result of this and similar actions, tensions between the colonists and some of the Indian groups quickly escalated. Hostilities back and forth ensued, in which the retaliatory actions of the Indians were answered by punitive expeditions, not always successful, of the colonists. An incident in August 1641 was of particular importance for the development of the administration in New Netherland. That month, Claes Cornelisz Swits, an elderly farmer on Manhattan, was murdered by a young Wecquaesgeek Indian. Kieft called all the heads of family together in the fort to discuss countermeasures, and at this meeting, twelve men were appointed to advise the director further. The *Twaalf Man* (Twelve Men) was the first of three advisory bodies to be created by the WIC authorities in the colony. The Twelve Men expressed the opinion that the murder of Swits should not be avenged until the right opportunity presented itself.[54]

If Kieft thought that the Twelve Men would limit themselves to giving advice on this matter, he was mistaken. In January 1642 the Twelve Men submitted a petition in which they addressed the administrative situation in the colony. First, they requested the director to staff the council of New Netherland as completely as possible, "the more so as in the fatherland the council in a small town consists of five to seven *schepens*." This shows the colonists' frame of reference: they wanted a government according to the administrative practices in the Dutch Republic rather than a Company-run trading post. The Twelve Men further wanted director and council to give four colonists access to council meetings, "so that the land may not be burdened without calling together the twelve." Kieft was not unwilling to acquiesce to the requests as they had been worded in this petition, although he rejected the last point:

> Concerning the Twelve Men, we are not aware that they have received further powers of the commonalty than only to give their advice on the murder committed on the late Claes Swit[s].[55]

This remark indicates that the members of the Twelve Men derived their position and influence from the fact that they acted as spokespersons for the community as a whole to advise the director on one specific issue, the murder of Swits and possible retaliation. They had not been granted any privileges by a higher authority, such as the right to meet on their own initiative or to give advice without having been asked for it.[56]

In January 1642 the Twelve Men advised director and council that in their opinion the time had come to avenge the murder of Swits.[57] Several weeks later Kieft thanked them for their services and discharged them. Thenceforth, they were not allowed to convene any further meetings,

> as this tends to a dangerous consequence and is to the great disadvantage both to the country and to our authority. Therefore we hereby forbid them to call in any way a gathering or meeting without our express order, under penalty of being punished as disobedient.[58]

The earlier unwelcome interference by the Twelve Men in administrative matters was undoubtedly a consideration of Kieft in deciding to disband them. However, after some time, developments in the colony's relations with the Indians forced him to reconsider his decision. Hostilities took place throughout 1642, culminating in February 1643, when Kieft allowed a number of colonists and soldiers to launch a gruesome surprise attack on a group of Indians in Pavonia which cost the lives of about eighty Indians. In retaliation many Indian groups in the vicinity of Manhattan set fire to houses, killed cattle, and murdered colonists continually throughout the summer of 1643.

The Eight Men

In September Kieft decided to ask the advice of the population once more. At a meeting of forty-six burghers, eight of them were elected to consult with director and council. The Eight Men advised that the war with the hostile Indian groups be resumed but that the Indians on Long Island be left alone, provided they refrained from hostile activities. Unlike the Twelve Men, the Eight Men were also given executive powers: on behalf of the free burghers they were permitted to recruit as many soldiers as possible. Meeting independently was not one of their prerogatives: every Saturday afternoon the Eight Men had to attend the meeting of director and council to give further advice. If at least five of them were present, "whatever shall be resolved or planned by them shall be held valid."[59]

All good intentions, but there is little indication that they were adhered to. When on 17 October 1643 the decision was made to launch an attack on the Wechquaesgeek Indians, only three of the eight, Cornelis Melijn, Thomas Hall, and Isaack Allerton, were present. And like the Twelve Men, the Eight Men also exceeded their authority by writing letters and memorials to the higher powers in *patria* without the approval and probably even the knowledge of Kieft and his council. Their letter of 24 October 1643 to the *Heren XIX* was harmless enough, containing only a description of the unfavorable situation and a request for help. About a week later they sent a similar letter to the States General. Herein, they again complained

> that we poor inhabitants of New Netherland have been persecuted here in the spring by these *bose heijdenen, ende barbarische wilden* [evil heathens and barbaric Indians] by fire and sword, daily men and women have been cruelly murdered in our houses and on the field, the small children in their parents' arms and before their doors clubbed to death with axes and mallets.[60]

However, the dramatic description of the colony's situation had little effect. The States General passed the letter on to the WIC for advice. In its answer, the Amsterdam chamber made it clear that "the Company has come into such inability and discredit, that, without considerable subsidies from the land it is no longer able to supply any distant places" and continued with the recommendation of their plan for a merger of the West India Company with the East India Company.[61] Nevertheless, the WIC did dispatch some reinforcements to New Netherland. By this time, it was already April 1644, and six months had passed since New Netherland had first cried for help. During this time, the colonists had gained some victories over the Indians, but they had been accompanied by monstrous cruelty. In spite of the brutality, a cessation of hostilities with a few Indian groups had been achieved. Even so, some of the colonists were greatly dissatisfied by Kieft's administration, whose action they believed had plunged the colony into unnecessary wars.[62]

The Eight Men again decided to turn to the WIC. At the end of 1644 they sent a letter to the Amsterdam directors in which they thanked them for their help but then directed their attention to Kieft's disastrous administration. They alleged that everything that had been built up over many years in New Netherland was "all together through a thoughtless bellicosity laid in ashes."[63] They were highly dissatisfied with the way in which Kieft dealt with them. From 4 November 1643 to 18 June 1644 he had not once called them together.[64] The Eight Men ended their letter with an impassioned plea to the WIC directors. They wanted new leaders and a new form of administration with delegates from villages and hamlet who could "issue their vote along the director and councilors on matters of state, so that in future the whole state of the country cannot be placed in peril again through a single man's discretion."[65]

The intention of the Eight Men was not lost on Kieft, who regarded it as a rebellion against his person and his legal authority. More important, their plea was directed to the wrong body. The Amsterdam chamber was little inclined to reform the administration of New Netherland or to recall Kieft. In contrast, the States General in The Hague were far more sympathetic and wanted in particular action taken "about the excess of the cruel shedding of blood committed against the *wilden*" so that "the punishment of blood that may be unlawfully shed may be averted from these lands." The representatives of the States General, including Hendrick van der Capellen, in a meeting of the *Heren XIX,* forced the WIC to take measures. The Company's Chamber of Accounts was to examine all documents relating to New Netherland and to compile a report with recommendations for improvement. Furthermore, Kieft was to be recalled to account for his actions, and Lubbert Dinclagen, Van der Capellen's protege, was to be sent there as temporary replacement. The directors of the Amsterdam chamber protested, but their opposition fell on deaf ears.[66]

Recommendations for Reform

In December 1644, the Chamber of Accounts produced its report, in which it first confirmed the necessity to recall Kieft. Second, the report recommended that the council consist of three men: the director, the vice director, and the *fiscael.* These three officers should deal with all matters concerning administration and justice, but in criminal cases the *fiscael,* who at that time still performed the duties of local public prosecutor, would be replaced by the highest military official in the colony, and two representatives of the burghers would also take a seat in the council. Third, the report recommended that a meeting of representatives of the patroonships should be held every six months to advise director and council about all matters on hand. This recommendation laid down the basis for the *landdag* (provincial convention or diet), not only with representatives of the patroonships (in practice only Rensselaerswijck) but also of all villages that in the years to come were to gain their own courts.[67]

The States General discussed the report at the end of December 1644, but some time elapsed before action was taken, probably because the WIC objected to Dinclagen, whom they knew as a recalcitrant man. It was not until May 1645 that Petrus Stuyvesant was appointed director, with Dinclagen as vice director. The instructions for Stuyvesant and his council in July 1645 were more specific than the recommendations of the Chamber of Accounts. For example, the two additional members of the council brought in for criminal cases were to be residents of the place where the crime had been committed. The innovative introduction of the *landdag* was, however, no longer mentioned in the instructions.[68] Finally, on 28 July 1646, Stuyvesant and Dinclagen were sworn in at the meeting of the States General, to depart for New Netherland in August in the WIC ships *Prinses Amelia* and *Groote Gerrit.* The new director general arrived in New Amsterdam in May 1647.[69]

A major task awaited Stuyvesant. He had to find a balance between establishing good relations with the colonists on the one hand and maintaining the authority of the West India Company on the other. During his first years in New Netherland, the conscientious Stuyvesant inclined toward the latter. Stuyvesant soon became enmeshed in the conflict between Kieft and the population. Undoubtedly, Kieft anticipated that things would be difficult for him after his return to *patria,* and he wanted to be well prepared. So, in an attempt to gather evidence, he asked the new director general and council for permission to subject some of the Eight Men to a written interrogation. Two of them, Jochem Pietersz Kuijter and Cornelis Melijn, reacted by petitioning for permission to question the members of the old council. This impertinence was too much for Stuyvesant to swallow. On his instigation, proceedings before director general and council were brought against both men. Ultimately, Melijn and Kuijter were banished from New Netherland.[70]

The Nine Men

Having shown what he considered to be unacceptable behavior, Stuyvesant next indicated what popular influence should look like. Eight days after Melijn, Kuijter, Kieft, and many other people who had played a role in the conflicts of the preceding years had left for *patria* on the *Prinses Amelia,* Stuyvesant and his council established the Nine Men. The instructions from director general and council had made no mention of the way in which the population was to be granted a voice. Establishing the Nine Men was the idea of Stuyvesant and his council, perhaps even of Stuyvesant personally. He may have looked upon it as a new beginning: a new director had arrived, the troublemakers were gone, scores had been settled, and the slate had been wiped clean.[71]

But practical considerations were of greater importance. The fort required repairs, and a school, a church, piling on the riverbanks, a pier, and other projects had to be undertaken for the common good of the colony. The cooperation of the population was needed. The burghers were asked to draw up a list of eighteen nominees, of whom director general and council would appoint nine. These *gemeentsmannen* or *gemeijnsluijden* (councilors of the community) were not entitled to meet at their own initiative but had to wait until called together by director general and council, "as is customary in our fatherland and elsewhere."[72] They were to offer their advice in matters only when requested. In this respect the rules governing the Nine Men differ little from that of their predecessors. But its composition was new: three men each from the merchants, the burghers, and the farmers. Also new was that three of the Nine Men, one from each of the groups, were to join the council every Thursday to deal with cases of civil law. Finally, succession was regulated. Every year, six members would step down. From a list of twelve nominees, director general and council would annually on 31 December select their successors. This introduced the practice of nomination of a double number, as was customary in the Dutch Republic.[73]

Like their predecessors, the Nine Men went further than had been the intention of director general and council. In February 1648 they met without the knowledge of director general and council to draft a petition. Director general and council approved the content but warned that in future they should adhere to their instructions not to meet without permission and not to make any decisions without the presence of a representative of director general and council. Above all, in any future petitions they should show more respect, "that is, that they must not [presume] to dictate to director and council what they ought to [do]."[74]

The petition probably related to the plan of 1648 to send a deputation to the States General, with the objective of gaining assistance against the continual intrusions from surrounding English colonies. According to Adriaen van der Donck, who may already have been one of the members of the Nine Men, Stuyvesant was initially not against this idea and supported it. But when it became clear that the director general wanted to have a major say in the content of the petition, the enthusiasm of the Nine Men waned. Collaboration with Stuyvesant would make any form of criticism of the WIC impossible. Nonetheless, after some delay the Nine Men decided to send a delegation to the States General, and requested Stuyvesant's permission consult the entire community. It is likely that they intended this to be a meeting of the population of New Amsterdam and not to involve the English towns. The director general tried to influence the orders to the delegation and made a number of proposals that, in the eyes of the Nine Men, "did not at all agree with our intention and were in our opinion impractical."[75] Stuyvesant probably preferred a meeting in the form of a *landdag* at which the English would also be present. As director general of the province, he could not agree to a general *landdag* from which part of the population was excluded. He therefore refused permission for a meeting of the population of New Amsterdam. This was no problem for the Nine Men:

> so we went and spoke to the commonalty house to house. From this time on, the General burned with fury…, although we did not know but that we had followed his order herein.[76]

This hypocritical attitude was as unhelpful as Stuyvesant's fury. The situation came to a head in March 1649, when it was discovered that Van der Donck had secretly drawn up a remonstrance for the States General. Stuyvesant was furious and immediately had Van der Donck locked up.[77]

The charges against Van der Donck included libeling some of the Company officials in New Netherland in his letter to the States General. He was eventually freed, whereupon he, together with Jacob Wolphertsz van

Couwenhoven and Jan Evertsz Bout, traveled to the Dutch Republic in the summer of 1649 as a delegation from the Nine Men to ask the States General to intervene. Their request contained a call for help of the States General in the furtherance of the growth of the population in the colony. The Nine Men insisted on the creation of "a competent civil government, such as your High Mightinesses will deem advisable to apply to this province, having something in common with the laudable government of our fatherland."[78]

The Representation of New Netherland

One of the supporting documents tendered to the States General was the *Vertoogh van Nieu-Nederlandt* (Representation of New Netherland), written by Van der Donck and published in 1650. This document squarely blamed the West India Company for the poor situation in the colony. In the opinion of Van der Donck, using the benefit of hindsight to the utmost, the WIC had pursued the wrong policy from the outset by concentrating more on its own profits than on the well-being of New Netherland. The *Vertoogh* made much of the faults of both the directors in Amsterdam and of Kieft. Nor did Stuyvesant escape Van der Donck's vitriolic pen: Stuyvesant "has been incomparably more diligent and bitter in finding personal lawsuits against his innocent enemies than his predecessor has ever been."[79]

Despite Van der Donck's personal animosity to Stuyvesant, his real target was the West India Company. The alleged tyrannical administration by the Company was denounced in language that was far from subtle. Clearly his objective was to have the States General discharge the Company from its administration of New Netherland and take it upon themselves. It was such a drastic suggestion that at the very least the Nine Men appeared to rebel against the legal authority. The attempt by the New Netherland colonists came after a number of years of heavy criticism of the WIC for the way it had conducted the war against the Portuguese revolting in Dutch Brazil. In the *Vertoogh*, Van der Donck tried to take advantage of the general opposition to the Company.[80]

The West India Company thus found itself under serious attack. Its situation was not improved when in early 1650 the States General received the documents that Melijn, with the support of Van der Donck and others, had assembled in New Netherland for the appeal against his sentence. Stuyvesant had also written to the States General. In eloquent words he condemned Melijn's behavior, ending with the remark that the circumstances and his duty compelled him to remain in New Netherland. He sent over the colony's secretary, Cornelis van Tienhoven, to provide the High and Mighty Gentlemen with all the information they required.[81]

From October 1649 to April 1650 a committee for West Indian Affairs of the States General investigated all these matters. At the same time several other people who believed they were the victims of injustice at the hand of

Stuyvesant turned to the States General. Also the issue between Kiliaen van Rensselaer's heirs and the other participants in Rensselaerswijck reared its head. The committee of the States General was also concerned with the considerably more important matters in Brazil, and some time elapsed before the appeal produced any result.[82]

The report of the committee of the States General was issued in April 1650 and was very critical of the West India Company. The directors of the Amsterdam chamber were blamed for the fact that "the good proposals and offers made to ensure the boundaries and the population of the lands are neglected or thwarted." But the committee stopped short of suggesting that New Netherland be placed under the direct authority of the States General. It did recommend some far-reaching changes in the administration of New Netherland and contained echoes of the 1644 report by the West India Company's Chamber of Accounts. The plans of 1650 were more drastic in giving the colonists a direct say in government. The council in New Netherland should consist of the director, a vice director, a council member jointly appointed by the States General and the WIC, and two council members selected from the colonists. These should be nominated in a double number at a meeting of the representatives of the patroons and the burghers of New Amsterdam, and each should hold his seat for a period of four years. Also, a "civil government" was to be established for New Amsterdam. The form this would take was obvious, and none of the parties disagreed upon it: it would be similar to the situation in *patria:* a small bench of justice with the addition of *burgemeesters* as urban executive officials and a *schout* as representative of the West India Company. Finally, Stuyvesant should be recalled to account for himself. Until all these changes were carried out, for which a period of three years was mentioned, the Nine Men were to remain in office and have jurisdiction over civil cases.[83]

The directors of the Amsterdam chamber protested vehemently. In their eyes there was little need to change the administration of New Netherland. Nevertheless, they were prepared to include two colonists in the existing council, to be appointed by the WIC from a triple number nominated by the burghers. The Amsterdam directors considered the recall of Stuyvesant completely unnecessary. They were prepared to recall Vice Director Dinclagen if the States General considered Secretary Van Tienhoven, who was already present, unable to provide them with sufficient information.[84]

The protests of the Amsterdam chamber could not prevent two members of the delegation from the Nine Men, Jacob Wolphertsz van Couwenhoven and Jan Evertsz Bout, from returning to New Netherland with a copy of the new but still provisional regulation. They acquainted Stuyvesant with its contents, but to the displeasure of the Nine Men the director general was unwilling to implement the reforms until he had received notification of their ratification by the States General from his superiors. The result was that during 1650 and 1651 the Nine Men dispatched a series of letters of complaint to the States General and to Adriaen van der Donck, who had remained in the Netherlands.[85]

Limited Reform

Some time elapsed before the States General reached a decision. One reason for this was that Alexander van der Capellen, the chairman of the committee for West Indian Affairs and a strong supporter of reforms in New Netherland, played a major role in the conflict between Stadholder Willem II and the States of Holland. The controversy led to an attempt by the stadholder to take Amsterdam by force, but his death later in 1650 defused the possibility of civil war. As a result of the fall of his master, Alexander van der Capellen lost most of his influence. In the meantime the Amsterdam chamber employed delaying tactics, in the hope that the radical plans for administrative reform would die a quiet death. The decision was also delayed by the States General's resolve to make a thorough examination of who was responsible for the wars with the Indians. In the meantime, Van der Donck in vain pushed for swift action. Not until February 1652 did the States General, still containing a small number of opponents of the WIC, send the provisional regulation for the administration of New Netherland to the chambers of the Company with a request for advice. The Amsterdam chamber was aggrieved. Not only had they already expressed their opinion in May 1650, but they were also surprised at the reappearance of this plan, "that so long ago had been considered dismissed." They requested that the plan be deferred until the States General had been fully informed of the situation in the colony.[86]

The States General were not impressed by the response of the Amsterdam chamber, and on April 27, 1652, they unilaterally ordered Stuyvesant to return. The Amsterdam chamber was informed of this in a brief note, which typified the relations between the States General and the WIC at that moment. It reacted by informing Stuyvesant that, as the decision had been made without consultation with either itself or the *Heren XIX,* the director general need not make too much haste. The Amsterdam chamber also sent Director Jacob Pergens to The Hague. He talked to a number of delegates to the States General and also obtained the assistance of two gentlemen from Amsterdam, *burgemeester* Cornelis de Graeff and Cornelis Bicker, member of the *Gecommitteerde Raden* of Holland. Together with six or seven other delegates of the States of Holland, these two on May 16, 1652, went to the meeting of the States General and asked for the resolution. After this had been read to them, they decreed that the recall of Stuyvesant required approval by the States of Holland before it could take effect. Thereupon the States General decided to rescind the order for Stuyvesant to return. Adriaen van der Donck was ordered to return the letter to Stuyvesant that had been handed to him for delivery. This completed the defeat of Van der Donck.

His plans for the reform of New Netherland government had been crushed by the internal politicking in the Dutch Republic. The close collaboration of the States of Holland, the City of Amsterdam, and the West India Company had thwarted his scheme to obtain a position of power for himself in New Netherland.

In the meantime Stuyvesant had acted decisively in the colony. In late 1650, director general and council had intervened in the composition of the Nine Men by not following the nomination. They only appointed men who were not opposed to the West India Company. This move created a new political atmosphere which made it possible to grant New Amsterdam its own court. In the fall of 1651, director general and council suggested to the directors in Amsterdam that the time was now ripe to transform the Nine Men into a city government. That had also been part of the proposals of Van der Donck, but his most important points were lifting all power from the WIC (which had not been approved in 1650) and a reorganization of central government with a vote for the patroons, of which he himself was one. That New Amsterdam would eventually be granted a city government and that it would take the form of a *schout,* two *burgemeesters,* and five *schepenen* was obvious, as New Netherland followed the example of the Dutch Republic in all forms of government. Much more important was the timing of the installation, as that would decide who would take up office. Early in April 1652, the directors in Amsterdam decided to follow the advice from director general and council:

> [We] have resolved hereby to approve your honors' proposal that your honors establish there a bench of justice formed as much as possible after the laws of this city. For this purpose we are sending printed copies relating to all benches of justice and the entire government. For the present, we believe that it will be sufficient to elect one *schout,* two *burgermeesteren,* and five *schepenen.*[87]

Of all of the recommendations of 1650, only this element was carried out. And it was ultimately the Amsterdam chamber that decided when to do so. The Nine Men, who already administered civil justice, were now transformed into a municipal government according to the Amsterdam model. In the years to come, the judicial and administrative duties of the municipal government would be expanded step for step.[88]

With the establishment of New Amsterdam's own court, the rancor disappeared from the relations between the colonists and the WIC. Of course, conflicts still occurred in the years that followed, but the colonists did not find it necessary again to approach the States General with their protests about alleged injustices.

New Netherland gradually developed from a trading post into a settlement colony, and the administrative form of trading post was not suited to this. As the population grew, the groups of colonists with local interests and a local identity evolved. Their interests conflicted with those of the WIC, the directors of which had difficulty adapting themselves to their altered role after they ceased to hold the monopoly in the fur trade, leaving only the function of supreme government on the basis of the charter awarded to the WIC by the States General. The governmental tasks included the central responsibilities for defense, for which taxes were levied, the function as the highest court of justice, and the supervision of lesser administrative institutions. By the time that New Netherland was undergoing the change from trading post to settlement colony, the WIC, because of its problems elsewhere, was financially not in a position to give the colony the impulse regarded necessary by the colonists and the States General.

A major catalyst in the conflict between the Company and the colonists was the wars with the Indians, which were caused by the policies of the WIC and which put into danger the interests of those colonists who were trying to build up an existence in the colony. The colonists were of the opinion that a government other than that of the West India Company would be better for the development of the colony. The possibility that the States General would ever accede to such requests from New Netherland was slight. The States General could only exert some pressure on the Company to give the colonists influence by the establishment of local courts. That was the form of administration asked for by the colonists.

Thus, the administrators in the Netherlands and the colonists in New Netherland were in agreement on the lines along which the administration should develop. Disagreement about the pace of such a development played a role, but it was not doubted that the expansion of the rights of lower administrative organs could come about only through the awarding of privileges and prerogatives by the higher authority. After the establishment of the city government of New Amsterdam, the discussion no longer related to the Company's authority but rather to practical responsibilities.

Small Benches of Justice

The desire of the people of New Amsterdam to be given responsibility for at least matters of civil law is understandable, for several local administrative bodies were already in existence elsewhere in New Netherland. Prior to the installation of the court of *burgemeesters* and *schepenen* on Manhattan in 1653, the provincial government had erected small benches of justice in six villages. More were to follow.[89] Most of the courts that had been established in the 1640s were located on Long Island, where English colonists had settled. The English towns of Heemstede, Vlissingen, and 's-Gravesande were given their own courts because the WIC realized that to maintain its claim to the territory, colonization was required, by Englishmen under Dutch rule if no Dutch colonists could be found. The first Dutch village to gain a court was Breuckelen in 1646; in 1654 other villages on Long Island followed. The growth of villages to a size that justified the establishment of a court was stimulated by a policy of population concentration. For reasons of safety, scattered farms were outlawed, and the inhabitants were compelled to live closer together. In 1645 the *Heren XIX* had already advised so in the instructions for director general and council, and after the problems with the Indians in 1655 the policy was pursued vigorously. Nevertheless, many villages in New Netherland never attained the required size to be endowed with a local court, such as Schenectady and Kinderhoek near Beverwijck, Nieuwdorp (Hurley) near Wiltwijck, and Arnhem on Long Island.[90]

The basis for local government was a stipulation in the 1640 *Freedoms and Exemptions:*

> And if it should happen that the settlements of the private colonists grow so much that the same should be considered villages, hamlets, or towns, then the Company will regulate the subaltern government, magistrates and ministers of justice (who will be nominated in triple number from the most qualified from the same villages or hamlets and will be elected by the governor and councilors), who will deal with all conflicts and suits in their district.[91]

It was the explicit prerogative of the overlord, the West India Company, to grant the privilege of local government and justice. A number of preconditions applied. The English had to swear allegiance to the States General and the West India Company; they were forbidden to build fortifications; and they were obliged to use the Dutch system of weights and measures. In exchange they were granted freedom of religion, free possession of land with an exemption from the payment of *tienden* for a period of ten years, and rights to fishing, hunting, and trading. Additionally, if they so desired, they were to be granted the privilege of nominating three or four men, one of whom would be chosen as magistrate by the director of New Netherland. This magistrate would be empowered to pronounce final judgments on all civil cases involving sums up to forty guilders. For higher amounts, appeal to director and council would be possible. The local magistrate would also try criminal cases, except those in which corporal punishment was applicable.

These preconditions were more specific than those in the *Freedoms and Exemptions* of 1640 and display some remarkable features. A nomination in triple number was uncommon, but a nomination in quadruple number was exceptional. The appointment of a single magistrate was also exceptional. In New England, however, a one-man magistracy was customary. One-man magistracy was highly uncommon in the Dutch Republic and would occur only this once in New Netherland. The privileges granted to the English on Long Island differed from those granted to Dutch villages and were much more an adaptation to English than to Dutch custom. It shows that the WIC made major concessions to the English in order to populate New Netherland.[92]

Later ordinances for the establishment of courts displayed more similarities with the practice in the Dutch Republic, to which explicit reference was regularly made. The first ordinances were quite summary. The placard by which a court was established in Breuckelen in 1646 does not even contain any demarcation of authority but merely states that, should the two chosen *schepenen*, Jan Evertsz Bout and Huych Aertsz, find the work too arduous, they could nominate a further two *schepenen*. The customs of the Dutch Republic were considered sufficiently known in Breuckelen and did not have to be spelled out.[93]

Wiltwijck

The founding of the court of Wiltwijck will here serve as an example. In the early 1650s, a settlement was established in the area around the Esopus Creek and the Rondout Creek, small tributaries of the North River halfway between New Amsterdam and Fort Orange. In the first years the area was under the jurisdiction of the court at Fort Orange, but with the growth in the number of inhabitants the prospect of having their own court became increasingly attractive.[94]

This happened in May 1661. The set of instructions for this court is one of the most expansive issued in New Netherland. The court, which had both judicial and administrative tasks, would consist of three *schepenen* and the *schout*. This body could pronounce definitive verdicts upon all civil cases involving fines of up to fifty guilders. Appeal to director general and council was possible against the imposition of larger fines. If the three *schepenen* were in disagreement, majority judgment would be applied, but the minority retained the right to have its opinion recorded in the protocol. The magistrates were not at liberty to make a minority opinion public: outwardly the unity of the court should be maintained. The *schout* was to chair the court and collect the votes.

The court in Wiltwijck would hold session once every fourteen days, except in harvest time. In matters requiring swifter action, extraordinary sessions could be held, but in civil cases this was permitted only when both parties so desired, and then they had to bear the costs. The court messenger had the duty of convening the *schout* and *schepenen* at least twenty-four hours in advance. Failure to attend incurred a fine of twenty stivers, with the chair of the court subject to a fine of double that sum. Late attendance by *schepenen* attracted a fine of six stivers. Such fines were not applicable in the case of illness, or if a member was out of the town on business.[95]

The area of jurisdiction of the small court of justice in Wiltwijck covered all the inhabitants around the Esopus. The court was empowered to deal with minor criminal offenses such as striking a person, fighting, verbal abuse, threats and the drawing of knives, provided it did not involve actual bloodshed. For more serious offenses, such as wounding, adultery, theft, blasphemy, and insulting the authorities, the task of the court was to arrest the offenders and transfer them to Manhattan. The local court assembled all the information, but director general and council tried the case itself. The only town that possessed complete criminal jurisdiction was Heemstede, although its judgments were subject to appeal to director general and council. In the cases in which a town had limited criminal jurisdiction, local magistrates were generally invited to join director general and council in trial deliberations.[96]

The court at Wiltwijck also had administrative responsibilities. It could issue orders concerning the construction of public roads, the enclosure of land, the building of churches and schools, and other public works, together with the financing thereof. However, such orders had to be approved by director general and council. The English towns on Long Island did not have to submit their ordinances for prior approval. Another difference between Dutch and English towns was that in the latter most of the administrative decisions were made in annual town meetings. The annual town meeting, like trial by jury, was not a feature of the Dutch towns, nor were either of these institutions known in the Dutch Republic.[97]

The *schepenen* of Wiltwijck were instructed by director general and council to ensure that the laws of the Dutch Republic, together with the ordinances of director general and council, were promulgated and obeyed.[98] Finally, the instructions contained stipulations concerning the appointment of magistrates. In accordance with the customs of the Dutch Republic, the *schepenen* were annually required to submit a double nomination, from which director general and council would make appointments.

One of the reasons why director general and council drew up such extensive instructions for Wiltwijck was their concern about the dearth of inhabitants with sufficient competence to carry out adequately the duties of *schepenen*. In such circumstances, the *schout*, who according to the practice in the Dutch Republic was the representative of the overlord, in this case the Company, was even more important. In a petition, Roelof Swartwout requested that he be appointed to the office of *schout* now that a court had been established in Wiltwijck. His instructions stated that he was not permitted to occupy any other position but that of *schout* and that he would preside over the meetings of the court. Together with two *schepenen,* he was to see to the publication of the ordinances of director general and council. It was the *schout*'s responsibility to maintain public order and to ensure that the town was purged "from all rabble and dicing." Neither were "whorehouses, pimps, or such lewd houses" permitted. Prisoners were required to appear before the court within a maximum of four days, to keep the costs down. The *schout*'s income would partly come from the fines for civil offenses, of which he received half, and from those for criminal offenses, of which he was to receive one-third. He was explicitly forbidden to accept gifts.[99]

The Schout

Swartwout's instructions also required of him that as *schout* he had to compile the list of people due to appear before the court in the same way that the *schout* of Amsterdam had been instructed to do four years earlier. This shows what the origins of the instructions to Swartwout are. On comparing the text with that of the 1646 instructions for the *schout* of Amsterdam, the similarities are great, not only in their purport but also in their wording. Naturally there were also some differences between them, just as there are differences between the largest city in the Dutch Republic and a small colonial town with less than a hundred inhabitants.[100]

No instructions for earlier *schouten* have survived. In the 1620s, when Jan Lampo was *fiscael,* that position was still combined with that of *schout,* initially throughout the whole of New Netherland. When at a later stage local *schouten* were appointed, a demarcation of responsibilities became necessary. The *fiscael,* who was in the employ of the Company, performed the duties of prosecutor in cases that came before director general and council, which were the more serious criminal cases. The local *schouten* also acted as prosecutor, but only for the lower courts, where the less serious cases were heard. The subordinate nature of the position of local *schout,* which displays some similarity to the relation between the functions of the *schouten* and *baljuws* in the Dutch Republic, is obvious in the right of appointment. The *schout* was appointed by the WIC, in most cases by director general and council. Most of the Dutch towns did not nominate candidates for the office of *schout.* This differed from the English towns, which were allowed a greater degree of autonomy. Heemstede was even permitted to appoint its own *schout.*[101]

Although the *schout* was, in formal terms, the representative of the overlord, in New Netherland the office was often filled by one of the inhabitants. This was not a prerequisite and indeed could not be so when one *schout* had more villages under his jurisdiction, as in the case of the *schout* of Breuckelen, Midwout, and Amersfoort. This was different for magistrates, who had to live in the town in which they held office.

Nomination and Appointment

In many instances the first nomination for local magistrates was put forward by the population. Subsequently, the incumbent magistrates drew up a nomination. The right of appointment remained in the hands of the West India Company and was exercised by director general and council. The procedure was different for the English towns, where the double nomination was made up by the town meeting before it was submitted to director general and council. The English towns did not always find it easy to reconcile themselves with the Dutch customs. The inhabitants of 's-Gravesande, where there had already been problems in 1651, had to be informed three years later that they did not have the right to appoint their own magistrates. Similar problems occurred in Heemstede in 1652, and two years later director general and council requested nominations for a third magistrate, since the bench had to consist of an odd number. Because of the difficulty that some of the lower courts had in adhering to proper procedure, director general and council often intervened in local matters. Stuyvesant visited Wiltwijck and Beverwijck on many occasions and also made several visits to the English towns on Long Island. In other instances director general and council sent a committee to announce the appointment of local magistrates and to administer the oath, which consisted of swearing allegiance to the States General, to the directors of the WIC, and to director general and council in New Amsterdam.[102]

Director general and council could, where they considered it necessary, suspend local courts and dismiss *schouten*. Their intervention was not always prompted by the failings of the local courts. In some instances the local courts invoked the help of the higher authorities in solving problems such as conflicts with the Indians or disputes with other towns about boundaries. Issues of the latter kind were most prevalent on Long Island, where the growth of the towns caused friction.

An institutional form of contact between the local courts and central authority was the *landdag*. Although meetings of all the heads of families of New Amsterdam had taken place earlier, the meeting on 8 March 1649 can be described as the first *landdag* in the sense of a meeting of representatives of the towns and other places in the colony, including the English towns. Other meetings took place in 1653, in 1663, and twice in 1664. The meetings were intended to advise director general and council, and in that sense they were a continuation of the earlier Twelve, Eight, and Nine Men. The difference lies in the fact that these earlier bodies represented only Manhattan and the surrounding area. Another difference is that the Nine Men administered a portion of the civil justice. In contrast, the *landdagen* were never given any administrative or judiciary powers. In the longer term, the *landdag* could have grown into something like the provincial meetings of estates in the Netherlands. But that stage was never reached.[103]

The gradual development of local government in New Netherland introduced a system in which both administration and justice operated on the same footing as in the Dutch Republic. It was thus a system firmly rooted in the traditions of *patria*, which remained the example both the colonial government and the colonists attempted to emulate.[104]

"This City of Amsterdam in New Netherland"

After the Amsterdam directors gave Stuyvesant and his council permission, a small court of justice was established in New Amsterdam. The installation took place on 2 February 1653, and the date was no coincidence. In Amsterdam, the election of *burgemeesters* traditionally took place on the eve of Lady's Day, the feast of the purification of the Virgin Mary. New Amsterdam had already adopted this custom in 1652, when it was applied to the installation of the Nine Men.[105]

It is no surprise that the date of the election of *burgemeesters* and *schepenen* referred explicitly to the mother city: the small court of justice was "to be constituted as far as possible and as the situation of the land allows according to the laudable customs of the city of Amsterdam." The *burgemeesters* were allocated the administrative tasks and also had the duty, together with the *schepenen,* to administer justice. This was not the case in Amsterdam, but the limited experience of the *schepenen* was an argument to arrange it differently in New Amsterdam. The court was restricted to civil cases involving less than one hundred guilders, double the amount applicable to the court at Wiltwijck, and to minor criminal cases. The jurisdiction of *burgemeesters* and *schepenen* extended over all burghers and inhabitants of New Amsterdam, from the tip of Manhattan to the Fresh Water, all those on ships in the roadstead and over the inhabitants of towns on Long Island and on the west side of the North River, insofar as no court had been established there. The sentences imposed by *burgemeesters* and *schepenen* were to be based on the laws of the fatherland and so far as possible in accordance with the ordinances of Amsterdam and of director general and council.[106]

Extension of the judicial authority of "this city of Amsterdam in New Netherland," as it was usually called, did not come until 1656. In a petition, *burgemeesters* and *schepenen* requested permission to deal with all criminal cases, with the exception of capital offences. Director general and council allowed *burgemeesters* and *schepenen* the authority to resort to corporal punishment, such as branding and flogging. Occasionally confusion about the extent of their powers arose, but whenever *burgemeesters* and *schepenen* experienced doubts they asked permission of director general and council which was generally granted. Even when the jurisdiction of *burgemeesters* and *schepenen* was not in doubt, they sometimes asked director general and council for advice on the correct procedure and degree of punishment.[107]

Administration

The situation was rather more complex with regard to administrative responsibilities. *Burgemeesters* and *schepenen* quickly reached the conclusion that their powers were too restricted. In December 1653 they requested the

NIEUW AMSTERDAM OFTE NUE NIEUW IORX OPT TEYLANT MAN

4. Nieuw Amsterdam ofte Nue Nieuw Iorx opt Teylant Man, by Johannes Vingboons, ca. 1664. Nationaal Archief, The Netherlands. Inv. no. 4. VEL 619.14.

directors in Amsterdam to extend their rights and expressed their wish that their instructions could be "as far as workable according with the form of government of the laudable city of Amsterdam—name giver of this our new [city]."[108] With this request the city government of New Amsterdam took the first steps in a continuing struggle with the Company. The responsibility of *burgemeesters* and *schepenen* in administrative matters was more flexible than that in the area of justice, and it was more affected by the peaks and troughs in their relations with director general and council. The issues that *burgemeesters* and *schepenen* were to take care of fell into four general areas: economic affairs, public works, issues concerning education, and defense.

The city government exercised influence on economic affairs in many ways. The use of the Amsterdam system of weights and measures was called for in ordinances of director general and council, but *burgemeesters* and *schepenen* could nominate the measurers, for instance sworn grain measurers, brand markers of casks, and gaugers, in double number. They also supervised tappers and taverns, both through ordinances and through licensing, as well as bakers, for whom they drew up stipulations about the size, weight, and price of bread. They supervised other trades less stringently. Another feature of government involvement in economic matters was the establishment of a public weigh house in New Amsterdam. Director general and council and the city government were not always in agreement on its supervision or on the income it produced.[109]

Burgemeesters and *schepenen* were responsible for constructing and maintaining public works, such as roads and canals, and for their financing. *Burgemeesters* and *schepenen* established rules concerning the throwing of rubbish into the canal, the nomination of fire wardens, the placement of fire buckets, and the establishment of a so-called rattle watch, who took care of the nightly watch for thieves and fire. The *burgemeesters* were in charge of the *weeskamer* (orphan chamber) and provided director general and council with nominations for *weesmeesters* (orphan masters). The role of the city government in educational matters was small. Schoolmasters had to be admitted by director general and council, although *burgemeesters* and *schepenen* sometimes supported petitions in this respect. This was also the case with the establishment of a Latin school in New Amsterdam.

Finally, as a matter of necessity, *burgemeesters* and *schepenen* involved themselves with the defense of New Netherland. While formally this fell under the duties of the West India Company, the Company was often not in a position to amass the necessary finances and was obliged to ask the city government for help. In return for such help, *burgemeesters* and *schepenen* requested and obtained some of the WIC's rights, such as the income from the duty on wine. On the other hand, the city government realized the importance of adequate defensive measures and were prepared to cooperate with director general and council. In 1653 two *schepenen*, Pieter Wolphertsz van Couwenhoven and Willem Beeckman, together with Johannes

La Montagne as the representative of director general and council, sat on the joint committee for the construction of the palisade, the wall that gave Wall Street its name. During the expedition against the Swedes in 1655, when both Stuyvesant and First Councilor Nicasius de Sille were absent, the remaining councilors invited Allard Anthony, at that time *burgemeester,* and Marten Kregier, former *burgemeester,* to the council for consultation. The relation between the city government and director general and council was never so bad as to rule out the cooperation on matters of urgency.[110]

City Government

For the exercise of all its tasks, the city government had at its command a growing body of officials, some of whom have been mentioned above. Besides these, the city government employed other lower officials with executive duties, such as a court messenger, a jailer, a dog catcher, a town crier, a harbor master, and weigh house hands. There were also several higher officials, such as a secretary, a receiver, and a treasurer.

The conflicts with the Company pertained mostly to the means of financing all the tasks of the city government. Gradually, albeit not without fits and starts, the magistrates gained from director general and council the control of some taxes, such as the duties on beer and wine and the charges levied by the weigh house. It also acquired the right to draw up deeds of conveyance and mortgage.[111]

The gradual expansion of their administrative tasks, coupled with the collection of the finances thereto, had repercussions on the organization and the working methods of the city government. The chairmanship of the meetings rotated on a quarterly basis between the two *burgemeesters.*[112] In about 1660, the *burgemeesters* began to meet separately to deal with administrative matters. The weekly meetings of *burgemeesters* and *schepenen* were maintained, and in the early years all decisions about administrative matters were made at these meetings, while the separate meeting of the *burgemeesters* was used to prepare and execute these decisions. Before long, the *burgemeesters* considered two meetings in the week too time-consuming, and they asked the director general to be released from their judicial obligations. However, their request fell on deaf ears, probably because Stuyvesant considered the judicial experience the *burgemeesters* had gained up to then to be indispensable.[113]

Nomination and Appointment

A similar consideration may have played a role in the appointment of *burgemeesters* and *schepenen*. The first *burgemeesters* and *schepenen* were appointed by director general and council without a nomination. Initially the city government did not possess the right to draw up a double nomination, and this obviously rankled. In the years that followed they petitioned for this privilege, arguing that the surrounding towns did have this right, while they did not. Ultimately, director general and council conceded the privilege, but not without an interesting, albeit rather inconsistent, consideration. They stated that the small courts of justice had been granted the right to double nomination because the small towns were scattered far and wide, with the result that director general and council were not able to be present at the nomination, and therefore not in a position to assess the candidates' suitability. In the opinion of director general and council, this was not the case for New Amsterdam, and therefore they had not wanted to grant the right of nomination. Nevertheless, they were now prepared to concede nomination to *burgemeesters* and *schepenen* on the proviso that they nominate only acceptable and suitable men and that a representative of director general and council be present at the drawing up of the nomination.[114]

The end of January was set for the nomination meeting. Each of the *burgemeesters* and *schepenen* would draw up nominations without discussing them with their counterparts. At the meeting all the nominations were laid side by side and the votes counted. In case of a tie, a second vote would be taken. The definitive nomination was then submitted in writing to director general and council, who made the appointment on Candlemas, 2 February. Director general and council were not always satisfied with those nominated. In 1656 the nomination contained several men who, because of earlier conflicts, were not acceptable. Director general and council therefore determined to retain the incumbent *burgemeesters* and *schepenen* and to fill only the two vacancies for *schepenen*. They did so without informing *burgemeesters* and *schepenen* of the true reason.[115]

Two years later *burgemeesters* and *schepenen* discovered that the regulations regarding the nominations were not a mere formality. The nomination was drawn up without the presence of *Schout* Nicasius de Sille as representative of the provincial government, although it was his duty to act as "head of the bench, convenor, and collector of the votes" and to cast a vote in the event of a tie.[116] Worse still, the representative had not even been officially invited. So director general and council returned the nomination, ordering *burgemeesters* and *schepenen* to draw up a new one. In the presence of the *schout* the nomination was once again approved by *burgemeesters* and *schepenen* and submitted to director general and council. Such relatively small differences of opinion on procedure continued to surface, including for instance whether employees of the Company could be nominated for office in the city and a question concerning the voting rights of the *schout*.[117]

The Schout and the Vroedschap

The *schout* played an important role in the city government, and it was a great source of irritation to *burgemeesters* and *schepenen* that in 1653 not one of the burghers was appointed, while the hated Cornelis van Tienhoven was. Van Tienhoven combined the position of *schout* with that of *fiscael,* but the *burgemeesters* and *schepenen* wanted a clear separation between the two. They also wanted the right to appoint the *schout,* or at least the right to submit a double nomination. These were matters about which Stuyvesant and his council were not permitted to decide for themselves. The directors in Amsterdam, not unsympathetic to the wishes of New Amsterdam, opined that the positions should indeed be separated. The request of *burgemeesters* and *schepenen* for "the election or at least the nomination" was refused, "because even here in this country all private lords reserve the granting of such offices for themselves."[118]

To the displeasure of the city government, the directors decided to keep Van Tienhoven in the dual function, albeit provisionally. Van Tienhoven's dismissal in 1656, when he fell into disfavor, gave *burgemeesters* and *schepenen* a new opportunity to petition for a separation of the positions. However, director general and council wanted to postpone their decision on this until they had received further advice from Amsterdam. In the meantime, Nicasius de Sille was appointed to both positions, again provisionally. This took the heat out of the discussion, as De Sille was a more acceptable person than Van Tienhoven. Another four years elapsed before New Amsterdam had its own *schout.* The appointee was Pieter Tonneman, who had been *schout* of Breuckelen. Tonneman retained his seat in the council, thereby again giving rise to a conflict of interest. Nevertheless, New Amsterdam had finally reached the long-awaited position of having its own *schout,* and the boundaries with the judicial authority of the Company's *fiscael* were determined.[119]

An institution of the Dutch Republic to which the sources for New Netherland only occasionally refer is a *vroedschap.* The commissioners of Amsterdam held out the prospect of a *vroedschap* to New Amstel with the proviso that the colony grow to two hundred families. Whether the West India Company would also have made such a concession may be doubted. Nonetheless, precursors of a *vroedschap* existed in New Amsterdam, such as the meeting of the heads of families in 1641. A restriction to the wealthiest burghers was not applied in New Amsterdam until August 1653. To hold consultations on providing financial support to director general and council for the defense of the city, *burgemeesters* and *schepenen* called together "some of the principal burghers and inhabitants."[120] Of the twenty-three men assembled, five were later to be either *burgemeester* or *schepen.* The meeting was intended to be only incidental and, as with the *landdag,* it was to be ten years before it was repeated. Again, the defense of the colony against the English prompted *burgemeesters* and *schepenen* to call together a number of burghers "in the way of a *vroetschap.*"[121] The thirteen men who were invited to attend were without exception former *schepenen* or *burgemeesters* or were later to become members of the city's government.

Even a few days before the surrender of the colony to the English, with the English frigates already lying before the fort, the burghers assembled in a meeting that resembled a *vroedschap*.[122]

Initially, *burgemeesters* and *schepenen* of New Amsterdam had powers that varied little from those of magistrates of other small courts of justice. Yet none of the members of other lower courts were appointed as *burgemeester*. While elsewhere the administration, the domain of the *burgemeesters,* and justice, the domain of the *schepenen,* were amalgamated into a single body, an exception was made for New Amsterdam, initially only in name. A number of years elapsed before a practical allocation of tasks was implemented. Yet the introduction of the office of *burgemeester,* typically an urban functionary, already indicated that New Amsterdam would be different. It would be the main city of New Netherland, its capital. The growth of its judicial and civil powers and its administrative apparatus indicates the quick development of New Amsterdam after 1653. Yet it remained subject to director general and council, as is evident in the appointments and in the position of the *schout*.

English Rule

The initiative for the conquest of New Netherland came from England, where the restoration of the monarchy had put Charles II on the throne. A hawkish faction in the English court, led by the Duke of York, the king's brother, urged an aggressive policy toward the Dutch Republic. The promulgation of a new Navigation Act in 1660, which was intended to impact Dutch shipping, was one of the first steps. On 12 March 1664 the Duke received letters patent for a large part of the North American coast, including the Dutch colony. Many arguments played a role in this grant, as they did in the resultant takeover of New Netherland, which was first of all a means of inspiring awe in the anti-monarchist New England colonies. The display of kingly might was intended to facilitate the expansion of respect for the throne elsewhere in North America as well. After the conquest, England would command the east coast of America from Nova Scotia to Carolina, and this would simplify both its government and its defense. Second, economic arguments played a role. New Amsterdam served as the port of transit for Dutch goods to the English colonies and for Virginia tobacco, among other goods, to Europe. The continued existence of the Dutch colony would make it easy for the Dutch merchants to flout the restrictions of the Navigation Acts. Finally, the Duke of York also had a personal reason for taking over the Dutch colony. The income from imposts would provide a welcome injection of funds to the ducal coffers.[123]

Three frigates, with a military force of three hundred soldiers, departed from Portsmouth in May 1664. The expeditionary force was commanded by Richard Nicolls, who knew full well that once the warships had departed it would be no simple matter to maintain control over so large an area with only three hundred men. It was necessary, therefore, to ensure that the population had no reason to resort to armed resistance. The terms that were agreed on for their capitulation were drawn up with this in mind, and they were therefore relatively mild.[124]

Articles of Capitulation

The twenty-three articles of capitulation dealt with administration, justice, and law, as well as other issues. In matters of inheritance, the colonists were given the right to maintain "their owne Customes," which was important, as English inheritance law varied considerably from the Dutch. Civil matters were resolved differently: disputes about contracts that had been entered into prior to the changeover to English law were to be settled "according to the manner of the Dutch," which implied that English law would apply to those entered into after the change. With regard to the administration, article sixteen specified that all magistrates would be retained for the period for which they had been appointed. Thereafter, new magistrates were to be selected, the terms of capitulation specifying that these were "to be Chosen, by themselves," the magistrates. This spelled the end of the Dutch system of double nomination and appointment by higher authorities, but whether the population was to be granted more say in their governance by the change-over to the English system remained to be seen. The new magistrates were obliged to swear allegiance to the English king. Finally, the terms of capitulation laid down that "the Towne of Manhattans, shall choose Deputyes, and those Deputyes, shall have free Voyces in all Publique affaires, as much as any other Deputyes."[125] No mention was made, however, of a meeting in which these deputies could convene.[126]

The rights granted to the colonists in the articles of capitulation were at odds with the concept of a proprietary colony as envisioned by the Duke of York. The patent had given him "full and absolute power and Authority to Correct, punish, pardon, Governe, and Rule."[127] Although the instructions to Nicolls have not survived, there need be little doubt that it was the Duke's intention to establish a powerful centralized administration, in which the governor was to be allotted all judicial and executive tasks without the hindrance of too great a measure of local autonomy.[128]

Nevertheless, Nicolls decided to call a "Generall Meeting of Deputyes," thus giving the impression that the population would be involved in its governance in some way. Only the towns on Long Island and in Westchester were invited. Representatives of neither New York City nor Albany were present, and the number of Dutch was limited to nine of the thirty-four delegates. Nicolls's particular intention for the meeting in Heemstede was to improve the administrative situation of the English towns, which, because of "their Subjection…to a forraigne Power," was not good. It was also his intention to solve the many conflicts among the towns.[129]

At the meeting, the English town of Southold, which lay on the eastern side of Long Island, came up with a number of proposals that in essence were suggestions for the maintenance of the independent form of administration that had been customary until then. Until 1664, Southold had fallen under the jurisdiction of Connecticut, and it wanted to keep matters this way, because of the easy communications across the Long Island Sound. It also wanted to retain the custom of the town meetings, with the right to choose its own magistrates and representatives. Such a degree of autonomy was unacceptable to Nicolls. The "Duke's Laws," which had been imposed on the English towns in 1665, did not provide for a chosen assembly that would have a Dutch majority and would therefore be acceptable neither to the English towns nor to the Duke of York. The governor was responsible for the day-to-day government of the colony, with the assistance of a council selected by him. In an annual session with the High Sheriff and the Justices of the Peace, the governor and council formed the highest judicial organ in the colony, the Court of Assizes. Appeal against the judgments of this court could be lodged with the English king. The Court of Assizes also played a role in the confirmation of local ordinances, the probation of wills, the drawing up of provincial legislation, and the supervision of the collection of taxes.[130]

Centralization

The new administration of the colony reversed the decentralization that had slowly been introduced under Dutch rule. This was a result of the royal patent. In England too, the power of the monarch began to acquire absolutist characteristics. In mid-1665 Nicolls wrote to Clarendon in England:

> the very name of the Dukes power heere, hath bine one great motive for weell affected men to Remove hither out of other Collonies, men well affected to Monarchy, and haue found that our new Lawes are not contriued soe Democratically as the Rest.[131]

Despite the centralist character of ducal rule, a form of regional government continued to exist. With the "Duke's Laws" the "county of Yorkshire" was created, consisting principally of areas in which the English colonists were in the majority: Long Island, Westchester, and Staten Island. Like Yorkshire in England, the county of Yorkshire in America was divided into three "ridings." In each of these, justice was administered by a Court of Sessions, consisting of justices of the peace and the "under-sheriff," all appointed by the governor. Among other things, their duties consisted of collecting taxes and of delivering judgments in cases in which an appeal had been made against the judgment of a local court.[132]

At the local level, the administration in the English towns was formed by a constable and eight overseers, who were elected by the freemen. Each year, four new overseers were elected, while one of the overseers who was standing down was elected constable. The task of the constable consisted of presiding over the local court and carrying out the orders of the governor. Although the administrative structure introduced for the English towns in New York displayed many similarities with that used in New England, an important difference was the absence of the town meetings. It is understandable that the "Duke's Laws" were not received with open arms by the English towns. The situation under Dutch rule had perhaps not been ideal, but the English towns did at least have their town meetings. Under English administration, however, their autonomy was reduced considerably. At the meeting in Heemstede, Nicolls met with some resistance, but nevertheless the changes were carried out.[133]

While for the English colonists the changeover to English administration was to their disadvantage, their Dutch neighbors initially experienced little change. In New York City the incumbent *burgemeesters* and *schepenen* remained in office up to the date for the appointment of magistrates, 2 February 1665. Then *burgemeesters* and *schepenen,* referring to the sixteenth article of the articles of the capitulation, appointed their successors themselves and requested Nicolls's approval of the appointments, which he gave without much ado. The situation changed only in June 1665 with Nicolls's decision that henceforth the city government "shall bee Knowne and Called by ye Name and Style of Mayor, Aldermen, and Sherriffe, according to the Custome of England."[134] *Burgemeester* Oloff Stevensz van Cortlandt protested this, with the argument that such a measure went against the terms of the capitulation, but his words fell on deaf ears. The opposition of the city government was weak because the majority of the magistrates, including the new *schout,* Allard Anthony, continued to be Dutch. The most important change was the appointment of Thomas Willett as mayor. As a merchant, Willett had years of experience with the New Amsterdam merchants and also knew Stuyvesant well. He was in Dutch eyes an acceptable non-Dutch magistrate. In the years that followed, the new members of the city government were appointed by the governor without having been nominated. Starting in 1669 double nominations were once again permitted, although on several occasions Nicolls's successor Francis Lovelace made appointments without resorting to nominations. Besides the titles and the composition of the city government, its duties and tasks also changed in the sense that the probation of last wills according to English law was added. A further important point was the introduction of trial by jury. As in the city government, the composition of juries shows a balance of English and Dutch, wherein the latter had few problems in adapting to the English customs.[135]

In Albany, as Beverwijck had been renamed, the administrative form continued to be Dutch for longer than was the case in New York City, even though in

1665 the court at Albany, which already had jurisdiction over Schenectady, was combined with that of Rensselaerswijck. Each of the three areas was to provide two magistrates. Gerrit Swart, who had been *schout* of Rensselaerswijck from 1652, became the *schout* over the whole area of Albany, Rensselaerswijck, and Schenectady. It was only after several years that Schenectady, situated at quite some distance from Albany, gained its own *schout*. The establishment of a separate court followed at the end of 1672. The problem of distance had already in 1671 prompted a change in the number of magistrates. Because the appearances of the representatives of Rensselaerswijck were few and far between, Albany was permitted a third magistrate so that a quorum was available more frequently. Despite these changes, both in composition and language the court in Albany remained Dutch for quite some time.[136]

In Wiltwijck, which had been renamed Kingston, changes were not put into effect until 1669. Until that time, *Schout* Willem Beeckman and Secretary Matthijs Capito had been retained. In 1669 a number of new officials were appointed by a committee that had been set up by Lovelace. In 1671 the administrative reforms went further: a Court of Sessions was established for Kingston, Hurley, and Marbletown, presided over by Thomas Chambers as justice of the peace. This court held session every six months and was endowed with the right of dealing with civil matters amounting to a maximum of £5. In criminal matters they had full jurisdiction, with the exception of capital offenses.[137]

Dutchmen continued to participate in the administration in both Albany and Kingston, where little changed, as well as in New York City, where the winds of change blew more forcefully. The English governors did not compel the Dutch colonists to accept radical changes. The accommodating attitude of the English went so far that Nicolls allowed the magistrates of Albany to write to him in Dutch, although he assumed that they could read English excellently.[138] Even so, the colony might once more fall into Dutch hands. In the articles of capitulation it was established, rather unnecessarily, that should the English king and the States General come to the agreement that the colony should once more come to fall under the authority of the Dutch Republic, and that orders to that end be given, then the appropriate actions thereto would be taken immediately. Yet in the Treaty of Breda, which in 1667 heralded the end of the Second Anglo-Dutch War, it was agreed that both countries would maintain the status quo after the events in the colonies. New Netherland remained in English hands, while Surinam, which was taken in February 1667 by a Dutch fleet under Abraham Crijnssen, remained Dutch.[139]

Dutch Again, Briefly

However, the peace was not accompanied by any reduction in rivalry between the two countries, and new hostilities were to be expected. With her allies France, Münster, and Cologne, England attacked the Dutch Republic in 1672. The States of Zeeland dispatched an expedition under the command of Cornelis Evertsen de Jongste with the objective of attacking the enemy in its colonial territories. Although New Netherland was not the primary target, the Zeeland fleet, in combination with an Amsterdam squadron under the command of Jacob Benckes, arrived at the Hudson at the beginning of August 1673. Evertsen decided to make an attempt to recapture New Netherland. The fleet came to lie before New York City, where three English representatives went aboard. After the objective of the fleet was made clear to them, they asked to see Evertsen's commission, to which he answered "that it was stuck in the mouth of the canon, as they would soon become aware if they did not surrender the fort."[140] After a brief exchange of fire, the English surrendered on 9 August 1673. Albany was recaptured a couple of days later.[141]

So New Netherland was once again in Dutch hands, and once more a number of places underwent a change of name: New York City became New Orange, Fort James became Fort Willem Hendrick, Kingston became Swaenenburgh, and Albany was renamed Willemstadt. The Dutch intermezzo lasted only fifteen months: on 10 November 1674 the colony was handed over to the English as a consequence of the Treaty of Westminster. In 1673, the new rulers did not suspect that their dominion was to be so short-lived, and they vigorously adopted measures to shape the administration to the Dutch model once more. This meant a return to the situation that prevailed prior to 1665, with some slight differences. Now, the highest authority was not the West India Company but the Admiralty of Amsterdam. The central administrative organ in the colony was initially the fleet's court-martial, in which Cornelis Evertsen and Jacob Benckes played the principal role, together with three captains of the fleet. With the departure of the ships imminent, Anthony Colve was appointed governor, Cornelis Steenwijck was appointed to the council, and Nicolaes Bayard was made secretary and receiver-general. The city government was requested, via Steenwijck, to put forward nominations, resulting in the appointment of three *burgemeesters* and five *schepenen*. Only Dutch were nominated, and among the eight appointees four had already held office in the city government prior to 1665. The appointment of magistrates in other courts in New Netherland was carried out by means of a double nomination and appointments by the higher powers. The rights and responsibilities of the courts were in many instances the same, although the amount above which the judgment could be appealed was increased to 240 guilders. English magistrates were appointed for the English towns. But all in all, the changes were minor. For a period of fifteen months everything seemed to have returned to how it had been prior to 1665.[142]

The Dutch population of New Netherland accepted English rule with an acquiescence that raises doubts as to its loyalty to the regime of the West

India Company. Yet infusing seventeenth-century people with nineteenth- and twentieth-century nationalistic sentiments is anachronistic. It is better compared with something else. To many of the colonists, the change to English rule was more like the arrival of a new government after elections in which the party you voted for lost. You may dislike it, but it is not a cause for widespread rebellion or departure. As the new rulers initially allowed trade and shipping to the Dutch Republic to continue, the takeover did not appear to have much impact on the economy and thus on their livelihood.

4   *Trade, Agriculture, and Artisans*

On the afternoon of Saturday, 28 December 1630, Michiel Pauw, delegate of the Amsterdam chamber to a meeting of the *Heren XIX,* presented three designs of coats of arms to the assembled gentlemen. One of the designs was quickly discarded, but the other two were provisionally approved. The first was entitled "*Sigillum Novi Amstelodamensis*" (Seal of New Amsterdam): two lions guarding a crest with the three Andreas crosses of Amsterdam, decked with the image of a beaver. The second showed the coat of arms of New Netherland: "a black beaver on a gold field, with embroidery of white *Zeewant* on a blue ground, decked with a count's crown," symbolizing the economic motives in the founding of New Netherland.[1]

    The trade in peltries with the Indians was the main motive for the colonization of New Netherland. Initially, "the Dutch came to New York City and established a trading post there to make a buck."[2] Of course, any division of motives for founding colonies into either economic or religious is contrary to how it was viewed in the seventeenth century. You couldn't expect to prosper if you didn't pray, and you couldn't live if you did nothing but pray. As New Netherland slowly changed from a trading post into a settlement colony, the Dutch colonists turned out to be there to make a living. The economic emphasis shifted, and the importance of local food supplies increased. Farming activities, which had been carried out since the earliest days of the settlement, were gradually expanded. Toward the end of the Dutch period, farming had grown to such an extent that it had become possible to export grain, albeit in limited amounts. Another agricultural product, tobacco, was mainly grown for export to Europe. Along with the growth in the number of inhabitants, a group of craftsmen evolved who provided for local needs. In spite of this, the colonists remained dependent on imports for a wide range of commodities, luxury items in particular. The export of peltries and tobacco and the import of diverse goods were controlled by the merchants in New Amsterdam. But unlike their colleagues in Amsterdam, they rarely received coins in payment. The currency of New Netherland was produced locally and consisted of *sewant* and beavers.

Trust and Shells

Trust was the basis of economic transactions in the seventeenth century, in the Dutch Republic as much as in New Netherland. Many people provided credit, but they sometimes had to wait months or even years for payment. In 1662 in Amsterdam, Maria Momma, the widow of Wouter van Twiller, re-quested her relative Jeremias van Rensselaer in New Netherland to recover an eleven-year-old debt. This was exceptional, but a number of months, even up to a year, was not. Nor was it uncommon for a borrower to exceed his or her payment deadlines, giving rise to many disagreements, sometimes accompanied by harsh words and exchanges of insults. As a last resort, matters could be taken to court, and indeed, the majority of cases brought before the courts in New Netherland concerned debts.[3]

In court cases in which the debt was disavowed, or disagreement arose over the exact amount, written acknowledgment of the debt or account books had to be produced. People regularly authorized relatives or friends to recover their outstanding claims. Inhabitants of New Amsterdam, for ex-ample, could be summoned to court under a power of attorney for payment of a debt incurred in the Dutch Republic, and people returning to *patria* gave power of attorney to someone remaining in New Netherland to claim any outstanding debts on their behalf. Departure for the other side of the ocean did not mean that you escaped debts.

Regulating Sewant

As in the Dutch Republic, accounts were made up in guilders (*guldens*), consisting of twenty stivers (*stuivers*), which again were divided into six-teen pennies (*penningen*). It was common practice to avoid having to pay in cash by canceling debts against each other. Coins rarely changed hands. As New Netherland, like other North American colonies, was hampered by a chronic shortage of silver coinage, payments were often made in *sewant*, beaver pelts, and tobacco. This was an important difference between New Netherland and the Dutch Republic, and it made the monetary situation in the colony very complex. In the Dutch Republic, payment in kind was not unusual, but it rarely took the form of beaver pelts or shell money. *Sewant* consisted of strings of beads made from shells, mostly found on Long Island. The Indians had many ritual uses for *sewant,* but for the colonists it quickly acquired the role of currency. Both the colonists and the Indians also used *sewant* as a gift in diplomatic negotiations.[4]

As governing body the West India Company issued ordinances with quality requirements for *sewant* and beaver pelts. These were regularly repeated, which is usually an indication that they were not adhered to. There were numerous complaints about loose, unstrung *sewant,* with glass beads mixed among the shell beads. The exchange rate was a constant source of concern to the government, and the rate for *sewant* had to be adjusted on a number of occasions. While in 1641 one stiver was paid for five white beads, in 1658 *burgemeesters* and *schepenen* asked director general and council to increase the rate to eight beads per stiver. A few years later it had risen to twenty-four white or twelve black beads per stiver.[5] The inflation was caused by the import of *sewant* from New England. The West India Company was aware of this, but few solutions to the problem could be found. As director general and council wrote to the directors in Amsterdam in 1660 on the suggestion of reducing *sewant* to the value of silver:

> it would be desirable if it could be put into practice without fear of trouble and without diverting the trade, [but] it is in our opinion not without considerable danger and peril, as the *zeewant* is the source and mother of the beaver trade, and no beavers can be obtained from the *wilden* for just trade goods without *zewant*, [and] if it is not imported, as we do not have it in our country, it would certainly cause a diversion in the beaver trade.[6]

Thus, *sewant* was essential for the beaver trade. But the beaver pelts too were subject to changes in exchange rates. An important difference between *sewant* and beaver pelts was that the latter had a commercial value in the Dutch Republic, while *sewant* did not. Because the beavers were merchandise, market conditions determined their value. However, the WIC set the exchange rate of beavers when used as payment of taxes and wages. In 1656 the rate was set at six guilders per pelt; a year later it was raised to eight and even ten guilders. The rate was reduced again in 1662 and 1663, first to seven and then to six guilders, to attune it better to the market value of beavers in Amsterdam.[7]

The continuous inflation of *sewant* was hardly conducive to smooth trading, and some attempts were made to replace *sewant* by silver coins as a means of payment. In 1649, Stuyvesant and his council suggested importing ten thousand guilders in coin from the Dutch Republic to reduce the use of *sewant,* but the directors in *patria* turned him down because of a shortage of money. Some years later they repeated the proposal, this time for twelve thousand guilders, and took preparatory measures, but again the proposal was dismissed by their superiors.[8]

And so *sewant* continued to be the most common method of payment. The consequence of the continuous inflation was that the relation between the methods of payment became more and more disproportionate, spawning onerous bookkeeping problems. In 1662 the price of a beaver was some twenty to twenty-four guilders in *sewant*. Although both currencies were calculated in guilders and stivers, the relation between the values of so-called *sewantstivers* and *beaverstivers* altered to such an extent that in 1658 the directors in Amsterdam decided not to object if the company's book-keeper in the colony were "to keep two cash accounts in the mentioned two species, if only the same are finally reduced to Dutch value." Some of the monthly wages had to be paid out in the colony at the nominal Dutch value.[9] But this was to the detriment of the WIC's employees, as director general and council tried to make clear to the directors in words that emphasize the complexity of the problem:

> Before [*sewant*] is reduced to beaver value and is reckoned at seven guilders per beaver, [it] suffers a loss of 50 percent, as the beaver, calculated at the usual rate of eight guilders, is bartered and estimated in public sales at fifteen or sixteen guilders in *sewant*, which would be about eighteen guilders, if the beaver is rated at seven guilders. Thus there is on *sewant* more than 50 percent loss, from which subsequently can be deduced how much damage your Honors' servants have suffered thus far by being paid their monthly wages at the Dutch value and what damage they who by lack of beavers will have to take *sewant* will suffer from now on.[10]

Merchants also suffered from the difference in value between the New Netherland guilder and the Dutch guilder. Two merchants from New Netherland complained in 1662 that one hundred guilders in *sewant* yielded no more than twenty-five guilders in the Dutch Republic, while one hundred guilders in beavers at eight guilders per pelt was worth fifty-six guilders and five stivers in Holland.[11]

Fur Trade

"The beaver is the main foundation and means why or through which this beautiful land was first occupied by people from Europe," Adriaen van der Donck wrote in 1655.[12] According to him no fewer than eighty thousand beavers per year were killed in New Netherland and its hinterland. Although other furred animals, like otters, were also traded in the early period, the beaver was by far the most important. Van der Donck's estimate of the number of beavers taken annually is one of the highest. Only Samuel Maverick, in his efforts six years later to convince the Earl of Clarendon of the benefits of conquering New Netherland, stated the even higher total of one hundred thousand pelts per year. Both men had reason to exaggerate and their estimates are too high.[13]

Little information is available on the period prior to 1623, the years of the New Netherland Company and other private traders. A remark by Isaac de Rasière in 1626 indicates that the private traders obtained some two thousand to twenty-five hundred pelts each year from the area round the South River.[14] This estimate fits in with later information on the early years of the West India Company as supplied by Johannes de Laet, a director of the Company. The information he provided, detailed and likely to be accurate, shows that between 1624 and 1635 the trade almost doubled in volume, rising to over 11,000 pelts with a total value of 91,000 guilders. The other figures for this period correspond with those provided by De Laet. De Rasière hoped to be able to export ten thousand pelts in 1626, but this was a little optimistic. In the same year the ship *Wapen van Amsterdam* arrived in the Netherlands with 7,246 beavers and 1,004.5 other pelts. A report from the West India Company of 23 October 1629 states that New Netherland expected to obtain no more than fifty thousand guilders' worth of peltries per year, quite a low estimate.[15]

In the early 1630s, the fur trade continued to grow. The ship *Eendracht,* which was seized by the English in Plymouth in 1632, carried more than five thousand pelts, roughly half of the total for that year, although an English report of the same year gives the higher figure of fifteen thousand. In 1633 Kiliaen van Rensselaer estimated that the fur trade in New Netherland could yield an annual maximum of sixty to seventy thousand guilders, which corresponds with a total of about ten thousand pelts. A year later John Winthrop estimated the Dutch trade at nine to ten thousand pelts per year. In the same year Kiliaen van Rensselaer wrote to Wouter van Twiller that he had heard that the new *commies* of the Company, Hans Jorisz Hontom, believed that he could send over some thirteen thousand pelts per year, which Van Rensselaer considered impossible. In 1636 the WIC received approximately eight thousand pelts.[16]

After the Company's monopoly on the fur trade had been lifted, the trade expanded, but quantitative details for the 1640s are scarce. Van Rensselaer noted in 1640 that in the preceding fifteen years, five to six thousand pelts were shipped annually from Fort Orange, the center of the beaver trade. But this applies to the trade from only one of the areas in the colony, albeit the most important. The other details available are limited to the trade of individual merchants. For example, in 1645 the ship *Rensselaerswijck* carried 1,585 beaver pelts. In 1647 Govert Loockermans hoped to dispatch approximately two thousand pelts. He also reported that merchant Willem de Key expected to export five thousand beaver pelts. With the wreck of the ship *Prinses Amelia* in 1647, no fewer than fifteen to sixteen thousand beavers disappeared under the waves. A year later, some fifty-five hundred pelts were shipped in the *Valckenier* for the firm Verbrugge, while the same ship carried a further two thousand pieces for the WIC. Although these figures do not cover the entire trade, they give the impression that in the second part of the 1640s, when the wars with the Indians were over, the fur trade grew to a volume that was considerably greater than that of the 1630s.[17]

Information on the 1650s is also quite hard to come by, but it can be assumed that the growth of the trade continued until 1657. Some authors cite the rather high figure of forty-six thousand beavers for Fort Orange alone. With a beaver price of seven to eight guilders, this would mean that the value of the export of peltries reached some three hundred thousand to three hundred and fifty thousand guilders. At least 37,940 beaver pelts were shipped from Beverwijck to New Amsterdam in the summer of 1657. Thereafter the volume went down slightly. In 1660, in a letter to Stuyvesant, Johannes La Montagne grumbled about the "bad trade of this year which barely mounts up to the number of thirty thousand." Director general and council estimated the number of beavers on which the recognition fee was paid at only twenty-five to thirty thousand. With a beaver price of seven guilders, this would yield the WIC sixteen thousand guilders. It was a rather low estimate, particularly as the recognition fee was levied not only for the beaver pelts from Fort Orange but also for those from New Amstel. The trade from that area in 1663 was estimated at ten thousand beavers per year. The authorities in New Netherland were clearly worried about the decline in the volume of the trade as well as about the drop in price.[18]

Decline

The cause of the decline is generally sought in problems on the supply side. Two factors have been put forward: intra-Indian wars and a gradual depletion of the beaver population as the result of overhunting. Intertribal warfare meant that the Indians devoted less attention to beaver hunting, and it jeopardized the safety of the trade routes to Beverwijck. Information about the second factor, overhunting, is scarce. It may have played a role, although the rate at which it occurred remains unclear.[19]

Demand was also a factor that determined the price of pelts and thus the total value of the export of peltries. Beaver pelts were shipped from New Netherland to Amsterdam, and a large number were sold to Muscovy to be processed. The market price in Amsterdam was, of course, subject to periodic fluctuations, but toward the end of the 1650s prices were lower than they had been in earlier decades. As a result of the large supply of beavers in the 1650s, the market suffered a glut, and subsequently demand fell, driving prices down to ƒ6 in 1657.[20] The beaver price quickly descended to ƒ4:18 in the middle of 1658 and after that fluctuated between six and seven guilders. If for the 1650s as a whole the average price for a beaver was six and a half guilders and if we estimate the average yearly export of peltries at thirty-five thousand pieces, then the total value of the export can be estimated at about 230,000 guilders.[21]

The volume of the trade and the price of the beaver were, of course, of great importance to the colonists in New Netherland, but other aspects of the fur trade also played a role. After the end of the West India Company's monopoly on pelts, private individuals took hold of the trade. The recognition fee on the export of peltries remained one of the sources of income of the West India Company. An extensive set of regulations was the result.

The Company's monopoly of the fur trade was already under pressure by the early beginnings of colonization. Colonists were allowed to trade with the Indians, but they had to sell the acquired pelts to the WIC at a price set by the Company, with the result that their margin for profit was minimal. The extent to which employees of the WIC and colonists were permitted to take beaver pelts back to *patria* is not completely clear. It is probable that, as with the VOC, a limited amount of private trading was accepted, but smuggling was an attractive option.[22]

Illicit Trade

At the introduction of the system of patroonships, the extent to which the patroons could engage in the fur trade had been limited: the patroons were allowed to trade only in areas where the Company did not have a trading post, and one guilder per pelt had to be paid as recognition fee. Van Rensselaer, interpreting this as a transfer of the WIC's monopoly of the fur trade to the patroons, tried to exclude the majority of his workers in the colony from the trade, although it is doubtful that he was successful. After the WIC had surrendered its monopoly, Van Rensselaer tried to keep a firm grip on the exclusive rights to the fur trade that, in his opinion, accrued to him according to the old *Freedoms and Exemptions* of 1629. Every so often he granted exemptions to his colonists, such as to Abraham Staets and Evert Pels, who as surgeon and brewer joined his service in 1642. They were permitted to export a limited number of beaver pelts, on payment of one guilder per pelt to the patroon.[23]

Smuggling and illicit trading could never be prevented completely. An ordinance of 1638 stated rather exaggeratedly that illicit cargo took up so much room in the holds of the WIC ships that hardly any room was left for the legal goods. Nevertheless, smuggling played a limited role in the discussion on the abolition of the fur monopoly. The pressure exerted by the States General on the West India Company to make immigration more attractive was more important. In this decade other government-granted monopolies were also under discussion in the Dutch Republic. By the 1640s, the WIC had not only lost the monopoly on the New Netherland fur trade, but shipping rights were also opened to all citizens of the Dutch Republic, provided a recognition fee was paid to the Company.[24]

This development forced the New Netherland authorities to tighten the regulations. On arrival at New Netherland, the ships had to anchor on the East River, to the southeast of the fort. The *fiscael* carried out an inspection before anyone was permitted to land. The cargo was unloaded into sloops, which then sailed to a landing stage. From there the goods were taken to the

WIC warehouse, where the contents of the chests were compared with the bills of lading. The goods were released to the addressee after they had been checked and the relevant excise had been paid.

The procedure for the export of goods was largely similar. During the ships' stay in port, the traffic between ship and shore was strictly regulated. The colonists were allowed to board ships only with explicit permission. The crew was not allowed to stay on land overnight, and journeys by sloop to and from the ships at night were forbidden. The cargo was transported in chests, which were identified with merchants' marks, usually the initials of the addressee. In the Company warehouse, the chests were re-verified and opened, and pelts for which excise duty had been paid were marked with the company's monogram in white chalk.[25]

No checks or severe punishments could prevent smuggling. The most common method was to load or unload goods out of sight of the Company authorities. As ships approached New Amsterdam, contraband could be put overboard in watertight chests, to be recovered later when the coast was clear. And when ships left New Netherland, beaver pelts that had been left on one of the uninhabited islands off the coast could be picked up. To prevent this, a guard ship was stationed near Sandy Hook (Santpunt), probably with little success. On the other side of the Atlantic, contraband was transported in small vessels to and from Edam, Medemblik, or Durgerdam, while the ship was on route between Texel and Amsterdam.[26]

Indian Trade

Apart from the loss of income caused by the evasion of excise duties, the relations with the Indians were another argument for the government to try to regulate the fur trade. At an early stage, probably within a couple of years after the Mohawk-Mahican War ended in 1628, the area around Fort Orange became the center of the fur trade.[27] Little is known about how trade was conducted there in the 1630s and 1640s. One of the few sources is the journal that Harmen Meyndertsz van den Bogaert kept during his journey into Mohawk and Oneida country in 1634 and 1635. Together with Willem Thomasz and Jeronimus Gerritsz and accompanied by a number of Mohawks, he set out in December 1634 to try to discover why the fur trade had turned bad recently. The cause turned out to be the competition from the French in Canada, who offered better rates.[28] Although Van den Bogaert was initially received with indifference, the Oneidas began to show some appreciation for his visit after a few days. They presented gifts and asked for a higher price and better availability of trade goods. Van den Bogaert was unable to agree on a higher price, but promised that they "would tell the chief at the Manhatas, who was our commander" of the Indians' request.[29]

Van den Bogaert's account highlights several aspects of the fur trade, such as the competition with other Europeans, the importance of *sewant,* the

een Mahakuaes Indiaen, met hun Steden en woningen

5. Een Mahakuase Indiaen, met hun Steden en woningen. Beschrijvinghe van Virginia, Nieuw Nederlandt, Nieuw Engelandt, en d'eylanden Bermudes, Berbados, en S. Christoffel. 1651. Engraving. I. N. Phelps Stokes Collection, Miriam and Ira D. Wallach Division of Art, Prints and Photographs, The New York Public Library, Astor Lenox and Tilden Foundations.

necessity of exchanging gifts, and the desirability of having sufficient stocks of merchandise to trade, in particular woolen cloth and hardware. But the journey was also atypical: the usual practice was that the Indians came to Fort Orange; only rarely did the Dutch venture out of their trading posts to meet the Indians in their own land, as did the French *coureurs de bois* (wood-runners). When the monopoly on the fur trade was abandoned, the system of fixed prices no longer applied. Each colonist could now decide for himself how much he wanted to pay for beaver pelts. This did not mean that all types of commodities could be traded with Indians in exchange for beavers. Trading in alcohol and weapons was not permitted.

Supplying the Indians with liquor was forbidden in many ordinances, starting in 1643. It was "a very dangerous offence, tending to the general ruin of the country." For the Indians, getting drunk was a way of going into a trance, bringing on visions and developing a closer contact with the spiritual world, albeit temporarily. To prevent excesses, severe punishments were promulgated: a fine of five hundred guilders, flogging, and banishment. In practice, however, punishments were much lighter. In Beverwijck, where the majority of offenses were committed, the *schepenen* tended to show mercy, especially if the guilty party showed remorse and promised to improve his or her behavior. And if a severe sentence was pronounced, such as banishment, it was usually not enforced.[30] In cases of hardship the courts were often inclined to impose relatively low fines.[31]

Guns and Powder

Even more unforgivable in the eyes of the authorities than providing the Indians with alcohol was to supply them with weapons and ammunition. Van den Bogaert reported that he and his companions were repeatedly asked to fire their guns, which suggests that the Mohawks were not much acquainted with firearms at that time and did not yet possess them. This started probably to change around 1640, although it is possible that the Algonquian groups acquired firearms earlier. A 1639 ordinance required the death penalty for the sale of weapons and gunpowder and lead to Indians, an indication of how serious the trade in weapons was considered to be. The death penalty was reiterated in an ordinance of 1645, and in this time of the wars with the Indians it was even said that "our enemies are better provided with powder than we." From the English colonies came accusations of the "dangerous liberty taken by many of yours in selling guns, powder, shott and other instrument's of warr to the Indians not onely at your forte Aurania," but also in other places.[32]

Thus, the arms trade put international relations in jeopardy and increased the risks in the event of conflicts with the Indians. But once the Indians had discovered the advantages of firearms it was impossible to stop the trade. To keep the situation under control, the arms trade in New Netherland was made the monopoly of the government. The directors in *patria* ordered director general and council not to risk war with the Indians by bluntly refusing to sell them arms and ammunition and ensuring that such trade took place as little as possible. But if the Mohawks would acquire their gunpowder and lead from the English, the beaver trade might be diverted. The authorities had to walk a fine line.[33]

Of course, some private traders tried to exploit the lucrative trade in arms illegally. Many were prosecuted for the offense, and ordinances concerning the trade in weapons were promulgated a number of times in the 1650s, a clear indication that the problem had not vanished. It is difficult to estimate the share of alcohol and firearms in the total package of merchandise traded by the Europeans with the Indians. Weapons are commonly found in archaeological excavations of Indian burial sites, and the same applies to textiles and metal objects. The information on payments for land and for ransoms for captured Netherlanders indicates that in addition to arms; gunpowder and lead; woolen, duffel and linen clothing; metal instruments such as knives, axes, kettles, and adzes were also traded.[34]

These were objects the Indians could also obtain in Beverwijck during the normal trading season. Most beavers were trapped in the winter. Each year from June to August, hundreds of Indians came down the Mohawk River in canoes to approximately thirty kilometers northwest of Beverwijck, the location of present-day Schenectady, where the Cohoes Falls and rapids make the river impassable for canoes. They walked from Schenectady with packs of beaver pelts on their backs to Beverwijck, where they sometimes slept in the homes of colonists, although in the English period separate huts were also built specially for them. Once they had arrived in the town, the Indians went from house to house to get the best price for their beavers.[35]

Beverwijck in Trouble

In the 1650s, the trade in beaver pelts could be crucial to individual colonists, making competition fierce. Handing out gifts to sway the Indians into selling all their beavers to a single trader was still relatively innocuous, but attempts to persuade the Indians could also take on more violent forms. Indians were sometimes beaten and obstructed as they went from house to house. Complaints from the Indians resulted in a few prosecutions. For example, Jochem Becker, no stranger to violence, was fined two Flemish pounds for assaulting an Indian.[36]

An undesirable result of the competition was the practice of traders to wait for the Indians in the forest before they arrived in Beverwijck. This practice had already been carried out by itinerant traders on the South River but was swiftly prohibited by director general and council. A similar prohibition was promulgated for Beverwijck some years later, as the authorities were of the opinion that it would make the Indians lazy and thus that it would be disadvantageous to trade. When trading in the forest was forbidden, inhabitants of Beverwijck tried to get around the letter of the law by using go-betweens, who would wait for the Indians and persuade them to do business only with specific traders. The use of such *maeckelaers* (brokers), both Indian and European, was prohibited in an ordinance of 1654, which was read out each year prior to the trading season.[37]

When the trade in peltries began to diminish, the competition in Beverwijck became increasingly fierce, with the result that many of the prohibitions were regularly contravened. The court in Beverwijck on several occasions had to make an exception to the general ordinances by allowing the use of Indian brokers for one year. The use of brokers was expensive and was therefore only possible for the larger fur traders, who in this way drove the smaller traders out of the market. And it was mainly the large traders who sat on the Beverwijck court and thus had the opportunity to draw up ordinances that promoted their own interests.[38]

In 1660 this situation led to a serious conflict within the community of Beverwijck. The *principaelste handelaers* (principal traders) wanted only *wilde makelaers* (Indian brokers) to be used. The *gemeene handelaers* (common traders) favored the use of both Indian and Dutch brokers. The vice director of Fort Orange, Johannes la Montagne, reported to Stuyvesant that "the matter led to insults and thereafter to heavy threats." The court was divided and with difficulty reached an unsatisfactory compromise: neither Dutch nor Indian brokers would be used.[39]

It soon became apparent that the compromise was untenable. A month of several violations followed, and on 17 June the magistrates had to decide to allow both Indian and Dutch brokers again. After the arrival of Stuyvesant on 22 July, order was quickly restored. He listened to the complaints from both sides and then decided that the use of both Indian and Dutch brokers would be prohibited. Without doubt violations had occurred in the years that followed, and it was therefore necessary to repeat the ordinance in 1662.[40]

The fur trade not only played an important role in the economy of New Netherland, it also had great influence on the relations with the Indians. The conflict in Beverwijck in 1660 demonstrates that the fur trade was of such importance that its decline exerted serious pressure on the community. At the same time the decline had such effect only in Beverwijck. In the rest of New Netherland the fur trade had become less important by the late 1650s. At its highest point at the end of the 1650s, the total value of the export was three hundred to three hundred and fifty thousand guilders.

Agriculture

The agriculture of New Netherland is a subject in which plans and expectations in the Netherlands contrast sharply with the actual development of the colony. Long before the founding of the WIC, Willem Usselincx had grandiloquent visions of settlement colonies that could provide the Dutch Republic with raw materials; for this he had Guyana rather than New Netherland in mind. For the directors of the West India Company such plans initially scarcely played a role, but the idea did not pass entirely into oblivion. It was one of the motives in the establishment of the patroonship system in 1629. In 1638 the *Heren XIX* were of the opinion that in the long run a considerable amount of grain could come from the colony. In the plans for New Amstel, one of the considerations was "not to be always dependent exclusively on the *Oostzee* [Baltic Sea]," from where most of the grain imported into the Netherlands came.[41]

A major problem with these ambitions was that the costs of transporting bulk goods from New Netherland were possibly twice as high as that from the Baltic area.[42] New Netherland was not considered a direct competitor to the Baltic area but rather as a complementary or strategic reserve in the event of the closure of the Sound, the narrow strait between Denmark and Sweden. In New Netherland, the colony's potential importance as a granary was also recognized, and it was used as an argument when requesting help from the Dutch Republic against the English:

> This well-situated province, where thousands of *morgen*[s] of land are still lying uninhabited, uncultivated, yes, which could even function as a retreat if (which God prevent) our Netherlands should be visited with heavy war, both within and without, and also as a granary in the case the easterly crops are lacking, or trade is prohibited by the northern king or rulers.[43]

Furthermore, the *burgemeesters* of New Amsterdam in February 1664 reported that a harvest of eight thousand *schepels* (6,112 bushels) of winter grain was expected. To gain the much-needed support, the magistrates may have indulged in a little exaggeration. Similarly, the communication made by the *burgemeesters* to the States General nine years later, when the province was once more in Dutch hands, is doubtful. According to them, the area around the Esopus alone, which consisted of three villages, had in 1672 produced twenty-five thousand *schepels* (19,100 bushels) of corn. The commissioners of New Amstel were also optimistic, and in 1664 estimated that within two years the South River could supply at least ten thousand *schepels* (7,640 bushels) of grain.[44]

Apart from these three estimates, the extent of agriculture in New Netherland is unknown. It may be assumed that from 1625 the total production initially grew at a rate roughly similar to that of the growth of the population of the colony. In the early years most of the local produce was probably consumed in the colony itself, and it is doubtful that it was sufficient to feed everyone. The colonists regularly supplemented their provisions by obtaining maize from the Indians, and this may have influenced Kieft and his council in 1639 in deciding to make the Indians pay contributions partly in maize. There is no indication of any grain exported to the Dutch Republic, but the WIC still thought that New Netherland could in time supply Brazil with foodstuff. Kiliaen van Rensselaer also believed that opportunities existed for grain trade with other Dutch colonies, such as Brazil and the trading forts on the West African coast. The great expectations for trade between the Dutch Atlantic colonies were never fulfilled, however, as Brazil was lost before agriculture in New Netherland produced any substantial surpluses. Indeed, one shipment of corn was sent to Curaçao in 1654, but that was the extent of it. In 1668 Jeremias van Rensselaer exported wheat to Boston, where he was able to obtain a better price for it than in New York. In the Dutch days of New York, the export of foodstuff never reached the importance that it attained later in the seventeenth and eighteenth centuries.[45]

Despite the lack of exportable surplus, agriculture was important in the economy of New Netherland, as it provided for the livelihood of the colonists. Three forms of agricultural activity stand out: crop farming, stockbreeding, and tobacco growing. Other plans, such as those to set up sericulture, illustrate the Dutch efforts to make New Netherland a success, but they never got off the ground. Fishery, too, after a half-hearted attempt at whaling in the South River, was never of importance.[46]

Planting and Sowing

Agricultural activities began when colonization started in 1624. In his instructions, Verhulst was ordered to give "each household as much land as they are able to cultivate." The *Provisional Regulations* instructed the colonists "to plant and sow first the lands allotted to them with such crops and fruits" as the West India Company would prescribe and make available.[47] As with the fur trade, agriculture for the first fifteen years was exclusively run by the West India Company, which concentrated its activities on Manhattan. The WIC retained ownership of the cultivated lands, the buildings, and the stock and installed the colonists as tenants. After a few years the WIC's hold loosened, as the stock was sold to the tenants. Until 1630 some eight *bouwerijen* (boweries) were set up on Manhattan, consisting of a farmhouse, a haystack, a barn, and fifty *morgen* of land, about a hundred acres. In the years that followed, some farms fell into disuse because the tenants abandoned them. The remaining farms were not very productive and rarely produced sufficient harvests to provide the WIC's employees with food, much less the export market. The Company gradually sold the farms to private individuals, some of whom installed tenants. The last farm to be in the hands of the WIC was the so-called Directors' Bowery, which Stuyvesant bought in 1651.[48]

The decline of the West India Company farms was accelerated by the implementation of the patroonship system. Cattle was purchased on Manhattan and transported to the patroonships, in particular by Van Rensselaer. Some Company tenants were inclined to move on to Rensselaerswijck after the expiration of their contracts, if they had not saved sufficient funds to set up farms of their own.

The tenancy agreements that were entered into for Rensselaerswijck provide some insight into tenants' rights and duties, even if these date from some time later. Tenants were obliged to maintain the house, the barn, and the haystacks at their own expense, and after the expiration of the six-year tenancy hand the property back in good condition. In many instances the cattle was rented *op halve aantelinge* (on half the increase), in which the tenant took care of the animals and had a right to half the offspring. If after six years the tenancy was transferred to someone else, the sown land would be valued. Every two years the tenant had to spread the accumulated animal dung over the fields and remove trees and tree stumps.[49] Finding good tenants was no simple matter, and for Rensselaerswijck preference was given to "highland" farmers from the east of the Netherlands over "lowland" farmers from Holland and Zeeland. Ex-director Wouter van Twiller was more specific when he hired two farmhands: they had to practice farming in the way it was done in the province of Gelderland. Despite having been so carefully selected, tenants regularly decided to set out for themselves, sometimes abandoning their rented farm before their master had found a new tenant. This may have played a role in the decision to sell off a number of Rensselaerswijck farms. But negligent tenants, who were to be encountered as frequently in the Dutch Republic as in New Netherland, were not the most important reason that productivity in Rensselaerswijck lagged far behind what had been hoped for in the Netherlands. Other factors played a role.[50]

Because of regular flooding, the farmlands along the North River were liberally provided with fertile river clay and were well suited for agriculture. In spite of this, constant manure spreading was necessary, but farmers did not carry out this task as often as they should. Moreover, stones could make plowing difficult, and the removal of "inconvenient trees" was no simple matter. The colonists adopted the Indian practice of burning down areas of forest, a practice not without risk. Many houses were destroyed in this way, particularly in the early years. Another method was to strip the trees of bark just above the ground, causing them to die slowly. Probably the second method was more prevalent. The disadvantage of both methods was that the stumps and roots remained in the ground for a long time and kept productivity low. Turning forest into farmland was a time-consuming affair, even when employing enslaved labor, and Van der Donck's remark that new farmers could be making a surplus as early as the third year was rather optimistic.[51]

In view of these problems, it is no surprise that New Netherland did not quickly grow into a grain-exporting country. In the early years, hardly enough foodstuff was produced to feed the colonists, and they had to purchase maize from the Indians to survive. The colonists also grew maize themselves to some extent, but wheat was considerably more important in the greater part of New Netherland, while rye, oats, and buckwheat were the most widely grown crops on the less fertile soil on Manhattan. Peas, beans, turnips, and clover were planted as fallow crops. Many houses had a kitchen garden and in some cases a number of fruit trees.[52]

The government considered farming important for the provision of food and because the taxes levied upon it were an important source of income. The general tax of ten stivers per *morgen* of land was nominally on the low side in comparison with Holland.[53] The most important land tax, as in the Dutch Republic, was the *tienden*. The traditional purpose of the tenths was to defray the costs of the church and the salary of the minister, although the revenues were not always sufficient and had to be supplemented from other means.[54]

The West India Company tried to help new farmers in New Netherland by exempting them from paying tenths for the first ten years, but attempts to collect it after that often met with resistance. But in 1647 the collection had to be postponed for a year because the harvest was very meager after the war with the Indians. A year later, director general and council again received a request for the cancellation of the tenths because of "the bad crop this year and many other impossibilities." Once again director general and council acquiesced. In 1649 the situation had not improved, and the export of grain was forbidden on a provisional basis, as was the brewing of beer. In 1653, the harvest was again disappointing, and the ban had to be repeated, although there are no signs that the attempts to collect the tenths were halted this time. On the contrary, according to the wishes of the Amsterdam directors a number of recalcitrant farmers were hauled before the court at New Amsterdam by *Fiscael* Van Tienhoven to compel them to pay. But in 1655 and probably also in 1654, director general and council managed to convince the directors that the collection of the tenths was not opportune that year, although according to the gentlemen in Amsterdam, in future the tenths were always to be collected, even in the event of a poor harvest. In the years that followed, difficulties with farmers who refused to pay the tenths or tried to frustrate the collection were a regular occurrence. It was deemed necessary in 1663 to warn the inhabitants of Breuckelen and surrounding district not to collect their harvest from the fields until Adriaen Hegeman, the local *schout,* had come through to count the yield.[55]

Cattle

Besides agriculture, stockbreeding was an important element in the agricultural sector in New Netherland, to provide both meat and dairy products but also because the manure from the animals was used in the fields. Many, if not all, farms had milk cows, horses, sheep, goats, chickens, and pigs. The first animals were imported from the Netherlands in 1625 in a transport organized by West India Company director Pieter Evertsz Hulft, who had received instructions to do so from the Amsterdam chamber. "One hundred and three stallions and mares, bulls, and cows," together with an unknown number of "hogs and sheep," were loaded into two ships, especially equipped for cattle transport.[56]

The costs of transporting animals across the Atlantic were considerable. The contract that Hulft made with the captains specified that 125 guilders would be paid for each horse or cow that was delivered alive to New Netherland, which with some 103 animals in all added up to a total of almost thirteen thousand guilders. The care that was taken paid off: only two animals died on the way. But another twenty died on Manhattan, probably because they ate "something bad from an uncultivated soil," even though it had been impressed on Director Willem Verhulst in the *Further Instructions* to make sure that the beasts did not gorge themselves in the changeover from dry to fresh fodder.[57]

In later transatlantic transports of cattle, less care was taken, and on many occasions animals died during the voyage. The journal of Anthony de Hooges, who made the crossing in 1641 on the *Coninck David,* contains many references to dead horses and cows being thrown overboard. According to Adriaen van der Donck, the greatest number of horses originated in the province of Utrecht, and animals were also imported from New England and from Curaçao and Aruba. But these were not of a quality that found favor in the eyes of Van der Donck: they were less suitable for farm work, as they were too light. They could, however, be used for riding. The horses from Curaçao and Aruba were not used to the cold and suffered in the New York winters. About the cows, Van der Donck reported that those of the Dutch kind were bought in the vicinity of Amersfoort. Cows were also brought in from New England.[58]

The main argument to import cattle from other colonies was that New England cattle were approximately forty per cent cheaper. Secretary Van Tienhoven stated in 1650 that a milk cow in New Netherland cost one hundred guilders, while one from New England cost sixty to seventy guilders. The price difference for a mare was about forty to fifty guilders, which may have been caused by a shortage of stock in New Netherland around 1650. This assumption is supported by the protests that arose when in November 1649 director general and council decided to allow the export of twenty horses to Barbados. When the States General reprimanded Stuyvesant, he reacted with the remark that he would of course comply with a ban on the export of animals, but he wondered whether this might cause trouble among the English in New Netherland, as their principal activity was the trade in grain and animals. Despite these indications, there was no shortage of animals. In Rensselaerswijck in 1651 farms averaged slightly over seven horses per farm, a rather high number, not only for colonial America but also for the Dutch Republic.[59]

Little trouble was taken in New Netherland to keep the animals in enclosed areas. The pigs in particular were allowed to roam free and forage for food in the forests, which caused many problems. The grazing by free-ranging horses and cows and the rooting by pigs on the walls of Fort Amsterdam were detrimental to the state of the defense works. Pigs rummaged in freshly sowed fields, and goats helped themselves to a snack in orchards or vegetable gardens, which unavoidably led to conflicts.[60]

Conflicts between the colonists were handled by the local courts, but dangerous situations could arise when Dutch settlers' livestock destroyed the Indians' maize fields. The fear of reprisals by the Indians is reflected in an ordinance of 1640:

> Whereas daily serious complaints are made by the *wilden* that the hogs and other cattle trample and uproot their maize pits and that consequently when the maize is growing great damage will be done, as a result of which the maize would be dear in the autumn and our good community would suffer want, the *wilden* would be caused to move and develop a hatred against our nation and some injury might happen to one or the other of us.[61]

So everyone had to take care that the animals were properly tended. Offenders had to pay a fine of several guilders as well as damages. Similar ordinances, mostly accompanied by warnings to keep gates and fences in good order, were frequently promulgated in the following years. In 1647 a *schuthuys* (pound) was built in New Amsterdam in which *Fiscael* Hendrick van Dijck could lock up stray animals until their owners had paid the fine. A similar measure was taken for the whole province in 1664. It was not only the crops that suffered from the attentions of the stray stock: in 1658 the city government of New Amsterdam prescribed that all pigs should have a ring put through their noses to prevent them from uprooting the streets and making them impassable for wagons and carts.[62]

Apart from the fact that straying animals caused damage, they could also easily come to harm. The Indians were quite inclined to kill any animals seen destroying their crops. And the livestock also had an enemy in wolves, which were numerous in New Netherland. Rewards were offered in many places for the shooting of wolves and foxes. In 's-Gravesande on Long Island, the bounty was two guilders for a fox and three for a wolf. A dead wolf was worth more in Rensselaerswijck: in 1650, Brant van Slichtenhorst paid twenty-four guilders for five wolves that had been captured. The death of a wolf was rewarded in Albany in 1671 with payment of six guilders in *sewant,* if a head, leg, or ear could be produced as evidence. In 1673 the price on Manhattan had risen to twenty guilders in *sewant* for a male wolf and thirty guilders for a female. Even more than the increasing amounts paid in premiums, the ongoing reappearance of these ordinances is a sign that wolves continued to be an unremitting plague. This was also the case in some parts of the Netherlands. In Amersfoort in Gelderland, for example, annual wolf hunts took place, and at the end of the seventeenth century premiums of 32 to 120 guilders were paid for killing a wolf.[63] A way of protecting the livestock was the appointment of a herdsman. Nolle Morisse was appointed to this function in Haerlem in 1667. From mid-April to All Saints Day, 1 November, he was paid four hundred guilders in *sewant* and one half pound of butter per cow in his herd. In total nineteen persons entrusted twenty-two oxen and fifty-eight cows to his care. Herdsmen were also used in Wiltwijck and in other settlements.[64]

Just as with agriculture, the government saw stockbreeding as a potential source of income. After the decision in 1654 not to collect the tenths that year, director general and council imposed a tax on animals and land. An annual levy of one guilder per *morgen* of land had to be paid to the WIC's collector. For each horned animal of more than three years of age, the tax was also one guilder, for animals of two years of age it was only twelve stivers. Two years later an excise duty was introduced on the slaughtering of animals. A tax of 5 percent of the value of oxen, cows, calves, pigs, goats, or sheep had to be paid prior to their slaughter. In New Amsterdam the slaughter excise was farmed out to Gerrit Hendricksz, who was also granted the right to charge the twentieth penny on any meat brought into the city. If the meat was intended for export, a license had to be bought for the sum of three stivers.[65]

A regulation for bringing animals for slaughter into New Amsterdam was more appropriate than elsewhere, as an annual cattle market was already held there on 15 October 1641, and an annual pig market was introduced on 1 November of the same year. Whether these were continued in the years that followed is doubtful, as in 1659 *burgemeesters* and *schepenen* renewed their decision to hold cattle markets, expanding it to include a market for lean cattle in May and for fat cattle from 20 October to 30 November. The *burgemeesters* took the trouble to have the poster advertising them translated into English, and copies were sent to several English towns on Long Island.[66]

Tobacco

Tobacco, the third branch of the agricultural sector in the colony, was already familiar in the Dutch Republic before the colonization of New Netherland began. At the beginning of the seventeenth century, Virginia tobacco was imported by the English Merchant Adventurers into the Dutch Republic via Middelburg. The high price paid for American tobacco not only played a role in the development of local tobacco growing in the Netherlands but may also have been an incentive for Kiliaen van Rensselaer to try it in Rensselaerswijck. In 1631 he made a tenancy agreement with Marijn Adriaensz van Veere, who went over with four farmhands to set up a plantation. Although

Van Rensselaer had great expectations for the venture, Marijn Adriaensz did not manage to make tobacco culture a success, even though he probably received advice from an English youth, Rutger Moris, who had gained experience in Virginia. His attempts may have failed because of inappropriate farming practices. The tobacco was sown in the autumn and protected from the cold during the winter with horse manure. In the spring, the germinated tobacco plants were then re-planted. In the Dutch Republic, however, sheep manure with high contents of nitrogen and potassium was used, which resulted in better-quality tobacco. Furthermore, in the 1640s cold frames were already used, which enabled the planter to sow the seed in early spring. Yet the growing season in Rensselaerswijck was still too short. Further south, on Manhattan, Rutger Moris had been able to set up a small-scale tobacco culture. Despite the lack of success, tobacco cultivation in Rensselaerswijck continued. The appointment of Brant van Slichtenhorst as director of Rensselaerswijck at the end of the 1640s may be due to his experience as a tobacco planter in Amersfoort. Kiliaen van Rensselaer's expectations for tobacco were as unrealistic as those for agriculture. Tobacco was a labor-intensive crop, and the shortage of experienced workers hampered production, even though Van Rensselaer recruited tobacco planters from Nijkerk, where the cultivation of tobacco had been set up with some success.[67]

While the first attempts to establish tobacco plantations in New Netherland had little success, Dutch merchants engaged in a lively trade in Virginia tobacco. Most of it was shipped to London and exported to Middelburg and later to Rotterdam. In the early 1630s, several attempts were made to evade the English customs duties by setting up direct trade with Virginia but, as David Pietersz de Vries discovered, this was not easy without a local agent. Better opportunities arose when the outbreak of the English Civil War made English shipping with Virginia difficult. Dutch merchants were quick to fill the gap.

Among them were the brothers Arent and Dirck Corsz Stam. They had gained experience with this trade while in the service of Van Rensselaer and decided to establish themselves in Virginia. They made a number of voyages between Virginia and Amsterdam, trading large amounts of tobacco: in 1639 a total of seventy-six thousand pounds, and two years later no less than a hundred thousand pounds, thereby surpassing the London merchants by far. In comparison, the amounts of tobacco that Kiliaen van Rensselaer received from Rensselaerswijck at the end of the 1630s were very small. In 1639, 1,258 pounds were shipped in seven barrels, of which (after the deduction for rotted tobacco and a standard percentage for stalks) 1,156 pounds remained. At eight stivers per pound, this yielded ƒ462:8. In the course of time the tobacco culture improved, and four years later the production had already quadrupled. Van Rensselaer's correspondence shows that the tobacco was shipped in the form of whole leaves in barrels. Further processing, such as saucing and spinning, took place in Amsterdam, although it is likely that a small amount remained in New Netherland for local consumption.[68]

In contrast with Virginia, tobacco culture on Manhattan and Long Island overcame its initial problems late, towards the end of the 1630s. Director Wouter van Twiller and his council already reported in 1635 that he could use a number of tobacco planters in the colony. The Manatus map of 1639 shows twenty-seven "*plantages*," most likely all tobacco plantations. Most of these were quite small in comparison with regular farms. The plantation of Christoffel Laurens and Raef Cardael, Dutch versions of Christopher Lawrence and Ralph Cardell, was only three *morgens* in size, which is roughly similar to the tobacco plantations at Nijkerk and Amersfoort. Other plantations, for example the three at Paulushoek on the west bank of the North River opposite Manhattan, had an area of only one *morgen*. As in the Dutch Republic, plots were screened against the wind with hedges made of branches. For drying the tobacco, special barns were built, some of which were of a considerable size. A tobacco barn built in 1639 for Thomas Hall was a hundred feet long, twenty-four feet wide, and ten feet high, with two doors. The frequent occurrence of English names in contracts makes it likely that planters from Virginia introduced the culture on Manhattan.[69]

The scattered details available on the tobacco production in New Netherland nevertheless allow some conclusions. In some instances, plantations were tenanted, and the due rent was given in pounds of tobacco, usually three hundred to three hundred and fifty pounds. If the rent amounted on average to one quarter of the total yield, then on the basis of twenty-seven plantations in 1639, a cautious estimate can be made that approximately thirty-five thousand pounds can have been produced in New Netherland at that time. This should be viewed as a minimum quantity. The increasing number of references to tobacco after 1639 show that in later years the production of tobacco grew considerably. The only other quantitative information available dates from 1663 and confirms this. In the plans for New Amstel an annual export of one thousand barrels of tobacco was conjectured, in total four hundred thousand pounds, of which the excise duty income (1.5 percent of the value) would amount to six thousand guilders. This would mean a total export value of four hundred thousand guilders of New Netherland tobacco. Even though this is an optimistic estimate, and only refers to tobacco from New Amstel, New Netherland's share in the total amount of North American tobacco shipped to Amsterdam was quite minor. In 1675, the imports of Virginia tobacco to Amsterdam were estimated at a much higher twelve thousand barrels.[70]

Not just the quantity but also the quality of the New Netherland tobacco left something to be desired. Already in 1638 the provincial government appointed Claes van Elslandt and Wijbrant Pietersz as tobacco inspectors to supervise the quality of the New Netherland tobacco. A week later the tobacco planters who concentrated more on quantity than quality were warned through an ordinance to produce tobacco that was well cured and properly made. Besides the quality of the tobacco, transport allowed an opportunity for fraud, as the directors in *patria* remarked in 1654. The to-bacco leaves were packed in the barrels in such a way that

> the top layers at both ends are the best, and in the middle the worst and most rotten is packed, which bad condition or rottenness often originates from mois-ture, as the same is packed too damp and not sufficiently cured, which causes the leaves to become wholly black and spoiled, while they are otherwise usually of a yellow color.[71]

The inspectors had to watch out for this problem. An improvement in the quality would lead to a higher price, and the aim was to make New Nether-land tobacco competitive with Virginia tobacco, which would benefit the economy of New Netherland.[72]

In 1657 further plans for the inspection of tobacco were drafted by di-rector general and council. A distinction was made among three qualities: good, merchantable, and poor, applying both to the tobacco from New Netherland and that from Virginia. The hogsheads had to be branded with letters that indicated the quality. The provincial government discussed the proposed ordinance with prominent merchants in New Amsterdam, who expressed their fear "that the trade in Virginia tobacco would be utterly diverted from this place, if a stricter ordinance was enforced." The directors in Amsterdam did not share this expectation but decided not to force the ordinance through against the wishes of the merchants.[73]

The growth of tobacco exports also provided the government with an additional source of income. In determining the rate of the excise duty, careful account was taken of the difference between tobacco from New Netherland and that from other areas. In 1649, at the request of the colo-nists, the directors in *patria* decided to reduce the excise on New Nether-land tobacco to the level of that of the worst Caribbean tobacco, in the hope of furthering the tobacco culture and thus the development of the col-ony. The competition with Virginia tobacco was also taken into account. In 1654 the excise duty on tobacco from Virginia was brought down from forty-five to thirty stivers per hundred pounds, but that for New Nether-land tobacco was kept at twenty stivers, due to the directors' fears that the tobacco production in the colony would be detrimental to grain cultiva-tion. A year earlier director general and council had decided, in view of the recent growth in the population and the expected number of immigrants that year, to order the tobacco planters to devote as much attention to growing crops for food as they did to tobacco.[74]

Apart from a 1674 ban on smoking in meetings of *burgemeesters* and *schepenen,* this was the only measure directed against tobacco. The govern-ment tried to promote the tobacco trade by levying relatively low excise duties on it and by introducing quality control. It is doubtful whether these measures were effective. Although tobacco growing in the colony was significant, the New Netherland tobacco continued to play second fiddle to Virginia tobacco. As the *burgemeesters* of New Amsterdam remarked in 1658, it was "the English that bring the most tobacco to this place."[75]

The agricultural sector in New Netherland could never meet the high hopes in *patria*. New Netherland would never become a granary for other Dutch colonies or for the Dutch Republic. But that the export of grain in particular never reached any significance did not diminish the importance of agriculture to the colonists. Toward the end of the Dutch period, most of the colonists were engaged in agriculture. The continued existence of the colony relied on the extent to which the colonists could be self-sufficient. Neither was agriculture confined to the internal economy of New Netherland. By 1664 the export of tobacco had risen to the value of four hundred thousand guilders, outstripping peltries as the main export item.[76]

Artisans

While the fur trade and the tobacco culture mainly served export purposes, by contrast the craftsmen in New Netherland served only the local market. No form of industry that produced a surplus for export ever developed. That was not the role of colonies, according to seventeenth-century economic thinking. As early as 1608 Willem Usselincx contended that it would be better if no industries were permitted and the colonies supplied only raw materials to patria.[77]

The directors of the West India Company, who generally ignored the ideas of Usselincx, in this case followed his advice. In the *Provisional Regulations* of 1624, the colonists were forbidden to carry out "any handicraft to which trade is attached," in particular *weveryen* (weaving) and *verwerye* (dyeing). A textile industry was thus not permitted in New Netherland, and it is doubtful whether the few textile workers who went to the colony, such as Willem Claesz and Lieven Jansz, ever worked in that trade. Other forms of industry, such as those using clay or paper, printing, sugar refinery, and suchlike were not explicitly forbidden, but there is no sign that these ever took place in the colony. Of greater importance was the wood industry.[78]

Industry

The wood industry in New Netherland consisted of shipbuilding to a minor extent and of saw milling for a more considerable part. In a few cases a seaworthy ship was built in New Netherland, one of them called, appropriately enough, the *Nieu Nederlant*. It proved its worth by sailing to *patria*. Other ships built were small yachts and sloops for river and coastal navigation.

Dutch ships returning from the Caribbean to the Dutch Republic were sometimes repaired in the colony, but not to a great extent. A number of sawmills were built that produced timbers for shipbuilding, but sawmills primarily served housing construction. Several types of mills were employed in the colony, for which up-to-date technology from *patria* was imported: windmills, water mills, and horse mills. New Netherland boasted a tide-driven mill, used both for sawing wood and for grinding corn. As early as 1626, François Vesaert built a horse mill for the WIC. He also planned to build a water-driven corn mill on Manhattan. His wind-powered mill sawed timber for the ship *Nieu Nederlant* in 1630 and 1631. The number of sawmills grew considerably during the existence of the colony. In 1638, Rensselaerswijck owned at least one corn mill and one sawmill. The sawmill was water-powered and could produce thirty planks per day. By 1651 daily productivity had increased: the mill now had the capacity to saw about forty planks. Unfortunately lack of running water hampered production that summer. By 1660, Jan Baptist van Rensselaer contemplated shipping two hundred well-sawn pine planks to the Dutch Republic, which had to be twenty-five feet in length, two inches thick, at least one foot wide, with as few knots as possible. His intended price was two guilders in *sewant* each, but he was unable to obtain the planks at this rate, and the experiment was abandoned. The export of wood from New Netherland never attained a significant volume, but the products from the sawmills were of great importance to the colonists for their housing.[79]

Other forms of industry sprang up in New Netherland after 1650. In a letter of 6 June 1653 the directors in Amsterdam noted that director general and council in New Netherland had granted patents to a few people for the setting up of a potash works, a pantile and brick-making works, and a salt works. They approved of the furtherance of such undertakings but were opposed to monopolies, as these would be detrimental to the development of the colony. Potash, potassium carbonate derived from wood ashes used in purified form in pottery making, was also produced in New Netherland, or at least attempts were made to produce it.[80]

Information on the manufacture of bricks and roof tiles is easier to come by. In the early 1640s Kiliaen van Rensselaer had difficulty in finding brick makers and considered attracting English workers from Connecticut, which indicates that, prior to this time, few brickyards existed in New Netherland, although it was already known that the area around Fort Orange provided good clay. In 1653 a brick maker traveled to New Netherland in the employ of Johan de Hulter to set up a brickyard near Fort Orange. The directors in Amsterdam instructed Stuyvesant to help him find a suitable location. Probably the enterprise flourished. After Johan de Hulter's death in 1656 his wife, Johanna de Laet, sold a pantile kiln for 3,717 guilders to Pieter Meese Vrooman, while retaining another one under her ownership. About 1660 at least six brick and tile yards could be found in Beverwijck, and bricks and tiles were sold to other places in New Netherland. However, it is unlikely that bricks were exported outside the colony during the Dutch period. In all probability, local production was only complementary to the large numbers of bricks that were imported from the Netherlands, to some extent as ballast. The ship *Wasbleecker,* which sank en route to New Netherland, carried sixty-three thousand bricks and roof tiles. Other ships also imported brick.[81]

Less successful than brick making was the attempt at salt extraction in New Netherland. Salt was imported into New Netherland principally from the Caribbean. Although Verhulst had already been ordered to explore the possibility to establish saltpans in 1625, it is unlikely that attempts were made prior to 1661. In March of that year, two Amsterdam merchants, Dirck and Abel de Wolff, father and son, who already had interests in New Netherland, were granted a monopoly by the WIC directors for the refining of salt. They bought land near 's-Gravesande on Long Island, *Conijne Eijlant* (Coney Island) and *Conijnehoek* (literally: "rabbit corner"), but their venture suffered as their land purchase was challenged by the English inhabitants of the town. After a campaign of harassment, sabotage, and threats, they managed to bring about the failure of the venture. A complaint of Dirck de Wolff to the directors in *patria,* who then urged director general and council to take severe action against the English, did not help.[82]

Crafts and Retail

Craftsmen and shopkeepers in the service sector played a much greater role in the economy of New Netherland than the forms of industry mentioned above. Many bakers, brewers, tailors, coopers, bricklayers, shoemakers, butchers, smiths, tappers, and carpenters provided for the needs of the colonists. In the Dutch Republic, these trades were regulated by the guilds, but in New Netherland guilds were nonexistent. In 1655 the bakers of Beverwijck tried to establish one, but this was rejected by the court, because the magistrates found it "for the present for certain reasons not advisable." They may have opined that a limit on the number of craftsmen, which could be the consequence of the introduction of guilds, was undesirable in a rapidly growing economy. Three years later the city government in New Amsterdam also contemplated the establishment of guilds. After a discussion about working hours and mealtimes of workers, *burgemeesters* and *schepenen* resolved to petition director general and council for the introduction of guilds. There is, however, no sign that such a petition was actually submitted. It is likely that the directors of the WIC, who by this time opposed private monopolies as well, considered the establishment of guilds not opportune "in such tender beginnings of a newly developing country." They may have preferred to give director general and council and the local courts some of the duties that were fulfilled by the guilds in the Dutch Republic.[83]

Such duties involved quality control and determining the permitted number of craftsmen per trade. The government in New Netherland regulated trades in which a lack of supervision could lead to social or economical excesses, such as those of bakers and tappers and, to a lesser extent, brewers. Director general and council had little involvement with tailors, coopers, bricklayers, shoemakers, butchers, blacksmiths, carpenters, or wheelwrights. When complaints about the quality of the work of these craftsmen were brought before a local court, judgment was frequently placed in the hands of "good men" from the same trade who had the required expertise. The admission of people to a trade was in most instances also arranged by the local courts. That was the case with the butchers in New Amsterdam. To facilitate the collection of the taxes on slaughtering, butchers had to take an oath and be versed in the instruction for butchers. Also, the slaughtering costs per animal were established, and the butchers were charged with keeping to the regulations for the slaughtering duty. Following the promulgation of these regulations in 1660, ten butchers took the oath.[84]

Blacksmiths, carpenters, bricklayers, coopers, and wheelwrights worked in the colony, but as these trades were not subject to government regulation, little is known about their methods or their exact numbers. The same applies to tailors, except for the detail that in 1648 Jan Verbeeck and Jan Michielsz were given permission to carry out in Rensselaerswijck "the tailor's trade to the exclusion of others." Their exceptional monopoly did not last long: six months later Evert Jansz was also admitted as a tailor. The number of tailors elsewhere in New Netherland is unknown. As to shoemakers, at least four worked in New Amsterdam in 1658, for they were called in on 1 August by the *burgemeesters,* as leather fire buckets needed to be made. One of them was Coenraet ten Eijck. Via his brother-in-law Engel Uijlenberg in Amsterdam he hired two helpers in 1659. Abel Hardenbroeck van Elberfeld and Pieter Jansz Schol van Den Haag were employed for three years as shoemaker's assistants, and in the summer had to work from five in the morning until nine in the evening. Working hours in the winter were shorter. They were expected to produce ten pairs of shoes per week. In addition to free passage to the colony and board and lodging, they earned 120 guilders per year. An earlier contract that Engel Uijlenberg entered into with shoemaker's assistant Harmen van Deventer, born in Groll, specified that he had to make twelve pairs of shoes per week, unless he was required to work at the tanning vat, which indicates that Ten Eijck tanned his own leather. He bought the raw materials locally, and for instance purchased some ox pelts from Jeremias van Rensselaer. Other shoemakers also carried out their own tanning. In most cases locally produced leather would have been used for regular shoes. Special materials, such as Russian leather, were still imported from the Dutch Republic.[85]

For trades that affected the general interests of the community, such as tapping, brewing, and baking, the government laid down extensive regulations.

In the case of the tappers, the main issue was the prevention of excessive drunkenness; for the bakers it was controlling the quality and quantity of the food supply. In addition, both baking and tapping played a role in the trade with the Indians, while in the case of tappers and brewers, as with the butchers, the collection of taxes required regulation.

Tapping and Brewing

A considerable number of tappers or tavern keepers carried out their trade in New Netherland. *Herberg* (inn) may be too grand a word for their establishments, as only a few provided sleeping accommodation as well as food and drink. Many of the *croegen* (bars) or *taphuyzen* (tap houses or taverns) were not much more than the front room of a house, with a table and a couple of chairs, where local residents could enjoy a drink after work. The drinks, beer, wine, and brandy, were drawn from small kegs and *ankers* (liquid measure, ca. thirty-five liters), and a record of the number of consumptions was chalked on a board or on the door. Tap houses provided an important location for socializing, and drinking was a social ritual that enhanced cohesion in the community. Yet it could also provide a threat, at least in the eyes of the authorities. An extensive ordinance of 1648 provides a colorful picture of the possible evils: if unregulated, almost a quarter of the town would consist of tap houses, honest trades would be neglected, and the youth would be led from the straight and narrow by the bad example of their parents. Exaggerated, of course, but director general and council nevertheless enforced a number of measures. New tap houses could only be established with prior permission of director general and council, the sale of drink to the Indians was once again forbidden, fights had to be reported immediately, and on weekdays the sale of alcohol was forbidden after nine o'clock. On Sunday the tap houses were allowed to open only after the afternoon church service was over, that is, after three o'clock. Finally, tappers had to be registered. A week later twelve men registered their names, a number that makes it unlikely that a quarter of the town actually consisted of tap houses. On the registration of the tappers in Albany in 1668, a license fee of one Flemish pound per three months was introduced. Although the colony was already under English administration, the license was called a *spinhuyssedul* (literally: "spinning house certificate"), a reference to Amsterdam, where the income generated by the tappers' licenses was used for the *spinhuis* (women's house of correction). That Albany had no *spinhuis* was no objection to using the name.[86]

Measures concerning the tappers had to be repeated regularly, as was true also for 1648 regulations to prevent the evasion of the beer and the tappers' excise. Brewers were forbidden to tap, and tappers were not permitted to brew, as in *patria*. A year later the regulation was repeated, with additional punishments for the unlicensed movement of alcohol. Maximum prices were also laid down: eight stivers for a *mutsje* (liquid measure: ca. 63.5 ml) of brandy and nine stivers for a jug of beer. Even the measures of beer jugs were determined by the powers that be.[87]

The government's intention with all these regulations is clear, but the question remains whether the rules were adhered to, as offenses occurred regularly. In January 1653, Pieter Adriaensz, an innkeeper in Beverwijck, was fined six guilders for tapping after hours. The many petitions for tapping licenses indicate that the trade remained under strict governmental control. In some cases a license was withdrawn, as happened to Jan Peeck in 1654. *Schout* Van Tienhoven had on several nights discovered "heavy drinking bouts" in his establishment where all sorts of people were engaged in "dancing and jumping" during the minister's sermon. The drunks were making a great noise on Sunday, 18 October, and one of them was so inebriated he had to be transported to the jail in a cart, obviously "a scandalous affair." After a few weeks Jan Peeck asked for permission to restart his tapping activities, which he obtained on condition of his future good behavior. Such incidents, as well as the permission granted to the *schouten* of New Amsterdam and Beverwijck to inspect tappers' cellars, give the impression that it was no simple matter to disregard the regulations.[88]

Tappers served beer, wine, and brandy. The most important drink in the seventeenth century was beer, the annual consumption of which in Holland was between two and three hundred liters per head. It is doubtful whether a similar quantity was drunk in New Netherland. In 1632 Kiliaen van Rensselaer indicated his intention to set up a brewery that could provide the entire colony with beer. That is a sign that the number of brewers in the first years of the colony was limited and that water was the principal drink. Unlike the cities in Holland, with their foul canals that served as sewer system, fresh water was easy to obtain in New Netherland.[89]

No brewery is known to have existed in New Netherland prior to around 1640, although beer may have been brewed in homes for the families' own consumption. The first mention occurs in 1642, when Hendrick Jansz sold his brewery on Manhattan with appurtenances to Willem Adriaensz for two thousand five hundred guilders. In the same year, Kiliaen van Rensselaer granted Evert Pels a monopoly to brew in Rensselaerswijck. His reasoning was that too many people in his colony occupied themselves with brewing, thus neglecting their other work and leaving their houses, which were the property of the patroon, "in peril of fire." Over the years, at least twelve breweries were established in Beverwijck, and there were quite a number in New Amsterdam too. Sadly, virtually nothing is known about the working methods of the brewers in New Netherland, about the recipes used or the amount of beer produced, although there is some information about its quality.[90]

The scarcity of grain in the colony influenced the quality of the beer. Brewers made the beer increasingly weaker, while still charging the same price for it. As a consequence, the main population felt hard done by while a few individuals could line their pockets, according to the complaints. In reaction, in 1655 director general and council produced an ordinance that set the price of beer at twenty guilders per barrel. Brewers were ordered not to decrease the quality any further, but they protested, stating that they could not possibly brew good beer for this price, since citizens and tappers paid in inferior, unstrung *sewant*. Director general and council thereupon raised the price of beer to twenty-two guilders.[91]

Because of the high costs of purchasing a wort boiler (brew kettle), brewers had to invest considerable sums of money. In Holland, many brewers were members of the city *vroedschap,* which was selected from the wealthiest inhabitants. In New Netherland brewers were also often part of the elite. For example, Beverwijck brewer Goosen Gerritsz van Schaick was also a magistrate for a number of years. In New Amsterdam, the brewers Oloff Stevensz van Cortlandt, Pieter Wolphertsz van Couwenhoven, Jan Vigne, Jacob Kip, and Willem Beeckman were at times members of the city government. In the 1650s and 1660s, Oloff Stevensz van Cortlandt was one of the most prominent magistrates and often acted as *burgemeester.* Van Cortlandt and other brewers probably had personnel for the daily brewing activities, enabling them to devote their attention to the management of the brewery and to their other trading interests. The regulations in New Netherland concerning brewers and beer merchants hardly vary from what was the custom in the Dutch Republic. In economic and fiscal matters, the laws of *patria* were used as a reference.[92]

Baking

The involvement of governmental authorities with the brewers was relatively limited in comparison with that of the bakers. Bread was the most important food, and no alternative was available in the case of scarcity. Therefore regulations were even more necessary. As far as is known, the first measures were taken in 1649. The bakers had started to bake white bread, *krakelingen* (pretzels or cracknels), and cookies for the Indians rather than the normal rye bread for the colonists. Director general and council condemned this practice in their customary colorful way:

> from a desire and inclination for the highest profit the *wilde en barberissche naturellen* [the wild and barbarous natives] are furnished best in preference to the Christian nation.[93]

A fine of fifty guilders was specified, but the prohibition on baking for the Indians had to be repeated regularly, an indication that it did not go unchallenged. In 1653, when the ban had just been repeated, the bakers of Beverwijck petitioned for an easing of the regulation. The local magistrates

were unwilling to grant this but promised to pass on the complaint to director general and council. Baking for the Indians was much more prevalent in
Beverwijck than elsewhere in the colony because of the concentration of the
fur trade there. It is therefore no surprise that in the court minutes of Fort
Orange most breaches of the law are to be found.[94]

The ban on baking for the Indians was not the only regulation that was
contravened. Baking bread that was too light in weight also occurred. The
price and weight of bread were laid down by the government in an ordinance, as in *patria*. In New Netherland this occurred in the aforementioned
ordinance of 1649, with a number of amendments in later years. The ordinance of 1649 stipulated that the bread must be baked in loaves weighing eight, four, and two pounds, but a policy on the price had not been
formulated. Prices were set down in 1651 at fourteen stivers for a whole
loaf of wheat bread and twelve stivers for an eight-pound rye loaf. Bakers
were permitted to bake white bread only for colonists, in the units of one
pound, half a pound, and a quarter of a pound, to be sold at three stivers
per pound. Later pricing systems illustrate the complex monetary situation
in the colony. In 1658 the price of a coarse wheat loaf of eight pounds was
set at seven stivers in silver money, ten stivers in beaver, and fourteen stivers
in *sewant*. For rye bread this was six, nine, and twelve stivers, respectively.
This pricing system created problems for the bakers in New Amsterdam.
They had to pay for grain at a beaver price, while the poor people paid
for the rye bread in *sewant*, which was detrimental to the bakers' profits. As
the result of their complaints, the city government raised the *sewant* price
of rye bread.[95]

In addition to the price and weight of the bread, the ingredients were
also subject to governmental regulation. After complaints in 1650 about the
"leanness and thinness of the common bread," director general and council
decreed that the bread be baked of "pure wheat or rye flour as it comes
from the mills."[96] As a result of the bakers baking excessive quantities of
white bread for the Indians, only undesirable bran bread remained for the
colonists. The magistrates requested measures,

> in the interest of the community here, especially of the plain and common
> people, who cannot bake themselves, so that if this continues the Christians
> must eat the bran and the *wilden* the flour.[97]

In the illegal bread baked for the Indians, the bakers used ingredients like
sugar, currants, raisins, and prunes. In 1655 the bakers in Beverwijck were
forbidden explicitly to enrich their product in this way. And even in New
Amsterdam, baker Hendrick Jansz was prosecuted in 1661 because he had
baked ginger bread and had not offered any normal bread for sale. His
excuse was that he had baked only a very small quantity of ginger bread
from dough that was left over because he had insufficient flour to bake

regular bread. *Burgemeesters* and *schepenen* accepted this explanation and acquitted him.

Compliance with the ordinances was enforced in two different ways. First, the manner in which the baking trade was carried out was supervised. In 1656 the bakers of Beverwijck wanted the baking of bread for sale to be permitted only after the government had granted prior permission. In this way it could be prevented that all sorts of people start baking for the Indians during the trading season, only to cease their baking activities in the winter. Director general and council acceded to their request and went on to create an ordinance requiring bakers to renew their license each quarter at a cost of one Flemish pound.[98] The city government of New Amsterdam agreed with the introduction of licenses but did not like the idea of the fees for them:

> it is not usual in any place that craftsmen pay anything in this form, and especially if this is now introduced, it would at the next occasion also be imposed on other artisans.[99]

Such considerations moved *burgemeesters* and *schepenen* later to petition for the introduction of a formal system of burgher right, in which the exercise of a trade was the sole prerogative of citizens.

Second, the price, weight, and quality of the bread were monitored. The *schout* in New Amsterdam was expressly ordered in 1659 to check the bakers on a regular basis. In 1661, special bread inspectors were appointed, Hendrick Willemsz and Christoffel Hooglant, both bakers themselves. Bakers were instructed to identify their bread with a mark. Seven bakers had their marks registered by the secretary of New Amsterdam. Likewise, it was customary for bakers in the Netherlands to mark their bread, although the monitoring thereof was generally carried out by the guilds. Such a system simplified the task of revealing which baker had baked bread that did not comply with the regulations.[100]

The regulations concerning craftsmen display a gradual development toward the Dutch model. As the community grew in size, the number of trades increased as well as the number of workers within each trade. This development lay at the root of the specification of regulations, and without fail the authorities adhered to the practices of the Dutch Republic. Naturally new elements existed, but these were to some extent inherent in the colonial situation and, as such, in essence not unique to New Netherland. The manner in which the new elements were encapsulated in economic life was determined by the pattern of thought that the colonists had brought with them from the Dutch Republic. The bakers provide the clearest example of this. As in the other trades, the government only regulated to further the common good, such as the relations with the Indians, the quality and quantity of the colony's food supply, and the levying of taxes. The craftsmen in New Netherland worked almost exclusively for the local market, and the few attempts to set up industries did not lead to exports of any magnitude. Neither the industry nor the craftsmen were able to fulfill completely the requirements of the colonial community, which for a number of products continued to rely on imports from the Dutch Republic. In this, the merchants of New Amsterdam played the leading role.

General Trade

Many goods required by the colonists were not manufactured in New Netherland. The most important among these were textiles, provisions, and ironware, including guns, supplemented with a varied assortment of diverse implements. These commodities were not intended solely for use by the colonists but were also used in the fur trade.

The textiles that were shipped to New Netherland largely consisted of woolen cloth originating from Amsterdam, Leiden, and Kampen. Duffel, a coarse woolen cloth with a thick nap, was intended for the fur trade. The Indians used the duffel in a way unfamiliar to the Europeans, one that surprised Isaac de Rasière: "They also use a great deal of duffel cloth, which they buy from us, and which serves as their blanket by night and their dress by day." He had found that it was virtually impossible to sell red or green duffels, "because the *wilden* say that it hinders them in hunting, as it is visible from too far off."[101] The Indians preferred black. Lead bale seals found many years later during excavations reveal that the cloth supplied to the Indians was of a high quality. Although wool was paramount, other types of cloth were also imported, such as Osnabrück linen and English damask. When cloth was intended for the use of the colonists, it was generally made into clothing by tailors in New Netherland. Other items of clothing were produced in the Dutch Republic and subsequently shipped to the colony, such as hats, linen, shirts, and stockings. Included in the latter were, for example, *ferousse* stockings from the Faeroe Islands, which were popular with the Indians because they were water repellent. An extensive selection of stockings was summed up in a notarial deed of 1659: men's gray stockings, crimson stockings, women's violet stockings, and white and yellow children's stockings, in numbers varying from ten to twenty-four pairs. These were probably intended for the colonists.[102]

In the second category, provisions, many items also recur that were not produced in the colony. Alcoholic drinks are the most numerous and mainly consisted of Spanish and French wines and, to a lesser extent, brandy and liqueurs, such as anisette. Wine was transported in hogsheads of 230- to 240-liter capacity, and in New Netherland it was sometimes mixed with local wine, water, and sugar. Brandy and liqueurs were mostly shipped in *ankers* of thirty-five liters and occasionally in bottles. In 1656, Jeremias van Rensselaer received a consignment from his mother, which he was to trade on her account. It consisted of thirty bottles in two chests, containing angelica, anisette, and several other types of cordial (princess, orange, lime, gin, and cinnamon), with a total value of approximately sixty-five guilders. Beer was imported from the Netherlands in only a handful of instances, and this was probably strong, high-quality beer. Besides alcoholic drinks, normal foodstuffs were also transported to the colony, especially in the 1620s and 1630s, when the agriculture in New Netherland could not feed all of the colonists. In the early years the quality of imported food was mediocre and the availability scant. *Predikant* Jonas Michaëlius complained in 1628 about the rations in New Netherland: it was "hard, old food, such as men are used to on ships."[103] Later, the food situation in the colony was improved as local produce increased, while the selection of imported provisions also became greater. In 1662 a shipment to New Amstel contained oil, vinegar, and wine, together with seventy-five pounds of cheese, six hundred pounds of prunes, fifty pounds of raisins, thirty pounds of currants, a pound of mace, one and a half pounds of clove, two pounds of nutmeg, five pounds of pepper, and fifty pounds of sugar. Both the amounts and the wide selection of what were essentially luxury food items is astounding. Not all the necessities had to cross the Atlantic: salt and sugar were imported mainly from the Caribbean.[104]

The third category of commodities for trade, ironware, consisted of nails, pins, kettles, axes, knives, swords, and the like. Also guns, muskets, *snaphaenen* (snaphances, matchlocks), and pistols were shipped from the Dutch Republic to the colony. The largest importer of firearms was the West India Company, which distributed the weapons to its soldiers. Although the WIC tried to stop the trade in firearms with the Indians, it did not prevent the spread of firearms among the colonists, who used them for defense and hunting and occasionally in trade with the Indians. The weapons used by the colonists were in some cases made to order. In 1657, Jeremias van Rensselaer ordered a firearm for his own use from the Amsterdam gunsmith Jan Knoop. Prior to shipment, the weapon was tested in the Dutch Republic by Jeremias's brother Nicolaes. Other ironware was imported specifically for trading with the Indians. The ship *Wasbleecker,* which in 1657 sank near Martinique, carried various types of ironware: small tin mirrors, thimbles, brass bells, copper kettles, scissors, and awls: all items that are also found in excavations of Indian sites. Farming tools for the colonists were also imported: plowshares, grain forks, scythes, and suchlike.[105]

The fourth category of commodities for trading is a catchall category. It contains pottery, large amounts of which were imported in a wide variety of both quality and origin: cheap white and red earthenware for daily use, faience from Delft in the Netherlands, but also items from other European countries, Dutch majolica and German stoneware, including some from the Rhine region. Other items of imported earthenware were pipes, which have been found in large numbers in excavations.[106]

The same is true of glassware, such as glasses and bottles. Dutch glassware shipped with an eye to the trade with the Indians were glass beads, which find little mention in the archives but which come to light to a greater extent in excavations. Despite the presence of shoemakers in New Netherland, shoes were also imported right up to the end of the Dutch period. In 1640, Arent and Dirck Corsz Stam imported ninety-six pairs of them, rain shoes, women's slippers, girls' shoes, and children's shoes. Luxury items were also shipped to the colony, although this was not a common practice. In 1643, Jan Tjebkensz Schellinger, captain of the *Hoop,* took with him part of his household effects, consisting of paintings, silverwork, clothing, jewelry, and furniture to sell in New Netherland. To some extent, luxury goods were ordered in *patria* to the specifications of the colonists, as the correspondence of Jeremias van Rensselaer shows. But that option was open only to the upper classes.[107]

The diversity and quality of the commodities imported indicates that for many products New Netherland still depended on imports. Colonists did not have to be deprived of the luxuries they were accustomed to in the Dutch Republic, if they could afford to import them. Transport costs made imported goods considerably more expensive than in the Netherlands. Van der Donck maintained in his *Vertoogh van Nieu Nederlandt* that commodities were two to three times as expensive as in the Dutch Republic. Director general and council tried to fix the prices of imported goods, as they had also done for bread. However, the directors in Amsterdam initially rejected this, arguing that

> the perspective of gain is the greatest incentive to make people go there, as experience has taught us sufficiently, whereas on the contrary the fear of a meager and uncertain profit discourages people and keeps them at home, as would certainly happen if they would come there with their merchandise on this basis.[108]

This would reduce the WIC's income from the duties. As with the export of beaver pelts and tobacco, the levies on imports were a source of income for the West India Company. However, the amounts charged were a bone of contention, and the delegation that in 1650 submitted diverse complaints to the States General protested strongly about it. In a memorandum of March 1650 the delegates stated that, in particular, the levies on dry goods necessary for the sustenance of the colonists stood in the way of the successful colonization of New Netherland. Levies on liquids or on goods intended for the Indians had fewer detrimental effects.[109]

Although the protests had no immediate effect, the WIC implemented the advocated distinction some years later. An ordinance promulgated in early 1654 states that the existing levy of 1 percent had so far not been collected, because it would make necessary items such as stockings, shoes, linen, shirts, woolen cloth, and soap more expensive. The unfavorable financial situation of the government now moved director general and council to introduce a new levy, although it was limited to commodities for trade with the Indians, *dosijntjes* (calico), kettles, and blankets, and less important goods, such as wine, brandy, liqueurs, imported beer, and salt. Protests from the merchants resulted in a reduction by a quarter.[110]

Apart from New Amsterdam, the WIC also charged levies in Amsterdam. The figures on the proceeds cover a number of years: in 1654 the Amsterdam chamber received ƒ32,603:7 in recognition fees on goods that private traders dispatched in six ships to New Netherland. The total for the following year was ƒ28,850; in 1656 ƒ24,624:4:8; in 1657 ƒ19,004:5; in 1658 ƒ32,196:18; and in 1659 ƒ26,772. Noteworthy is that the amounts per ship vary quite considerably. The goods on the *Vergulde Beer* which sailed in 1654 were taxed at ƒ10,619:19:8, but those on the *Abrahams Offerhande* only ƒ424:12. The lack of any specifications implies that it is impossible to discover the reason for this difference. The figures provide an indication of the total value of the stream of goods from *patria* to colony. If the recognition fees were maintained at the same level in this period, namely 4 percent, then the total value of the export from the Dutch Republic to New Netherland between 1654 and 1659 would have fluctuated between five hundred thousand and eight hundred thousand guilders annually. As shipping increased after 1659, the value of the goods dispatched from the Dutch Republic to the colony must have been even higher. At some point the collection of the recognition fees was transferred from Amsterdam to New Amsterdam to give the colonial government more financial leeway. Later, this measure was reversed. Since the bookkeeping records of the WIC have been lost entirely, little more is known about the collection and the proceeds of the recognition fees.[111]

Merchants

After the WIC had abandoned its monopoly on the fur trade and shipping, the key role in the trade between colony and the Dutch Republic went to a group of Amsterdam merchants. They made use of factors in New Amsterdam, usually family members, to maintain their trading activities in the area. After the expiration of their contracts, many of the factors who were sent over by Amsterdam families to take care of their affairs began trading on their own account, and in doing so they continued to make use of their connections in Amsterdam. Included in this group were merchants such as Cornelis Steenwijck, Govert Loockermans, and Johannes de Peijster. As a result of their prominent position in New Amsterdam, many of them acquired a seat in the city government and were therefore in a position to negotiate the conditions and levies of the WIC with director general and council and, in some instances, with the directors in Amsterdam. This applied not only to the direct trade with the Dutch Republic in textiles, provisions, ironware, and pottery on the one hand, and peltries and tobacco on the other, but also to the transit trade with other areas of America.[112]

An important aspect in the development of New Amsterdam into the central point in the trade was that the WIC, in the *Freedoms and Exemptions* of 1629, had designated Manhattan as its staple. Such a measure was unnecessary while all shipping and trade remained in the hands of the Company, but the freedom of the patroons to use their own ships made it necessary to require all imports and exports to go via the WIC warehouse in New Amsterdam. When the shipping and trade were de-monopolized in 1640, this requirement was maintained. Although the staple right remained in the hands of the WIC, which levied the import and export duties, the merchants of New Amsterdam found it to be to their advantage, especially as it applied not just to transatlantic but also to intercolonial shipping. The staple right was not undisputed: some English towns on Long Island in vain sought permission for direct trade, which meant that ships would not put in at New Amsterdam. The commissioners for New Amstel were more successful. In 1663 the directors in Amsterdam allowed ships from the Netherlands to sail directly to the South River without first calling at New Amsterdam. The direct shipping from the Dutch Republic to the English colonies and vice versa was also subject to the WIC monopoly and after 1640 could be conducted only after payment of recognition fees. At the end of the 1640s several ships were seized in New Amsterdam for having broken the regulations in an attempt to increase their profits. Direct shipping was continued illegally, although this was not made any easier by the introduction of the English Navigation Acts. For the merchants who were not prepared to take such risks, the opportunity still remained to trade legally via New Amsterdam.[113]

The number of ships traveling from the Dutch Republic to New Amsterdam gradually increased over time. The amount of traffic was small until 1623: it consisted of small-scale private shipping, organized by Amsterdam merchants, who were granted a monopoly from the States General for a short period. Although much information is missing, it probably involved only a few ships each year. From 1623 to 1640, when the monopoly on shipping was released, the amount of traffic increased slightly to about two to three ships per year, largely dispatched by the West India Company. The patroons had the right, under specific conditions, to send out their own ships but only occasionally made use of it. After 1640 the average number of ships increased, at first to four or five per year. At the end of the 1650s it had risen to seven or eight. The vast majority of the ships were fitted out by Amsterdam merchants, and the WIC's share of the shipping fell to between 10 and 20 percent. At the end of this period, part of the shipping was already financed by New Amsterdam merchants. The English Navigation Acts, which stipulated that shipping from English colonies had to be carried out in English ships, caused this trend to increase after 1664. The New Amsterdam merchants, in collaboration with those in Amsterdam, looked for opportunities to arrange part of the financing via Amsterdam. Initially, direct shipping was permitted in the conditions of capitulation, but after the Second Anglo-Dutch War goods had to be cleared through customs in Dover or London and thereafter shipped to Amsterdam. This increased costs to such an extent that direct shipping between New York and Amsterdam decreased to two to three ships per year.[114]

This development had severe consequences for the economy of the colony, according to a petition from Stuyvesant to the Duke of York in 1667: "all the Dutch inhabitants of New Yorke must inevitably be brought to ruyne," if direct shipping was forbidden. If "the Comodities brought from Holland as Camper, Duffles, Hatchetts, and other Iron worke made at Utrick &c much esteemed of by the Natives" were not available anymore, the fur trade in New York would collapse, and the French in Canada would take over the trade. It would also be detrimental to the other English colonies, since "the Dutch lost their former trade, by which also many thousands of His Ma^tyes subjectes in Virginia Maryland and New England were furnisht with necessaries."[115]

The statement makes clear how important the transit trade had become. From New Amsterdam the merchants distributed the imported goods in small yachts or other craft throughout the rest of New Netherland, as well as to New England, Maryland, and Virginia. Director general and council wrote the directors in *patria* that Virginia

> yearly draws a great quantity of mixed goods, brandy, and distilled waters from here, and exchanges it for tobacco, which is the main trade here and without which there would be few returns from here.[116]

Excavations in Virginia and New England, including Boston and Jamestown, show that large amounts of Dutch pottery were also shipped to these colonies. What goods were shipped back from New England is less clear. Close contacts existed between the colonies, but as yet little is known about the scope of the transit trade or the intra-American shipping.[117]

In contrast, how the shipping and trade between the Netherlands and New Netherland was carried out in practice can be clearly determined. Although for a number of years it was principally in the hands of the WIC, this did not mean that all the ships were owned by the Company. In the 1630s and 1640s, to cut costs, the WIC began to make increasing use of chartered ships, a practice that private merchants also adopted in the 1640s. Collaborating in a partnership, they hired a ship for a number of months. In such an arrangement it was the task of the charterers to acquire a cargo. Part of the cargo consisted of their own trading commodities, while the rest of the hold was filled with goods belonging to others, which were shipped for a prearranged price. Generally, a WIC supercargo sailed with the ship to prevent smuggling.[118]

As the trade in the 1640s and 1650s expanded, some of the private trading companies were moved to buy their own ships, such as the families Van Rensselaer and Van Twiller, who in 1647 together owned the *Prins Willem* and in 1651 bought the ship *Gelderse Blom*. Such purchase indicates that the trade on the colony had gained a sound and long-lasting nature. The shipowners expected that the use of their own ship over a couple of years would be less expensive than chartering a ship every year. The *Gelderse Blom* made annual voyages to New Netherland between 1651 and 1657, captained first by Cornelis Coenraetsz van Kampen and later by Sijmon Claesz van Graft. Besides transporting trading goods, it also carried contract workers for Rensselaerswijck.[119]

The merchants in Amsterdam and their agents in New Netherland maintained a close correspondence about the commodities that could fetch a good price at any particular time, as is apparent from the exchange of letters between Govert Loockermans and the Verbrugges. Loockermans was reprimanded because he did not include sufficient information about the trade:

> In your honor's letter your honor writes us one-and-half page full of news, such as [the journey of] our little ship to the north [New England] and further about the situation of the land, which is unnecessary as we learn that sufficiently orally from the captain and the passengers, but the trade, that really concerns us.[120]

The trade really concerned the merchants, both in Amsterdam and in New Amsterdam, and it was obviously of great importance for the founding of New Netherland. In the literature dealing with the economy of New Netherland, the emphasis is placed for the most part on the export side, that is, the economic significance of the colony for the Dutch Republic, a perspective on the role of colonies put forward by Usselincx. But for the colonists themselves, the internal economy of New Netherland—its agriculture and its industry—was of higher importance in achieving prosperity. And for prosperity, God's grace was essential.

5 The Reformed Church and the Others

The *Provisional Regulations* to the first colonists of New Netherland in 1624 were quite clear. It stipulated that the colonists were not allowed to practice any

> other divine worship than that of the Reformed religion in the way it is at present practiced here in this country..., without however persecuting anyone on account of his religion, but leaving to everyone the freedom of his conscience.[1]

There would be no right of worship for other denominations in New Netherland. However, the freedom to believe whatever one might like was considered sacrosanct, with the proviso that no disturbance was caused by speaking one's mind or by meeting with the like-minded. It may be a far cry from modern ideas on freedom of religion, but by seventeenth-century standards it was not too bad, at least on paper. As in the Dutch Republic, the extent of religious tolerance depended on the interplay between ecclesiastical and secular authorities, especially the position of the latter. The preference for the Reformed Church, as stipulated in the *Provisional Regulations*, shows the Calvinist origins of the West India Company.

In the first decades of the Company's existence, a large number of the shareholders and directors, including a number of merchants who had fled the southern Netherlands, were strict Calvinists. The founding of the Company was prompted by the end of the Twelve Years' Truce between the Dutch Republic and Catholic Spain, and religious considerations played an important role. The WIC's charter does not explicitly refer to religion, but it had an obvious duty to ensure that the Reformed religion played an important role in the colony, as it did in *patria*.[2]

The WIC took a first step in its religious duties in New Netherland in 1624, when it decided to send Bastiaen Jansz Krol, a *ziekentrooster* (comforter of the sick), to New Netherland with Director Willem Verhulst. Although the West India Company bore a responsibility for the spiritual care of its employees, there was initially little clarity about which organizations were responsible for appointments, what procedures had to be followed, and how the costs were to be met. The situation changed when New Netherland gradually developed into a settlement colony.

Supervision from *Patria*

The supervision of religious matters in the colonies was more the result of ad hoc decisions than of preconceived plans, a characteristic it shares with the development of the administrative organization. Initial measures included employing a minister or comforter of the sick on ships going to the colony, but as the colony became more firmly established, the creation of a fully fledged church was necessary. During the entire existence of New Netherland, the secular and religious authorities, both in *patria* and in the colony, maintained a stable relation in appointing comforters of the sick and ministers.

During the first decades of the seventeenth century, the consistory of Amsterdam appointed comforters of the sick and ministers for the areas under control of the East India Company chamber in Amsterdam. When the West India Company was founded, the committee extended its task to include the religious affairs of the colonies of the WIC chamber of Amsterdam.[3] Its position was challenged by several provincial synods, and supervision over overseas churches was transferred to the Amsterdam classis in the mid-1630s. Delegates of the Amsterdam classis had to report to the synod of North Holland, in which representatives of the other provincial synods were present. By the 1640s, candidates from other provinces who wished to be considered for the colonial churches could present themselves to the Amsterdam classis. This agreement confirmed the authority of the Amsterdam classis over North America, which would last until 1772, when the Dutch Reformed Church in America gained its full independence from the mother church in the Netherlands.[4]

As with the Amsterdam consistory earlier, the Amsterdam classis transferred some duties to a committee, which operated under several different names: *deputati ad res Indicas, ad res exteras, ad res maritimas,* and *ad causas Indicas* (deputies for Indian matters, for foreign matters, for maritime matters, and for Indian affairs). Their work consisted of preparing and executing decisions made by the full classis. The most important matter was the appointment of ministers. From 1636 onwards, a continual interaction took place between the Company directors, the classis, and the deputies.

Calling a Minister

The first step was for the directors of the WIC to decide whether a minister should be appointed for a particular place under the government of the Company. The classis then summoned potential candidates to report to it, although this task was sometimes left to the deputies. The full meeting of the classis checked the references of the candidates and examined them. After the classis had made its choice, the two oldest deputies presented the candidate to the directors. These had the right to either accept or reject the candidate: the so-called right of approbation. This was a customary right in many places, and the Amsterdam chamber adopted it as well. After a trial sermon in the classical meeting and the candidate's final examination, the confirmation of the appointment took place. The deputies drew up the instruction and issued a letter of call, both of which were signed by the two oldest of them and by the elders of the Amsterdam church. The procedure for comforters of the sick and schoolmasters was roughly the same.[5]

The general procedures on the calling of ministers only provided the framework for the relations between the administrative bodies. The religious authorities and the secular authorities in Amsterdam, that is, the classis and the West India Company directors, occasionally had conflicting views. Disagreements arose over the necessity to appoint a new minister, which the directors usually considered less pressing than the classis, in part because of the costs involved. Sometimes the directors rejected a candidate nominated by the classis, as was the case with Jonas Michaëlius in 1637. Michaëlius was minister on Manhattan from 1628 to 1631 but became involved in the conflict between Pieter Minuit and Jan van Remunde, and as a result he incurred the displeasure of the directors. When in 1637 a new minister had to be found for New Netherland, the classis asked Michaëlius to make himself available as candidate. The deputies subsequently recommended him to the directors, who answered that they would invite him if they needed him. The classis was dissatisfied with that answer, and the deputies pressed the directors again, but in vain.[6]

The appointment of ministers in New Netherland was not always exclusively decided in Amsterdam. In some instances, director general and council in New Netherland played a role, as in the case of Johannes Backer, and later of Johannes Megapolensis. When Joannes Backer arrived in New Netherland in 1647, in transit between Curaçao and *patria,* the incumbent *predikant,* Everardus Bogardus, was on the point of leaving for *patria.* Because it was undesirable to leave the congregation in New Amsterdam without a minister, Backer allowed himself to be persuaded by director general and council to stay. The post proved not to his liking, and a year later the classis and the directors permitted him to return to *patria*. In Backer's case the initiative was taken by director general and council, but this was not so in the case of Johannes Megapolensis. The directors hoped to persuade Megapolensis, who had recently left his ministry in Rensselaerswijck, to fill the vacancy left by Backer in New Amsterdam. However, Megapolensis was unwilling, and the fear that there would not be a single minister left in New Netherland caused director general and council to keep him in the colony "blanda vi et quasi nolens volens" (with friendly force and almost willy-nilly).[7] In most cases, decisions on the appointment of ministers were made in the Dutch Republic, and the secular authorities in New Netherland simply carried out instructions.

If ministers wanted to return home, they informed the classis, which then tried to obtain their discharge from the Company directors. Of the eleven ordained ministers who arrived in New Netherland before 1664, five returned to *patria* after their contract expired: Johannes Backer, Hermannus Blom, Jonas Michaëlius, Henricus Selijns, and Samuel Megapolensis. The five who stayed were Johannes Megapolensis, Samuel Drisius, Johannes Polhemius, Gideon Schaets, and Everardus Welius, who died soon after his arrival. Johannes Megapolensis had to be persuaded to stay in New Amsterdam. Everardus Bogardus drowned on the return voyage, but presumably did not intend to leave New Netherland forever.[8]

Among the reasons why ministers wanted to leave New Netherland, problems with their pay was paramount. The salary promised in *patria* turned out to be difficult to obtain once the ministers arrived in the colony, and it was generally insufficient. In the first decades of the existence of New Netherland, the salary was paid in its entirety by the directors in Amsterdam, but in later years director general and council in the colony were charged with arranging the income, which they partly did via the *tienden*. Part of the salaries of the ministers had to be provided by the community, and collection was not an easy matter. On a number of occasions it was necessary to appeal to the classis to obtain payment of overdue salaries. Salary concerns also played a role in the recruitment of ministers in the Netherlands.[9]

The procedures for calling ministers to the colonies, the interventions regarding their return, and their salary problems were without doubt the most important tasks of the classis, and it corresponded regularly with the overseas ministers. This could cause problems for the West India Company, as it did in the case of the Lutherans. It is therefore not surprising that the directors in Amsterdam wished to examine the correspondence. They even sent a letter to *predikanten* Megapolensis and Drisius in which they expressed their surprise that they had not received copies of their letters to the classis. The classis had no objection to the directors examining the letters and even went so far as to encourage the ministers in New Netherland to correspond actively with the WIC authorities in the Dutch Republic, thus underlining the fact that control over religious matters lay in Amsterdam, with the classis and the directors.[10]

Local Ecclesiastical Organization

In the Dutch Republic, the Reformed Church was the official public church, but it was not a state church. The government provided it with all the facilities necessary to carry out its tasks. The civic authorities were charged with protecting it, which included prohibiting public worship by nonconformists. But although the Reformed Church occupied a privileged position, the Dutch Republic did not follow the rule of *cuius regio, eius religio* (Whose rule, his religion) established at the Peace of Augsburg in 1555. While that rule could apply in areas where the rulers were individual kings and princes, it was much more difficult when no single ruler was present, as in the Dutch Republic with its governmental elite of about two thousand regents. Yet the ties between church and state were close. Although some theocratically inclined ministers would continue to disagree, the Reformed Church was in practice under the supervision of the regents, not only on the provincial level, as in the approval of the convening of synods, but also on the local level, through the appointment by the city government of *commissarissen-politiek* (political commissioners), who attended the ecclesiastical meetings. Within this general framework, the extent of supervision and, with it, the character of the relations between church and state were of course dependent on local and personal circumstances, in which the inclinations of magistrates and consistories and the characters of regents and ministers played an important role.[11]

The relations between the ministers and the authorities in New Netherland were not always smooth. Particularly in the early period, when only a few ministers served in the colony, conflicts got out of hand. The colonial isolation, in which the ministers had no opportunity for swift consultations with colleagues or classis, catalyzed conflicts. After 1650, when the number of ministers in the colony increased, the relation between the church and the civic authorities improved. Undoubtedly the character of Director General Stuyvesant played a role, just as the characters of those involved in earlier conflicts had to some extent determined the course of events.

However, another factor puts a different complexion on the conflicts in the early period, as the religious developments in the Dutch Republic show. In the early part of the seventeenth century the Reformed religion was still in the early stages of its development and displayed a variety of schools of thought, one of which was a movement of popular pietism that was strongly influenced by English Puritanism and which was later to develop into the Further Reformation. Its aim was a further purification in religion and society than the Reformation had so far provided, particularly as to lifestyle and morals. The Further Reformation contained two strands: the first militant, theocratic, and externally oriented, the second much more internally oriented.[12] Some ministers in New Netherland, certainly Bogardus and Backer, but also to some extent Michaëlius, were influenced by the theocratic version of the Further Reformation and tried to establish ecclesiastical primacy. In contrast, later ministers, such as Selijns, Megapolensis, and Drisius, were less inclined to demonstrate opposition to the secular authorities publicly and followed more faithfully the authority model propagated by the colonial authorities. Also, later ministers had more links with the higher classes than ever before. Selijns came from a family of Amsterdam merchants, Megapolensis's daughter married Cornelis van Ruyven, secretary to director general and council, and Drisius married a daughter from a prominent Amsterdam–New Netherland merchant family. Partly as a result of these factors, differences of opinion no longer escalated into all-embracing conflicts in the later years. Several aspects of the conflicts shed light on the relation between church and state in New Netherland.[13]

Minuit and Michaëlius

First, the problems between Minuit and Michaëlius. The latter had arrived in 1628 as the first minister in New Netherland and began to form a consistory, recruiting Bastiaen Jansz Krol, Minuit himself, and his brother-in-law Jan Huygen as elders. According to Michaëlius, these were both "persons of very good fame," who had already gained experience in religious functions in Wesel. Of the four members of the consistory, Krol, Minuit, Huygen, and Michaëlius himself, three held public office, which was of considerable concern to the *predikant*. He hoped to keep ecclesiastical matters separate from civil matters. It is doubtful whether the consistory meetings under Michaëlius were very frequent. The atmosphere cannot have been very pleasant, in light of the far from amicable terms used in 1630 by Michaëlius when describing Minuit:

> We have a leader, who is most unworthy of his leadership: a slippery man, who under the treacherous mark of honesty is a compound of all iniquity and wickedness. For he is accustomed to the lies, of which he is full, and to the imprecations and most awful execrations; he is not free from fornication, the most cruel oppressor of the innocent and deems no one worthy of his favor and protection, who is not of the same kidney as he is.[14]

Minuit and some members of his council tried to enrich himself at the cost of the Company, or so Michaëlius alleged. After a while, he spoke out about Minuit's practices, but the latter tried to silence him and to persuade the directors in Amsterdam that Michaëlius should be recalled. The minister also contacted the directors and, together with the secretary, Jan van Remunde, formed the core of the opposition to Minuit.[15]

It was not just a lack of chemistry, as the letter from Michaëlius shows. In his opinion, Minuit did not fulfill his duties as representative of the Company's interests. This was a standard accusation of disobedience and self-interest, frequently made of employees of both East and West India Company, and it should not be taken at face value. Yet open conflicts between the minister and the highest-placed Company employee in a small, isolated community such as a colony could escalate all too quickly into a feud, especially as neither the religious nor the secular authorities in the Netherlands could intervene swiftly. Furthermore, it was difficult to determine from the Dutch Republic which party had right on his side. Hence both Michaëlius and Minuit were recalled in 1631.

Bogardus and Van Twiller

Their successors were Everardus Bogardus and Wouter van Twiller. During his youth, spent in the orphanage at Woerden, Bogardus had had a mystical experience, after which he was given the opportunity to study theology at Leiden. He soon left university and was dispatched to Guinea as comforter of the sick, thus giving him experience in other Dutch colonies, as did several other ministers of New Netherland. After his return to *patria* he was examined and ordained by the Amsterdam classis and sent to New Netherland as *predikant*. Bogardus featured prominently in the conflicts of the 1630s and 1640s.[16]

Before long, Bogardus and Van Twiller were at loggerheads. In the eyes of the *predikant,* Van Twiller's incompetent performance of his duties, his taste for alcohol, and his improper behavior did not set a good example for the community. Like Michaëlius before him, Bogardus was unequivocal in his criticism of Van Twiller. In a letter of 17 June 1634, Bogardus called Van Twiller "a devil's child, a villain in his skin," to which several threats were added for good measure. Even so, these sparks did not kindle a major fire, and there are indications that Van Twiller's behavior improved later on. In any event, the number of complaints about him decreased during his later years in New Netherland.[17]

Van Twiller and Bogardus had a good opportunity to bury the hatchet when they were both attacked by Lubbert Dinclagen, who in 1634 was appointed as *fiscael*. Dinclagen shared Bogardus's criticism of Van Twiller: the director had neglected his duties and was unfaithful to the Company. However, his motives in seeking a conflict with the minister are unknown. The conflict between Dinclagen and Bogardus focused on what was more important in the colony: the religious or the secular authority. Dinclagen was suspended from his church membership by Bogardus and his consistory, the most severe disciplinary sanction that the Reformed Church could inflict upon its members. But Dinclagen was not a man to take this lying down. He returned to *patria* in 1635, full of resentment toward Van Twiller and Bogardus. He turned first to the consistory of Amsterdam, which referred him to the classis, the normal body of appeal for such matters. Initially, he was strung along, as it was expected that Bogardus would shortly return from New Netherland.

In August 1635, Wouter van Twiller and his council requested the Company directors to dispatch a new minister to the colony to replace Bogardus, "as he is not at all inclined to continue for whatever reason." It is not clear why Bogardus did not follow up on his intention to leave, but it is possible that the classis and the Amsterdam chamber did not want to let him return to *patria* until his replacement had been arranged. When it became apparent that Bogardus would not return to *patria* in the near future, Dinclagen once again urged for his rehabilitation, but his request fell upon deaf ears. The classis continued to stand by Bogardus. Because Dinclagen was back in the Netherlands quite soon, the conflict had few repercussions in New Netherland, although it remained a thorn in the flesh in the Dutch Republic for quite some time as a result both of the time-consuming correspondence with the colony and of the persistence of Dinclagen himself. He was supported by friends in high places, such as Hendrick Feith, *burgemeester* of Elburg, and Hendrick van der Capellen, who were later to bring about his appointment as vice director.

Bogardus and Kieft

The controversy between Bogardus and Kieft was much more important and, because of the tragic outcome, certainly more dramatic.[18] It was catalyzed by the wars with the Indians and its dire consequences for those colonists who had chosen to build a permanent existence in the New World. Bogardus was part of that group and acted as its spokesman. In the early years Bogardus and Kieft got on with each other reasonably well. It was not until after the massacre of the Indians in February 1643 that Bogardus decided to take action. Although he had not previously opposed the policy of imposing contributions on the Indians, Bogardus turned against Kieft when he took on the defense of Marijn Adriaensz van Veere, a tobacco planter in the service of Kiliaen van Rensselaer. In March 1643 Marijn Adriaensz attempted to murder Kieft, believing that the director was trying to blame him for the bloodbath. Kieft retaliated by sending Adriaensz back to Holland in captivity for trial. According to Kieft, Bogardus had protested against this from the pulpit, thereby making his conflict with the secular authorities public and, in a way, defaming the director. In 1644 Bogardus took another opponent of Kieft under his protection: Laurens Cornelisz, who was accused of having slandered the director. Kieft in turn accused the minister of having appeared drunk in the pulpit, of having cursed at the consistory members, and of having behaved in such a way that it would lead to "a general ruin of the land, both in ecclesiastical and in political matters." Kieft and his council warned Bogardus in writing that he should not resist the "magistrature, placed over you by God," but the minister initially refused to answer and only after repeated pressure wrote a few letters in reply which, according to the director, were unsatisfactory. Kieft subsequently refused to attend church and persuaded many other employees of the Company to do the same. He even tried to obstruct the services by ordering his soldiers to beat their drums loudly and to fire cannons outside the church.[19]

Of course, such measures ensured that the conflict took on a bitter character, with reconciliation becoming ever more difficult. But it is worth taking a closer look at Bogardus's motives. Apart from the fact that he was on the side of those colonists who were trying to put down roots in the colony, he regarded the Reformed Church, and therefore himself as its main exponent, as the sole source of moral authority, a source that he held to be higher than the secular authority of the WIC and its director, even if Kieft was of the belief that his authority also stemmed from God. Just as in the conflict with Dinclagen, the theocratic bias of Bogardus's religious convictions manifested itself.[20] Thus the question of authority became the central issue in the conflict, and that meant it could only be resolved by the authorities in the Dutch Republic. In 1644 the Amsterdam directors had already decided to recall Kieft. For many reasons it was not until August 1647 that the director boarded the ship *Prinses Amelia*. Also aboard was Bogardus, who wanted to gain justification in Holland. Both lost their lives when the *Prinses Amelia* was wrecked on the south coast of Wales.

Stuyvesant and the Ministers

So, in 1647, as in 1631, both the minister and the director left the colony. Their successors were Stuyvesant and Backer. Backer had no intention of remaining in New Netherland any longer than was strictly necessary. Any initial enthusiasm for extending his stay was quenched when on 8 May 1649 he was warned by Stuyvesant not to

> read or have read to the community from the pulpit in the church or elsewhere any writing or proposal regarding political affairs and the general government, be it in general or in particular, at the request of anyone of the inhabitants.[21]

It later emerged that Backer had "made common cause with the complainants," that is, the 1649 delegation of the Nine Men to the States General. At the same time, during the first half of 1649, the tension between Stuyvesant and the Nine Men escalated. By visiting Backer privately and giving him this warning, Stuyvesant tried to deny the Nine Men an easy means of communicating with the community. But by keeping the warning private, Stuyvesant also avoided an open breach with the *predikant,* rather a change from the policy of his predecessor. Since Backer repatriated soon after, his antagonism with Stuyvesant had no sequel.[22]

Stuyvesant was a staunch Calvinist. In 1661, the classis in Amsterdam described him as "a great *liefhebber* [devotee] and advocate of the true reformed religion." Right from the start of his period as director general,

Stuyvesant became a member of the consistory in New Amsterdam and remained an elder after the English conquered New Netherland. His predecessor Minuit had also been an elder. Whether the same was true for Van Twiller and Kieft is unknown. Neither in the minutes of director general and council nor in those of the authorities of New Amsterdam or other places is anything to be found of the formal institution of political commissioners, who in the Dutch Republic represented the city government on the consistory. However, since some of the directors in New Netherland were elders in a personal capacity, the situation did not need to be formalized.[23]

Generally, Stuyvesant enjoyed good relations with the ministers in the colony, in particular with those in New Amsterdam. Apart from this, a few slight disagreements arose, such as that with Gideon Schaets. Schaets was a *Duits klerk* (Dutch clerk, a minister without university training) and had served as schoolmaster in Beesd in Gelderland. In 1652 he was enlisted by the Van Rensselaers to succeed Megapolensis as minister in Rensselaerswijck. Two years later Schaets interfered in the conflict between the WIC and Rensselaerswijck. After a number of months' imprisonment in New Amsterdam, the director of Rensselaerswijck, Brant van Slichtenhorst, had recently returned to the patroonship. During his sermon on the morning of Sunday, 25 January 1654, Schaets proclaimed that whosoever had any complaints about Van Slichtenhorst should go immediately to the court in Rensselaerswijck or must thereafter remain silent. This did not please the *commies* of Fort Orange, Johannes Dijckman. On leaving the church after the afternoon sermon, he read out a protest in which Schaets's proclamation was declared invalid since, among other reasons, it tended "to make the good inhabitants disobedient and rebellious against their just government." Schaets was forbidden to make any further announcements of that nature. A conflict of authority may have played a part. Van Slichtenhorst had been summoned to appear before the court of Fort Orange on a number of occasions but had refused to do so since, according to him, that court had no jurisdiction over him. Yet Schaets referred his audience to the other court, that of Rensselaerswijck. The *commies* of Fort Orange felt it necessary to bring the matter to the attention of Stuyvesant, who visited Beverwijck in March 1654. It is not known what action the director general took then, but the conflict was apparently smoothed over.[24]

After 1650 scarcely any conflicts erupted between the authorities and ministers. Quite the reverse, in fact. Stuyvesant and the ministers acted in unison when problems with the Lutherans, Quakers, and Jews arose. The relations of the director general with the ministers were such that Stuyvesant used one of them, Samuel Drisius, as an envoy to Virginia during the First Anglo-Dutch War.[25]

Stuyvesant's benevolence toward the ministers and his concern for religious affairs also shows in his attitude toward Henricus Selijns. When

Selijns arrived in New Netherland in 1660 as the new minister for Breuckelen, it turned out that the population of the town could not raise their share
of his pay. Stuyvesant offered personally to pay 250 guilders annually to the
WIC, with the provision that Selijns would preach on Sunday evenings at
the Director's Bowery on Manhattan, where Stuyvesant's farm hands and
colonists living nearby formed the congregation. This arrangement meant
that Selijns had to travel each Sunday from Breuckelen to Manhattan, which
involved crossing the East River, easy enough in summer but rather trying in
winter. Hence the services at the farm were discontinued during the winter
months.[26]

Paying the Predikant

Not only the inhabitants of Breuckelen had difficulties in paying the salary
of a *predikant;* it was a problem in other towns as well, and it persisted
throughout the existence of New Netherland. In the first decades, the salary and board and lodging were paid entirely by the West India Company.
However, the Company was a notoriously bad and slow payer, as Michaëlius had already discovered in 1628. In lieu of the customary free board, the
directors in *patria* had promised him six or seven *morgens* of land, but the
promise was worthless, as there were no horses, cows, or farm laborers to
work the land. In the early days of the colony it was the Company's custom
to pay the salaries when the minister or any other employee returned to the
Dutch Republic after the expiration of the contract. However, since the directors in Amsterdam waited for details to arrive from the colony concerning the exact period of office and of the *predikant*'s behavior, they always
had an excuse to delay payment.[27]

The help of the classis thus had to be called in regularly. In the case of
Bogardus, who died in the shipwreck of the *Prinses Amelia,* his heirs had
great difficulty in obtaining his overdue salary, which had been 46 guilders
per month, plus 150 guilders for board and lodging per year. Later ministers were paid 100 guilders per month and 250 to 300 guilders per year
board and lodging. Nominally, ministers in the Dutch Republic were paid
substantially less, with an average of 600 guilders per year. However, taking into account the level of prices in New Netherland together with payment in beavers or *sewant,* the later ministers, who received their pay in the
colony, were worse off than their colleagues in *patria.* Consequently, count-
less complaints were made. In 1656 the minister on Long Island, Johannes
Polhemius, even threatened to leave if his salary were not increased and its
payment made on a more regular basis.[28]

When after 1650 increasing numbers of towns acquired their own administrative bodies, the custom evolved that the congregation paid a portion of the pay, generally one half. In contrast to the practice in the Dutch
Republic, this was not usually paid from general funds, such as the *tienden,*

but by separate voluntary contributions. The collection was a predictable source of problems, particularly in small towns such as Breuckelen, Midwout, and Wiltwijck. If the amounts raised proved to be insufficient, director general and council allowed local benches of justice to impose a tax on all inhabitants, including the nonmembers of the Reformed Church, who protested against this. For instance, in 1658 Nicolaes de Fransman and Abraham Jansz in Breuckelen refused to pay their share, the first because he was Roman Catholic, the other because he did not understand Dutch and thus could not benefit from the sermons. Both arguments were rejected as "frivolous" by director general and council. It is tempting to infer from this incident that religious reasons were prominent in the problems concerning the salaries of ministers, but it is more likely that the small towns were simply not wealthy or populous enough. It was much less of a problem in New Amsterdam, which from 1652 onwards had two ministers: Megapolensis and Drisius, who presumably preached in English as well. The difficulties about the collection of the salaries of the ministers were rather of economic than religious origin. Besides this, an aversion to such special taxes, which were a break from the practice in the Dutch Republic, may have played a role.[29]

The increase of the population led to the existence of eleven congregations with a total of six ministers at the time of the surrender to the English. In contrast to Brazil, the growth did not lead to the formation of a classis in New Netherland. Johannes Polhemius, who had gained experience of a colonial classis in Brazil, argued that "communication, after the style of our fatherland, in the form of classis" was desirable, although he thought the long distances would make regular meetings difficult. Although Polhemius again voiced his opinion in 1664, the classis in Amsterdam did not take the issue up. The opportunity of forming a classis was reduced when after 1664 the number of ministers in the colony initially declined. Not until the eighteenth century was a coordinating body formed.[30]

Consistories

Below the level of the classis, the religious organization was similar to that in the Netherlands: a consistory per congregation, consisting of the minister, several *ouderlingen* (elders), and a few *diakenen* (deacons). Since only sparse minutes of the consistories in New Netherland survive, lists of members of the consistories are not available except for New Amsterdam. However, some conclusions can be drawn from other sources. Reference has already been made to the role of Minuit and Stuyvesant as members of consistories, but consistory members were also recruited from a lower administrative level of the Company as well as from the city government. An overlap in religious and secular administration existed in New Netherland, just as in the Dutch Republic. The overlap was continued through the use of co-option by the consistory to make up its numbers, which did not change after the English takeover.[31]

One of the tasks of the consistory was to exercise discipline over the church members, but unfortunately little is known about this. A few reports from Beverwijck and New Amsterdam indicate that the court was sometimes consulted on delicate matters. As the help of the court was enlisted in only a few cases, much of the enforcement of discipline remains shrouded in mystery.[32] In fact, only the minutes of the consistory of Breuckelen in the period from 1660 to 1664 provide a clear picture of the supervision of the church members' conduct. Included in matters that were examined were the sale of another man's pigs, the use of bad language, fighting, prolonged absences from church services, drunkenness, marital differences, child neglect, and precipitate remarriage. Extensive attention was devoted in the protocol of the consistory of Breuckelen to one case, because the position of the minister himself was at stake.

In April 1662 Gerrit Dircksz Croesen, born in Winschoten, had *predikant* Henricus Selijns summoned to the court in Breuckelen. Selijns, together with elder Willem Bredenbent, had called Croesen to account outside his house ("not inside the house, lest he be embarrassed in front of his wife") because of the rumor that on the previous day of prayer, Wednesday, 15 March, he had taken away several fruit trees that were not his. The rumor was confirmed, and Croesen was denied participation in the celebration of the Lord's Supper for the time being. He reacted by summoning Selijns to the court. The consistory, in which Selijns's vote was of great influence, was "very displeased with the aforementioned improper procedures and with the unheard-of citation" but did not know exactly what action to take in this serious issue. It therefore asked Selijns to seek the advice of Johannes Megapolensis. The latter found that Croesen should appear before the consistory, which also requested the court to provide further information.

When Croesen was asked by the consistory why he had summoned Selijns, he replied "that it was due to his own dullness" and "that he had sought his honor, the sooner the better." He denied stealing the trees and stated that it was rather those who had gossiped about him that should be denied participation in the Lord's Supper. As the court in Breuckelen would not hold session prior to the next communion, Croesen believed that by making this complaint he could deny the entire congregation that had gossiped about him participation in the Last Supper. The consistory was especially vexed by the fact that, with this accusation against Selijns, Croesen had tried to make ecclesiastical discipline subordinate to a secular court, "where, according to Christ's precepts, no Church disputes can nor may be settled, neither [those] between members and the consistory or its delegate." The consistory decided to deny Croesen participation and asked the court to annul the complaint.[33]

Church Membership

The importance of honor and the role of malicious gossip are illustrated by this incident. It also shows the dividing lines between the spheres of influence of religious and secular authority, in any event as viewed by the minister and the consistory and to a lesser extent by Gerrit Dircksz Croesen. The incident emphasizes the importance of unity and peace within the community, symbolized in the Lord's Supper. Prior to the celebration of Lord's Supper, church members were required, according to the Rules of Church Government adopted at the Synod of Dort in 1619, to examine themselves on their worthiness to partake in the sacrament of the Lord's Supper. Furthermore, the minister, accompanied by an elder, was required to visit the homes of church members prior to communion to instruct them and inquire whether there were any obstacles for participation.[34] Such visits are not mentioned in the consistory minutes of Breuckelen, although they undoubtedly took place. *Predikant* Hermannus Blom of Wiltwijck does note the visits, but he rarely reported any difficulties or conflicts among his flock, which is remarkable.[35] The contrast with the minutes of the Breuckelen consistory is such that Blom probably chose to exclude negative items from his notes, with a few exceptions.

During the weeks prior to the Lord's Supper, new members of the church were admitted. Stringent requirements were placed on the conduct of members, and becoming a full member and partaking in the Lord's Supper was a major step. The correspondence between Jeremias van Rensselaer and his mother, Anna van Rensselaer, in Amsterdam illustrates this. In 1658 Jeremias complained about misfortune in trade and with his cattle. In answer, she wrote that the best advice that she could give was "that you question and examine yourself whether it is not your own fault, that perhaps you do not serve God as you should." His mother had heard from his brother Jan Baptist, who had recently returned from New Netherland, that he tried to persuade Jeremias on several occasions to become a church member, but without success. That made his mother unhappy:

> It is, namely, plainly written that God wants to be found by those who seek him and that one must first of all seek the kingdom of God and his justice and that all other things will be bestowed upon us. Therefore, let the fear of the Lord be planted in your heart, for that is the beginning of all wisdom.

Membership in the church was also important because Jeremias, as director of Rensselaerswijck, now occupied the place of the patroon, and he needed to set a good example in his conduct and church attendance, following the saying "*Soo de heer is soo de knechten*" (As the master is, so are the servants). A year later, Jeremias reported to his mother that he had been admitted as a member and regularly participated in the Lord's Supper.[36]

The minutes of the Breuckelen consistory indicate that the confession of faith had to be carried out in the presence of the consistory and several witnesses. Those who were members upon their emigration to New Netherland or when they moved within the colony had to produce a certificate of membership from their previous congregation. In principle, the services of the Reformed Church were open to all. The ordinary attendees (often called "*liefhebbers* [devotees] of the true religion") attended services and availed themselves of baptism and marriage, as provided by the minister. *Lidmaten* (full members) made a public confession of their faith, put themselves under the discipline of the consistory, and were eligible to partake in the Lord's Supper. Anna van Rensselaer thought that it was fitting for Jeremias to be a *lidmaat,* as it was appropriate for the position the director of Rensselaerswijck held in the local society. This opinion was reflected by the magistrates of New Amsterdam. At the installation of the magistrates in 1653, a reference was included to the rule that *burgemeesters* and *schepenen* should be members of the Reformed Church. Of the twenty-eight men who were *burgemeester* or *schepen* between 1653 and 1664, only three are not included in the list of members.[37]

Although the New Amsterdam membership list is incomplete, it does provide information about the proportion of women to men in the membership. Until 1660 a small majority of members were women: 202 of the 371 (54.5 percent). From 1660 up to and including 1664, 260 new members joined, of whom again a small majority (53.5 percent) were women. The proportion of women increased gradually after the English takeover: of the members admitted between 1665 and 1695, 59 percent were female. In 1686 62 percent of the membership were women, and they generally joined the church before their twentieth birthday. In comparison, in the Dutch Republic a small majority of church members were women, while in Batavia in 1674 it reached two-thirds of the membership. Considering the ratio of the sexes in New Netherland, the female preponderance becomes even more surprising.

Women in the Reformed Church were also important in other respects. Their loyalty to the denomination continued when their husbands adopted a different religious persuasion. During the commotion about the Lutheran attempts to call a minister, many women continued to attend the Reformed services, while their husbands preferred Lutheran services. After 1664 Dutch women whose husbands were English remained members of the Reformed Church and did not convert to the Anglican Church.[38]

What the New Amsterdam membership list does not reveal is what percentage of the total population were members of the Reformed Church. Some information about this can be gleaned from other sources, but the matter is complicated by the lack of reliable population figures. The first figures for Manhattan date from the time of Michaëlius. He reported that in 1628 "fully fifty communicants, both Walloons and Dutch," attended the services. In Bogardus's period little increase had taken place: the pamphlet *Breeden-Raedt* reveals that prior to the minister's conflict with Kieft, around 1644, the community consisted of more than 70 members, and thereafter roughly half as many. This is a low estimate, as Backer reported in 1648 that the New Amsterdam church had 170 members, "most of them very ignorant concerning religion and much inclined to drunkenness." In 1666 the number had increased to between 300 and 400 members, according to Megapolensis. Eight years later his successor Wilhelmus van Nieuwenhuysen counted between 400 and 500 in New York.[39]

More detailed than the information above about New Amsterdam is what Gideon Schaets in 1657 reported to the classis about Beverwijck. When he arrived there in 1652, the congregation had 130 members, and since then membership had increased by 30, although not all of these behaved as the minister wished. Schaets then gives a number of interesting details about church attendance. Normally 300 to 400 people were present at the services. If everyone were to attend, there would be some 600 people in the church. Many *liefhebbers* attended the services of the Reformed Church as nonmembers but did not join the church. In 1660 the number of members in Beverwijck had grown to 200, an increase of 40 in three years. Twenty-one years later in Albany, it had doubled to 400 members.[40]

Information about the other places is sparse. The congregation on the South River showed some growth. At the end of 1659 Jacob Alrichs reported that church membership there had increased from 19 to 60. When Selijns arrived in 1660 in Breuckelen, 24 of the 134 inhabitants were members. After four years the number of members had quadrupled. In Wiltwijck Hermannus Blom had seen to it that the congregation had grown in 1663 from 16 to 60 members, before the Indians wreaked a bloodbath that cost many lives.[41]

To transform these figures into percentages, we need to set them off against the estimates of the size of the population. In 1629 New Amsterdam had some 300 inhabitants, of whom 17 percent were members. Taking the revised estimate of 2,500 for New Amsterdam in 1664, the percentage drops to about 15 percent. Beverwijck and the surrounding area had 1,051 inhabitants in 1664, so the percentage of members was 19 percent. For New Amstel, Jacob Alrichs gives the figure of 800. But due to an epidemic the city-colony had recently lost at least 100 colonists. It is safer to estimate the population there as 600, and as a result the percentage of members comes out at the rather low figure of 10 percent. On the basis of Selijns's figures, the membership at Breuckelen stood at 18 percent in 1660. No data exist on the population numbers there in 1664, but it is unlikely that the total population in that town quadrupled in four years. This implies that the percentage of church members must have risen. And finally Wiltwijck: the total number of inhabitants was 200 to 300 hundred, and so the percentage of members was between 20 and 30 percent.[42]

These figures are not exact, and the percentages may have been somewhat lower than my calculations suggest. Even so, they provide a sufficient basis for comparison. The percentage of full adult members in New Netherland in its entirety rarely reached 20 percent in the 1650s and 1660s. This is lower than in the Dutch Republic, where in the first half of the seventeenth century the proportion of members of the Reformed Church in the total population gradually grew to approximately 37 percent around 1650, with variations according to place and time. Of course, the percentage of members in the total population is not the same as the percentage belonging to the Reformed congregation, which also included children of members. In Haarlem in 1617, for instance, about 4,000 members partook in the Lord's Supper. Doubling this figure to include the children and setting it off against an estimated total population of 40,000, about 20 percent of the total population belonged to the Reformed congregation. All of this does not simplify the comparison. Yet it is safe to say that a general percentage of 20 percent for church membership in New Netherland around 1660 is quite low in comparison with the Dutch Republic. However, as Schaets's figures for Beverwijck indicate, the number of church attendees was considerably larger than that of church members. These were not all devotees of the Reformed Church. A number of them were sufficiently God-fearing to attend the Reformed services but may have preferred other churches if these had been available.[43]

A Tolerant Colony?

For the magistrates in New Netherland, both at the central and local level, the Reformed Church was paramount. The oath that the new commissaries of Beverwijck had to swear in May 1656 shows what was expected of them. Besides loyalty to the States General, the Company directors, and the director general, the magistrates had to swear

> that we shall help to maintain here the Reformed Religion according to God's Word and the regulations of the Synod of Dordrecht and not publicly tolerate any sect.[44]

The last six words were added in 1656 and were inspired by the first ordinance against "conventicles," which had been proclaimed earlier that year. The ordinance stipulated a fine of one hundred Flemish pounds for preaching at such illegal religious gatherings and a fine of twenty-five Flemish pounds for those attending. The measures were taken to prevent "disasters, heresies and schisms" as well as God's wrath, which would occur if public exercise of a religion different from the Reformed was permitted. Freedom of conscience was allowed as well as "the reading of God's holy word, family prayers and worship, each in his household," but not public worship.

The ban on conventicles was repeated in 1662, on this occasion also in English.[45]

Both decrees went back to policy documents that were conceived in about 1640, when colonization was in the ascendant. They contain an interesting motivation for countering religious diversity: it was "highly necessary... that in the first beginnings and fostering of this population proper order on religion is established" without inflicting on anyone "in his conscience any constraint or burden." The view of New Netherland as a young and growing society was seen as an additional argument for permitting no other public exercise of religion other than that of the Reformed Church. On the other hand, freedom of conscience was guaranteed, and everyone was allowed to

> believe his own in peace and quiet, provided he takes care not to frequent any forbidden meetings or conventicles, much less to gather or instigate the same; and further to abstain from any public scandals and annoyances, which the magistrates are ordered to prevent with appropriate warnings and punishments.[46]

Seventeenth-century authorities thought that an unmanageable, disorderly situation would arise more quickly in a colonial situation and that permitting religious diversity could have detrimental consequences. The growth of the colony would be best served by order and peace. Public manifestation of religions other than the Reformed Church was forbidden, but other than that everyone in New Netherland was allowed to think and do what he or she wished in peace and quiet. However, this was not enough for some colonists.

Lutherans

In 1656 Tjerck Claesz was fined six guilders in Beverwijck "for having been found last Sunday in the company of the Lutherans, performing divine service."[47] Tjerck Claesz was not the first Lutheran in New Netherland, and many of the Scandinavians and Germans in New Netherland adhered to the Unaltered Augsburg Confession of 1530. For instance, several Lutheran books can be found in the 1643 inventory of the estate of Jonas Bronck.[48]

The Lutherans first attempted to obtain their own minister in 1649. Quite likely it was only then that the number of Lutherans in the colony was large enough to pay the salary of a Lutheran *predikant,* for which no contribution from the government could be expected. The first attempt consisted of a letter of the Lutheran community in New Netherland to the Lutheran consistory in Amsterdam, where a Lutheran church had been established for some decades. As the Amsterdam Lutheran community was the largest in the Dutch Republic, its consistory acted as a coordinating body for Lutheran communities in the Netherlands. The Lutherans in Amsterdam were informally allowed public worship, and yet the Amsterdam Lutheran consistory hesitated to take any action after reading the letter from New Netherland,

> as it is a matter of far-reaching consequence and the most serious consideration to engage therein, in view of the state of the country and the situation of our churches at this juncture in time.[49]

It was four years before the next attempt was made. In early October 1653, the Lutheran community in New Netherland, which according to its own statement amounted to approximately 150 families, drew up petitions to the States General and the directors of the Amsterdam chamber, requesting freedom of worship and permission to appoint their own *predikant*. The petitions were handed to Stuyvesant, who said that in view of his oath and instructions, he could not allow them. He promised to forward the petitions to the authorities in Amsterdam. At the same time the Lutheran community sent a letter with copies of the petitions to the Lutheran consistory in Amsterdam. If the decision of the authorities proved favorable to them, the Lutherans in the colony could subsequently request the consistory in Amsterdam to enlist a suitable *predikant,* for whom they offered a salary of eight hundred guilders per year and free accommodation.[50]

Acting as intermediary was merchant Paulus Schrick, who had arrived in New Netherland in 1651 and, as the most prominent among the Lutherans there, was preeminently suitable to be their spokesman. Both the signatories of the letters to the Lutheran consistory in Amsterdam and the list of sixty-six people who signed a petition in 1659 show that a large number of them had a background in farming and soldiering rather than trade.[51]

The action of the Lutherans caused the authorities in New Netherland to contact their superiors in the Dutch Republic. Stuyvesant and his council wrote to the directors, and the *predikanten* Megapolensis and Drisius stepped in by writing letters to both the classis and the directors. In their letter to the classis, the ministers emphasized that granting the Lutherans' request would be disadvantageous to the advancement of the Reformed Church in New Netherland, since it would considerably reduce the size of the congregations. Some leading Lutherans had made a confession of faith and participated in the Lord's Supper. Granting the Lutherans permission would also create a precedent. All sorts of sects would be encouraged by it, resulting in New Amsterdam becoming a haven of refuge for heresies. The ministers' only comfort was Stuyvesant, who was

> good of the religion and says rather to quit his position than to allow the same, as it would be in contravention to the first article of his commission, which was

sworn to by him with an oath, not to admit any other than the true reformed faith.[52]

Maintaining order and peace was not mentioned by Megapolensis and Drisius, but that argument was used by the directors in Amsterdam in a letter to director general and council. They refused the request "because of the consequences which could follow from it." Also, it was "against the custom observed by us and the East India Company." Director general and council were instructed not to accept any such petitions but "to turn these down in the most decent and least offensive way." They added that attempts should be made to convert the Lutherans to the Reformed religion, "to thus stay and remain in greater love and concord among each other."[53] Established practice, fear of the creation of precedents, a preference for the Reformed Church, and the desire for unity in the colony played a role in the decision.

The decision of the West India Company was the result of a process of lobbying in which the Amsterdam classis had also played a role. On receipt of the letter from the ministers in New Netherland, the classis immediately sent the deputies for Indian affairs to the *Heren XIX* to express their concern. On 23 February 1654 the deputies reported to the classis that the WIC had decided not to allow Lutheran ministers, and shortly afterwards the decision was communicated to Megapolensis and Drisius.[54]

In the meantime, Paulus Schrick had called at the Lutheran consistory in Amsterdam with the letter from the Lutherans in New Netherland and the copies of the petitions. The consistory advised that the petitions be withheld, as they could be counterproductive. That advice came too late. The formal request had already been denied, and that made it less likely that a blind eye would be turned toward public Lutheran services. Nonetheless, this was the course that the Lutherans subsequently followed. Over a year later Schrick again met with the Amsterdam Lutheran consistory. He was about to return to New Netherland and requested a written reply to the letter of October 1654. Upon receiving that, the Amsterdam consistory wrote to their co-religionists in the colony that formal permission for the public exercise of religion in the Dutch Republic was almost never given but that informal permission by connivance might be possible after some time. The consistory advised the Lutherans in New Netherland to follow this route, and they would look out for a suitable *predikant*.[55]

As a result of the petitions and of the subsequent refusal of the West India Company to formally approve the public exercise of the Lutheran religion, the relation between the government in the colony and the Lutherans in New Netherland polarized. The proclamation of the decrees against conventicles and the conviction of Tjerck Claesz in 1656 are signs of this. A problem with the wording of the baptismal formula used by New Netherland's Reformed ministers played a role as well. The parents of the child to be baptized had to answer whether they believed in the doctrine as it was taught "here" in the Christian church. The small word "here" was the stumbling block, as it referred to the Calvinist rather than to the Lutheran doctrine. If that word had not been used, most of the Lutherans would have had no problem in having their child baptized by a minister of the Reformed Church.

The Gutwasser Affair

In mid-1656 the Lutheran consistory in Amsterdam received complaints about persecution of Lutherans in New Netherland. The news prompted the consistory to approach informally several people who were friendly with the Company directors to request freedom of worship. The directors were also dissatisfied. They deplored the promulgation of the decree against conventicles, because it had always been their intention "to deal with them [the Lutherans] in all quietness and peacefulness." Director general and council were ordered to allow the practice of religion in their houses and not to issue any further ordinances on the subject without prior permission. Yet this reaction of the Amsterdam chamber gave the Amsterdam classis reason for concern, since they had heard a rumor that the Lutherans had again asked for the freedom of public worship. The deputies were informed by the directors that this would certainly not be allowed, but the answer did not dismiss their fears completely, even though they were handed an extract of the letter the directors had sent to director general and council. Vigilance remained their watchword.[56]

In the meantime, the Lutheran consistory had acquainted the Lutherans in New Netherland of its efforts, and they petitioned Stuyvesant once again. Rather prematurely, the Lutherans stated that their friends in the Dutch Republic had obtained the promise from the directors that "the faith of the Unaltered Augsburgh Confession should also be tolerated, as happens in the fatherland under the laudable government there." They therefore requested that they no longer be obstructed in the exercise of their faith, especially as that they were shortly expecting the arrival of a *predikant.* Stuyvesant promised to send the petition to the directors in Amsterdam, but until an answer had been received the decree would remain fully in force, although "household readings, prayers, saying grace, and singing" were permitted. Since Paulus Schrick was once more departing to *patria,* the Lutherans sent a letter with him to the Lutheran consistory in Amsterdam in which they informed the latter of Stuyvesant's answer. They also asked for a good preacher, "eloquent and God-fearing, since among the Reformed here there is one who formerly was a Jesuit and who on that account is very politic and disputatious." This fanatical apostate was Johannes Megapolensis.[57]

The expectations of the Lutheran community were too optimistic. The pressure of the classis made it impossible for the Lutheran consistory in

Amsterdam to obtain explicit freedom of public worship from the directors. However, it was

> by one person and another...suggested in private that in case we sent a *prædi-cant* thither, public worship would be tolerated by connivance and winking of the eye.[58]

In a letter to the Lutherans in New Netherland it was even stated that the majority of the directors had so promised. In view of the practice in the Dutch Republic, the Lutheran consistory, in consultation with Paulus Schrick, decided to send a Lutheran minister to the colony. Their expectation may have been fueled by the fact that, despite the opposition of the New Netherland ministers and the classis, the presence of a Lutheran minister was tolerated in the former Swedish colony on the South River. The Amsterdam Lutheran consistory chose Johannes Ernestus Gutwasser, who sailed to New Netherland aboard the ship *Vergulde Meulen* almost at once.[59]

Immediately after Gutwasser's arrival, Megapolensis and Drisius submitted a petition to *burgemeesters* and *schepenen* of New Amsterdam in which they expounded their objections to the Lutheran minister at some length. The magistrates agreed with the ministers and in turn addressed director general and council, in whom they found a ready ear. Director general and council warned Gutwasser to adhere strictly to the decree against conventicles, which caused him to request the Lutheran consistory in Amsterdam to obtain formal freedom of worship as quickly as possible. In the meantime, Megapolensis and Drisius urged that Gutwasser be sent back to *patria*. On 4 September 1657 director general and council decided that Gutwasser had to depart at the first available opportunity. The reason they gave was that he posed as a Lutheran minister, "without, however, exhibiting for that qualification any proof from political or ecclesiastical authorities in our fatherland (in conformity with the practice and order observable there and also here)." This was of course a formalistic argument, but no less valid, as the admission of a minister without formal appointment, regardless of the denomination, would impugn on the government's right of approbation and counteract the powers of the secular authorities over religious appointments, Reformed or otherwise. Gutwasser delayed his departure in the hope that in the meantime permission would still arrive from the Dutch Republic. He was supported by a new petition from twenty-five Lutherans, who stated that Gutwasser had obeyed the decree to the letter and that further orders were expected from *patria*. The answer from director general and council was that Gutwasser's failure to depart, although two ships had already left New Amsterdam for the Dutch Republic, displayed contempt for the rightful authorities. This alone was sufficient to refuse the Lutheran request and to order Gutwasser once more to embark as quickly as possible.[60]

The conflict escalated further when Gutwasser went into hiding at a farm on Long Island, from where he could easily flee to English territory if it became necessary to avoid deportation. In the meantime, reports of the proceedings had reached Amsterdam, where the Lutheran consistory continued its efforts to obtain the support of highly placed persons. The consistory informed the Lutheran community in New Netherland that patience and endurance were necessary and that freedom of worship would be permitted eventually, even though this would be because the authorities turned a blind eye. It was a rather optimistic assessment. The classis, egged on by Megapolensis and Drisius, continually pressured the directors in Amsterdam. In May 1658 the Amsterdam chamber approved the decision to deport Gutwasser, "although the procedures used herein could have been applied with less sharpness." However, at the same time the directors in *patria* tried to placate the Lutherans by giving them their own way on the issue of the wording of the baptismal form.[61] Megapolensis and Drisius were not pleased with this, but in a separate letter to the ministers, the directors indicated that the measure was necessary

> to prevent schism and separation, and to win over the dull and resentful emotions hereto in due time, which is especially necessary in such a tender and newly developing church.[62]

The attitude of the directors gave director general and council a free rein to deport the Lutheran *predikant*. Gutwasser sailed back to Amsterdam in the summer of 1659. A petition from sixty-six Lutherans, in which they emphasized that they were good and loyal subjects and that without freedom of worship many farmers would leave the country, was to no avail. It was only after the takeover of New Netherland by the English that the Lutherans were given permission to appoint their own *predikant*.[63]

Six different groups played a role in the Lutheran attempt to gain freedom of worship: the Lutherans in the colony and the Lutheran consistory in Amsterdam, the ministers in New Amsterdam and the classis in the Netherlands, and director general and council and their superiors in the Dutch Republic. The Lutherans in the colony made the wrong choice in requesting freedom of worship by means of petitions. The Lutheran consistory in Amsterdam, which based its opinion on its experience in the Dutch Republic, did not consider formal permission realistic goal. It believed it was more likely that the authorities would choose to turn a blind eye to the problem. However, the ministers in the colony, with the support of the classis, also tried to prevent that outcome, with the result that the decision ended up in the hands of the directors in Amsterdam. Their constant wish for unity and harmony in the young and fragile colony is evident from their actions. They were not very strict, as their decision on the baptismal formula shows. Although they did not explicitly say so, it is conceivable that they would have turned a blind eye to the presence of a Lutheran minister provided that it did not lead to troubles. However, the attitude of the ministers and the provincial government preempted this option, and because of the pressure put to bear by the classis, the directors in *patria* could do nothing but subsequently approve the decision to deport Gutwasser.

Quakers

The problems with Quakers in New Netherland were of an entirely different nature. The Quakers were one of the most radical among the religious movements that sprang up during the English Civil War. Their belief in the rebirth of God's truth and the mercy and light within each human individual led to their eschewing all forms of authority that did not directly stem from God. Thus the Quakers posed a much more direct threat to the established order than the Lutherans. In the first decades of their existence, the Quakers were still mainly a radical prophetic movement whose members actively sought martyrdom. In the late seventeenth century, they became a more institutionalized sect. Their anti-authoritarian attitude became clear immediately when the Quaker ship *Woodhouse* arrived in New Amsterdam in August 1657. The ship flew no flags to indicate its origin, nor did it fire its guns in the customary salute. When the captain was summoned to Stuyvesant's presence, he showed "no respect at all, but stood there with his hat firm on his head, like a goat," according to Megapolensis, whose account in a letter to the classis is the only source about these events. The following day the ship left the roadstead of New Amsterdam via the East River. Megapolensis thought it was headed for Rhode Island, "where all kind of rabble lives and which is nothing but the latrine of New England; all the bandits of New England retire thither." Two female passengers from the ship remained in New Amsterdam, and

> these began to quake, putting their fury at work, preaching and calling out in the streets that the last day was near. The people got excited and assembled, not knowing what to do; the one called fire, the other something else.

The two women were locked up by the *fiscael* and, after a few days in prison, were expelled from the colony.[64]

Without doubt the turmoil in New Amsterdam caused by the Quakers' first activities played an important role in the decision to arrest the two women and to expel them from the colony. Two other points are worthy of note: Megapolensis's evident animosity and the absence of the normal expressions of respect by the Quakers for secular authority.

A couple of months later, Robert Hodgson, a young Quaker of twenty-three or twenty-four years of age, began to hold conventicles in Heemstede on Long Island. One of the magistrates of the English town, Richard

Gildersleeve, thereupon decided to imprison the man in his house. That did not prevent Hodgson from continuing to preach, so Gildersleeve informed Stuyvesant, who sent the *fiscael* with twelve soldiers to the town. Two women to whom Hodgson had provided accommodation were also taken prisoner, and the three were transported to New Amsterdam by cart—the two women in the cart while Hodgson was trailed behind on a rope. On arrival in New Amsterdam, the women were quickly set free, while Hodgson was brought to trial. During the reading of his sentence in Dutch, which he did not understand, his hat was pulled from his head. He was sentenced to a fine of six hundred guilders "or forced labour for two years at the wheelbarrow with the *negers* [Negroes]." It turned to be the latter, as Hodgson refused to pay. As he also refused to work, he was chained to the wheelbarrow, whereupon he was beaten and fell to the ground. After he had been helped up, he was beaten again and fell down once more. Meanwhile he shouted that he had done no harm, and if anyone believed that he had, they should produce evidence of it to him. He was locked up without bread or water and was again beaten. Ultimately he was given permission to have his wounds attended to. The treatment meted out to Hodgson aroused the pity of many of the New Amsterdam burghers, including Stuyvesant's sister Anna, who tried to have the man banished from New Netherland. Thereupon he was freed on condition that he should leave New Amsterdam immediately.[65]

This is the nineteenth-century version of events, which is largely based on hagiographic Quaker publications from the beginning of the eighteenth century, forty years after the event.[66] Although the broad outlines are in agreement with what Megapolensis and Drisius wrote in their letter to the classis, some details in the Quaker publications give the impression that the account has been embroidered upon to emphasize the parallel with Christ's Passion. Undoubtedly, Hodgson refused to carry out the penalty that was imposed upon him and was flogged for it. Yet Hodgson was not asked to renounce his religious persuasions, and it was not the intention to force his conscience. His crime was organizing conventicles, and excessive violence was applied in the attempts to carry out the sentence, not to make him abandon his Quaker persuasion. In the view of the authorities, his refusal to obey legal authority was much more important than the Quaker convictions from which that refusal stemmed. In this, the New Netherland authorities concurred with the opinion of the classis. Earlier in 1657 the classis had asked the *burgemeesters* of Amsterdam and the commissioners of New Amstel to prevent the emergence of Quakerism there. As the classis informed Megapolensis and Drisius, the answer was

> that they could not force the conscience of people (which we also expressly said not to request by any means), but that if there was news that the sects committed their public exercises and religions, that they would then see and according to the circumstances prevent it.[67]

The treatment of Hodgson shows where freedom of conscience ended. Quakers may have been of the opinion that paying a fine or acquiescing to a sentence of forced labor constituted an acknowledgment of the worldly authority of government that they could not conscientiously agree with. But to government officials, the origins of the refusal were irrelevant. Freedom of conscience provided the liberty to believe whatever one might like, not the liberty to act upon that belief. That explains why such violence was used in the case of Hodgson. In earlier situations, such as that of the women from the Quaker ship, banishment had been sufficient, though their gender may have played a role. In another case, a shoemaker who had left his wife and children to organize conventicles was banished, as he was unable to pay the fine imposed on him. In both cases no corporal punishment was used, so why was Hodgson subjected to this? The answer lies in the fact that in his case the authorities in New Netherland decided to stop the "evil at the first opportunity." In Hodgson's case it was decided that enough was enough and that an example had to be set. However, in doing so, director general and council overplayed their hand by applying methods that were considered out of bounds by the population of New Amsterdam.[68]

The Flushing Remonstrance

It was no coincidence that Hodgson held his conventicles in one of the English towns on Long Island under Dutch rule, which were a rich breeding ground for dissidents, as the absence of ministers left the way clear for them. At the end of December 1657 the magistrates and populace of Vlissingen protested the new edict against the Quakers that had been proclaimed. In what has come to be called the Flushing Remonstrance, they refused to carry out the ordinance:

> wee desire therefore in this case not to iudge least wee be iudged neither to Condem least wee bee Condemned but rather let every man stand and fall to his own Maister.[69]

If this remonstrance was intended as a plea for freedom of conscience, it was out of place. It was never the intention of director general and council to infringe upon freedom of conscience, only to prohibit conventicles. In fact, the Flushing Remonstrance was a veiled plea for disobedience on conscientious grounds. The magistrates of Vlissingen refused to implement an ordinance; after the earlier incidents, director general and council could not allow this to pass. The local *schout,* Tobias Feake, who was the first signatory and had presented the Flushing Remonstrance, was arrested, as were several magistrates of the town. The clerk, Edward Hart, was interrogated to discover whether the insubordination was instigated by a specific individual, but he initially answered that he did not know.[70]

It turned out that part of the motivation for the remonstrance from Vlissin-gen was the presence of Quakers on Long Island. They had been given ac-commodation in Rustdorp by Henry Townsend, who had earlier been fined for this. Quakers were also spotted in 's-Gravesande, in the house of John Til-ton. Director general and council felt they had to act. Tilton was fined twelve Flemish pounds and Townsend three hundred guilders. In the meantime, To-bias Feake, who presented the remonstrance, in which they supported "the abominable sect of the *queeckers* [Quakers] who vilify both the political regents and the teachers of God's word," was to be removed from office and banished from New Netherland unless he paid a fine of two hundred guilders and kept his promise to behave himself in a proper manner. The ac-tual author of the document, Edward Hart, received the lightest punishment. After the intercession of the inhabitants of Vlissingen and on his promise of better behavior, also taking into account his history of good service and his age, he was forgiven and had to pay only the costs of his trial.[71]

Of course, this was not the end of the problems with the Quakers; a num-ber of them were arrested and expelled from the colony. Several years later, Henry Townsend was again caught harboring Quakers. After investigation, he was fined and banished. In other cases, soldiers were billeted with inhabi-tants of Rustdorp to ensure that Quakers were not provided with lodgings. It was only after a number of the inhabitants had signed a written promise to stop offering accommodation to Quakers and to inform the authorities if Quaker preachers turned up that the billeting was partially lifted. The soldiers were then billeted exclusively with those who had not signed. These probably decided to sign before long.[72]

After the incident with Townsend, a few more banishments followed, one of which deserves special attention. Quaker John Bowne was arrested in September 1662 for holding conventicles. He refused to take his hat off in the presence of the director general, and as he refused to pay the fine im-posed upon him, he was banished. It is remarkable that he was not expelled just from New Netherland but was sent to the Dutch Republic. Perhaps director general and council intended this punishment to be a deterrent ex-ample. In Amsterdam Bowne appealed to the Company directors, achieving little. When he wanted to return to New Netherland, he encountered no obstacle. A little later the directors wrote to Stuyvesant and his council that, although it was their desire that New Netherland be rid of such sects, they did not believe that rigorous action could be taken "without impoverishing and diminishing the population, which on the contrary in such tender begin-nings of a state must be continued by all suitable means." The authorities in New Netherland therefore had to be moderate, "leaving everyone free in his conscience," as long as the inhabitants behaved themselves and did not create any difficulties. Such "moderation" was always practiced in Amster-dam, and the directors did not doubt that New Netherland would also be the better for it.[73]

Of course, this did not amount to explicit permission for the public exercise of religion, and freedom of conscience had never been violated in New Netherland. In fact, the instructions did not even constitute a change in policy. Rather, it stressed the directors' preference for peace and quiet. Director general and council shared this sentiment, but their assessment of what constituted a disturbance of peace and quiet differed from their superiors. After this letter from the directors, no more arrests on religious grounds were made in New Netherland. Yet even this cannot, in the absence of available sources, be taken as proof of tolerance. The edict on conventicles was still in force, and as to whether there were any that were tolerated or not, is impossible to tell due to the lack of evidence. It is clear, however, that in the interplay of forces between colony and *patria,* it was ultimately the tough attitude of Stuyvesant and his council, working closely with the ministers in New Amsterdam, that stood in the way of New Netherland displaying the same extent of tolerance as Amsterdam.

Smaller Denominations

In addition to Lutherans and Quakers, two smaller denominations featured among the colonists in New Netherland: the Mennonites and the Roman Catholics; among the English on Long Island, many religious movements, "many Puritans, Independents, many Atheists, and various other *dwaal-geesten* [erring spirits]" could be found.[74] They caused little public disorder, although Megapolensis in particular saw their presence as a threat. Action had to be taken in only a few cases, as in 1652. Undoubtedly more Anabaptists lived in New Netherland than just Anna Smith, who at the request of Megapolensis in that year had to answer to the religious and secular authorities for "her slanderous and ill-speaking mouth with which she slanders God's word and the servants thereof."[75] The result is unknown. Another case was that of William Wickendam, who held Baptist conventicles in the autumn of 1656 in Vlissingen. This incident took place at the same time that the Lutherans were campaigning for their freedom of worship. Megapolensis believed that the Lutheran example encouraged others to hold meetings as well. Yet no further problems with the Anabaptists arose.[76]

Such incidents did not take place with the Roman Catholics. Only a few of them lived in New Netherland, and they seem to have obeyed the edicts against conventicles and probably limited their worship to the family circle. They had the opportunity of contact with a priest only occasionally, such as when Canadian Jesuits were captured by the Indians and brought to Fort Orange. In 1642 the French Jesuit Isaac Jogues was taken by the Mohawks to Rensselaerswijck. He managed to escape and went into hiding on a Dutch ship. Ultimately, Joques was able to return via New Amsterdam and France to Canada, where he was murdered by Indians a few years later. Another Jesuit, Giuseppe Bressani, regained his freedom thanks to the Dutch colonists.

Both were helped by Megapolensis, who at the time was minister in Rens-selaerswijck. It is not known whether Jogues and Bressani came across any Roman Catholics in Fort Orange. Joseph Poncet, who arrived in Beverwijck in 1653, found at least two: a merchant originating from Brussels and a young Frenchman who worked as an interpreter. Megapolensis wrote of Simon Le Moyne, who in 1657 visited Fort Orange and New Amsterdam from Canada, that he had come "without doubt to encourage the Papists, both Dutch and French, and to examine the situation of the land." Mega-polensis was held in high esteem by the Jesuits due to his role in freeing the priests captured by the Indians, and he had good relations with them, which were not put to the test since they did not react to his attempts to get into discussion on religious matters.[77]

Conversion Attempts

Although slavery was permitted in the colonies, in contrast to the Dutch Republic, many people had doubts about its legitimacy. Tracts were writ-ten against the growth of slavery, in particular by Pietist ministers. In some of these, the existence of slavery was grudgingly accepted, but the duty of the slave owners to bring their slaves in contact with the gospel remained intact. It is difficult to establish whether the ministers and colonists in New Netherland shared such doubts. However, attempts were made to impart the basic principles of Christianity, and more particularly of the Reformed Church, to the enslaved and free blacks in the colony. This had far-reaching consequences, because of the belief that Christians could not hold fellow Christians in slavery.[78]

The conversion of blacks had to begin with knowledge of the gospel, and education was the appropriate tool for this. As early as 1636 Bogardus asked "for a schoolmaster to teach and train the youth both Dutch and blacks in the knowledge of Jesus Christ." Adam Roelantsz van Dokkum, who had in 1633 been in the service of the WIC as *bosschieter* (able seaman) in the colony, was appointed for this task and was from 1638 employed as school-master on Manhattan for a number of years. Whether this first schoolmaster on Manhattan was able to teach much to the blacks is unknown, but that Bogardus attempted to promote the teaching of black children indicates the missionary zeal of the early ministers. Other indications are the marriages and baptisms of blacks.[79]

The majority of marriages in New Netherland were carried out by min-isters, although as in *patria*, religious marriage was not the only legal man-ner in which to marry. Secular magistrates, such as director general and council or local *schepenen*, had the authority to marry and usually did so in the absence of a minister. Even if the marriage ceremony was carried out by the *predikant*, this does not necessarily imply that it was an indication

6. Nieu Amsterdam. 1642–43. Engraving. I. N. Phelps Stokes Collection, Miriam and Ira D. Wallach Division of Art, Prints and Photographs, The New York Public Library, Astor, Lenox and Tilden Foundations.

of conversion to Christianity. Rather, it could be an indication of the social acceptance of blacks and slaves and thus point at the degree of racial conviviality in New Netherland. If free or enslaved blacks, with or without their owner's permission, manifestly lived together outside formal wedlock and procreated, this could be regarded by the white colonists as a threatening departure from the normal pattern. The blacks' participation in marriage according to the Dutch model may have made the union more acceptable for the colonists. However, there are some arguments against this. The number of marriages between blacks recorded in the New Amsterdam register of marriages before the English takeover is relatively small: approximately twenty-seven out of 441.[90] The register of marriages prior to 1639 is lost, and the later years only pertain to New Amsterdam. A number of free and enslaved blacks may have cohabited without being formally married. Yet the annual number of black marriages displays scarcely any increase, while the number of blacks in New Netherland grew. The black marriages that took place in New Amsterdam involved both free and enslaved blacks. The first group was in the majority, but there also is, for example, a marriage between Franciscus Neger and Catharina Negrinne, slaves belonging to Cornelis de Potter. From this it appears that marriage did not automatically lead to freedom.

A lingering question is whether the parents of any resulting children were expected to bring them up in the Reformed religion, although it is not known if a clause of this nature was included in the marriage ceremony in New Netherland. A better indicator of the intention of a Christian upbringing is the baptism of blacks. It is here that the conflict between slavery and the conversion to Christianity becomes most evident. Up to the takeover in 1664 a total of fifty-six children of black parentage were baptized.[81] However, it is not always clear whether these were the children of enslaved or free blacks. All fifty-six baptisms took place prior to 1656. In Bogardus's time, up to the middle of August 1647, at least forty black children were baptized. After his departure, at least sixteen baptisms took place, the majority before 1652, the last in 1655. After that it was not until 1665 that a black baptism is shown in the baptismal register. This does not mean that in the whole period between 1656 and 1664 no blacks were baptized, but it is definitely an indication that a change had taken place.

The motivation for a possible change is indicated by a letter that Henricus Selijns wrote to the classis in Amsterdam in 1664, shortly before his departure from New Netherland:

> As for the Holy Baptism, [we] were sometimes asked by the *negers* [Negroes] to baptize their children, but [we] refused, partly because of their lack of knowledge and faith, and partly because of the physical and wrong aim on the part of the aforementioned *negers* who sought nothing else by it than the freeing of their children from corporeal slavery, without pursuing piety and Christian virtues.[82]

Selijns added that the other ministers in New Netherland did not baptize black children either. The two elements of his motivation touch on two aspects of the baptism of blacks. The first point, the lack of knowledge and faith, applied both to enslaved and to free blacks. Selijns had indeed made some efforts toward catechism but had little success with "the old people, who do not understand." Things went slightly better with the black children. The second point is more important. The baptism of the children of slaves generally implied that they could no longer be slaves. There is at least one exception to this, the manumission of Christina, who had been baptized on 18 February 1645. Although at the Cape of Good Hope many baptized blacks remained in slavery, this was regarded impossible in New Netherland after 1650, as is emphasized by an incident in 1664. Stuyvesant had sent a number of slaves with children to Curaçao, from where they were sold to Spanish colonies. Only later it turned out that a mistake had been made. The children had been "presented for baptism with good intentions by Mrs. Stuyvesant, your honor's beloved"—and as Christians should never have been sold. Vice Director Matthias Beck wrote to Stuyvesant that he would do everything to buy the children back, but he feared that this would be extremely difficult. The incident raises several questions. If the children had been baptized at the insistence of Judith Bayard, Stuyvesant's wife, then the baptism must have taken place either in New Amsterdam or at Stuyvesant's bowery. No record of this can be found in the New Amsterdam register of baptisms, nor in the list of those baptized at the bowery. If these small children were baptized there, it must have been done by Selijns, who from 1660 to 1664 provided the church services there. But it was Selijns who in June 1664, shortly before he returned to *patria,* spoke out against the baptism of blacks. Possibly the 1664 remark reflects a very recent change in attitude. The incident implies that the number of baptisms of black children after 1655 might well have been larger than can be assumed on the basis of the baptismal registers. A possibility is that at a given moment a separate register of baptisms for blacks was kept in New Amsterdam and that this was lost at a later stage.[83]

One step further than baptism was the confession of faith and becoming a member. Although later in the seventeenth century, a small number of blacks became church members in New York, prior to 1664 there is only one: Susanna Negrin. It is tempting to assume that this is the same woman who as a seventeen-year-old was baptized on 14 April 1647 and who thirteen days later as "Susanna van Nieuw Nederlandt" entered into matrimony with Jan Augustinus.[84]

That all the missionary work led only to the membership of one black woman indicates where the problems lay. The conversion of heathens may have been advocated with enthusiasm in the Dutch Republic, but in the colony practical objections stood in the way. Many, if not all, ministers made attempts to catechize blacks, but the teaching of religious knowledge was not easy. It was for good reason that Selijns vested any remaining hope in children. Complete conversion was a question of extreme patience and required answering all 129 questions in the Heidelberg Catechism, the Reformed Church's primary teaching tool. It is particularly in the reduction of the number of black baptisms that the changing ideas on conversion become evident. The change in 1655 was not absolute; nonetheless, the abruptness of the disappearance of black baptisms from the baptismal register raises some questions. The change in baptismal practice may be the result of the crumbling of the convivial societal model adhered to by some of the early Pietist ministers. It is evident that the later ministers were less inclined to baptize blacks, even though the difference may not have been as great as the figures in the incomplete baptismal registers might suggest. A change took place from a humanitarian outlook on slavery toward a productivistic view. The possible change in baptismal practice is an indication that the social distance between colonists and blacks in New Netherland increased.[85]

Christianizing the Indians

The situation of the conversion of the Indians was entirely different from that of the blacks. A variety of differences existed, mostly emanating from the geographical and cultural distance between the Indians and colonists. The consequence of the Dutch pattern of settlement, which meant that after 1650 the population was mostly concentrated in towns and villages, coupled with prohibitions on going into the woods to engage in trade, resulted in some contact during the trading season, when the Indians came to the Dutch settlements. This was in sharp contrast to the situation in Canada, where the French *coureurs de bois,* with Jesuit priests in their wake, visited the Indians in their settlements. The cultural distance between colonists and Indians was greater than that with the blacks. This was partly because the blacks were part of the colonial community and the Indians were not. Both the language problems and the absence of sufficient common ground for transmitting the ideas of Calvinism were obstacles.

This does not mean that no enthusiasm existed for the conversion of the Indians or that the no missionary effort was made. As early as 1624 the *Provisional Regulations* stated that the colonists must "by their Christian life and conduct seek to draw the *Indianen* and other blind people to the knowledge of God and His Word." The colonists' role to act as examples of Christianity was emphasized in Verhulst's instruction a year later. Such expressions of missionary zeal also occur in the WIC's 1638 instruction for ministers, and it became a trope in many pamphlets. The Amsterdam classis continued to point out to the West India Company that the "propagation of the true religion among the *blinde heijdenen* [blind heathens] under the authority of your Honorable Company" was of great importance. The patroons too considered the conversion of Indians to be one of their duties. The contract that Johannes Megapolensis entered into with Kiliaen van Rensselaer included a reference to "the edification and instruction of the inhabitants and the *Indiaenen.*" On the appointment of his successor, Gideon Schaets, it was specified that he should employ "all Christian effort... to encourage the *heijdenen* and also the *heijdense kinderen* [heathen children] in the Christian religion." If it was necessary to board Indian children in his house in order to catechize them, the costs would be reimbursed by the patroon.[86]

So the classis and the patroon in Rensselaerswijck clearly wished to convert the Indians in New Netherland. But did the directors in Amsterdam share this desire? The early instructions suggest this, but in 1650 the directors were accused of not having made sufficient efforts to promote the conversion of Indians and blacks. Their reaction was revealing:

> Everyone who has been in the company of the *indianen* in and around New Netherland will be able to say that it is not humanly possible to bring the adults to the christian faith, also it belongs to the position of the *predicant* to make an effort in that, and it is the duty of the director to assist him therein.[87]

The directors considered it the duty of the ministers to take this in hand. With the appointment of ministers, their contribution to the missionary activities ended. Naturally this sharp division of tasks was a point on which differences of opinion arose. Johannes Polhemius, who had experienced in Brazil that some ministers were exempted from other ecclesiastical duties to apply themselves exclusively to missionary work, opined that the Company was showing too little zeal. That does not alter the fact that in the first part of their reaction the directors recognized that considerable practical drawbacks had to be overcome.[88]

The reports of the ministers about their contacts with the Indians indicates this problem as well. Michaëlius wrote in 1628, when he had only been in New Netherland a couple of months, that he was surprised that many in the Dutch Republic thought that the "docility" and the "good nature" of the Indians would make conversion a relatively simple matter. His experience indicated otherwise: "If we want to speak to them of God, it seems a dream to them." Of course, poor communication was part of the problem. Many colonists talked with the Indians about trade, "but this is done almost as much in pointing with thumb and fingers as by speaking, which in matters of religion could not be done." Even if the language difficulties could be overcome, the cultural differences between with the Indians were still such that Michaëlius proposed a rather drastic solution, namely to separate a few Indian children from their parents at an early age and bring them up as Christians. These children would later be used "to spread the knowledge of religion amongst the entire nation." This plan encountered an obvious practical difficulty: the Indians were not inclined to give up their children. Michaëlius remained in the colony for only a few years, and it is unlikely that he achieved any success.[89]

In all probability his successor Bogardus also made attempts to convert the Indians, but no sign of any success can be found. The minister had made some progress among the blacks, but it was an uphill struggle as far as the Indians were concerned. While the names of many blacks appear in the New Amsterdam baptismal register, no signs of any Indians appear whatsoever. The wars with the Indians in the 1640s did not help the missionary efforts, of course.[90] Whether Bogardus took the trouble to learn any of the Indian languages is unknown, but Megapolensis, who worked in Rensselaerswijck in the 1640s, did. His observations indicate that he did not find it an easy task, but his description of the creation myth of the Iroquois shows that he was able to discuss abstract subjects. Still, listening to and understanding stories such as this was quite different from explaining the fundamental principles of Calvinism. Megapolensis intended to preach among the Indians:

> When we hold a sermon, they sometimes come with ten or twelve, more or less, each with a large long tobacco pipe, made by themselves, in the mouth and stand around and look. Afterwards they ask me what I am doing and what I want, that I stand there alone and make so many words while no one of the rest may speak? I tell them that I admonish the Christians that they should not steal, fornicate, get drunk, murder and that they should also not do it. And that I intend to preach the same to them and come to them in their land and castles (about three days' journey from here, lying further inland), when I know their speech. Then they say it is good that I teach the Christians, but immediately add *diatennon jawij assyreoni hagiouisk,* that is, why do so many Christians do it?[91]

The bad example set by some of the colonists did not make the task of the ministers any easier. Yet the "propagation of Christ's realm among the *blinde heydenen* [blind heathens]" continued, "although not with such success as could be wished," as was remarked by the classis as a reaction to the meager results that Megapolensis and Drisius achieved with a specific Indian.[92] They had instructed the Indian for two years, so that he was able to read and speak good Dutch. He also received instruction in the basic principles of religion, and had even attended church services. He was given a Bible, so that he could work among the Indians, but

> it has all turned to naught, he has lapsed to drinking brandy, sold the Bible and turned into a *rechte bestia* [true animal], who is doing more harm than good among the *Indianen.*[93]

The result was such that Megapolensis and Drisius saw no more opportunities of converting the Indians, until

> the time that they are subdued by the number and power of our nation and reduced to some government, and that our people provides them a better example than they have done before.[94]

In this, Megapolensis and Drisius create an interesting link between conquest and missionary work. It was also the experience in the East Indian colonies that the propagation of the Christian religion could only be brought about successfully under the protection of a Christian government. No success could ever be achieved as long as the Indians were outside the sphere of authority of the Dutch colonial authorities, as had been learned from the experience of thirty years of fruitless work among the Indians. During the existence of New Netherland, no attempt was made to subdue the Indians in such a way that attempted to proselytize were feasible.[95]

The reports of early ministers of New Netherland make clear that the spread of the Christian religion, by which they meant their specific brand of Calvinism, among the Indians was no unstoppable tidal wave. The Indians did not automatically see the light of Christianity upon hearing the ministers preach. But the lack of Indian converts should not be mistaken for a lack of effort. The result is hardly surprising, especially when taking into account the situation of the Dutch Reformed church in the first part of the seventeenth century. In the Dutch Republic, as in New Netherland, it was in many ways a vanguard church, not intended to encompass all of the population. It set high standards for its members, standards that many could not or would not meet. For the Indians, the conditions attached to becoming a member of the Dutch Reformed Church were simply not attainable within one or even two generations. Later in the seventeenth century and especially in the eighteenth century, the Dutch Reformed Church in the Dutch Republic gradually became more inclusive: its membership as a percentage of the total population grew, while at the same time the exercise of discipline over members relaxed. The same development took place in New York, and it allowed for a change in attitude toward the proselytization of Indians. The work of Bernardus Freeman in Schenectady, who over the course of years baptized a number of Indians, is evidence of that. It was made possible by a change in the meaning attached to baptism as applied to children of non-Christian parents. No longer was it required for them to promise to rear their children in the Christian faith. In these cases baptism no longer functioned as the first step that, via catechism and confession of faith, would lead to membership of the Calvinist church. It became a sign of inclusion into a Christian society controlled by Europeans, rather than conversion, and thus it took on a role not unlike that for which Catholic priests had already used it in the seventeenth century. In New York, this development took place long after the Dutch Republic had lost control of New Netherland.[96]

6   Burghers and Status

Achieving economic prosperity was an important aim for prospective colonists, especially after 1650, when the economic growth of the Dutch Republic had slowed. But did New Netherland really offer immigrants better opportunities for social betterment? Were colonists better off by going to New Netherland?

That question implies a difficult comparison with the Dutch Republic. In the long run, an individual immigrant might have achieved a position in the colony that was better than that which he had left behind in the Netherlands, but that itself was not the sole result of the opportunities open to him in the colony. Establishing a career and achieving a better standard of living and position in society takes time anywhere. A valid evaluation therefore involves the comparison of the position of a colonist with that which he could have reached had he remained within his own province, elsewhere in the Dutch Republic, or indeed if he had pursued his fortune elsewhere in Europe. Yet, such a comparison is in many cases impossible, both because of its speculative nature and because of the relative lack of information on individuals.

So the answers have to be sought not on an individual level but on a collective level. As a result the questions require some modification and require an examination of the social stratification and status system of New Netherland. Status in early modern society was related to, among other factors, material things, such as possessions and salary. It could be acquired by holding administrative functions. It can also be deduced from judicial regulations, such as those for civil rights.

Money Matters

For an analysis of the social stratification of New Netherland, a number of tax and loan lists are available, of which five pertain to New Amsterdam.

These lists date from the years 1653, 1655, 1664, 1665, and 1674 and were drawn up for various reasons. The 1653, 1655, and 1664 loan lists were compiled in order to get quickly gather funds to improve defense works. In all three cases there is a direct cause: the threat of an English attack in 1653 and 1664 and the recent Indian attack in 1655. The 1665 list was compiled to pay for the billeting of English soldiers. And the 1674 loan was decided upon to pay off the loans of 1653 and 1664. The number of people per list and the amounts of money involved are quite varied.

All five lists concern special direct taxes or loans, levied exclusively to meet the costs of defensive measures. There are hardly any records of the normal, indirect taxes and duties. The lists contain mostly white, self-employed men, the "middle-class" and elite citizens of New Amsterdam. Women's names appear only sporadically in the lists, and these are almost exclusively widows. Blacks do not feature on the lists, and Indians were never taxed. The five lists provide no information about the lowest members of society. The lists principally consisted of names and numbers; the trades have to be found in other sources. But many people did not confine themselves to a single economic occupation and combined many activities. Apart from being brewers, men such as Oloff Stevensz van Cortlandt were also merchants. It can rarely if ever be ascertained which occupation was the major source of income. Yet, taking all the idiosyncracies of the sources into account, the hundreds of names on the lists can be categorized and combined with other information, and a general stratification of the New Amsterdam society emerges.

The top tier consisted of major merchants, in many cases related to the merchant families in Amsterdam and Haarlem, and high Company officials. Many new names turn up in the early 1650s, showing that the men that were to dominate New Amsterdam both commercially and administratively for a long period of years for the most part arrived in the colony after 1647. These were men such as Cornelis Steenwijck, Johannes Pietersz van Brugh, Jacob Backer, and Johannes de Peijster.

The second tier was composed mostly of merchants as well. This group was larger in number, slightly less prosperous, and less likely to hold office. This category also includes the two New Amsterdam ministers, Megapolensis and Drisius, and middle-ranking WIC officials.

Artisans and small merchants form the third category. Craftsmen such as shoemaker Coenraet ten Eijck, surgeon Hans Kierstede, tapper Jan Peeck, and yacht captain Claes Bordingh are included in this category, together with a number of masons, tailors, carpenters, and coopers. They were well-to-do artisans, with one or more servants. This category also contains a number of minor merchants, notaries, and a small number of military personnel, mostly petty officers.

The less prosperous artisans are to be found in the fourth category, which also contains a number of people about whom little is known as to how they supported themselves. Yet they were their own masters, Also in this category are those who provided a nonmonetary contribution to the construction of the defensive works. A small number of them, mainly carpenters, chose to work on the construction for several days without pay.

Not included in the lists are tradesmen's hands, servants, soldiers, sailors, and other people in a lower employed position. As was the case in the Dutch Republic, they were not subject to direct taxes and had insufficient funds to contribute to city loans. They rarely owned property and were mostly lodged by their master. Neither is the lowest category included: the poor of New Amsterdam, about whom very little is known.

Merchants in particular were able to amass fortunes. Noticeable is that the differences in the wealth of the most prosperous inhabitants became greater as the seventeenth century progressed and the size of the colony's population grew. The link between wealth and the holding of administrative office was obvious, but magistrates were not recruited exclusively from the richest inhabitants, and sometimes they can be found in the lower categories. The connection between wealth and holding office is stronger for the top level (*burgemeesters* and, after 1664, mayors) than for *schepenen* and aldermen. The elite in New Amsterdam was therefore not a closed group, and it had a dynamic character. On the one hand, the elite contained a number of older inhabitants, including Oloff Stevensz van Cortlandt and his brother-in-law Govert Loockermans. They had been in the colony since the late 1630s and took the opportunity to strengthen their personal position in tempo with the increase in population. On the other hand, from the early 1650s, when New Amsterdam was granted its own city government, a continuous stream of newcomers arrived who in many cases would have been well-to-do before they came to the colony. The newcomers swiftly established a position within the economic elite, but it generally took more time for them to join the governmental elite.[1]

Income

Another way to gain insight into the differences in status in New Netherland is by examining differences in income, although this is also not without problems. Little is known about the amounts the independent merchants, craftsmen, and farmers in New Netherland earned from their labor. Better information is available when they were employed by someone else. The most important sources are the contracts of employment, principally from the notarial archives in Amsterdam, together with a few lists from the West India Company and the city of Amsterdam concerning employees' salaries. A comparison of salaries is not easy, because some employees were also given free board and lodging, and to place a value on this is difficult; other employees had their income supplemented. For example, in addition to their basic salary, many schoolmasters were paid a fixed sum per pupil by the parents, and it is rare that the number of pupils they had is known. Furthermore, some posts could easily be combined with other positions, such as that of precentor in the church. The people for whom information is available can be divided into four categories, which correspond to the types of immigrants outlined in chapter 2.

First, the higher employees of the Company. A list dating from 1644, when the WIC was reviewing the government of New Netherland, provides the monthly salaries of the most senior officials. The director would be paid 250 guilders. His "second," the vice director, who would also act as a merchant and collector, received less than half this amount, namely 120 guilders. The minister was on par with the vice director. The *fiscael* and the secretary were each paid 60 guilders per month, as was the *commies* of the merchandise and of the store. A commander was to be appointed as military leader, and he would also receive 60 guilders per month. All officials were also given yearly money for board and lodging, which varied between three and five times their monthly salary.[2]

In the second category, the lesser Company employees, the salaries were significantly lower, as is to be expected. In 1638, the *commies* of the victuals had a salary of thirty-six guilders per month. A schoolmaster earned thirty guilders, as did the workmen's supervisor, while an assistant *commies,* a surgeon, and a captain of a sloop were a little lower down the ladder, with twenty-five guilders per month. The majority of the craftsmen working for the Company earned twenty guilders or less per month: for example, a master mason received twenty guilders and a carpenter eighteen guilders. The less highly trained workers earned several guilders less per month. Common soldiers were not paid much, but their superiors did reasonably well. The 1644 list indicates that an ensign was paid forty-five guilders, a sergeant twenty-five guilders, and a corporal eighteen guilders. The lower ranks appear on the list at a little more than ten guilders per month: the drummer received thirteen, *adelborsten* (cadets) fifteen, and soldiers thirteen guilders per month. The 1650 list shows all these amounts at a couple of guilders less. The yearly board and lodging allowance was relatively high for the lower-ranking employees: between five and eight times their monthly salary.[3]

The third category consists of the Amsterdam merchants' factors. Their salaries were at the same level as those of the second tier of Company employees but display a greater range and development: experience and ability in private employment led to better pay. Fifty to seventy-five guilders per month were normal salaries for independent factors in New Netherland, which suggests that the income of a major merchant trading on his own account would have exceeded that. In New Amsterdam many of the large merchants were members of the city government. The remuneration for this work, which would have taken up one to one and a half days per week, was 350 guilders per year for *burgemeesters* and 250 guilders for *schepenen.*

In Beverwijck and Rensselaerswijck the salary for the magistrates at 150 guilders and 50 guilders per year, respectively, was considerably lower.[4]

The fourth category consists of the contract workers. Here too, experience and a higher age resulted in a higher salary. Yet in general the pay was lower than in the three previous categories. An adult farm laborer could expect eight to ten guilders per month, plus board and lodging; this was even less than soldiers were paid. Farm boys received a starting wage that was dependent on their age and that increased gradually.[5]

The social stratification in New Netherland was similar to that in the Dutch Republic. A classification made for Amsterdam in 1696 shows four categories: the common people as the lowest category; above that the shopkeepers and craftsmen, with one category higher the notables and rich merchants; and the highest being the "gentlemen of the government."[6] The same categories are found in New Netherland. Little is known about the poor in the colony, the tramps and beggars, even though the people that appealed for charity made up a considerable part of the population, in Beverwijck as much as 10 percent. It is a little easier to gain a picture of the farmhands, laborers, and soldiers who formed the following category, but its size is unknown. Above this are the broad category of burghers: artisans, notaries, shopkeepers, farmers with their own land, captains, and the like. The highest category is comprised of the relatively small group of merchants, from which the magistrates were recruited, flanked by several highly placed Company employees. A wide range of degrees of wealth was to be found within the two highest categories.[7]

In comparison with the Dutch Republic, there was more social mobility in New Netherland, and many examples can be given of people who arrived in the colony in a low social position and managed to work their way up. Govert Loockermans and Oloff Stevensz van Cortlandt are the most striking examples of this. In other cases, such as with some of the merchants, their careers were helped by family connections in *patria*. Men such as Cornelis Steenwijck, Johannes Pietersz van Brugh, and Johannes de Peijster were unlikely ever to achieve office in the city government of Haarlem, from where all three originated. In New Amsterdam, however, they managed to become part of the elite. The same kind of mobility was available to farmhands in the settlements that were established after 1650, such as Hendrick Jansz van Schalkwijck.[8]

The rapid increase in the population of New Netherland created economic circumstances that provided several people with the opportunity of reaching a social level that they might not have achieved in the Dutch Republic. This does not mean that the opportunities were limitless. The opportunity to gain a prominent position in the less stratified society in the 1630s and 1640s was greater than in the 1650s and 1660s. The development toward a more extensive stratification as the result of the increase in population was evident earlier in New Amsterdam than in Beverwijck, and the same applies to the settlements that were established in the mid-1650s. As the New Netherland population grew, so did the concomitant need to establish the customary societal and legal mores of the Dutch Republic in the colony, such as membership in the burgher guard and burgher right.

The Status of Magistrates

In the seventeenth century, governmental authority was generally legitimized by an appeal to God. This was accepted to such an extent that only a few references to it can be found. Director Kieft referred to it when he attempted to reprimand Bogardus for cursing at "your magistrate, placed over you by God."[9] It features more clearly in the prayer that preceded the meeting of *burgemeesters* and *schepenen* of New Amsterdam. It had pleased God "to promote us to the government of your people in this place." God's help was called upon for the execution of this task. The magistrates had to justify their decisions in the eyes of God, and it was not up to His subjects to question this: "Incline the hearts of the subjects to proper obedience, that through their love and prayers our burden may be made lighter." In protecting God's laws, the city government implored God to arm it with "strength, courage, boldness, and frankness."[10]

In the Dutch Republic, power was vested in the most prominent citizens, those men who were considered best qualified to wield it. The most important criterion for this was wealth, which was seen as a sign of God's favor. The same mentality prevailed in New Netherland. In the establishment of the city government of New Amsterdam, the WIC had stipulated extensively the criteria that magistrates had to satisfy. They were to be qualified, honest, rational, intelligent, and prosperous men, who were not opposed to the WIC but who were peace-loving people who owned property. They had to have been born either in the colony and, according to the customs of Amsterdam, to have been citizens for at least seven years or to have been born and brought up in the Dutch Republic. And of course they had to be members of the Dutch Reformed Church.[11]

The first appointments were made by decision of director general and council, but after 1656 the city government was permitted to submit a nomination. The nominees had to be of people of good reputation, considered worthy to hold such a position, and who would be disposed to fulfill the office with honor.[12] With a few exceptions, *burgemeesters* and *schepenen* nominated men that met with all these criteria. In the early years of the city government, in 1653, director general and council were not convinced that the right people would achieve office if the WIC's right to appoint magistrates were to be delegated. Undoubtedly, lingering resentment from the preceding years, when the directors of the WIC locked horns with the advisory boards of Twelve, Eight, and Nine Men, played a part here.[13]

Wealth was required to become *burgemeester* or *schepen*. Governmental experience, either in *patria* or in the colony, also counted, as did having held a position in the burgher guard, the civic guard of New Amsterdam. Although it was explicitly stated of only two men that they were merchants, this was actually true of most of the others as well. Trade was the quickest way to wealth and thus to a seat in New Amsterdam's city government. The people best qualified were also appointed as magistrates in other places in New Netherland. The magistrates there were less well-to-do than their colleagues in New Amsterdam; nor were most of them of the merchant classes, with the exception of some of the magistrates in Beverwijck.[14]

The distinction in rank between *burgemeesters* and *schepenen* was confined to the New Amsterdam city government. All *burgemeesters* had first gained experience either as a *schepen* or as a member of the Nine Men, which earlier administered civil law. However, former *burgemeesters* were never again appointed as a *schepen* but often graduated to the office of orphan master. In the Dutch period the office of *burgemeester* rotated among only six men. Two of them were in office for only a few terms. The other four were appointed five or six times, and their appointments show a clear pattern: in most cases they were in office for two years, as was the norm in *patria*. During the second year, they were the senior *burgemeester*. Before a new term as *burgemeester*, they usually served for two years as orphan master. Only a few exceptions to this pattern occurred.[15]

No such system is ascertainable for the position of *schepen*. Twenty-six men, four of whom went on to become *burgemeester*, were appointed as *schepen* a total of sixty-three times. It is not clear what the basis was for the nominations of *burgemeesters* and *schepenen* or the appointments of director general and council, but all candidates were prominent citizens. In New Amsterdam no subordinate posts existed that could function as a springboard to the office of *schepen*. The office of orphan master, which could have been used in that way, was performed almost exclusively by former *burgemeesters* and *schepenen*.[16]

A general explanation for the alternation of appointments is that the function of *burgemeester* or *schepen* was very time-consuming. Although the positions carried an honorarium, time considerations made it hardly surprising that some people were not keen to be nominated. However, taking on a role in government was considered a duty if a prominent position in society had been attained.[17] In New Amsterdam no appointments were ever refused, but it did happen in Rensselaerswijck. In 1648, Goosen Gerritsz van Schaick, who later served a number of times as a magistrate in Beverwijck, refused to serve on the patroon's court because he did not consider himself suitable. Furthermore, he claimed he did not have a house in the patroonship and was therefore not bound to serve. Another argument was that he was not "on a free basis with the patroon." These arguments were not accepted by the court, and Gerritsz thus accepted the position.[18]

The case of Jan Evertsz Bout shows what the penalty for refusal could be. In 1654 he declined to accept his appointment as *schepen* in Breuckelen and said that he would rather depart for Holland than fulfill such obligations. That was not a remark with which director general and council could be fobbed off, especially as Stuyvesant had not had good experiences with him. Bout was told:

> If you will not accept to serve as *scheepen* for the welfare of the town of Breuckelen with others, your fellow inhabitants, then you must prepare yourself to sail in the ship *Coninck Salomon,* agreeable to your own statement.[19]

Status Symbols

Such cases were exceptional. Usually those nominated accepted their appointments without objection, not only because it was seen as a duty but also because it was a public recognition of the status a person had achieved in society. This was symbolized in the decorations in the courtroom. The city magistrates had special cushions made, and in 1659 the windows of the city hall were decorated with the city's coat of arms in stained glass.[20] The magistrates' clothing was also an expression of their authority. In Rensselaerswijck the magistrates wore black hats with a silver ribbon, while the patroon equipped the *schout* with "a silver-plated rapier with baldric and a black hat with plume."[21] Under the English administration, the English governor Francis Lovelace, on behalf of the Duke of York, gave the city magistrates a city seal, a silver scepter, and "Gownes both for the Mayor & Alderman" as a "Perticular Testimony of his R. Highnesse grace and fauour to this his City of New Yorke."[22]

The magistrates also displayed symbols of their status beyond the confines of the court building. They had their own pews in the church. The Nine Men had been granted this honor earlier.[23] Another status symbol of the city government was the stained-glass windows in the church that Evert Duyckingh placed in 1656 to honor *schout, burgemeesters,* and *schepenen.* The costs were not paid for by the city; each magistrate was obliged to contribute two and a half beavers to defray the costs. In Beverwijck too, stained-glass windows showing the coats of arms of the magistrates were installed.[24]

Apart from the church, the status of administrators of city and Company was indicated by several other means. Gun salutes were fired for both Kieft and Stuyvesant, sometimes with disastrous consequences, as in 1636. When Kieft and a few others returned to Manhattan from Pavonia, Cornelis van Vorst organized the gun salute. A spark landed on the thatched roof of a house, causing it to burn down in half an hour. Every time Stuyvesant arrived at or departed from New Amsterdam, a gun salute was fired from the fort, each shot consuming sixteen pounds of gunpowder. Another expression of status can be found in the titles with which the magistrates were addressed. Director Kieft was addressed as *"Mijn Heer Directeur"* (My Lord Director), and in the register of baptisms he was registered as "the Lord Willem Kieft," with as suffix "commander" or "governor." Prior to 1647 no one else was given the title of "Lord" in the baptismal register. Shortly after his arrival, Stuyvesant instituted the form of address "My Lord General." The members of the city government were sometimes distinguished from other citizens, although this was done in a less prominent manner than with the highest WIC officials. From the 1650s onwards the magistrates of New Amsterdam are referred to as *schepen* or former *schepen* whenever they appear in notarial acts.[25]

Although the position in society of officials and magistrates manifested in many ways, they were not always treated with the respect they felt they were entitled to. In several instances criticism was expressed about judicial decisions, and magistrates were sometimes insulted or even threatened. It usually happened in anger over a judgment considered unjust by the person involved, but the magistrates nevertheless took the incidents very seriously. Insulting a government that was approved by God was a form of blasphemy and therefore fell within the category of offenses that the local bench of *schepenen* itself could not try but had to be passed on to director general and council. Yet in Beverwijck the court regularly dealt with these situations itself. In the case of baker Thomas Paulusz and his wife, who were caught infringing the ordinance on baking and who then called the inspecting magistrates extortionists and devils, the customary fine was increased. Even more serious than insults were the incidents in which a judgment of the court was explicitly criticized. In such situations, fines of six hundred or even twelve hundred guilders, sometimes in combination with a number of years of banishment, were imposed. Such sentences were used as a deterrent but were usually mitigated if the culprit showed remorse and apologized.[26]

In New Amsterdam too, a distinction was made between major and minor incidents. A double fine was imposed in the case of a fight between two men in 1660, since it had taken place in the presence of the *schout* and his deputy.[27] In another case, *burgemeesters* and *schepenen* had to invoke the power of director general and council. In a matter concerning a bill of exchange, Walewijn van der Veen had made known his displeasure to *schepen* Jacob Backer by announcing that the magistrates did not know what they were doing, adding some insults for good measure. *Schout* Pieter Tonneman demanded that Walewijn van der Veen be condemned to make amends for the insult,

> honorably and profitably; honorably, by praying with uncovered head God, justice, and this government for forgiveness; profitably, by paying as a fine the sum of twelve hundred guilders with costs.

Since Van der Veen refused to do this, *burgemeesters* and *schepenen* asked director general and council to confirm the sentence, as they were of the opinion that the injury to their court also damaged the authority and esteem of the higher court. Director general and council probably agreed.[28]

Begging forgiveness with bared head and on bended knee was of course not exclusive to New Netherland and happened elsewhere in Europe and colonial America also. Occasionally another form of public punishment was applied in New Netherland. For cursing the magistrates of Boswijck and the writing of a "scandalous letter," Jan Willemsz IJsselstein van Leiden was sentenced by director general and council to be bound to a stake at the place of public executions "with a bridle in his mouth, rods under his arm, and a note pinned to his chest with these words: squib writer, false accuser, and thief of the honor of his magistrates."[29]

Burgher Right

Below the group of magistrates, a broad layer of reasonably prosperous self-employed citizens existed. In the cities of the Dutch Republic, this was the group of burghers that formed the burgher guard. The basis of this institution was the ideal of a community of citizens, bound in solidarity, who stood up for one another and who were collectively responsible for the maintenance of peace, order, and security. In the Dutch Republic burghers had specific rights and duties, such as the exclusive exercise of some trades and a degree of legal security, against which stood the duty to pay taxes and to perform guard duty. In *patria* this community spirit and the institutions that emanated from it were the result of a centuries-old evolution. But what was the situation in a new colonial society?

As the free colonists in New Netherland began to play an important role in the transition from trading post to settlement colony and as the colony grew in size and importance, more references occur in the documents to the burgher right and the burgher guard.[30]

Although explicit rules on burgher right were not promulgated in New Amsterdam until 1657, a number of indications show that burgher right was already in existence, or at least that many inhabitants envisioned themselves in terms of citizenship. The Twelve Men in 1642 spoke of themselves as "*borgers* [burghers] and inhabitants of New Netherland."[31] People were known as "burghers" in many places. It is tempting to interpret this as a distinction between burghers and inhabitants, comparable to the difference between burghers, who had sworn the burgher oath, and inhabitants, who had not. This distinction was already fading in the Dutch Republic, and the same may apply to New Netherland.

The oaths that colonists in New Netherland had to take show what was expected of burghers. In 1639, a number of Englishmen living on

7. Schuyler coat of arms of 1656 in a rendition executed in the mid-nineteenth century. Wood engraving. Emmet Collection, Miriam and Ira D. Wallach Division of Art, Prints and Photographs, The New York Public Library, Astor, Lenox and Tilden Foundations.

Manhattan had to swear an oath that contained two elements: loyalty to the government and loyalty to the community. Loyalty to the government was indicated by pledging allegiance to the States General, the Prince of Orange, and to director and council. Loyalty to the community was in-dicated by the requirement that the English "to the best of [your] ability help, support, and protect with your life and property the inhabitants [of New Netherland] against all the enemies of the land." Such solidarity was explicitly required of the English, but it was considered a matter of course for the Dutch colonists.[32]

Although an oath of loyalty to the government was normal for magistrates and employees of the Company, a general oath for burghers and inhabitants, known as the burgher oath, did not come into use until the 1650s. It first occurred in Rensselaerswijck in 1651. The implementation of the oath, which included loyalty to the patroon, was triggered by the conflict taking place at that time between the patroonship and the WIC. In the case of Jan Verbeeck, one of the people who had earlier sworn an oath in Rensselaerswijck, a new oath was required. As his house was located in Beverwijck, which had recently been founded on land that was originally considered part of the patroonship, he took an oath of allegiance a couple of months later in his new community. This indicates that in the event of a changeover of authority over an area, the population was relieved of the previous oath and took a new oath of loyalty to the new powers. This also happened when New Amsterdam became New York in 1664.[33]

The oath sworn by Jan Verbeeck was "the customary burgher oath." The text is unknown, but the two elements outlined above would have been present in it. By swearing the oath, one became a member of the community, with all the rights and duties. Yet a number of questions remain. For instance, it is not clear which inhabitants were eligible for citizenship. Probably citizenship was open only to free men, those who were in the employ neither of the Company nor of private individuals. The ownership of real estate may also have been a requirement, as such a stipulation was later laid down in New Amsterdam. The rights of burghers are easier to deduce. The problems involving the bakers in Beverwijck indicate that a distinction existed between burghers on the one hand and the ordinary inhabitants and strangers on the other. The profits that could be made by baking white bread or sugar bread for the Indians had attracted some itinerant people who were not Beverwijck burghers. The regular bakers immediately protested, and they convinced the court that measures had to be taken, as nobody without a burgher oath was allowed to conduct any trade. The exercise of a trade or craft was thus clearly a prerogative of burghers.[34]

Another advantage that burghers had over ordinary inhabitants and strangers was their legal status. In the Dutch Republic burghers were protected by the *jus de non evocando,* the right to be summoned before the court only in one's own city. No indications exist that this right was formally invoked in New Netherland prior to 1657. However, in a number of cases heard in the court of New Amsterdam, citizenship was used as an argument. In 1655, Pieter Dircksz Waterhont, captain of the *Witte Paert,* demanded that merchant Augustijn Heermans, who was on the point of leaving for Maryland, should provide surety for the payment of 840 guilders for a number of slaves that he had bought. Heermans stated that as he was a burgher of New Amsterdam and possessed real estate that was worth more than his debt, he did not have to provide surety. The court accepted his argument.[35]

Great and Small Burghers

Prior to 1657 burgher right existed in New Netherland, but it was only in this year that a formal ordinance on it was promulgated. The main motivation was the continuous exasperation about the "Scotch" merchants in the colony. These itinerant traders were not inhabitants of New Netherland but traveled to the colony only for the trading season. Usually, they went straight to Beverwijck, where most of the fur trade with the Indians was carried out. Their itinerant status allowed them to keep their costs low and offer their goods cheaper than the resident traders, who had homes in New Netherland, paid the usual taxes there, and contributed to the defense of the community as members of the burgher guard. The irritation caused by the itinerant merchants in 1657 led to an attempt to exclude them from the fur trade, which was then at its peak.[36]

In January 1657 the city government of New Amsterdam submitted a petition to director general and council, which pointed out that the practices of the itinerant merchants were in contravention of article twelve of the *Freedoms and Exemptions* of 1640, in which Manhattan was designated as staple for the transport of goods to and from the colony. *Burgemeesters* and *schepenen* stated that the community in New Amsterdam had to bear the heavy costs of defending the city against the English and the Indians, while the traveling merchants profited from them. They thought it reasonable that the burghers be granted specific privileges, and as they considered the burgher right one of the most important privileges, the city government requested that the right to trade be limited to burghers of New Amsterdam.[37]

Director general and council acknowledged the validity of the arguments of city government, but the issue was complicated. An earlier attempt to deal with the problem of the itinerant merchants had met with opposition from the Amsterdam directors. The combination of staple right and burgher right offered a new opportunity. Staple right could be used to force the itinerant merchants to offer their goods first in New Amsterdam, while burgher right was made compulsory for keeping an open shop. A further regulation could require payment for the granting of burgher right, while at the same time a rule could be instituted that the burgher right would lapse if a merchant left the city for a longer period of time. Thus itinerant merchants could be kept at bay.[38]

An ordinance along these lines was drawn up and promulgated on 30 January 1657. Director general and council went further than laying down criteria and rights for burghers. They also introduced a distinction between the small and the great burgher right, with a reference to the situation in Amsterdam, where such a system had been introduced in 1652.[39] In New Amsterdam, the two-tier system introduced different rights and duties for great and small burghers. For the small burgher right, required to keep an open shop or to exercise a trade, a fee of twenty guilders was set, and small burghers were obliged to contribute to the direct taxes and to perform guard duties. This created a solution to the problem of the itinerant merchants. Small burgher right was awarded to all those who had been resident in the city for one year and six weeks and kept "fire and light" (occupied a house), all inhabitants that had been born in the city, everyone who married a burgher's daughter who had been born in the city, and finally all those who wished to carry out trade or exercise a trade in the city and to that end had paid twenty guilders to the *burgemeesters*. Great burgher right was a requirement for the fulfillment of functions in the city government. Other features were that the great burghers were exempt from guard duty and were not liable to arrest by the lower courts in New Netherland.[40] Great burgher right was automatically awarded to members of the provincial government, to *burgemeesters* and *schepenen,* to the ministers, and to the officers of the burgher guard above the rank of *vaandrig* (ensign). Others could obtain great burgher right on payment of fifty guilders to the *burgemeesters*. This was applicable in all cases to current and former magistrates, and great burgher right was hereditary via the male line. Both great and small burgher right were invalidated if the burgher left the city and did not keep "fire and light" there.[41]

The details of these ordinances caused complications, and in the years that followed supplementary measures became necessary. The criteria laid down in 1657 show that burgher right would be free for longstanding inhabitants, while newcomers had to pay for it. However, it was not clear where precisely the dividing line lay. On 9 April 1657 the *burgemeesters* announced that anyone who wished to obtain great or small burgher right free of charge should report to them at the city hall between two and five in the afternoon during the following eight days. Twenty people applied for great burgher right and almost two hundred for small burgher right. The number of burghers increased gradually during the months that followed, although the later burghers had to pay for the privilege. In total some 277 people applied, although there may have been more. The burghers had to swear an oath that contained a promise of loyalty to all governmental authorities but was vague about the duties of a burgher. It was required only that the burgher should behave as an "obedient subject and good *borger.*"[42] If he so wished, on payment of a sum of money the burgher could acquire a certificate as proof of his citizenship.[43]

On the list of great burghers many names are missing. Stuyvesant was among the twenty listed great burghers, but not his secretary, Cornelis van Ruyven. *Predikant* Megapolensis was listed, but not his colleague Drisius. Also on the list were former *burgemeester* Marten Kregier and former *schepen* Jacob Gerritsz Strijcker, but not the incumbent *burgemeesters* Allard Anthony and Paulus Leendertsz van der Grift. It is possible that members of the city government were not required to register, as they automatically qualified, but this does not explain the other omissions.[44]

The large number of small burghers makes it more difficult to track down the omissions. Of course, the list includes many carpenters, surgeons, bakers, coopers, butchers, and shoemakers who appear on the taxation lists discussed earlier. The list does not contain all the adult males in New Amsterdam. Company soldiers and officials, for instance, do not appear in it, nor in the taxation lists. The large group of servants are absent as well. The few women who applied were widows, and their aim was to continue the trade of their deceased husbands, for which small burgher right was a requirement.[45] The regulation of burgher right in New Amsterdam was initially aimed at keeping the itinerant merchants out. It provided the burghers of New Amsterdam with advantages in the trade with Fort Orange, although it did not put a complete stop to the competition of itinerant traders.

The irritation of parasites preying upon the available trade was not exclusive to New Amsterdam. In the latter years of Dutch rule of the colony, it was also directed at other outsiders. In March 1664 the inhabitants of Beverwijck submitted a petition that was aimed against the trade of the burghers of New Amsterdam and their wives. According to the petitioners, they spoiled the fur trade to the great disadvantage of the inhabitants of Beverwijck, who had to come up with all the community's costs and were obliged to perform guard duties. The complaints sound similar to those uttered a couple of years earlier in New Amsterdam against the itinerant merchants. The delegates of Beverwijck brought the matter up at the *landdag* of April 1664 and managed to persuade director general and council to restrict the trade with Christians in Beverwijck to house-owners, men who had resided there for a minimum of one year and six weeks or had kept "fire and light," or who had been granted burgher right. This was of course a reference to the burgher right of Beverwijck, although it was not made explicit. Nevertheless, the inhabitants of Beverwijck were not too pleased with the reply, as their main aim had been to restrict the fur trade with the Indians, whereas the answer of director general and council pertained only to the trade between Christians.[46]

In New Amsterdam as well, displeasure arose about colonists elsewhere in New Netherland. Several months after the Beverwijck petition, the *burgemeesters* asked director general and council whether it was just that the colonists in New Amstel were permitted to trade freely in New Amsterdam, while the reverse was not allowed. The provincial government had earlier reported to the directors in Amsterdam that the monopoly on the South River was a source of irritation and thus were favorably inclined towards the request. Director general and council allowed the city government of New Amsterdam to introduce the requirement that merchants from New Amstel purchase burgher right in New Amsterdam before offering their wares for sale. Both the petition from Beverwijck and that of New Amsterdam indicate that local particularism, prevalent in the Dutch Republic, was beginning to find its way into New Netherland. Toward the end of the

Dutch period, the population of New Netherland had grown to such an extent that one's own community had become more important than the interest of the whole colony. The adoption of a system of great and small burgher right straight from Amsterdam indicates the extent to which the colonial society fell back on customs from *patria* to create order and structure in its burgeoning society.[47]

Burgher Guard

A recurring point in the petitions about burgher rights was the complaint that outsiders, while profiting from the trade, neither contributed to the costs of defense nor participated in the burgher guard. That complaint is directly related to the issue of the *schutterij,* or citizens' militia, in New Netherland. The *Freedoms and Exemptions* of 1640 required the colonists to make a contribution to the defense of the colony. The Company would

> take all colonists, both free men and servants into its protection, defend the same in domestic and foreign wars with the power that it has there, as much as it is capable to.[48]

That implied that the WIC would provide defensive works and a garrison of soldiers. But the colonists were expected to assist, and to this end every male immigrant had to be in possession of a firearm. This was a formalization of a situation already in existence. A couple of months earlier, Director Kieft had taken measures to organize the colonists in the area of Fort Amsterdam into a burgher guard. It was limited to the requirement that the individual colonists have their own weapons and be assigned to units. Also the alarm signals ("three cannon shots fired in quick succession") were agreed upon. Nonetheless, it was the beginning of the burgher guard.[49]

With the exception of a remark about the units, each under the command of a corporal, nothing is known about how the burgher guard was organized in 1640. More information is available for later years. A petition of 1648 shows that the burgher guard in New Amsterdam was led by officers, although neither their names nor ranks were mentioned. Named as burgher officers a year later were Captain Jacob Wolphertsz van Couwenhoven, Lieutenant Marten Kregier, Sergeants Philip Gerardy and Pieter Cock, and Ensigns Borger Jorisz and Augustijn Heermans. This indicates an organization in two units, with officers in the rank of captain and lieutenant above the others. The rank of colonel, which in Dutch cities was customarily held by one of the incumbent *burgemeesters,* was not used in New Netherland. Appointed to the highest ranks in the colony were mostly men from the city government, as a muster roll from 1653 or 1654 of the Amsterdam burgher guard shows. At the time, the captain and lieutenant were *burgemeester*

Arent van Hattem and *schepen* Paulus Leendertsz van der Grift, while a Van Beeck, possibly Johannes, was an ensign. Collectively, the officers formed the court-martial. The burgher guard in New Amsterdam consisted of two units, the orange company and the blue company. Each company was formed by two units, each consisting of a sergeant, a corporal, a lance corporal, four *adelborsten* (cadets), and twelve to fifteen regular soldiers. In 1659, the number of companies in New Amsterdam was increased to three.[50] Burgher guards existed in other places in New Netherland, but these were probably smaller in size. In Breuckelen, Beverwijck, and Haerlem the officers were appointed by director general and council from the incumbent magistrates.[51]

The task of the burgher guard was twofold: assisting the West India Company in the defense against enemies from outside and conducting the regular patrols within the city, which were aimed at maintaining peace and order, principally at night. In a few instances the threat of an attack from outside was so acute that orders were given to enlarge the guard, as in 1653 during the First Anglo-Dutch War and in 1663 during the Second Esopus War. But in such exceptional circumstances simple defensive patrols were not sufficient. Yet the burgher guard was not suited for offensive action, as it could not be ordered to serve outside its own city. In the few instances that the Company's troops needed supplementing, such as for the expedition against the Swedish colony on the South River in 1655, a call was made for volunteers. No great enthusiasm was forthcoming. Four years later, during the First Esopus War, Stuyvesant found it difficult to recruit volunteers for an expedition to relieve the settlement in the Esopus that was under siege by the Indians.[52] A call was also made for volunteers during the Second Esopus War in 1663, both for the expedition to Wiltwijck and as a supplement to the defense of New Amsterdam. No volunteers were to be found in Beverwijck, while Amersfoort, 's-Gravesande, Midwout, and New Utrecht answered that they were prepared to help in the defense of their neighbors on Long Island but refused to cross the East River.[53]

Such incidents might call into question the fighting spirit and morale, but risky expeditions beyond their own communities were not a traditional task of the burgher guard. Danger was rarely present in the normal task of night patrols. The first ordinance on guard duty stems from 1643 and does not contain much more than a handful of instructions. Swearing was forbidden, as was speaking ill of one's comrades. The guards had to turn up for duty both sober and on time. A few years later a separate guardhouse was built, of which the costs were borne by the WIC. The Company had to ensure that sufficient firewood was available and on several occasions found it necessary to make sure that the guardsmen were adequately armed.[54]

A comprehensive ordinance for the burgher guard in Beverwijck from the early 1650s shows that performing the watch was generally regarded as a tiresome duty. Fines were laid down for absenteeism, arriving late or drunk for duty, and for falling asleep on guard duty. The ordinance also contained rules on obedience to officers and a few stipulations about marching and handling weapons. During marching, no one was allowed to leave or change his line without orders. Neither could a guardsman discharge his gun without an explicit command. Firing at the flag, or windows, or gables, or weather-vanes, or any signs hanging on houses was absolutely forbidden and carried a fine of five guilders. Recalcitrant behavior and expressions of displeasure were clearly not appreciated. A further indication that guard duty was not much enjoyed is that at the end of their term of office, the magistrates of Beverwijck were exempted from serving again for a period of one year.[55]

With all this reluctance to carry out the regular nightly patrols, which was also evident in the Dutch Republic, it is hardly surprising that a solution was sought. In 1654 a first attempt was made in New Amsterdam to set up a so-called *ratelwacht* [rattle guard], but no one was interested. Four years later, it was tried again, and eight men signed on. They were divided into two shifts of four, which were deployed on alternate nights. They had to patrol the city from nine in the evening until sunrise, rattling their rattles at every street corner and calling out the time. In 1659 a rattle guard was established in Beverwijck on the express request of burghers who wanted to be relieved of the burden of guard duties. In the event of fire, the rattle watchmen had to warn the burghers, either by banging on the door or by ringing the church bell. They had to arrest any thieves caught in the act, and the help of the burghers could be called upon for this. And, of course, all forms of unruly nighttime activities and breaches of the peace had to be prevented. If fights broke out, the rattle guard could rely on the magistrates to pay for any damage, and here again explicit reference was made to regulations governing the burgher guard in Amsterdam. In both New Amsterdam and Beverwijck, the salary of the rattle guards was paid by the members of the burgher guard. In this way, the burghers could avoid the onerous night duty that came with membership of the burgher guard and enjoy a good night's sleep instead.[56]

Yet the burgher guard also had its pleasurable sides. The ideal of fellow-ship that lay at the foundations of the burgher guard was cultivated in a parade held during the annual fair. With roll of drums, the companies marched under their respective pennants. Powder for the gun salutes, and pennants, halberds, and drums were supplied by the Company. Although a single mention of parrot shooting shows that in Beverwijck shooting competitions were held, there are no other indications in the records of any other social activities engaged in by the burgher guard. It probably organized communal meals, but no trace can be found of any collective portraits of the burgher guards, such as were painted for the Dutch cities. Such expressions of self-importance were beyond the budget of the colonists.[57]

Burgher right and the burgher guard gave the inhabitants of the communities in New Netherland the opportunity of distinguishing themselves from outsiders and of increasing their sense of self-worth. The regulations for burgher right and the organization of the burgher guard show that the customary forms from the Dutch Republic, and in particular those of Amsterdam, were adopted. Both the aversion to itinerant traders from elsewhere in New Netherland and the unwillingness to come to the aid of other communities point to a gradual shift in what were considered the boundaries of one's community. In the later years of the Dutch rule in the colony, little solidarity existed with the inhabitants of other communities in New Netherland. In this way too, the colony was in conformity with the local particularism that prevailed in the Dutch Republic.[58]

Jews

The burghers saw themselves as the core of colonial society. They were adult, white European men, many of whom were members of the Reformed Church. Other denominations were also present in New Netherland, such as the Lutherans from Germany and Scandinavia and the English Quakers. In the case of individual Lutherans, their religious persuasion was not an insurmountable obstacle in achieving status. However, the situation was fundamentally different for Jews, blacks, and Indians, who had in common that they were not Christian.

At the beginning of the seventeenth century, a Jewish community had sprung up in Amsterdam, consisting mainly of Sephardic Jews from Portugal and Spain. From Amsterdam, they had access to the Dutch colonies in the Atlantic, and it was especially Brazil that attracted their attention, as it allowed them to take full advantage of their Portuguese background, language, and contacts. A number of Jews settled in Brazil after the West India Company conquered Pernambuco, the northeastern part of the Portuguese colony. Objections to their presence arose swiftly. The Amsterdam classis protested, because it saw the Jewish presence as a threat to the spread of the Reformed religion. Great displeasure also arose among the sugar planters in Brazil about the high rate of interest applied by the Jews, who played an important role in financing trade, especially the slave trade. Despite the objections from diverse sides, the West India Company directors in *patria* and their officials in Brazil did not institute measures against the Jews in Pernambuco, who had more rights than was customary in the Dutch Republic.[59]

In the autumn of 1654, a small group of Jews, consisting of twenty-three men, women, and children, arrived in New Amsterdam. They had sailed with a French ship from Recife, which had fallen into Portuguese hands in January 1654, after which the inhabitants had three months to leave. No one was pleased with the arrival of twenty-three destitute Jews. On 22 September 1654, Stuyvesant and the council requested the directors to refuse the Jews permission to remain in the colony. In itself, this was not an exceptional request; in the Netherlands many cities did not permit Jews to take up residence. This was particularly true of the Generality Lands, the southern provinces that the Dutch Republic had conquered over the course of the Eighty Years' War. For example, Jews were not admitted to Tilburg until 1767 or to Maastricht until 1785. The Reformed ministers in New Netherland were not enthusiastic about the arrival of the Jews either, and they supported the request of director general and council in a letter to the classis. According to Megapolensis, the Jews had

> no other God...than the unjust Mammon and no other aim...than to obtain the Christians' goods and to abuse all other merchants, and draw the trade to them alone.[60]

Furthermore, Megapolensis alleged, it caused a great disturbance among the people of New Amsterdam. The aim of the *predikant*'s letter is clear: he wanted the classis to help prevent the Jews from settling in New Netherland.[61]

Just as with the problems surrounding the admission of a Lutheran minister a year earlier, the final decision had to be made in Amsterdam. It is probable that the Jews in New Amsterdam turned for support and intercession to their relatives in Amsterdam, whose assistance they also sought for paying the money they owed for their passage. In January 1655 a number of Jewish merchants in Amsterdam submitted a petition to the directors there, requesting permission for the Jews to remain in New Amsterdam. They also requested permission for Jewish merchants in Amsterdam to trade with the colony. The petition emphasized the great losses the Jews had suffered in Brazil, where they had risked both their livelihood and their lives. The WIC directors granted the Jews permission to live and trade in New Netherland, on the condition that they would not become a burden to the Company or to the deaconry.[62]

In their letter to director general and council, the Amsterdam directors were rather more specific about their motivation for this decision. They wrote:

> We would gladly have put into effect and carried out your wish and request in order that that new conquest [that is, New Netherland] would not be infected any more by any Jewish nation, as we foresee from this the same difficulties which you anticipate.

However, after ample consideration they found that a hard attitude would be somewhat contrary to the "*reden ende billickheijt*" (reason and fairness), not only because of the losses that the Jews had suffered in Brazil, but also because of "*de groote capitalen die sij alsnoch inde compagnie sijn heriderende.*" At the end of the nineteenth century this was translated as "the large amount of capital, which they have invested in shares of this Company."[63]

In my view this translation is faulty. A better version would be "the large sums of money for which they are still indebted to the Company," which would refer to the sums that the Jews still owed the Company.[64]

Some Amsterdam and New Amsterdam Jews were "*hoofdparticipanten*" of the West India Company, as is indicated in the January 1655 petition. This does not mean they were "principal shareholders," as it is often translated, but rather that they had invested a sufficient amount to obtain permission to conduct private trade to Brazil once the monopoly of the Company had been partly lifted. The two extant lists of large shareholders in the Amsterdam chamber, dated 1656 and 1658, contain only a few Jewish names, making it less likely that as a group the Jews had acquired a considerable number of WIC shares. The West India Company did not have to pay much heed to its investors, a trait it shared with the East India Company.[65]

A further question is why the New Amsterdam or the Amsterdam Jews owed the West India Company money. The explanation is that many of the tax farmers in Brazil were Jewish. In total, 63 percent of the tax farming business in Brazil was in Jewish hands. The tax farmers had agreed with the West India Company on the right to collect specific taxes and duties, such as the impost of the weighing in Recife and the *tienden* on sugar cultivation. Although the tax farmers would pay the WIC later, the risk of collection was theirs. It involved considerable sums of money, usually thousands of guilders, occasionally tens of thousands. The *tienden* on sugar cultivation in Pernambuco, for instance, was granted in 1645 to Moses Navarro for ƒ74,000. The Portuguese revolt in Brazil made it impossible, however, for the tax farmers to collect the taxes; yet they still owed the West India Company the lump sum. As the West India Company owed many former soldiers and merchants large sums of money, quick collection of some of its outstanding debts, such as from former tax farmers, was important to its cash flow. Allowing the Jews access to New Netherland and allowing them to trade there would provide them with a way of making money from which the debts to the West India Company could be repaid. It would also further the economic development of New Netherland. Even so, financial arguments were not the sole consideration of the WIC in its decision to grant the Jews access to New Netherland. The other argument that was mentioned, "reason and fairness," referring to the suffering of the Jews in Brazil, was equally important to the Amsterdam directors.[66]

In New Netherland the Amsterdam chamber's decision came as an unpleasant surprise. Director general and council had in March 1655 already informed the New Amsterdam city government that they had decided that the Jews should depart as soon as possible. *Burgemeesters* and *schepenen* replied that they had absolutely no objection to this. Although part of the correspondence between New Amsterdam and Amsterdam is missing, it is reasonable to assume that director general and council attempted to change the Amsterdam directors' minds. From July 1655 onward they made a number of decisions with the objectives of preventing the Jews from becoming permanent residents and of making it so difficult for them that they might leave of their own accord. A request from the Jews for their own burial ground was put off, since there was no immediate need for it. The situation in Amsterdam had been similar. Requests for a Jewish burial ground there had been rejected in 1606 and 1608, and only in 1613 did the Amsterdam Jews buy a plot in Ouderkerk aan de Amstel. In New Netherland, obstacles were also put in the way of the Jews becoming members of the burgher guard. In a petition, the burgher officers referred to

> the aversion and disinclination of the *borgerije* [citizenry] to be partners with the aforesaid nation and to mount guard in the same guardhouse.[67]

They reminded director general and council that Jews were not admitted to the burgher guard anywhere in the Dutch Republic. It was decided that the Jews should pay a special tax instead. When Jacob Barsimson and Assur Levy protested about this to director general and council, they were told that they were free to leave New Netherland whenever they liked. A request from Abraham de Lucena, Salvador d'Andrado, and Jacob Cohen to trade on the South River was refused "for important reasons." The Jews' purchase of real estate was also prevented, again with a reference to "important reasons." In October 1655 five Jewish merchants received exorbitantly high demands in the tax for the defense of New Amsterdam.[68]

Despite all these measures, the Jews decided to stay in New Netherland for the time being. They were strengthened by the policy of the directors, who were disinclined to change their decision. As a result, a number of the anti-Jewish measures were reversed shortly afterwards. In February 1656 the Jews were allotted a piece of land outside the city for a cemetery. A month later, the trade on the South River was opened to them. However, there were limits. As the Amsterdam directors outlined in March 1656, their decision to allow the Jews access to New Netherland applied only to their political and civil rights. The privilege of exercising their religion in a synagogue was not granted, but then, the Jews had not yet asked for this privilege. If such a request were to be made, it should be referred to the Amsterdam chamber. The Jews were permitted to

> exercise their religion within their houses in all quietness..., whereto they will without doubt seek to build and choose their houses close to each other on one or the other side of New Amsterdam, like they have done here.[69]

As in Amsterdam, the Jews were not allowed to practice crafts or "keep open shop." Consequently, a request from Jacob Cohen to open a bakery was refused by the *burgemeesters* of New Amsterdam, even though Cohen promised that it would be "with closed doors" and so would not be public. However, when the *burgemeesters* tried to exclude the Jews from obtaining the small burgher right, they were reprimanded by director general and council. Although the Jews thus had fewer rights than other inhabitants in New Netherland, in court cases they were treated as equals. Account was taken of their Sabbath, even a year before the same happened in Amsterdam. Some consideration was shown to them several years later, when an exception was made for Assur Levy and Moses Lucena during the appointment of sworn butchers. The other butchers were obliged to slaughter any animals brought to them, but Levy and Lucena were granted exemption from slaughtering pigs. They were also given permission to swear an adapted version of the oath. Despite these concessions, the Jews in New Netherland were second-class burghers. Although they were finally granted burgher right, most of the trades, the burgher guard, and the magistracy remained closed to them. They did not obtain freedom of public worship. The decision to allow the Jews to stay in New Netherland was a consequence of the financial problems of the WIC chamber in Amsterdam and the more liberal views of the directors. It is not evidence of a desire for tolerance in the colony. On the contrary, colonists, city government, the ministers, and director and council were united in their anti-Semitism.[70]

Blacks

In the Dutch Republic enslaved labor was not permitted, but it was practiced in all Dutch overseas colonies. In New Netherland, a distinction must be made between slaves and free blacks. It seems an obvious difference to modern eyes, but for the most part it is not indicated in the sources for New Netherland.

Most of the enslaved Africans were owned by the West India Company. At the end of the 1630s Jacob Stoffelsz was overseer of the Company blacks. They were deployed in building and repairing the fort, chopping wood, developing land, burning lime, and gathering crops.[71] All of these activities were physical work for which little training was necessary. In later years the Amsterdam directors were of the opinion that the black slaves should be given instruction in useful crafts. Since experienced craftsmen were expensive, "such trades as carpentering, bricklaying, supervising, blacksmithing, and others, ought to be taught to the *negros* [Negroes]," as was tried in Brazil and Guinea. However, director general and council replied that no blacks were sufficiently competent to be instructed in these trades. Besides physical labor, slaves were also used for household duties. In 1662, director general and council manumitted three older female WIC slaves on condition that every week one of them would do the housework at the director general's residence. Blacks were also deployed in the wars with Indians, both in fighting functions and in supporting duties. Some historians have judged the contribution made by slave labor to the economy of New Netherland as high, and some even doubt whether the transition from trading post to settlement colony could have taken place without the input from slavery. Although without question slavery was important, the supposed indispensability is undermined by the fact that the number of slaves in the colony began to take substantial form only after 1645, when the transition from trading post to settlement colony was already at full pace.[72]

From 1647 to 1654 the WIC slaves were under the supervision of Paulus Heymans and lived together in a house in the *Slijcksteeg* in New Amsterdam. They were regularly hired out to private individuals. The Amsterdam directors disapproved, opining that the blacks could be better employed in repairing Fort Amsterdam.[73]

Becoming Free?

Both slaves in private ownership and those belonging to the Company could gain freedom. Running away was one of the options, but it occurred only on a few occasions. Manumission was fairly common in New Netherland, in most cases under specific conditions, depending on whether they were privately owned or Company slaves. In some instances, the former were set free during the lifetime of their owner. Philip Jansz Ringo granted Manuel de Spanjaard his freedom in 1649, on condition that the latter pay him one hundred guilders on 15 February each year for three years. In the event of default, Ringo would have the right to reclaim Manuel as his slave. In some instances, slaves were freed after the death of their owners. Jan Jansz Damen determined in 1649 that after his death his "West Indian servant maid, named Cicilje, shall be emancipated and completely released from her slavery." No form of payment was required.[74]

Much more extensive and far-reaching were the conditions attached to the freeing of Company slaves. In 1644 eleven slaves who had been in the Company's service for eighteen or nineteen years asked for their freedom. They argued that they had served the Company for a long time and since they had a large number of children, it was impossible to support their wives and children if they remained in the WIC's service. Kieft and his council decided to set them "free and at liberty, like other free people in New Netherland," but under conditions that rightly have been labeled "half freedom." It could equally well have been called "half slavery." The first condition was that per person they had to pay to the Company thirty *schepels* of maize, grain, or other agricultural products annually, together with one fat pig at a value of twenty guilders. This was a lifelong obligation, and in the case of default the blacks would relapse into slavery. The second condition was that, if their services were called for, they would be obliged to serve the WIC on normal terms of payment.[75]

The third condition was the most controversial. Both their existing children and any children as yet unborn would "remain bound and obligated to serve the honorable West India Company as *lijffeygenen* [serfs]."[76] Van der Donck, who had been trained in law, protested against this in his *Vertoogh van Nieu Nederlandt:*

> There are also several other *negers* [Negroes] here in the country, of which some have been made free, because of their long service, yet their children remain slaves, [which is] against all natural law, that someone who is born of a free Christian mother, yet is a slave, and must remain servile.[77]

The reasons of Kieft and his council to attach such conditions to manumission are unknown. Possibly financial arguments played a role. Slaves were expensive, and labor was scarce. Requiring an annual payment and obliging the freed slave to serve the Company when asked can to some extent be explained by this. The third point, child slavery, is the most complicated. As slavery did not exist in the Dutch Republic, director and council could not fall back on existing practices in their decision. It is by no means certain that authorities in New Netherland in 1640s were aware of customary manumission regulations in other Dutch colonies. Inventing a regulation of their own without precedent was a novelty into which the seventeenth-century mind was hesitant to wander. Possibly director and council based their reasoning on Exodus 21:4, which stipulates that if slaves marry during slavery, the wife and their issue remain the property of the slaveowner. It is not inconceivable that this is the basis for the concept of "half freedom," although it would have required consultation with the WIC directors. Van der Donck was trained in Dutch-Roman law, and his condemnation suggests that in the Dutch Republic there might indeed have been legal opinion forming about slavery in the colonies, but the question then is whether Kieft and his councilors were aware of this. The matter was raised again in 1650 during the inquiry by the States General into the complaints of the delegation from New Netherland, but little sign can be found of a clear decision in the Dutch Republic. Nevertheless, the stipulation that children would continue to be slaves was not repeated in later manumissions. In several instances the condition that a regular payment had to be made was applied. There were also cases of once-only payments. In December 1663, Domingo Angola was obliged either to pay three hundred guilders or to provide another slave in exchange for the freeing of the eighteen-year-old Christina, who had been baptized in 1645. Two months later she married Swan van Loange, a slave of Govert Loockermans, who supplied the money to purchase her freedom.[78]

At the same time that they were granted their "half freedom," the blacks were allotted pieces of land on Manhattan, for the most part a few acres in size. The parcels were situated beside the *gemeene wagenweg* (common wagon road), to the north of New Amsterdam and near the director's farm. Gradually, a settlement developed there consisting of some free blacks and some of Stuyvesant's slaves. Both in that neighborhood and in New Amsterdam, the blacks had considerable freedom of movement. As a result, they could find their own marital partners, although they may have had to seek the permission of their owners prior to the solemnization of marriage, in the same way that the permission of the parents or guardians was required before the marriage of a minor. In some instances the slaveowners took the marital partners into consideration. When in 1664 Jeremias van Rensselaer bought a slave from the WIC, Stuyvesant insisted that Jeremias also purchase the woman with whom the black had a relationship.[79]

In addition to freedom of movement in their personal lives, the blacks, both free and slaves, had some legal rights. Anthony de Portugees, one of the slaves freed in 1644, lodged a complaint in 1638 against Anthony Jansz van Salee, because the latter had injured his pig. This case indicates that the slaves not only had rights of ownership but could also start legal proceedings against free persons. Other instances indicate that slaves were paid for work and that their statements of evidence were also legally valid.

Enslaved people were protected against ill treatment by their masters or others. In 1638, Gijsbert Opdijck had to make a statement about an incident with his black boy, Lourviso Barbosse, who during an argument with his master had fallen onto a knife and sustained fatal injuries. He stated that it had been an accident, and thus no action was taken against him. In a few cases blacks were injured in fights, and the court dealt with the matter in the same way as when other colonists were involved. An illustration of the fact that slaveowners could not inflict unlimited punishment on their slaves is provided by the request made by Pieter Cornelisz van der Veen in 1659, when he asked the *burgemeesters'* permission to chastise his female slave. He was granted permission but did not make use of it.[80]

In cases in which blacks were charged, the courts in New Netherland showed little distinction between blacks and whites in their treatment of them. Besides a number of civil cases involving blacks, several criminal incidents occurred. Theft was the most common offense. In 1661, the ten-year-old Lijsbet Anthony, property of minister Drisius's wife, stole some black *sewant* from her mistress. The New Amsterdam court sentenced her to a whipping, to be carried out by her mother in the presence of the magistrates. In instances of sodomy, too, the court displayed clemency for children. Jan Creoly in 1646 was sentenced to strangulation, after which his body was burned. Manuel Congo, the ten-year-old boy upon whom Jan Creoly had committed this offence, got away with a whipping, although he was compelled to watch the execution of Jan Creoly. In the well-known case of the murder of Jan Premero in 1641, charges were brought against eight Company slaves. Lots were drawn, indicating which one of them was to be hanged. The ropes broke as the sentence was carried out, and at the request of the onlookers, who saw this as a judgment of God, pardon was granted. In the case of the black girl Lijsbet Antonissen, who had started a fire in the house of her owner, former *burgemeester* Marten Kregier, the court displayed equal clemency. The sentence was that she be strangled and her body burned, but although she had to undergo all the preparations for the execution of her sentence, she was granted mercy at the last moment and was returned to her owner.[81]

Slavery in New Netherland is usually characterized as a relatively mild form, especially when compared with English colonies to the south and in the Caribbean, where slave labor was of major importance to the sugar and tobacco plantations. This does not alter the fact that blacks, whether free or slave, were at the bottom of the social ladder in New Netherland and had little chance of improving their situations. The blacks' low status compared with that of the whites is apparent from the fact that being compelled to work with the Company slaves was also occasionally handed down as a punishment for whites who had committed a felony. Slaves were also employed as executioners, a job that was generally seen as dishonorable and repugnant. Sexual contact with slaves was forbidden, as is apparent from an ordinance of 1638, the same year that Sergeant Nicolaes Coorn was demoted to the rank of common soldier for this offense. Although they were treated equally in court cases, examples show that the blacks were looked down upon. Michaëlius described a few female Angolan slaves as "thievish, lazy, and unseemly raggety people." Jeremias van Rensselaer displayed no less disdain when in making mention of a situation in 1664 he said that as little attention was paid to his words "as if my *neeger* [Negro] had said it.'[82]

Even when blacks had become free they still found themselves at the bottom of colonial society. Although they could support themselves by farming their own land, their lack of financial means, education, and training prevented them from bettering their position. In many ways, they were worse off than the contract workers and farm laborers. No blacks are listed among the burghers, nor were free blacks included in the burgher guard.[83] New Netherland never became a slave society or a creole society. Although its regime may have been of a mild nature, it was still slavery. The status of blacks, enslaved or not, was low.

Indians

The relations of the colonists with the Indians were of a completely different nature. From the perspective of the colonists, Indians were not members of the community. They remained outsiders, who in some cases lived nearby, visited the Dutch settlements regularly (especially Fort Orange and Beverwijck), engaged in trade, and at times worked for the colonists. Many of the contacts between colonists and Indians involved land agreements, negotiations, and peace treaties. These are "foreign" policy agreements, to which regular judicial procedure did not apply.

Most of the contacts between the colonists and the Indians stemmed from the fur trade, which prompted the illegal sale of alcohol and arms. It is apparent from various examples that the Indians were of service to the colonists in different ways in exchange for payment. The instructions for Krijn Fredericksz contained the suggestion to employ the Indians to help the construction of Fort Amsterdam. They were to receive a salary equal to half that of the colonists. Whether Fredericksz followed the instruction is unknown. A later example shows that eight Esopus Indians assisted Thomas Chambers in Wiltwijck in bringing in the maize crops. It is possible that Indians helped at harvest time on other occasions as well, but the sources are mostly silent on this. Indians were also used as couriers. Letters within New Netherland were usually sent by ship, but in the event of urgent news an Indian was dispatched overland on foot, as when Wiltwijck was besieged by the Esopus Indians in October 1659. Indians were used regularly as couriers for the correspondence between director general and council in New Amsterdam and the director of New Amstel, Jacob Alrichs. In the winter, when the river was frozen over, it was customary to send an Indian at least once on the overland trip between Beverwijck and New Amsterdam to deliver letters. This practice was continued after the Dutch period. In December 1680, for example, Thomas Chambers wrote to Maria van Rensselaer, Jeremias van Rensselaer's widow, that he had given "a very fit, young *wildt*" among other things a duffel coat to deliver a letter.[84]

In both these instances, Thomas Chambers paid in kind, in 1659 in the form of alcohol, in 1680 in textiles. Other colonists were not so prompt in paying. In September 1648 director general and council promulgated an ordinance in which the colonists were warned that if they had Indians working for them they should pay them properly. Defaulting on payment was "against all public law," but a second argument was also used in the motivation for the ordinance: the "*Indianen* threaten, if they are not satisfied and paid, to pay themselves or to revenge themselves with other improper means." Just as in the prohibition of the sale of alcohol and weapons, the importance of good relations with the Indians played a significant role. The ordinance specified that colonists could be ordered to pay by the courts, "on the representation and complaint of *wilden*, who for good reasons in this case will be given credence."[85] This suggests that in other instances Indians may not have been accepted as legal witnesses.

There are very few instances of notarial statements involving Indians being used as evidence in court cases. Neither are there general laws or ordinances on the admissibility of Indian testimony. It is therefore interesting to examine how Indians were looked upon in cases in the smaller courts of law and the extent to which their testimony was legally valid. In many cases the courts came into contact with the Indians. For the most part, the Indians were victims of unlawful actions of colonists. If a colonist was the accused party, the question whether the court was qualified to pronounce sentence was relatively simple, and the only concern was whether the evidence of Indians was admissible. Matters were more complicated if an Indian committed an offense within what the colonial government considered its area of jurisdiction.[86]

Conflicting Jurisdictions

First the cases in which charges were brought against colonists. On 28 October 1638 Cors Pietersz was summoned for assaulting and robbing an Indian. The charge was based on a complaint made by the Indians and the testimony of two colonists. Both Sivert Cant and Frederick Lubbertsz were heard by the court, and on the basis of their evidence Cors Pietersz was sentenced. The Indian did not give evidence, but the stolen goods were returned to him. This is the pattern repeated in many instances. Indians could draw the attention of the *fiscael* or *schout* to an incident, but their statements were accepted as admissible evidence only in specific instances, for example, in cases in which alcohol had been sold to them. An ordinance of 1654 required that drunken Indians be locked up until they revealed the names of the people who had supplied them with the alcohol. Such a revelation was considered to be admissible evidence. The stipulation was repeated at the time of the problems with the fur trade in the early 1660s. An interesting point mentioned here is that the suspect might be obliged to deny his guilt under oath, even when the Indians did not swear an oath. An oath sworn by non-Christians and dishonorable people was not valid. It is probable that the Indians were implicitly placed in these categories, which would explain the exceptions laid down in this ordinance.[87]

The sale of alcohol was a constant problem, and in 1662 director general and council even went so far that they empowered Oratam and Mattano, two *sachems* of the Hackensack,

> to seize the brandy brought into their country for sale as well as those offering to sell it and report them here, to be punished as an example to others.[88]

Although this did not go so far as to give the Indians the right to try colonists, it does indicate how the separation of geographical jurisdictions was perceived. Two months after this authorization it appeared that the onus of proof was difficult in such cases. Jacob Wolphertsz van Couwenhoven was caught trying to transport alcohol to the "Nevesing, a pl[ace] whereabouts no Christians are residing, and only *wilde barbaren* [wild barbarians], but a lack of evidence meant that the case did not result in a conviction.[89]

Incidences of theft and assault were regular occurrences. Manslaughter or murder were less common and attracted severe penalties. When in 1660 colonists killed three Indians on the South River, Stuyvesant dispatched *Fiscael* Nicasius de Sille to investigate the matter. He also empowered a number of men, both WIC officials and magistrates from New Amstel and New Amsterdam, to try the case. De Sille was given the explicit order to ensure that a few *sachems* were present both at the trial and the execution. This was obviously intended to prevent matters from escalating into a war.[90]

Second, we turn to the cases in which the Indians were the offenders. Although numerous incidents can be found in which drunken Indians caused trouble, virtually no cases occurred in which the court pronounced sentence. In a small number of cases Indians were arrested and locked up to sleep off their drunkenness, but even when the incident involved fighting, the magistrates were principally interested in discovering who had supplied the alcohol.[91] In serious cases, such as murder and manslaughter, the provincial government had virtually no means at its disposal for dealing with offenders in a way it considered appropriate. Sometimes the colonial government requested the extradition of an Indian, but even when the Indians were not prepared to jeopardize the peace, they rarely acceded to such a request. Noncompliance with requests for extradition was one of the causes of Kieft's War in the 1640s. In later years, this sort of problem was generally solved by means of negotiation.

Sex

Another form of contact between the colonists and the Indians lay in the sphere of sex. In his *Historisch Verhael,* Nicolaes van Wassenaer displayed his interest in the sexual mores of the Indians. He established, probably on the basis of accounts given by people who had returned from the colony, that chastity could be found among the Indians, but that some women were more casual. A number of reports confirm that sexual relations between Europeans and Indians were a regular occurrence. *Predikant* Megapolensis stated:

> The women are exceedingly inclined to whoring; they will be bedfellows for the value of one, two, or three *schellingen* [shillings], and our Dutchmen debauch themselves very much with the whores.[92]

David Pietersz de Vries heard from a *sachem* that several children among the Indians had been fathered by colonists. And during negotiations in Beverwijck in 1659, the Mohawks demanded that white men who had carried on a relation with an Indian woman should provide gifts to her family on her death.[93]

Sexual relations between whites and Indians were a regular phenomenon, then, virtually always between a white man and an Indian woman. Nothing indicates that the opposite ever took place in the Dutch period. That these relations occurred does not of course imply that they were generally accepted. Kiliaen van Rensselaer warned Arent van Curler:

> And above all be careful not to mix with the *heidense off wilde vrouwen* [heathen or Indian women], for such things are a great abomination to the Lord God and kill the souls of the Christians when they debauch with themselves. Therefore work and move in the council that an ordinance be issued imposing severe fines and punishment on those who are found guilty of it.[94]

In 1638, sex with heathens, whether they be blacks or Indians, was forbidden, and several convictions followed. It was not only the salvation of the soul that was at risk but also honor. In a court case in 1641 Jan Jansz Damen stated that Jan Platneus was "a perjurer and incompetent to give any testimony, because he has committed adultery with *wildinnen* [Indian women]."[95]

Both the convictions and the remark made by Jan Jansz Damen date from around 1640. Expressions of disapproval are also found in later years, but these had no legal implications. Van der Donck wrote of Cornelis van Tienhoven that he

> has run about the same as a *wilt* [Indian], with a little cloth and a small patch in front, from lust after the whores to whom he has always been mightily inclined, and with whom he has so much to do.[96]

It is probable that the scarcity of women played a role in the extent of sexual interaction with the Indians. But this was not true in every individual case. Arent van Curler was married to a Dutch woman but despite Kiliaen van Rensselaer's warning had a child by a Mohawk woman, possibly conceived prior to his marriage. Cornelis Teunisz van Slijck also had children by a Mohawk woman. One of them, Hilletie, grew up with the Mohawks, married a colonist, Pieter Daniëlsz van Olinda, and subsequently lived in Schenectady for a long time. She acted as an interpreter between Indians and whites but was viewed with contempt by both. The repugnance and disdain that writers such as Van der Donck, Megapolensis, and De Rasière displayed for the Indians surfaced in only a single occasion in the court records of New Netherland, and it did not concern the treatment of Indians but colonists calling one another "Indian" and "Indian dog."[97]

Some colonists developed good personal relations with the Indians. Arent van Curler was on good terms with both the Mohawks and the Mahicans. He acted as an intermediary in purchases of land and in diplomatic negotiations, and his death by drowning in Lake Champlain was mourned greatly by both the colonists and the Mohawks.[98] While Van Curler attained a prominent position in both societies, several others overstepped the boundaries between both nations. In 1660, director general and council asked the directors in Amsterdam to arrest "a certain person, commonly called Jacob *mijn vrient* [my friend]," of whom it was understood that he wanted to return to Holland via Virginia. He had

> some years ago fled from here with sums of money given to him by several people to go to the South River to trade with the *wilden* [Indians], has since that time lived for years as a *wilt* [Indian] among the *mincquaesse wilden* [Minquas Indians], married a *wildin* [Indian woman] or used her as concubine and procreated several children with her, [has] by his flight and sojourn among the *wilden,* caused much damage, diversion of trade and troubles to the Honorable Company and the inhabitants here.[99]

The main motive for his arrest was not that Jacob had consorted with the Indians; it was the embezzlement, which marked him as a dishonorable man. Sexual interaction with Indian women added to the dishonor. Another one who sought salvation with the Indians was Harmen Meyndertsz van den Bogaert. Toward the end of 1647 he was accused of sodomy with Tobias, a young Company slave, and took refuge with the Indians, where Hans Vos, *gerechtsbode* of Rensselaerswijck, tracked him down. In an attempt to defend himself, Van den Bogaert set fire to one of the Indian houses, and the food supply for the winter, together with a quantity of *sewant* and beaver pelts, went up in smoke. The Indians demanded payment of damages, and Van den Bogaert's garden in New Amsterdam was sold to defray the costs. Van den Bogaert himself died when, in a second attempt at flight, he went through the ice of the North River and drowned. Both "Jacob mijn Vrient" and Harmen Meyndertsz van den Bogaert had specific reasons for leaving the colonial society and joining the Indians. There may have been more such incidents about which no information is available.[100]

Indian Slavery

Finally, the few instances of Indian slavery deserve our attention. During Kieft's War, a number of Indians were captured. Some of them were killed in a brutal manner, but in April 1644 a captive was given to two Company soldiers who were returning to the Dutch Republic. In September 1644 these soldiers, Pieter Ebel and Pieter Cock, entered into a contract with Harmanus Meijer to display the "*wilde Indiaen* named Jaques given to them by the governor there" at fairs in *patria*. The notary reminded them that it was not permitted to keep "in these United [Nether]lands any slaves or serfs." The references to Jaques are tantalizing, especially considering the engraving Wenceslaus Hollar made of "Unus American ex Virginia" in 1645. As

"Virginia" was regularly used to indicate New Netherland, and as Hollar spent some time in the Netherlands in these years, there is a distinct possibility that the depicted Indian is in fact Jaques.[101]

Both soldiers later returned to America, where they settled. Nineteen years later, Pieter Ebel acted as an interpreter in negotiations with the Wappinger Indians and the Esopus Indians. Apparently the Indians did not think that the incident in 1644 made him an unacceptable interpreter, although they may not have connected him with the incident. Yet the gift of a prisoner of war to soldiers did not go unchallenged. The Eight Men complained to the Amsterdam chamber:

> The captured *wilde,* who could have been of great service to us as good guides, have been given to the soldiers as presents, and allowed to go to Holland; the others [have been sent off] to the Bermudas as a present to the English governor.[102]

The objections thus were on practical grounds and not a matter of principle.[103]

Indian children are sometimes found in the sources in the Dutch period, but the question remains whether they were slaves. It is possible that they were raised within a colonist's family in an attempt to convert them. In the inventory of the insolvent estate of Willem Quick, the last item is "1 *wilt* [Indian] child."[104] However, such references are so scarce that it is safe to assume that Indian slavery occurred only rarely, if at all.

The relations with the Indians were of a fundamentally different character from those with the non-Christian groups such as the Jews and the blacks. The essential difference was that the Indians were not part of the colonial society. In the trade with and the employment of Indians, some degree of respect is evident in the ordinances on problems with alcohol, weapons, and the payment of salaries. The correct treatment of the Indians was laid down explicitly, although this does not mean that it was always adhered to. In diplomatic negotiations, the principal objective was to prevent friction and war, which rendered circumspection and a little willingness to please necessary. The conduct of proceedings in the courts displays the same tendency, but it is clear that Indians were not really treated as equals. The specifications concerning the depositions and the furnishing of proof are demonstrations of this. On the other hand, it is evident that the colonists' attitude changed in the course of the seventeenth century. The inequality is also apparent from the general condemnation of colonists engaging in sexual relations with Indians. Although Indian slavery was extremely rare and mainly the result of wars, its existence also indicates the low status of Indians in European eyes.

7   *Living in a Colony*

In 1929 Helen W. Reynolds published her book *Dutch Houses in the Hudson Valley before 1776*. Franklin Delano Roosevelt, at that time governor of New York State, wrote an introduction. Roosevelt was proud of his Dutch background.[1] In his introduction, he stated that

> the mode of life of the first settlers of New Netherland and of their immediate descendants was extremely simple, a statement which is true not only of the smaller landowners but of many of the patentees of large grants. From high to low their lives were the lives of pioneers, lives of hardship, of privation and often of danger. Roads were few and rough, household belongings modest, and the dwelling that contained more than four rooms was an exception.[2]

The achievements of the settlers, founders of the new America, were emphasized, and increasing the difficulty of the colonial circumstances heightened their status. But were living conditions in New Netherland really much different from those of simple farm laborers in seventeenth-century Drenthe, one of the poorest regions of the Dutch Republic, or even the slightly more prosperous province of Zeeland, from where Roosevelt's ancestors are supposed to have originated?

Houses and Belongings

Roosevelt's statement about "the first settlers of New Netherland" was not justified by the content of Reynolds's book. Most of the houses Reynolds described date from the eighteenth century. Few seventeenth-century houses remained in the 1920s, when her book was published, and of those the majority were built after 1675. Her descriptions are to a large extent of

8. New Amsterdam of 1660. Few images are extant from daily life in the Dutch colony. To fill this gap, nineteenth-century artists produced their own, like this one, often including details that modern scholarship would not regard as authentic. Print. Picture Collection, The Branch Libraries, The New York Public Library, Astor, Lenox and Tilden Foundations.

farmhouses built in stone or brick, and few wooden houses have been preserved. Little is left of buildings from the New Netherland period. The two most important remaining houses are the stone Bronck House dating from about 1663 in Coxsackie, now a museum, and the wooden Wyckoff House in Brooklyn, believed to have been built between 1638 and 1641. If so, it would be the oldest house in New York State and possibly in the entire United States.[3]

In the early years of New Netherland, dwellings were undoubtedly primitive. A 1650 description provides detail:

People who in the beginning do not have means to build farm-houses as required, in New Netherland and especially in New England dig a square pit in the ground like a cellar, six to seven feet deep, as long and as broad as they think fit, [and] cover the earth inside with timber against the wall, and cover the timber with bark of trees or something else against the caving in of the earth, put over the cellar beams and woodwork to form a ceiling, put a roof of spruces on it, and cover the spruces with bark and green sods, so that the people can live dry and warm for two, three, or four years in such cellars, with their families, as in the same cellars rooms are partitioned off depending on the size of the family.[4]

In later decades new colonists may still have started with simple dugout houses if they were unable to buy existing houses. Such houses are similar to the *plaggenhutten* (literally: "sod houses") that were used in Drenthe as late as the nineteenth century.[5]

Better accommodations than covered dugouts were constructed quickly. A number of contracts for the construction of houses built in New Netherland in the 1640s have survived. Some were built of stone or brick imported as ship's ballast, but most of the contracts are for wooden houses. Using these contracts, three types of houses in New Netherland can be found: one-, two-, and three-aisle houses. These houses were principally rural structures similar to wooden houses in the province of North Holland, particularly those in the Waterland area, from where some of the colonists originated.[6]

In both the Waterland and the New Netherland houses, timber frame construction was used, in which the frame of beams, often H-shaped, was surrounded with *clapborden* (clapboards). These planks, constructed on a stone or brick footing, overlapped to ensure the adequate drainage of water. The length of the houses varied according to the number of aisles from thirty to sixty feet (8.25 to 16.5 meters, based on an Amsterdam *voet* [foot] of eleven *duim* [inches] of 2.5 centimeters). The rooms were between eighteen and twenty-four feet wide (4.95 to 6.60 meters). Such dimensions meant that generally the houses had only two rooms, plus an attic, used for storage. In one or more of the rooms, or in a side aisle in the case of multi-aisle houses, *bedsteden* (box beds, beds partitioned off from the rest of the room by paneling) were built. The flue was generally situated in the middle of the house, but in the early period chimneys were made of wood, while the roofs were thatched. Some houses had no chimney at all, with the smoke escaping through a hole in the roof. The costs of building a house, which took up to eight weeks, generally amounted to several hundred guilders.[7]

Wooden houses, thatched roofs, and wooden chimneys implied a considerable risk of fire, especially as the density of the housing in New Amsterdam and Beverwijck increased. Early in 1648 fire had broken out in two houses in New Amsterdam because the chimneys had not been properly swept. This prompted the provincial government to appoint three fire masters to inspect the chimneys. At the same time, the new construction of wooden chimneys was forbidden. After the Indian attack on New Amsterdam in 1655, director general and council decided that the farms in the hamlets had to be built close to each other for mutual defense. The use of thatched roofs for new houses was also prohibited. Similar measures were adopted in New Amsterdam. Despite some resistance from the population, a gradual changeover to stone or brick construction took place in New Amsterdam and Beverwijck. In less densely populated settlements, this process probably proceeded slower.[8]

Although this changeover began in New Amsterdam and Beverwijck, little is left of the Dutch colonial architecture in these places, due to the fires in New York at the end of the eighteenth and the beginning of the nineteenth centuries, as well as the development of both places into modern cities. Elsewhere, for instance in the stockade parts of Schenectady and Kingston, old houses are extant, but the majority date from the eighteenth and nineteenth century. Additionally, many eighteenth-century houses and barns spread around the states of New York and New Jersey show traces of Dutch architecture.[9]

Yet these eighteenth-century houses are not similar to contemporary Dutch buildings and are evidence of a divergence of style. The construction contracts of houses built in New Netherland prior to 1664 show that building practices were still closely modeled on Dutch origins. In some instances locally available building materials were used, such as stone, brick, and timber, but this did not lead directly to a change in the essential characteristics of the houses. A change did not come about until the middle of the eighteenth century. Several factors contributed to this. The influence of English architectural styles, the availability of local building materials that required other techniques, and the sparse contact with the Dutch Republic created the blend of styles that has been labeled as Dutch-American. This divergence of the lines of development of the colony and *patria* led to changes of sufficient magnitude that few modern Dutchmen would identify the old houses along the Hudson and in New Jersey as typically Dutch.[10]

On the Inside

Houses are often included in inventories drawn up for inheritance purposes, but these usually provide more information on the furnishings and goods inside. Unfortunately, the number of inventories from the Dutch period is small, and they are quite diverse. Several inventories were drawn up for farmhands and sailors, whose possessions consisted of a chest containing some clothing and, in some instances, a little merchandise. Eight inventories are those of established colonists, but only three extensive inventories list clothing, household effects, and books.[11] A number of conclusions can be drawn from the furniture, clothing, tableware, ornaments, and books described in the early inventories, in combination with information from other sources and from archaeological excavations.[12]

First, the items that are rarely or never mentioned in the inventories. Papers of value, such as shares or bonds do not appear in the New Netherland inventories. In exceptional cases a list contained outstanding debts. Houses are usually included. For example, the inventory of the possessions of Jonas Bronck includes his stone house roofed with tiles. But in the case of Jan Jansz Damen, the house that he had built three years before his death is not included. Neither is his land, while it is certain that he owned land on Manhattan.[13]

Silver money is rarely mentioned in New Netherland inventories, nor in other North American colonies. An exception is the list of the possessions of Vrouwtje Ides and Jacob Stoffelsz. The estate included a sum of about 185 guilders in coins, mostly *gouden Jacobussen* (golden Jacobs), *Hollandse schellingen* (Dutch shillings), and *rijksdaalders* (rix-dollars, worth two-and-a-half guilders). They also had an amount of *sewant* in the house. Coins appear relatively infrequently in the inventories, while occasionally some money in *sewant* and beavers was included. Virtually no mention is made of money in the inventories of the less well-to-do, and even in the case of the not impecunious Jonas Bronck, no cash appears in the inventory.[14]

Gold, silver, and jewelry on the other hand feature regularly in the inventories: golden jewelry and silver spoons or other cutlery. Probably, most of the rings listed were wedding rings. After Daniël van Krieckenbeeck was killed by Indians in 1626, Secretary Isaac de Rasière sent his ring to the directors in Amsterdam to be passed on to his wife. Other items of jewelry also appear in the lists, such as silver pendants with pearls or *oorijzers* (literally: "ear irons"). In 1661, magistrate Rutger Jacobsz in Beverwijck used a number of objects as collateral against a debt, including three gold rings, a gold chain, a golden pin, two pairs of gold *oorstricken* (ear ornaments), a pair of *halve manen* (crescents), fourteen silver spoons, two silver beakers, a silver dish, and a silver salt cellar. Gold and silver objects without exception were imported from the Dutch Republic. The correspondence of Jeremias van Rensselaer shows that orders were placed regularly for jewelry. For example, in 1660 Jeremias asked for gold *oorijzers* for Margaretha van Slichtenhorst, wife of Philip Pietersz Schuyler. A silver chalice for the celebration of the Lord's Supper in the Beverwijck church was also ordered in the Dutch Republic in 1660. In the later seventeenth century, objects in precious metals began to be made in America, and these followed the Dutch style for many years.[15]

Because of their small size, items of jewelry were easy for colonists to take with them from the Dutch Republic. Furniture was a different matter. Often, chairs and tables were sold prior to going to New Netherland or given to someone in the Dutch Republic to look after. In most cases household furniture was made in the colony, probably by carpenters or by the colonists themselves. In the early years chests were used as chairs or tables. Some scarce references to furniture can be found in correspondence. In 1661, Jeremias van Rensselaer took delivery of, among other things, eight Spanish chairs, a mirror, a *leedekant* (bed), and a *kassie* (small cupboard) from the Dutch Republic. The chairs had been ordered on the account of the patroonship and were intended for sessions of the court of Rensselaerswijck, which had previously used pinewood benches.[16]

Little pre-1664 furniture remains. The collections of the Albany Institute of History and Art and of the Museum of the City of New York contain "Dutch" chairs, tables, cupboards, and chests, but these date from the late seventeenth century and the eighteenth century. This concurs with the evidence from inventories: chairs and tables are included in only a few cases. Jonas Bronck's inventory contains an extending table and two mirrors, one with an ebony frame, the other with a gilded frame. Aeltje Jans possessed, among other things, three old chairs and an old mirror. The inventory of Jan Jansz Damen lists six green doeskin cushions in the front room and three old chairs in the barn connected to the house. His other furniture consisted of a single small table. Surgeon Gijsbert van Imbroch, whose inventory is very extensive, owned but a few items of furniture: two benches, seven chairs, a barber's chair, and a square table, while a round table also appeared at the auction of his goods. The proceeds from the sale of his furniture amounted to thirty-six guilders and thirty stivers, while the total value of the goods sold was more than 2,500 guilders in *sewant*. Few chairs and tables were available in New Netherland, and they were of little value. In this, the colony was no different from the Dutch Republic.[17]

Other furniture was more common. Chests in particular can be found in virtually all inventories. They were used to transport goods and, once in the colony, served as storage space and as seating and tables. Whenever chests are listed in the inventories, a summary was made of their contents, but little is known about the chests themselves. Sometimes their size or color is indicated. The majority were made of wood, although there may have been a few iron chests, serving as strongboxes. Cupboards seldom appear, for the same reason that few chairs and tables occur. Later in the seventeenth century and the eighteenth century, chests were made that resembled those of the Dutch Republic, although the type of wood used and their construction were generally different.[18]

Beds are rare in the inventories, as people usually slept in box beds, of which none appear in the lists, as they were unmovable goods. If a bed is listed, it usually indicates mattress, and these are more common. The mattress, among the meager possessions of Hans Nelisz, was filled with straw, a rare specification. Jan Jansz Damen's large front room contained an old half bed with a bolster, a whole bed with a bolster, four pillows, two green blankets, a white woolen blanket, and two white sheets, as well as a chamber pot. The box bed, evident from the construction contract, was not listed in the inventory. Bedclothes can be found in almost all inventories. The exceptions are the few lists of possessions of the itinerant merchants, who rented rooms. The insolvent estate of Willem Quick included a mattress, a pillow, three blankets, five sheets, and two pillowcases, which was the full extent of his bedclothes. In a few cases, curtains were also listed along with the bedclothes, sometimes with the specification that this referred to box-bed curtains. Curtains for windows are not mentioned.[19]

Textiles

Apart from bedclothes, other textile goods also feature in the inventories. Towels, handkerchiefs, tablecloths, napkins, and diapers appear in the lists, but table linen is not usually to be found in the estates of the less well off. Other textile piece goods measured in yards are listed in several estates. This was cloth destined either to be made into clothing or to be traded with the Indians. By far the majority of textiles mentioned in the estates occurs in the form of clothing. Little clothing appears in the inventories of poor colonists; if it did, it was often worn out. The estate of Willem Quick and Anna Metfoort included four skirts, three shirts, six undershirts, three aprons, and two pairs of stockings. Most of it was women's clothing. While Anna Metfoort kept the clothes in which she was clad, making the inventory incomplete, it is nonetheless notable that no men's clothing is listed.

Probably Willem Quick owned little more clothing than that in which he was buried. Luxurious items of apparel made of expensive material in colors other than black or brown are only included in the inventories of prosperous colonists. Jan Jansz Damen owned a new crimson waistcoat, a suit made of colored bombazine, a colored doeskin suit with piping, and a red nightcap. Some clothing in the inventory of Gijsbert van Imbroch also indicates prosperity, such as a leather jacket with silver and golden braiding, silk stockings, and a velvet cap. Shoes appear in almost all inventories, but the eighty pairs of men's shoes that Jacob Jacobsz Roy kept in a chest were without doubt intended for commercial purposes. In the colony's early years, shoes were imported from the Dutch Republic, mostly to order. Anna van Rensselaer wrote to her sons in the colony: "If you again order shoes, write me what kind of leather you want, for I cannot dream that."[20] The fur used in clothing in New Netherland was obtained from the trade with the Indians. The estate of Vrouwtje Ides and Jacob Stoffelsz contained a fur hat with beaver lining. Gijsbert van Imbroch owned two Indian nightcaps, probably made of fur.[21]

In addition to clothing, tableware, such as pewter plates, bowls, and beakers, is the most prominent category of goods in the inventories. The estate of Vrouwtje Ides and Jacob Stoffelsz contained ten plates, one jug, one dish, two beakers, four funnels, one small goblet, one mug, and one mustard pot, all made of pewter. Wooden plates are rare. Pewter tableware was more common in the estates of wealthy colonists, but there also is earthenware. This was often the red, lead-glazed variety and occasionally majolica, which is often found during excavations. China is rarely found in the inventories. An exception was Jonas Bronck, who owned a chest containing many pieces of china. He also had six alabaster saucers, equally exceptional. Normal kitchenware, such as kettles and pans, was mostly made of copper, iron, or bronze. Cutlery is found less frequently than crockery. Spoons are regularly included, the majority of which were of pewter. Forks were extremely rare and do not appear in the inventories. The only man known to have possessed forks was Jeremias van Rensselaer who, when he went to the colony in 1654, took fourteen pairs of knives and forks with him, possibly for trading purposes. Knives feature in a few inventories, but it is likely that more than those listed were present. It was common for men to carry a knife with them, both for defensive purposes and to eat with. Glassware is encountered regularly in excavations but is relatively rarely found in the inventories. Most of it consisted of beer glasses, *roemers* (rummers; green wineglasses with a wide top part), and bottles.[22]

Food and Drink

The inventories provide little information on the daily victuals that filled the pewter plates. Some farm house inventories list stocks of grain, and it may be assumed that part of the grain was intended for trade or sowing. The meager estate of Hans Nelisz contained a barrel of bacon fat, and in the case of Jan Reijersz, we find some butter and maize meal.[23] Up to about 1635, the colony did not yield sufficient victuals to meet the needs of all the colonists. *Predikant* Jonas Michaëlius complained in 1628 that "food here is scanty and poor." The hard fare consisted of "beans and gray peas, which are hard enough, barley, stockfish etc. without much change."[24] The minister may have been used to a better standard of living, but such fare was normal for the lower classes in the Dutch Republic as well as on board ships. Stockfish, for example, was regularly eaten by the poor in the Dutch Republic. Butter and milk were scarce in the colony. After the hard early years, most of the daily fare was produced in the colony itself. Detailed information can be gleaned from the instructions in 1654 to the Company's jailer. He was allocated twelve stivers per day for the provisions for the ordinary prisoners to provide them with the standard Company rations: "1 1/2 lbs of meat, 3/4 lb of bacon, 1 lb of fish, 1 gill of oil, 1 gill of vinegar" together with soup and sufficient bread.[25]

No alcoholic drinks occur in most of the descriptions of food. Alcohol, in the form of weak beer, can be found, however, in the 1658 instructions of the jailer of New Amsterdam. The prisoners were supplied with:

> three pounds of beef, one-and-a-half pounds of bacon, one loaf of bread a week, in the summer two cans of small beer, and in the winter one can of small beer a day, pottage, and dairy produce as is fitting.[26]

The rations in New Netherland correspond with what is known of the menus of orphanages and other institutions in the Dutch Republic, although it is possible that a little more meat was included in those of the colony, due to the easy availability of venison. The rations pertain only to the food of soldiers, prisoners, and new colonists. Wealthy colonists had a richer and more varied diet. The correspondence of Jeremias and Maria van Rensselaer includes references to oysters, sugar cakes, and oranges, for instance. One difference between New Netherland and the Dutch Republic was the adoption of an Indian dish, *sappaen*. This pap of maize meal and water or milk continued to be a regular component of the diet after the Dutch period. Yet on the whole, the colonists carried on cooking their meals in the way they had learned in the Dutch Republic. The collection of the Historic Hudson Valley in Tarrytown contains a cookbook, *De verstandige kock* (*The Sensible Cook*), part of the collection entitled *Het vermakelycke landt-leven* (*The Pleasurable Country Life*). It was intended for a well-to-do public, like the Van Cortlandt family, and was first published in 1668, although the copy in Tarrytown is a later edition, from 1683.[27]

Books

De verstandige kock is an exception. Cookbooks do not appear in the inventories from the period prior to 1664, although other books do, albeit in limited numbers. All books had been imported from the Dutch Republic, as New York's first printer, William Bradford, did not begin his activities until 1693, and in his first year printed one small work in Dutch. Of the early inventories, only five contain references to books. In three of these, the number of books is limited, and titles are not mentioned. A total of three books, without further specification, are referred to in the estate of Willem Quick. Jacob Roy possessed only two old books, plus a pocket book, probably a notebook or an almanac. Jan Jansz Damen left a folio Bible, an old quarto Bible, and a chronicle. Jonas Bronck and Gijsbert van Imbroch, however, had substantial libraries. Bronck had a total of fifty-six books, including "eighteen old small books, printed, by various authors, both German and Danish" and "seventeen written books that are old." The majority of the remaining twenty-one books were religious works, some of Lutheran, some of Calvinistic origin, evidence of the mixed marriage of the Lutheran Bronck to the Calvinist Teuntje Jeuriaens. His library contained a Lutheran Bible, a book of psalms, an ecclesiastical history, and a catechism next to Calvinistic works: a folio Bible, the "Institutie calvinus in folia" (John Calvin's *Institutio Christianæ Religionis*), Heinrich Bullinger's *Huysboeck* (House Book, a collection of fifty sermons), and the "Schultetus dominicalien" (*Idea concionum dominicalium, ad populum Haidelbergensem habitarum,* by Abrahamus Scultetus). Bronck also possessed a few general works on religion and a small number of works on navigation such as a *Seespigel* (probably

the *Zeespiegel, inhoudende een korte onderwysinghe inde konst der zee-
vaert, en beschryvinghe der see'n en kusten van de oostersche, noordsche en
westersche schipvaert,* by Willem Jansz Blaeu), a cosmography, and a few
helmsman's handbooks, which were relics of his time as a captain. Finally,
he owned a children's book, a book on law, a calendar, and a chronicle, all
in Danish.[28]

Gijsbert van Imbroch's background is also reflected in his books. He was
a surgeon from Aachen, and his library contained anatomical and medi-
cal works by Christoph Wirtsung, Ambrosius Paré, Johannes de Vigo, and
Nicolaes Tulp. He also had an extensive collection of schoolbooks, dozens
of copies in some instances: 102 ABC books, 27 *"letterconsten"* (Arts of
Letters, writing manuals), 19 large *"corte begrypen"* (*Short Understanding,* probably catechisms), 20 small *"corte begrypen,"* and 9 *"trappen der
jeught"* (*Steps of Youth,* general schoolbook). Among the schoolbooks were
also the 83 "written and printed histories of Tobias" and "100 catechisms."
It suggests that he also acted as schoolmaster. Remarkable in Van Imbroch's
collection is a rare "handbook of the Catholic faith in High German." Besides these, he also owned other religious books, including works by Jean
Taffin, Albertus Huttenus, Johan Sarcharson, Jacobus Borstius, and one
"korte manier [Short Way] *van Megapolensis,"* the lost catechism of the
New Amsterdam *predikant.* Lastly, some historical works were mentioned
in Van Imbroch's inventory, such as Van Meteren's *Historie* (*History*), a
Dutch translation of Livy, Commelin's *Frederick Hendrick,* and Richard
Baker's *Chronyck van het leven en bedrijf van al de koninghen van Enge-
landt* (*Chronicle of the Lives and Works of all the Kings of England*).[29]

If Van Imbroch had purchased all these works for his own reading, his
interest would have been wide. At least some of them, in any event the
schoolbooks, were intended to be sold. Even so, this is an extensive library,
furnished with both books related to Van Imbroch's profession and a good
selection of religious and general books. In the cases of other colonists,
their total literary collections are an unknown quantity, but some indications exist. The correspondence and accounts of Jeremias van Rensselaer
show that he regularly ordered books from the Dutch Republic, sometimes
for trading purposes. In 1654 he bought Commelin's biography of Fred-
erik Hendrik, Hooft's biography of the French king Henry IV, and Vondel's
Josep (either *Joseph in Egypten* or *Joseph in Dothan,* or perhaps even both),
while at a later date he also received *Buyten leven op Zorgvliet,* by Jacob
Cats, first printed in 1658. Newspapers and *prijscouranten* (printed price-
lists) were also available in New Netherland.[30]

Although secular literature was sent to the colony, the emphasis lay on religious books. In the early 1630s, Kiliaen van Rensselaer sent over a book of
sermons by Scultetus, so that religious services could be held when no minister was present in Rensselaerswijck. He also sent eight copies of the *"Prack-
tijcke der Godtsalicheyt"* (*The Practice of Godliness*) for the families in his

colony. This was possibly *De practycke ofte oeffeninghe der godtsaligheydt* by Lewis Bayly in the 1633 or 1620 edition, or Voetius's *Meditatie van de ware practijcke der godtsalicheydt* of 1628. In 1660, when Blom and Selijns were called to Wiltwijck and Breuckelen, the Company sent a number of "psalters, prayer books, and verse books to be used in the education of the congregation."[31] After Jeremias van Rensselaer joined the church in 1660, he asked his mother to send him a book of psalms. It had to be long and thin to fit in the pocket of his coat, and he wanted it to be furnished with gold clasps. Ten years later he also ordered a few prayer books by Casparus Sibelius. However, his brother Rijckert was unable to obtain for him the second volume of *Theologiae praxis, de ware practycque der godt-geleerdtheit* (*Theologiae praxis, the True Practice of Theology*) by Adrianus Cocquius that he would dearly have liked to receive.[32]

Another category of books was the handbooks for administrators and law officials. The *schout* in Rensselaerswijck was provided with a notary's book and a copy of Joost de Damhouder's *Practycke in criminele saecken* (*Practice in Criminal Matters*). Kiliaen van Rensselaer sent *Commies* Arent van Curler De Groot's *Inleydinge tot de hollandtsche regts-geleertheyt* (*Introduction to Dutch Law*), probably the same copy that was later discovered among the papers of Brant van Slichtenhorst. A book with examples of legal acts was used in New Amstel.[33] In November 1674, several Dutch books were present in the City Hall of New York. As these were no longer needed now that the English legal system was used, they were handed to *Burgemeester* Johannes van Brugh for safekeeping.[34]

The inventories in the Dutch period present a sober but recognizably Dutch picture with more similarities to rural parts of the Dutch Republic with small towns than to the affluent cities in Holland. Many goods had to be imported from the Dutch Republic, and these were expensive. New Netherland was no rich society with a broad spectrum of refined implements and luxurious consumables. Later in the colony's existence, specialized craftsmen immigrated, and it may be assumed that prices then fell. Many colonists in the period up to 1664 had not had time to amass any significant fortune. That was different for their successors in the later years of the seventeenth century and certainly in the eighteenth century.

Living and Dying

In early December of 1670, Jeremias van Rensselaer wrote in his letter book:

> In the year of our Savior Jesus Christ, on the 1/11 December, was born my fourth son. [On] Thursday night about two o'clock, my wife was through God's mercy very hastily delivered, we having only with us the midwife and

Maria Loockermans Pieterss. On the 4/14 December, Sunday, he has received Christian baptism and was named Joannes, after my wife's brother Joannes deceased and after my uncle Johan van Weely, my grandfather, and my half-brother Joannes van Rensselaer deceased. His godmother, who presented him for baptism, [was] Margrita Schuylers, and his godfathers [were] his grand-father Oloff Stevens (in whose place Phlip Schuyler) and my uncle Johan van Weely, in whose place stood Gerret Swart, former schout. Who baptized him was our pastor, *do*[*minee*] Gidion Schaets. May the Lord God let him grow up in virtue, amen.[35]

This long quotation contains several points of interest. First, Jeremias's wife, Maria van Rensselaer, gave birth in their own house at Watervliet. The location is less obvious than it would appear. In some instances a woman, either accompanied by her husband or not, returned to the Dutch Republic for the confinement, presumably to be close to family. Such travels were the prerogative of the wealthy colonists, who could afford to make the crossing. For Maria van Rensselaer it was not an option. She had been born in New Netherland, and it would have been more likely that she would have traveled to her parents' house in New Amsterdam than to the Dutch Republic. However, as far as is known, she bore all her children in her own house in Rensselaerswijck.[36]

At the birth of Johannes van Rensselaer in 1670 only the midwife and Maria Loockermans, a relative of Maria van Rensselaer, were present. Both women were collected by sleigh two hours earlier, at about midnight. Jeremias later wrote to his father-in-law that the "little fellow, thank God, [was de-livered] so quickly that there was no time to send for our nearest neighbor's wife."[37] Jeremias's correspondence does not reveal who were present at the birth of his other children, but a midwife was certainly there, as midwives had been working in New Netherland since the 1630s and possibly earlier. Neighbors and female family members also came with all haste to the house, as was the custom in the Dutch Republic. Births were preeminently women's affairs. In general, the husband waited in an adjoining room. In 1662, War-naer Wessels, who had been imprisoned because of a debt, was freed at the request of several women who declared that his wife was in labor. For Hen-drick Jochemsz, innkeeper in Beverwijck, his wife's confinement caused him to neglect paying duty on a barrel of beer. When summoned to the court, his excuse was accepted by the magistrates. Three days later his daughter Christina was baptized.[38]

Jeremias van Rensselaer named his son Johannes and gave four reasons for this choice of name. It was also the name of one of his wife's brothers, an uncle on his mother's side, his maternal grandfather, and finally Jeremias's own half-brother. Jeremias had named his earlier children after other family members as well. The first son had been named after Jeremias's father Kili-aen, while the second child, a daughter, was called Anna, after her paternal grandmother. The second son was given the name Hendrick. Jeremias wrote to his brother-in-law Stephanus van Cortlandt: "We have named him Hendrick, after my grandfather and eldest brother, deceased, as the Hendricks had quite died out of the family."[39] It all matches the customary naming pattern in the Dutch Republic and in New Netherland.[40]

Baptism could show a connection between the choice of name and the name of a godparent, although this was no hard and fast rule. At the baptism of Johannes, Jeremias van Rensselaer had nominated his uncle Johan van Wely as godfather, but as the latter was in the Dutch Republic, his place at the font was taken by the former *schout* of Rensselaerswijck, Gerrit Swart. This system of substitutes was used regularly with the baptism of the children of Jeremias van Rensselaer, and in most cases the name of the child was not that of one of the godparents. At the baptism of his first son, Kiliaen, Jeremias had chosen four godparents: his brother Jan Baptist and his father-in-law, his mother, and his mother-in-law. None of these was present at the baptism. They were substituted by Abraham Staets, Pieter Claerbout, Margaretha Schuyler, and Anthonia van Rijswijck, respectively. At the baptism of Kiliaen it was impossible to have one of the child's namesakes present as a godparent. Grandfather Kiliaen had already died, and no adult member of the family bore the same name. Four of Kiliaen's sons named a son after their father. Only in the case of Rijckert van Rensselaer was it not his first but his second son, as he had named his first son after his maternal grandfather. It is not surprising that more godparents were present at the baptism of Jeremias's first son, who was the first candidate to continue the family line, than at those of the children that followed. The choice of four absent godparents gave Jeremias the opportunity of strengthening his network within the community in which he lived.[41]

The choice of godparents reflected the familial and social networks and is closely linked with religion and status. That becomes evident in the case of *schepenen* and *burgemeesters,* who regularly appear as godparents of the children of their colleagues, who of course in many cases were also family members. Often WIC employees acted as godparents to colleagues' children. At the baptism of Stuyvesant's first son in 1647, the majority of godparents were members of the council. A year later, Stuyvesant asked the directors in Amsterdam to be godfathers to his second son. This strengthened his position in the colony at this time of conflict with the population. The directors acquiesced to the director general's request, although they wrote that previously the Amsterdam chamber had always refused such requests. The WIC directors asked to be advised of the child's name, so that they could make an appropriate baptismal gift as soon as the Company's financial situation permitted it.

Such gifts could involve considerable sums of money. On 13 August 1673, the Admiralty of Amsterdam and the States of Zeeland were godfather to the son of *burgemeester* Ægidius Luyck, and Admiral Cornelis Evertsen de

Jongste acted as one of the witnesses. The value of the baptismal gift for Cornelis Jacob Luyck was 630 guilders, quite a large sum. The correspondence of Jeremias van Rensselaer contains a reference to two silver salt cellars as baptismal gifts, also a valuable present. Other baptismal gifts were silver spoons, examples of which still can be found in museums.[42]

In New Netherland no trace can be found of special meals or other festivities to celebrate a birth or a baptism, although these very likely took place, as such customs were widespread in the Dutch Republic. Nor is much known about what went on at a baptism. The only account available of a baptismal ceremony is devoted mainly to a description of the clothing of the baptized child, which in this case was rather exceptional. The child was the illegitimate son of Arent van Curler, a married man, and Anna Schaets, the daughter of the minister in Beverwijck. The child was presented for baptism in heavy mourning clothing and bedecked with black ribbons and bows. Stuyvesant disapproved of the attitude of the *predikant* toward his daughter's behavior and deplored the schism in the congregation that resulted from it. At a recent celebration of the Lord's Supper, half of the membership stayed away. As Stuyvesant wrote, even down in New Amsterdam word had spread that, in place of mortification and conversion, to "the scandal of the holy sacrament of baptism, uncommon and before this never used ceremonies and waggery [were] carried out with a child of whoring." Stuyvesant wrote in sarcastic tone to Vice Director La Montagne at Fort Orange:

> I readily leave to anybody's choice and approval in what kind of napkins or swaddles children are presented for baptism, [as well as] how to name them, but concerning this subject, it seems, under correction of a better judgment, that this child of whoring might better have been named Barrabas, that is frolicsome father's son, than Benoni, child of grief.[43]

Stuyvesant's personal disgust is clear, but his letter was also prompted by the fact that in the absence of a classis in New Netherland, he considered it his duty to prevent "vexations and offences in [God's] tender church in this far-away land." Apart from reporting the presence of the black ribbons and bows, the account actually tells little about the baptismal ceremony itself.

Prenuptial Intercourse

Another form of extramarital sex was prenuptial intercourse. Of the earliest 150 marriages (1639–ca. 1652) recorded in the register of marriages of New Amsterdam, the name of the first child can be found in the register of baptisms in ninety cases. In seven of these, the period between the first publication of the banns of marriage and the birth of the first child is less than 211 days, or seven months, and premarital conception may be assumed. In comparison with the Dutch Republic, this number is not exceptional.[44]

Although prenuptial sex was frowned upon by some in the Dutch Republic, there are no traces of general moral outrage about it in New Netherland. Sex was generally thought permissible after a couple had become betrothed, as a token of which they gave each other a gift, such as a ring or a handkerchief. It was a different matter if a child had been conceived and father did not wish to marry the mother. A number of women in New Netherland entered into legal proceedings to compel the father to marry or at least contribute to the cost of the upbringing of the child. The demand for marriage was in most instances intended to emphasize that the child had been born of a steady relationship, rather than adulterous fornication. Actual marriage was rarely the real intention, as the couple's relations were already strained. In many cases, the woman succeeded in obtaining financial and honorary compensation, especially if the man admitted paternity.[45]

The case of Grietje Hendricks Westercamp in Wiltwijck provides an interesting example. Pieter Jacobsz would not admit that the child was his and also declared that he had made no promise of marriage. Grietje, however, claimed that intercourse with him had taken place eight days before Christmas in the millhouse of Pieter Jacobsz and that the child had been born in mid-September. Seven women present at the birth stated that Grietje had sworn three times that Pieter was the father, but this traditional evidence was not considered sufficient to reach a verdict. Pieter was able to prove that he was not the only one to have slept with Grietje. He also contested the chronology: intercourse had taken place much earlier than Grietje alleged, so if the child was indeed his, then she would have been pregnant for thirteen months and four days, which is impossible. Ultimately, Pieter Jacobsz was able to extract himself from the affair by swearing under oath that he was not the father of the child. However, he had to pay two hundred guilders for sleeping with Grietje. The child had in the meantime been baptized. Initially, *Predikant* Hermannus Blom had filled in the words *adhuc nescio* (as yet unknown) where the name of the father was normally written. Later he changed this to Pieter Jacobsz, "miller of this place." Pieter's oath had not convinced the minister.[46]

A step further than giving presents and exchanging marriage promises was the publication of the banns of marriage. Rose Joele and François Soleil had reached this stage, whereupon they had "conversation of the flesh with each other." François subsequently refused to marry Rose. He defended himself before director general and council with an unsavory mishmash of arguments:

> that she is not fit to have a man, because she has a bad breath, and also because she has agreed to marry someone else in the West Indies, and third, because

they do not agree with each other, as she is very choleric, and further because she is able to let all men die who be with her, as she has a white lung.[47]

He therefore requested that Rose be examined by experts to determine whether or not she actually had tuberculosis. Director general and council did not acquiesce to this and put François in jail until he decided to make the best of a bad job and agree to marry Rose. An affair such as this one, and several instances of unmarried cohabitation, in particular among the English on Long Island, prompted director general and council, by means of several ordinances, to underline that, once the banns had been read out three times, marriage should took place soon afterwards. A blind eye was turned to sex before marriage, provided it did not give rise to problems. On the other hand, unmarried cohabitation was considered absolutely impermissible, like it was in the Dutch Republic.[48]

Marriage

On 12 July 1662, in New Amsterdam, Jeremias van Rensselaer married Maria van Cortlandt, the seventeen-year-old daughter of *Burgemeester* Oloff Stevensz van Cortlandt. A day later he requested his brother Jan Baptist in Amsterdam to inform their mother Anna of the event. Had they not been separated by such distance, he would not have had the nerve to marry without first asking for his mother's prior approval of the match. But he had no doubt "that she would be pleased to hear of ~~my house wife~~ [*sic*] I shall still call her bride." Jeremias did not find it fitting to sing her praises too greatly:

> but I thank the good Lord for having granted me such a good partner and we shall beseech him that He may let us live together long in peace and health.[49]

The difference in age between Jermias and Maria was considerable, as he was thirty years old. His mother's permission was therefore no longer a legal requirement to his marrying. Nonetheless, it is remarkable that he did not consult his family before settling on a wife. For a merchant family like the Van Rensselaers, any marriage was first and foremost an alliance with another family, in which business interests played a major and sometimes decisive role. Jeremias's mother must have been aware that a match with a member of the Van Cortlandt family was a good move. The Van Rensselaers had maintained business contacts with the Van Cortlandts for quite some time. Yet Jeremias's tone was apologetic when on 19 August 1662 he wrote to his mother:

> I know that you must have thought it strange to hear this, fearing perhaps that in haste I had taken a foolish step, because I had not informed you of it before.

This is due to my timidity, for I had been thinking of her already a year or two before, when now and then I did an errand at the Manhatans.[50]

Jeremias was afraid that his mother would think "that she is still a little young and therefore not well able to take care of a household," but he assured her that all was going well. Alas, Anna van Rensselaer's reaction is not extant, but she sent two silver salt cellars as a baptism present for Jeremias's first son, which can be interpreted as a sign of approval.[51]

Jeremias was very happy

that the Lord God has granted me such a good spouse, with whom I can get along so well and live with peaceably in such a far distant country separated from all the friends.[52]

Jeremias made the choice who was to be his partner for life himself. We do not know this of other New Netherlanders. On the other hand, Jeremias wrote absolutely nothing about the details of the wedding. The little information available shows that a wedding was a good reason for festivities, unsurprisingly. But the few reports of wedding celebrations contain little more information than that food and drink was served, that in some instances quarrels occurred, that once in a while something was stolen, and that the bridesmaids present wore decorated coronets. These are all expressions of gaiety that were also prevalent in the Dutch Republic.[53]

As in the Dutch Republic, in New Netherland poems were written in honor of weddings. The nuptials of Ægidius Luyck, rector of the Latin School in New Amsterdam, and Judith Isendoorn, were graced with two works by *Predikant* Henricus Selijns. The first is an ode to be sung to the tune of *"O Kersnacht"* (O Christmas Night), known from the chorus of the nuns of the Order of St. Clara from Vondel's *Gijsbrecht van Aemstel,* a well-known play by the most prominent of Dutch seventeenth-century playwrights.[54] It was an appropriate choice, for the marriage ceremony took place on 26 December 1663. In the song, Selijns makes a link between the coming of the Christ-child and the couple's union:

> And as they bring this child before them,
> Luyck comes and marries Isendooren
> Standing before this Christ-like crib;
> And finds when her consent is shown
> Flesh of his flesh, bone of his bone,
> For Judith is his second rib.

The second ode, *Bruydloft Toorts* (Bridal Torch), begins in somber tones. The "fire of love" has been extinguished by "fire of war," and Cupid has been chased away by the Indians, who in June 1663 had created a blood-bath in Wiltwijck.

> His [Cupid's] words are yet still warm, and does he not behold,
> Alas! house after house, with *wildt* [Indian] monsters posted?
> Child upon child taken away? and man on man killed
> Barn upon barn consumed. And pregnant woman roasted?
> People flee, wherever they can. From Wiltwijck I too flee.[55]

Selijns finds the cause of the disaster in "three lamentable general sins," namely "lechery, drunkenness and wicked haughtiness." As a result, Cupid has lost his bow and arrows. Ultimately he recovers them when a peace settlement is reached with the Indians, and the first thing he does is hit Luyck and Isendoorn with his arrows of love. These are fine works of poetry, which were either recited or sung at the wedding. Jacob Steendam too has written odes for such occasions in New Netherland, as he had done earlier for weddings at Fort Elmina. Of course poems were written for weddings in the Dutch Republic too, but Selijns's *Bruydloft Toorts* differs from these through its reference to the Indians.[56]

A couple of times public opinion was expressed when a marriage took place. An incident in Haerlem is, as far as is known, the only instance of charivari-like behavior in New Netherland. Pieter Jansz Slot, son of a former *schepen* of Haerlem, was to be married. The banns were published on 2 February 1663. On the same day, a maypole was erected before the door of the house of Pieter's father "in his honor" by a number of young men from the town. The maypole was then festooned with pieces of old stocking, symbolizing that the bride was no longer a virgin. The bridegroom, taking a dim view of this scorn and mockery, chopped the maypole down. The following day another maypole was erected, which was also chopped down. This occurrence repeated itself a third time. The placing of the maypole was accompanied on each occasion by the "music" of kettles and pans. The father, Jan Pietersz Slot, had alerted the *schout,* Jan La Montagne, but when he attempted to prevent the young villagers from assembling, he was threatened with firearms and axes. Further incidents of vandalism and fights took place. What had aroused the displeasure of the youth of Haerlem is not reported, but perhaps the husband and wife-to-be had refused to provide them with *kwanselbier* (literally: "barter beer"), a customary treat for adolescents in the Dutch Republic on the occasion of an engagement. No clear references to this custom occur in New Netherland, but the context makes it a possibility.[57]

Love and Marriage...

Married life proved a bumpy road for some colonists. Occasionally the authorities became involved, and in almost every one of those instances the magistrates tried to restore peace and tranquility. Pieter Jansz Metselaer, for example, was caught by his wife Trijntje Pieters in the whorehouse of Paulus Heymans. An argument ensued, and Pieter hit his wife, who then went to director general and council and asked them to forbid her husband from ever going there again. Otherwise, so she said, she would have little pleasure with him. Pieter Jansz was told by director general and council that he had to live, eat, drink, and sleep with his wife, as befitted an honorable husband. On the same day, the provincial government warned Paulus Heymans that if he and his family did not improve their behavior, they would be sent back to the Dutch Republic.[58]

This is one of the few situations in which prostitution played a role in marital discord. Most cases involved simple quarrels, ending in fisticuffs, sometimes as the result of incompatibility of character. During an argument in 1656, Jacob Jansz Stol assaulted his wife Geertruit Andries and threw pieces of burning wood at her. Even blood was drawn, but nonetheless the magistrates of Beverwijck opined that this did not fall under the ordinances concerning fighting since it had taken place between man and wife. Stol got away without even a warning. A further explanation is that Geertruit would not make a statement and that dissension was an exception in this marriage.[59]

That cannot be said of the squabbles between Arent Juriaensz Lantsman and Belitje Lodewijcks. He originated from Oldenzaal in Twente; she came from Amsterdam and was the daughter of Lodewijck Pos, captain of the *ratelwacht* (rattle guard) in New Amsterdam. Arent and Belitje married in New Amsterdam in 1660. No problems were apparent in the early years of their marriage, and two children were born to the couple. However, in October 1664 Arent was arrested in his own house by *Schout* Pieter Tonneman. The noise of the argument with his wife had caused a nuisance to their neighbors, and the drunken Arent made matters worse by threatening the *schout* with a firearm. In the meantime, Belitje had fled the house with the children and gone to her parents to stay with them for several months. However, this separation had taken place without permission of the authorities, and it is therefore not surprising that, when Arent petitioned the magistrates to order his wife to return, his words did not fall on deaf ears. In an attempt at reconciliation, the couple promised the court to behave properly. They then went home together.

Three months later new trouble arose. Belitje, accompanied by her parents, came to ask the court for a divorce. The magistrates did not want to acquiesce without another attempt at reconciliation and asked the two *predikanten* of New Amsterdam, Megapolensis and Drisius, to mediate. The ministers were also unable to reconcile the parties. In the meantime it had become clear that Belitje's parents-in-law were the cause of the problem. Hence the magistrates instructed Arent and Belitje to try once again to patch things up. All went well enough for a while, and in May 1666 the couple had a third child baptized. However, in March 1667 Lodewijck Pos went to court to complain that his son-in-law had hit his daughter, whereupon she had again moved in with her parents. Only then did the court agree to a temporary separation, ordering Arent to pay four guilders per week toward the upkeep of his children. After a cooling-off period of several months, Arent and Belitje decided to live together again. This was not to last, and the pattern of argument, leaving home, and reconciliation repeated itself.[60]

A bad marriage in which the parents-in-law tried to intervene is not exceptional, and neither is the intervention of the ministers in the attempt at reconciliation, even though Arent and Belitje were not members of their church. However, the magistrates were reluctant to grant a temporary separation, much less a definitive divorce. For years endeavors were made to preserve the marriage and to compel the couple to live in peace and tranquility by means of extracting promises from them to do so. The restraint of the magistrates in New Netherland was no more pronounced than that of their counterparts in Holland. The New Netherland sources reveal nothing about the background to the magistrates' attitudes, although for the Dutch Republic it has been determined that the conviction that marriage was a holy institution played an important role. Any marital difficulties were to be dealt with in acquiescence and borne patiently. That the court in New Amsterdam was not prepared to consider divorce in the case of Arent and Belitje is more understandable when compared with the sort of instance in which they did so.[61]

Adultery

Adultery was the most prevalent and accepted ground for divorce, in the Dutch Republic and New Netherland alike. Another reason, accepted rather less generally, was wrongful desertion. The case of John Hickes, *schout* of Vlissingen, was very clear. In a petition to director general and council, he stated that his wife Hardwood Longh had run away and for nine years had been living with another man, by whom she had had five or six children. Director general and council did not hesitate in granting him a divorce, thus giving him the possibility to remarry. In other cases adultery and wrongful desertion were also accepted as grounds for a divorce.[62]

Several cases of bigamy occurred in New Netherland, equally good reason for the dissolution of a marriage, although such cases formally are not divorce. Michiel Anthonisz van Utrecht had heard nothing from his wife Grietje Jacobs for five years, until he received news that she had died in the Dutch Republic. He subsequently married Femmetje Alberts in Beverwijck. It was a surprise when Grietje suddenly turned up in New Netherland. The reported death turned out to have been that of her mother and not herself. The consistory of Beverwijck brought the matter to court. After extensive deliberation, and in consideration of the fact that Femmetje Alberts, the second "wife," was prepared to give up her "husband" since Grietje Jacobs possessed the oldest rights, the magistrates of Beverwijck declared the marriage null and void and restored Femmetje to "her former liberty."[63]

Death

Just as in the Dutch Republic, last wills drawn up in New Netherland contain the standard expression that nothing is more certain than death itself and nothing less certain than when it shall occur. The mother of Jeremias van Rensselaer died at one o'clock in the afternoon of 12 June 1670 in Amsterdam, in the presence of four of her children. The same day, Jan Baptist wrote to his brothers Jeremias and Rijckert in New Netherland to impart the sad tidings. The letter was also signed by his other brother Nicolaes and his sisters Leonora and Susanna. It is the only letter in the entire correspondence that bears a joint signature, an indication of the importance placed on the announcement of a death.[64]

The death of Anna van Rensselaer at almost seventy years of age, after seven weeks of debilitating illness, was not a surprise. That was different from the passing away of Maria, the five-year-old daughter of Jeronimus Ebbingh and Johanna de Laet.[65] In October 1665 she caught a cold and was administered a syrup by surgeon Hans Kierstede. It was of little help. The cold worsened, and Maria's chest became constricted. On 12 October her worried parents sent for *predikant* and doctor Samuel Megapolensis, son of Johannes Megapolensis.[66] He also prescribed a syrup. The same evening she was administered a enema of sweetened milk by Hans Kierstede to see whether the problems had been caused by worms. This too had no effect. The following day Maria played by the fireside with her silver trinkets, but she became increasingly weaker and at night tossed and turned with a high fever. On 14 October she joined the family at table for the midday meal but had no appetite. By the evening, she had become weaker, her fever had increased, and when she asked to be allowed to sleep with her parents, her request was granted. An hour before her death she sat up in bed without assistance. Her mother came to stand beside the bed with Paulus de Hulter, a son from her earlier marriage to Johan de Hulter, and asked if she knew who he was. "That is little Paul, little Paul who is crying," answered Maria. Her father asked her if she also loved her father. "So much, dear Father" she replied fervently. Moments later she gave two little sobs, and with her last gasp her little mouth stayed half open.[67]

It is an emotional account, which shows how much the death of his daughter affected the father. Jeronimus Ebbingh described the last days of Maria's life in detail, but while he appears to have been a religious man, his notes contained no religious observations. On her deathbed Maria Ebbingh did not quote from the Bible, as was done in abundance in some of the descriptions of the deaths of children. And in his family notes written at the time of Maria's death, the father did not include the phrase that she "passed away quietly from this world in God," as he had done a few years earlier on the death of his daughter Francyna. She had died in 1662 at the age of one and was interred in the church at New Amsterdam in front of the bench of the incumbent *schepenen*, to be followed a year later by her only weeks-old brother, Albertus. Child death was common, but the account of the death of Maria Ebbingh is exceptional, as few other descriptions of the deaths of colonists in New Netherland are extant.[68]

Just as in New Amsterdam, burial sometimes took place inside the church in Beverwijck. When *predikant* Gideon Schaets died in 1694, breaking open the church floor and digging his grave cost two guilders and ten stivers. A grave inside the church was the prerogative of people of wealth and standing, both in the colony and in the Dutch Republic. For those of more modest means, a cemetery was available outside the church, usually in the churchyard. In New Amsterdam the cemetery was on the Heerestraet, a little to the north of the present Morris Street. In 1656 this burial ground was already overfull and rather dilapidated, and other locations were sought. Some years later, a new cemetery outside the city was put into use.[69]

Interments also took place outside the church in Breuckelen. Carpenter Aucke Jansz requested of the consistory that the whole churchyard be fenced off and in particular that section in which his wife was buried. He was told that the consistory was not the owner of the churchyard but that they would ask the court at Breuckelen to enclose it with boarding as protection against the pigs, which had been, and were still, rooting among the graves. The court placed the ball once more in the consistory's court, saying that the church should take care of the matter, so a contract was entered into with Aucke Jansz. The costs were to be met by all the inhabitants. In the Dutch Republic it was not customary that the consistory undertook such tasks, as secular authorities owned the church buildings. When several years later, for the same reason, the churchyard in New Amsterdam had to be enclosed, the magistrates allotted the task not to the consistory but to the churchwardens, Govert Loockermans and Johannes de Peijster. This was more in line with the practice in the Dutch Republic.[70]

Care of the graveyard was generally in the hands of the churchwardens appointed by the local authorities, as was the practice in the Dutch Republic. Gravediggers and *aansprekers,* who announced deaths, were functions which in New Netherland were often combined with that of sexton and precentor. Both were appointed by the local court and enjoyed a monopoly. Hendrick Rooseboom, gravedigger and *aanspreker* in Willemstadt, as Albany was then known, complained in 1674 that the Lutherans buried their own dead and had appointed their own gravedigger. His protest resulted in a confirmation of his exclusive position by the local magistrates.[71] In New Amsterdam Claes van Elslandt Sr. in 1661 was one of the gravediggers, but his conduct left much to be desired. He was told by the *burgemeesters* that he should take better care of digging the graves inside the church and in the graveyard. It was his duty

> to look after the bier being fetched and brought back to the proper place; to invite, according to old custom, everybody to the funeral, to announce [the death], to walk steadily before the corpse, and to collect, demand, and receive pay only for his service, without demanding and requesting more money on this account.[72]

Some of the other burial duties were carried out by Jan Gillisz Kock. It was his responsibility to ensure that the bell was tolled and that the fee for hiring the funeral pall was paid. He was also to keep a list of who was buried. The hire of palls was, as in the Dutch Republic, one of the sources of income for the poor relief funds. In New Amsterdam the cost of hiring a funeral pall was eighteen guilders. It was less costly in Beverwijck, five guilders for the small pall and ten guilders for the large one. These sums, which were often paid in *sewant*, were nominally a little larger than in the Dutch Republic, but otherwise few differences existed between the funeral rites in the colony and *patria*.[73]

Another item of expense at a funeral consisted of the refreshments provided for the guests. The sources reveal nothing about elaborate funeral meals, but liquid refreshments were consumed in some volume. After the funeral of Jacob Claesz Coppen, a half *aam* (approximately twenty gallons) of French wine to the value of five beavers was drunk. At the interment of WIC soldier Jems Bronck, the cost of the refreshments amounted to about fifty guilders. Perhaps *doot coekjes* (death biscuits) were also served. The flour and milk included in an undertaker's bill in Bergen in 1690 is an indication. Recipes for "funeral biscuits" occur in eighteenth-century cookery books. Of a more lasting nature was the silver spoon that was made for the occasion of the funeral of Oloff Stevensz van Cortlandt in 1684. In the case of such costly gifts, it is likely that they were given only to family members as a memento.[74]

Another memorial of the deceased were the epitaphs composed by Henricus Selijns. A quarter of all his poems come from this genre. A number of these relate to deceased colonists, but Selijns also wrote poems on the death of friends in the Dutch Republic. On the occasion of the death of Johannes Megapolensis, Selijns, who at the time was minister in Waverveen, wrote:

> New Netherlander, weep,
> Check not the gushing tear.
> In perfect shape, doth sleep
> Megapolensis here,
> New Netherland's great treasure.

His never-tiring work
Was day and night to pray,
And zeal in th' church exert.
Now let him rest, where may
He scorn all worldly pleasure.[75]

The particulars on the funeral of Jeremias van Rensselaer are of a somewhat less poetic nature. In the invoice of *aanspreker* and gravedigger Hendrick Rooseboom, almost all of these elements appear. Announcing the death in Bethlehem, the area to the southwest of Beverwijck that still bears this name, Beverwijck itself and Schenectady together accounted for more than half of the costs. The digging of the grave cost twelve guilders, tolling the bell eight guilders, and the rental of the pall amounted to ten guilders. Eight broken rummers were also charged for, adding another ten guilders to the total. In all, Maria van Rensselaer paid 101 guilders for her husband's funeral.[76]

Most of the details of important moments in the lives of the people in New Netherland come from the correspondence of Jeremias van Rensselaer. This is a valuable source of information, but then, he was a member of the colony's elite. Little is known about the less eminent colonists. Still, customs in the colony display great similarities to those in the Dutch Republic.

Cursing and Fighting

In August 1636, the gunner of Fort Amsterdam gave a *foy*, a farewell dinner. A tent was set up on one of the points of the fort, in which a table and benches were placed. When the banquet was in full swing, the trumpeter began to play his instrument, according to David Pietersz de Vries, whose eyewitness account is the only source for this occurrence. He does not report why the trumpeter began to play. Perhaps he wanted to brighten up the festivities with a little music, but his trumpeting may also have been the signal for the beginning of curfew, indicating that the feast should be brought to a close. The trumpeter's call aroused the displeasure of two WIC employees, Andries Hudde and Jacob van Curler, who began to curse him. The trumpeter rewarded this with a *santerquanter* (cuff) to the ears of each, whereupon they went home to get a sword to wreak their revenge on him. They ended up in the house of Wouter van Twiller, who dissuaded them from further action. Nevertheless, "many unpleasant words" were spoken. "One of them shouted that I am still the same man that took the life of Count Floris [Floris the Fifth]." These final verses from "*History lledt van Graef Floris ende Geraert van Velsen*" are the answer to the question "how is your temper now?" and indicate that the tempers were still running high. A night's sleep restored the calm.[77]

Rows such as this can be encountered regularly in the New Netherland sources, although the reference to a late medieval Dutch song is unique. The cause of the conflict is shrouded in the mists of time, but it contains elements that recur in other disputes: swear-words, fisticuffs, and pointed weapons, present but not used in this case. And while not explicitly named, it may be assumed that alcohol also played a role. That arguments occurred in New Netherland, and that these sometimes escalated into vituperation, fights, and manslaughter is not remarkable. What is more interesting is to see how these began, when and how curses and insults were exchanged, under what circumstances this led to physical violence and, finally, how conflicts were resolved or dealt with by the courts.

A considerable number of fights can be found in the minutes of New Netherland courts. In most cases the magistrates were not interested in the cause but in who was the first to draw a knife. In the incidents for which more information is available, a variety of causes played a role, such as damaging another's property, damage caused by free-roaming livestock, or the late payment of debts. The latter played a role in an uncharacteristic outburst by the usually calm Ludovicus Cobus, the secretary of the court at Albany, who may have been drunk. On the evening of 24 June 1670, Cobus stood in the street in front of the house of Wijnant Gerritsz, shouting that the latter owed him money:

> You devilish fool, you are lying abed and hear this perfectly well; come out and clear yourself; you owe me at least a hundred *daelders* and now you are sponging on some one else.

When Wijnant's wife, midwife Trijntje Melchers, came out, Ludovicus directed his swearwords at her:

> you mother Melchels with your license, you big slut with your fat legs, you will give birth to a big turd to which *kackkedorus* [a quack doctor] will be midwife.[78]

By shouting his insults at the top of his voice from the street, Ludovicus Cobus made the conflict public to pressure Wijnant into paying the debt. However, he was sufficiently circumspect not to enter Wijnant's house. He would have done his case little good by committing trespass. His challenge to Wijnant to come outside was intended to hurt Wijnant's pride. If Wijnant refused, he would be seen as a coward. The insult to Trijntje Melchers was a mixture of attacking the midwife's professional good name and declaring her to be foul by verbally throwing excrement. However, the evidence of the witnesses shows that Ludovicus overplayed his hand. His public mudslinging brought himself into discredit rather than Wijnant.

Honor

This incident shows the importance of honor in conflicts. Honor can be defined as "someone's good name as seen by others." Formulated differently, in the early modern period it concerned the good name of an individual in the eyes of a collective. The contrast between individual and collective in this definition also explains why Ludovicus Cobus's verbal abuse toward Wijnant Gerritsz was fruitless. In this instance the matter was limited to the two individuals, without the collective component, which turned honor into a social mechanism and linked it to the prevalent ideal of a community of honest citizens, bound in solidarity. Honor was one of the aspects by which citizens could distinguish themselves from foreigners, for example. Imputations that cast a smirch on someone's good name involved matters that attracted collective disapproval. This covered a large variety of insults, accusations, gossip, and slanderous utterances, which involves diverse aspects of honor.[79]

Of course, honor was not the issue to the same extent in all instances. In many cases the cause was not a question of honor but became one when the conflict escalated. An example is the incident between Catelina Trico and surgeon Paulus van der Beeck in January 1645 in New Amsterdam. Catelina demanded to know why he had hit her daughter. Paulus denied the accusation and called Catelina a liar, to which she replied that he was a lying villain. She raised her hand, but Paulus was quicker, and struck out at her. He then called her a whore and a *sewant* thief, thus calling into question her sexual honor and her honesty. Catelina had Paulus van der Beeck summoned by director and council. The cause of the argument, the alleged assault on Catelina's daughter, no longer played a role in the matter. The charge brought against Paulus concerned only the verbal abuse and the blow. Supported by the testimony of Egbert van Borsum, Catelina Trico demanded redress for the damage done to her reputation. Paulus van der Beeck was instructed to prove the validity of his accusations or otherwise declare that he knew Catelina to be only honest and virtuous. Paulus chose the latter way of settling the conflict but was nonetheless fined two and a half guilders for the blow he had struck.[80]

In this case, the council in New Amsterdam restored the peace. Many cases of defamation did not come before the court. Having the testimony of a witness recorded was in some way a final warning to the other party, who then still had the opportunity of trying to achieve reconciliation in a less formal manner. In the Dutch Republic this took place via the consistory or via *buurtmeesters* (neighborhood leaders), for example. In New Netherland the neighborhoods are evident only in the latter years and then only in the largest community, New Amsterdam. The function of *buurtmeester* in New Amsterdam may have been fulfilled by the local magistrates in the early period. Parties involved in minor conflicts may also have reconciled through the intervention of friends or neighbors.[81]

Curses

For women, the most commonly heard insult was the word *whore,* which Paulus van der Beeck used against Catelina Trico. This did not necessarily refer to prostitution as such but rather more generally to wanton behavior. Sometimes it was elaborated upon to form *allemans hoer* (whore of all and sundry) or *jodenhoer* (Jews' whore). The terms of abuse applied to men show rather more variation. *Schelm* (scoundrel) was the most used in New Netherland as well as in the Dutch Republic. *Dief* (thief) was also used regularly, as was *hond* (hound), with the variants *bloethondt* (bloodhound) and *reeckel* (dog). *Vercken* (pig) and *swijn* (swine) were less common in the animal category. Calling someone a *leugenaer* (liar) was a widely used form of insult, occasionally also seen in its expanded version: "the biggest liar in the colony." Such supplements to terms of abuse occur with some frequency. For example, Brant Aertsz van Slichtenhorst, director of Rensselaerswijck, then over sixty years of age, was called an "old grey thief and scoundrel." In other instances too, the choice of the insults was adapted to the person at whom they were directed. Hans Vos, court messenger at Rensselaerswijck, was called *verklicker* (informer) and *diefleijer* (thief catcher), an honorific also bestowed on Willem Bredenbent, deputy *schout* on Manhattan. The men appointed to inspect chimneys in New Amsterdam for their safety against fire were sometimes dubbed "chimney sweeps." Ethnic terms of abuse are relatively rare, while in view of the widely varying backgrounds of the population of New Netherland, they were to be expected. *Mof* (kraut) and *Danish dog* appear in only a few instances. The term *Turk* crops up now and then, in one instance applied to Anthony Jansz van Salee, who had been born in Morocco. Occurring once is the expression *wild dog,* possibly meaning Indian dog. This was followed by the equally unique riposte of *spitter baart* (spitter beard).[82]

Both insults and gossip were seen as calumnies. Gossip was an important instrument in social regulation, but it became slander if something was alleged that could not be proven. The party that felt that his or her honor had been besmirched first had to provide evidence in the form of statements from witnesses to prove that the disputed remarks had been made. The defending party then had the choice either of proving what had been said was true or of making an immediate retraction by means of *amende honorable.* That was the usual outcome, as the injured party would be unlikely to bring a case if producing the evidence to justify the alleged slander were a simple matter. The content of the slander was extremely diverse and, for example, had to do with the theft of firewood, a stay in the *spinhuis* (women's house of correction) in Amsterdam, fraud in making up a bill, and the malicious desertion of a spouse.

Honor did not depend only on one's own behavior. In some cases a man was made a figure of fun because his wife was alleged to have committed adultery. One of the first cases dealt with by the newly installed court of *burgemeesters* and *schepenen* in New Amsterdam concerned a complaint from Joost Goderis. He related that he had taken a canoe to *Oestereiland* (Oyster Island), the present Ellis Island, where he met eight men. One of these, Guilliaem de Wijs, asked Joost for permission to "fuck the plaintiff's wife, because" he said, "Allard Anthony does it." Joost was then called a *hoorenbeest* (horned animal, meaning cuckold) and sung to mockingly: "Joost Goderis should wear horns like the beasts of the forest." Isaac Bedloo and Jacob Buys then shouted that Allard Anthony had had his wife. When Goderis later asked Bedloo why he had insulted him, the latter answered that Goderis had been an idiot and had himself said it. At this point, Joost hit him, whereupon Isaac Bedloo drew a knife and wounded Joost in the neck. It was difficult to persuade the witnesses to make a statement under oath. *Burgemeesters* and *schepenen* designated two of their number to hear the witnesses, a procedure possibly inspired by the fact that at that time Allard Anthony was also a *schepen*. It is remarkable that all the witnesses claimed that the name of Allard Anthony had not been mentioned. On other details of the incident, their evidence also differed. Words such as *horned animal* and *cuckold* had been used, but the witnesses denied that these had been directed at Joost Goderis. It is probable that Joost dropped his case because he had insufficient evidence.[83]

Fighting

While insults and scandal-mongering started as matters between individuals, as soon as it led to fights, the officer came into play and the incident became a matter for the authorities. As early as 1638 a ban on fighting was included in a general ordinance. Four years later a specific ordinance followed against drawing a knife and inflicting wounds. An offender could expect a fine of fifty guilders or a sentence of three months' forced labor, in this case working with the Company's slaves. Explicit reference was made to an ordinance of the States General of a year earlier. When the ban on fighting was repeated in 1647, New Netherland was under the exclusive supervision of the Amsterdam chamber, and reference was thus made to the "commendable customs" of that city. In the by-law of 31 May 1647, a fine of hundred guilders was set for the drawing of a knife, to be increased to three hundred guilders if someone was injured. The fines actually imposed were smaller, particularly if the knife had been drawn in self-defense. Again in 1657, all "fighting, wounding, knife-drawing, and mischief" was banned. Surgeons, when treating cuts and stab wounds, were obliged to question the patient and notify the *schout*. It was also the duty of innkeepers and tappers to report all incidents to the *fiscael*.[84]

The majority of the fights that led to court appearances in New Netherland took place between two men. Violence between men and women was rare. An exceptional case is that of Trijn Herxker, who after an exchange of abuse with Huych Aertsz, drew a knife, which was subsequently taken away from her by bystanders. It was much more usual that the women tried to keep matters in hand, for example by urging the men not to draw knives. Maritje Damen intervened when her husband, Hendrick Andriesz van Doesburg, stood drunk in the street in Beverwijck at ten in the evening with an unsheathed saber in his hand. He was not threatening anyone at that moment, but as a preventive measure she took the weapon away from him anyway. Women also fought among themselves. In 1657 Engeltje Cornelis was charged because she was alleged to have entered the house of Wijnant Gerritsz and insulted and struck his wife Trijntje Melchers. Engeltje did not deny striking the other woman but argued that this had taken place in self-defense and not in the house but on the threshold, which made the charge less serious. In the few other instances of female fights, blows were struck, people were kicked, and in one case someone was bitten in the ear.[85]

In some fights between men, attempts were made to inflict a cut in the opponent's cheek, so-called *bekkensnijden* (face-cutting). On one hand this was literally a loss of face, on the other hand the "red line" that resulted was worn by some as a sign of standing, as it showed daring and ability to withstand pain. The two meanings are not mutually exclusive, but no trace can be found of anyone in New Netherland having pride in carrying such a scar. In the southern Dutch province of Brabant this type of injury took place mostly during fairs or the annual market. The same timing occurred in an incident in Rensselaerswijck in 1649. On 21 September, a day before the usual date of the so-called Amsterdam fair, Jan Dircksz van Bremen was the subject of an attack by Abraham Stevensz de Croaet and Dirck Hendricksz van Hilversum. Jan Dircksz was

> cut with a knife from the right to the left side from above to below his lower lip in his chin, so that the right side is hanging completely loose.[86]

Face-cutting was punished severely by the courts. For disfiguring Meuwis Hoogenboom in this way, Jacob Loockermans was fined three hundred guilders, and he was also ordered to pay the costs of the surgeon.[87]

More serious than fights in which a knife was drawn, of course, were the incidents resulting in death. All cases in which a death occurred were fights in which manslaughter was committed. In 1631 Jonas Fredericksz and Roelof Hendricksz had words about a net with which Roelof had been fishing. Jonas complained that after Roelof had used the net, he had left it lying about for others to clear away. Later, during a meal, the argument turned nasty. Jonas grabbed a knife from the chest at which they were eating, said "Ho! Defend yourself," and attacked. Roelof also drew a knife, and in the struggle Jonas was stabbed twice in the chest. Nonetheless, he chased after Roelof, stabbed him in the back and then fell to the ground. He died of his wounds shortly after. For the benefit of his heirs, the witnesses to the incident stated later in Amsterdam that Roelof was pardoned in New Netherland for the manslaughter at the request of the friends and relatives of the victim. That Roelof Hendricksz was not punished can be explained by the fact that he was not the first to draw a knife and had inflicted the fatal wounds in self-defense. Interesting here is the role of the friends and relatives, of whom several were present in the colony.[88]

Forgiveness by victims' next of kin can be encountered frequently in New Netherland. After the death of Claes Cornelisz Swits, who in 1663 was shot in the back in Schenectady by Philip Hendricksz Brouwer, the family set down in a notarial statement that they

> from the bottom of their hearts, forgave said Phillip Hendricxsz and acquit him of said unfortunate manslaughter committed upon said Claes Cornelisz, not desiring or meaning to take any revenge therefor, nor that any should ever be taken by their kin, begging all honorable courts and tribunals before whom these presents may come to grant the like immunity, pardon, and forgiveness to said Philip Hendricxse.[89]

In this case, the family acquiesced with the wish of the victim, who had forgiven Philip Hendricksz immediately after the incident, since he did not intend to kill. That the members of the family so expressly declined to exercise their right to revenge indicates that taking revenge was seen as a realistic alternative, even if this rarely occurred. It could lead to a feud that might split the whole community. The magnanimous forgiveness of manslaughter was a reasonable alternative for the restoration of a family's good name, especially if the perpetrator had expressed remorse and provided redress. This is a continuation of the medieval practice to regard manslaughter primarily as a private matter between the perpetrator and the victim's family.[90]

However, as far as the courts were concerned, the forgiveness of the victim or his family did not automatically imply exemption from legal proceedings, as can be seen in the case of WIC soldier Jacob Jeuriaensz, who was stabbed by fellow soldier Jochem Beeckman. Jacob Jeuriaensz on his sickbed forgave Beeckman, as he had himself provoked the fight. More important was that Jeuriaensz disobeyed the instructions of surgeon Hans Kierstede by getting up, causing the wound to reopen on several occasions. The patient lost a large amount of blood and subsequently died. The act of forgiveness was not considered in the acquittal, but reference was made to Exodus 21:19, which specifies that if a victim shall rise again from his bed, he that struck him shall not be punished.[91]

Violent Colonists?

All these insults, fights, and cases of manslaughter create the impression that the colonists were aggressive people who resorted to violence over the most trifling of matters as soon as honor was called into question. But was this really so? Even including the doubtful incidents, the tally adds up to a total of fifteen in the period prior to 1664, a figure that is probably incomplete for the first part of the colony's existence. Nonetheless, fifteen is quite a large number when compared with the only two incidents in the small town of Graft in North Holland in the whole of the seventeenth century. Of course, with its approximately three thousand inhabitants, Graft was smaller than New Netherland, which in about 1664 numbered some seven to eight thousand colonists. On the other hand, however, the period for Graft is considerably longer than the roughly forty years of New Netherland. Rather less problematic, and therefore more revealing than a quantitative comparison, is the qualitative similarity that existed between colony and the Dutch Republic in case of conflicts and violence. Attitudes toward these phenomena were essentially the same, the government played the same role, and the epithets and curse words were also generally the same.[92]

A Time to Every Purpose

The Gregorian calendar was used in New Netherland, as in Holland and Zeeland. As a result, a ten days' difference exists between the chronology in the colony and that of the English colonies in North America. In New Netherland the New Year began on 1 January. Besides the holiday of New Year's, many days served as landmarks, on which specific rituals were carried out.[93]

The most important instrument to herald daily and weekly occurrences was the bell, which was sounded every evening at nine o'clock to mark closing time for the taphouses and to summon the members of the burgher guard who were on duty to assemble in the guardhouse. The summoning of fugitive criminals and the proclamation of ordinances took place at the court building, after the sounding of a bell had first alerted the population. The bell was also rung in the event of emergencies, such as fire. When no bell was available, a trumpeter or drummer was used. In New Amsterdam and Beverwijck the nocturnal hours were eventually marked from the time of curfew until four in the morning by the night-watchman, whose duty it was to sound his rattle every hour at each street corner and to cry out the time.[94]

Each week, days were allotted to justice, commerce, and religion: days for the court to be in session, market days, and Sundays. Most of the adult population of New Netherland came into contact with the local court, and the importance of the court was such that it was widely known when it was in session. The choice of the day for the session varied from town to town, although Tuesday, the traditional day for justice, was generally preferred. However, in the 1630s and 1640s the court sessions of director general and council were held on Thursdays. From 1653 onwards the meetings of *burge-meesters* and *schepenen* of New Amsterdam took place on Monday morn-ings starting at nine o'clock. In 1658 it switched to Tuesdays. In later years, separate meetings of the *burgemeesters* were held on Thursday mornings, during which they dealt with administrative matters. In Beverwijck the court held session every week at ten on a Tuesday morning. This was changed to Thursday under English rule. In smaller settlements in New Netherland, court meetings were not held weekly. In Wiltwijck, for instance, the Tuesday meetings were in principle held every fortnight. After the English takeover, the first Tuesday of the month was the appointed day for all cases that had to be heard before a jury. No judicial sessions were held during some peri-ods of the year, for example at the end of July and the beginning of August, during harvest time. In New Amsterdam the regular court sessions were suspended from mid-December until three weeks after Christmas, although exceptions occurred.[95]

Another important day in the week was market day. In 1656, Saturday was designated as market day in New Amsterdam. The beach in front of the house of surgeon Hans Kierstede, today the corner of Pearl Street and Whitehall Street, became the place where the inhabitants of the towns and villages around New Amsterdam could offer for sale their meat, but-ter, cheese, turnips, carrots, and other wares. Thursday was market day in Breuckelen.[96]

The Day of the Lord

Sunday was the day of rest and worship, as laid down in the Bible in the Fourth Commandment and confirmed by the Synod of Dort. Bell ringing marked the commencement of the church services. Nonobservance of the Sabbath had already been forbidden in New Netherland in the instructions to Willem Verhulst in 1625.[97] While that ban was worded in general terms, later ordinances were more specific. Several edicts were issued for the ad-vancement of rest on Sundays, which until 1663 differed only in less impor-tant details. In principle, all work was forbidden, although exceptions were made for some activities that could not be put off. Further,

> exercises and amusement, drinking [themselves] drunk, frequenting taverns or
> taphouses, dancing, playing cards, *ticktacken* [backgammon], *balslaen* [liter-
> ally: "hitting the ball"], *clossen* [bowling], *kegelen* [nine pins], going boating,
> traveling with barges, carts, or wagons, before, between, or during the Holy
> worship

were not permitted.[98] The wording indicates that such activities were per-missible only after the two Sunday services. This distinction can also be seen in the many court cases brought against offenders. Numerous reports were made of beer being served in taphouses while divine service was under way in the church. Generally, the offense resulted in the imposition of a fine of six guilders for the tapper. The person being served had to pay a fine of four guilders. Contraventions of the ban on Sunday working were considerably less common than those of drinking at the time of the service, but some incidents occurred, such as that of Jan de Wit, miller in New Amsterdam, who cleaned his millstone on a Sunday and was fined six guilders for his industry.[99]

In 1663 a growing lack of clarity among the people whether all these interdictions applied to the whole Sunday or only a part of it prompted director general and council to draw up a much stricter ordinance. The description of what was not permitted was expanded, for example, with "the much too licentious and dissolute play, bawling, and shouting of the children in the streets and highways." Also stipulated was the explicit precept of rest for the whole Sabbath day, from sunrise to sunset. The usual fine remained, but repeat offenders faced the prospect of corporal punishment. *Burgemeesters* and *schepenen* received this new ordinance on 15 September 1663 but left it aside for several months without promulgating it. After a few offenders had been charged, they voiced their opinion to director general and council that "many points in such are too severe and at too great a variance with Dutch freedoms." In May 1664, the city government requested director general and council to give this further consideration, but whether this happened and what the result was is unknown. What the content was of those "many points" is also unknown. Possibly it was a reflection of the controversy in the Dutch Republic about the observance of the Sabbath. In 1673 the city government had different thoughts about it than in 1664. The magistrates of New Orange at that time issued an ordinance concerning the day of rest, in which was specified that it applied to the whole of the Sabbath. The precepts for Sunday observance and the attempts to ensure that everyone adhered to them indicate that these did not apply only to the members of the Reformed Church, who were expected to attend the church services anyway, but to the entire population.[100]

Days of Fasting and Prayer

The same holds true for *bededagen,* days of general fasting and prayer proclaimed by the provincial government. On *bededagen,* services were held and the same regulations applied as on regular Sundays. These days were proclaimed in the Dutch Republic to invoke God's blessing in the event of exceptional occurrences or to thank the Lord for His grace and favor. In New Netherland, some of these *bededagen,* always held on a Wednesday, were designated for matters that concerned the whole colony. In 1645, a *bededag* was proclaimed to acknowledge the peace agreement with the Indians and in 1655 another was proclaimed when the expedition against New

Sweden was about to start. Other *bededagen* were proclaimed as the result of occurrences that affected the Dutch Republic, such as the Treaty of Münster, which was marked in the colony by a *bededag* on 1 February 1649, or the end of the First Anglo-Dutch War in 1654. Toward the end of the 1650s, the wording of the letters in which the local authorities were informed of the proclamation of the *bededag* became increasingly general. The *bededagen* gradually took on a more general character and turned into annual or monthly occurrences, as first happened in 1648. Over the course of time this tailed off, and in later proclamations once again the first Wednesday of the month was designated for *bededagen*. The Dutch Republic also tended toward fixed annual *bededagen,* but while for a short period weekly *bededagen* were held in *patria,* no fixed *bededag* on the first Wednesday of the month occurred. In New Netherland all the *bededagen* were proclaimed by director general and council, in a few cases at the request of a minister. The *bededag* letters instructed the ministers to match their sermons to the character of the *bededag.*[101]

Religious Feasts

Besides the monthly *bededagen,* a number of religious feast days took place during the year, such as Christmas, Easter, Ascension Day, and Pentecost. After the Reformation only four of the original Roman Catholic feast days and holy days remained. The celebration of the Lord's Supper mostly took place four times a year on or near these four days, especially Christmas and Easter. The dates of the other two celebrations of the Lord's Supper varied from place to place. The Lord's Supper was celebrated at Pentecost in Breuckelen; in Wiltwijck, on the other hand, it did not generally take place until a few weeks later. The fourth celebration of the Lord's Supper mostly took place at the end of September or the beginning of October.[102]

Apart from these days sanctioned by church and government, several other days of the year were connected with specific customs and traditions. Some of these were, in the eyes of the two governments, remnants of the period prior to the Reformation, and several attempts were made to ban them. Many ordinances were promulgated, but that they had to be repeated year after year suggests that they met with little success. Nonetheless, the minutes of the court contain a few expressions of popular customs that were punished by the court of *schepenen*. Descriptions of them are so brief that they can be seen only as an indication of the existence of a particular tradition or custom. A few customs spread throughout the year were not overly frowned upon by the government.

Many small references indicate that special significance was attached to New Year's Day. In 1647, 1 January was the day allocated to the taking of office of the newly appointed Nine Men. New Year's wishes were common in letters written during the first half of January, even if in many cases these epistles were read months later on the other side of the Atlantic Ocean. The transition from the old year to the new was generally celebrated with festivities and drink. One of the more noisy customs was the habit of discharging firearms in the air. This met with the disapproval of the government, as director general and council considered shooting at night a waste of gunpowder and a possible cause of nasty accidents. In December 1655 director general and council banned a number of other customs observed around New Year's, such as the erection of maypoles, the beating of drums, and public drunkenness. Similar ordinances were also regularly issued in December of subsequent years. At the beginning of 1650, Abraham Stevensz de Croaet was fined forty guilders by the court at Rensselaerswijck for "the offense of shooting at night-time." He was not the only one to observe this custom. On their expedition into Mohawk and Oneida country, Harmen Meyndertsz van den Bogaert and his companions were regularly asked by the Indians to fire their weapons. One of the few occasions when they acquiesced was on 31 December 1634: "And on this night we fired three honor salvos in honor of the year of our Lord and Savior Jesus Christ."[103]

A last New Year's custom that made its way to New Netherland concerns the *duivekater*. In the Dutch Republic this bread, in the shape of an animal, was baked specially for the period between Christmas and Epiphany, or Twelfth Night, and was regularly given as a present to laborers and maidservants. On 1 January 1664 two women in Breuckelen who were regularly supplied with provisions by the deacons received a *duivekater* on the occasion of New Year.[104]

Several other feast days, such as Epiphany, followed New Year's Day, but no trace of celebrations can be found in New Netherland. Several other customs are linked with the season of winter, such as sleigh riding, skating, and *kolven* (precursor of golf) on the ice. These activities were engaged in regularly, but they were not without danger. In 1659 Jeremias van Rensselaer reported to his brother Jan Baptist that the past winter had been fairly cold,

> so that we could have all the racing with the sleigh we wanted. But I have been in trouble again, for my sleigh turned over with me on the river, or was upset by another sleigh, so that I severely hurt my left hand, from which I suffered much pain, but now it is again nearly all right.[105]

Jeremias had already been injured in a fall from a horse three years earlier on Christmas Eve, when he went out riding with several others. Riding horses fast was also a favorite winter pastime. However, Director Brant van Slichtenhorst of Rensselaerswijck disapproved of the sport when the farmhands used their masters' horses for this entertainment, risking the chance of the animals becoming crippled. The director's warnings had the opposite effect. One of the farmhands, Claes Teunisz, also known as Uylenspiegel, deliberately rode several times past the director's door very quickly, "out of pure mischief and in spite of the court." He was of course punished. Other pastimes were more innocent. After Jeremias van Rensselaer had become a member of the church, a husband, and a father, he no longer mentioned tobogganing and pleasure rides in his correspondence. Now he devoted the long winter evenings to the singing of psalms and visiting around the neighborhood. In December 1664 he wrote to the new English governor, Richard Nicolls: "There is no special news here, except [that we follow] the old winter custom, namely, of one neighbor visiting the other."[106]

Candlemas, 2 February, the celebration of Christ's presentation at the temple in Jerusalem, did not have a special place in the calendar of the Reformed Church. However, in Amsterdam 2 February did have a special significance as the day on which the new city administration took office. This was also adhered to in New Amsterdam, the first time in 1652 on the appointment of the new members of the Nine Men, and afterwards yearly on the appointment of *burgemeesters* and *schepenen*.

Of importance to a larger group were the customs surrounding Shrove Tuesday. Although this festival had lost much of its meaning after the Reformation, the evening before Ash Wednesday was still held in honor. Its celebration was limited to small groups, as a statement from Dirck Hendricksz van Hilversum shows. When questioned about a fight, he told the court that "Adriaen Huijbertss invited him on Shrove Tuesday to his house out of friendship." Probably a few others were there for a couple of drinks, something that the courts did not frown upon as long as it did not result in fighting. "Dressing up," a tradition on the evening of Shrove Tuesday, also took place within the home without any objection from the court, although walking the streets in fancy dress was not permitted. Only one incidence is recorded. In 1654 Abraham Stevensz de Croaet was fined six guilders for appearing on the streets dressed in women's clothing on Shrove Tuesday. Since it was the first offense and he excused himself by ignorance, he got off lightly. The court assured him of a heavy penalty in the event of a repetition.[107]

A traditional custom on Shrove Tuesday was *ganstrekken* (pulling the goose), in which a live goose was suspended on a rope, head down, between two trees. The animal's neck was greased with soap or oil. Participants then rode past on horseback and attempted to pull off the goose's head. This custom also crops up a few times in New Netherland, to the horror of director general and council. In their view, it was

> at the feast of Bacchus on the Eve of Lent completely frivolous, needless, and disreputable by subjects and neighbors to celebrate such pagan and popish festivals and to introduce such bad customs into this country.[108]

The farmhands who engaged in this, despite having been given prior warning, were fined. Harmen Smeeman received a heavier fine because he had also threatened Stuyvesant and some other members of the council.[109] Several years later a request for permission to engage in *ganstrekken* was addressed to director general and council, who, of course, turned it down.[110]

Much information can be found about Shrove Tuesday, but little is known about Easter. The only thing that can be found in the New Netherland sources is that the Lord's Supper was held. More is known about the first of May. As far as popular festivals are concerned, only the attempts of director general and council to forbid the erection of maypoles are worthy of mention. This occurred not immediately prior to May Day but was included in the ordinances outlawing breaches of the order at New Year. In Beverwijck, May Day was the day on which new magistrates were installed. Further, it was, as in the Dutch Republic, the customary day for moving household. It was one of the days on which payment became due for the tax on immovable property, and the date therefore appears in contracts referring to the sale or rent of property or as a date on which payments became due. From 1658, 1 May marked the beginning of the market for lean cattle to be fattened up over the summer; the market continued until the end of May.[111]

Two days of religious significance took place during late spring: Ascension, the day on which Christ ascended to Heaven, and Pentecost, when the Holy Ghost descended on the Apostles. Shortly after Pentecost the burgher guard in Beverwijck engaged in *papegaaischieten* (wooden parrot shooting). In Zeeland, for example, *papegaaischieten* also took place around this time. It is possible that in the summer months the New Netherlanders made pleasure trips to places in the neighborhood, but the sources contain little information, except for Selijns's remark about Stuyvesant's farm, "which is the place for recreation and pleasure in Manhattan where people from the town come for evening prayers as well." Summer was also the time for the harvest, which demanded the time and attention of the colonists, especially in the small towns and villages where the majority of the population was involved in agriculture.[112]

A date referred to frequently in the New Netherland sources is 22 September, the day of the annual fair in Amsterdam. Whether there actually was a fair or annual market in New Netherland on 22 September is unknown, but this date is mentioned regularly as one of the dates upon which payments came due. More is known about the markets held in October and November. The annual cattle market in New Amsterdam took place on 15 October, while the pig market was held on 1 November. This was later changed into a single market for fat cattle, to be held from 20 October to the end of November. Strangers who came to New Amsterdam in that period were not subject to arrest or summons but could go about their business with impunity.[113]

If any form of the celebration of *Sinterklaas* (the feast of St. Nicholas) took place in New Netherland, this has left no traces in the early sources.[114] With regard to Christmas, apart from the celebration of the Lord's Supper, extra food and drink were stocked up. For example, in 1667 the English governor Richard Nicolls ordered from Jeremias van Rensselaer "four barrels of good beer, which must be well malted and as good as we can make it." It was to be delivered before Christmas. From the nineteenth century onwards, American authors have written much about Sinterklaas and Christmas, and to a lesser extent about other Dutch festivals. For the most part these are reinvented traditions, part of a "Holland revival."[115]

Epilogue

*"It has pleased the Lord [to ordain] that
we must learn English"*

No Dutchman turns English overnight, even if he would like to. Four years after the English takeover of 1664, Jeremias van Rensselaer had learned very little English as yet. "The reason is that one has no liking for it." Jeremias had not expected New Netherland to remain in English hands. Yet the 1667 Peace of Breda brought a halt to the Second Anglo-Dutch War at the expense of the Dutch colonists in former New Netherland. From a geostrategic perspective, the decision of the States General is understandable: the colony was a small enclave, an island in a sea of foreigners, never as well populated as its English neighbors, and it would thus remain vulnerable. The Dutch Republic derived little benefit from it and could easily replace colonial produce from New Netherland, such as tobacco and fur, with goods obtained in trade with English and French colonies. By 1664, New Netherland did not fit any more into the changing Dutch Atlantic economy. Despite its early Brazilian adventures, the Dutch Atlantic empire was by this time based on shipping and trade—the main strength of the Republic's economy—not on colonial territorial conquests, for which it had neither the required surplus population and military power nor the repressive regime and depressed economy that had earlier sparked the emigration to England's overseas exploits. Both in 1667 and 1674, New Netherland was merely a convenient bargaining chip for the Dutch Republic. It was expendable.

The takeover of New Netherland was the result of a change in England, with the recently restored monarchy asserting itself on the road to absolutism. Extending royal power to the colonies was part of that. It was not a sign that colonial children were suddenly considered of paramount importance to its European parents. Colonial interests at home and abroad remained subordinate to the requirements of foreign relations with the European theater. No colonial issue lay at the root of a European war until the mid-eighteenth century, whereas on the other hand warfare in the colonies was always an extension of conflicts in Europe. Even so, while especially in the Caribbean colonial trading posts and islands had changed hands frequently, by the second half of the seventeenth century some form of stability prevailed as colonial populations grew and fortifications became more extensive, hampering easy takeovers. In a way, both the 1664 and 1673 takeovers of New Netherland were the last of their kind. If only New Netherland could have held out a decade longer, then perhaps it would have attained a population and defensive posture sufficient to keep English forces at bay and remain Dutch. If an English conquest had taken place a century later, like it did in the case of New France, then perhaps the Dutch language would still be used today in upstate New York, like French is in Quebec. For New Netherland's imaginary continued existence, such a perspective ignores the fact that the Dutch Republic had little to gain in persisting with its North American settlement. Perpetuating Dutch culture was not one of the aims of its founding, but the remarkable fact remains that New Netherland's existence had a substantial impact on early America.

The most obvious impact comes in the form of the persistence of Dutch culture after 1674. Although some of the Dutch colonists left New Netherland after 1664 and again after 1674, many stayed, either out of choice or because their property was in the form of land ownership. Merchants could return to *patria* more easily, but few of them did. The new English rulers initially allowed some trade and shipping to the Dutch Republic to continue, and gradually Dutch merchants began to integrate into English economic patterns. The Dutch colonists did not leave in droves, but the virtual standstill of emigration from the Dutch Republic meant that while their number rose through natural increase in absolute numbers, it dropped in comparison with other ethnic groups that arrived later. At the time of the first United States census in 1790, about a hundred thousand Americans, 3.4 percent of the total population, were labeled as of Dutch descent, well below the English, Scots, Irish, and German. This may have included descendants of New Netherland colonists not born in the Dutch Republic but in Germany or Scandinavia, who had gradually become culturally Dutch, partly through marriages with colonial Dutch families. Dutch Americans had largely stayed in the former New Netherland area; in New York and New Jersey they made up 17.5 percent and 16.6 percent of the population, respectively. It is no coincidence that during the debate over the Constitution in 1788, a translation of the draft proposal in Dutch was printed in Albany.

That is an indication that the Dutch language was still in use, although it was in decline. Its slow disappearance would take more than another century and fits into a general pattern. Dutch cultural elements first disappeared from the sphere of government. The imposition of English rule resulted in the removal of Dutch forms and procedures. Content followed form after a while, and some practices, such as the mutual will, persisted longer than others.

9. Joan Vinckeboons. De Manatus. Op de Noort Riuier. 1639. Photograph of map. I. N. Phelps Stokes Collection, Miriam and Ira D. Wallach Division of Art, Prints and Photographs, The New York Public Library, Astor, Lenox and Tilden Foundations.

The second sphere is that of religion. Theological tenets, as laid down at the Synod of Dort, are still adhered to in the Reformed Church in America. Specifically Dutch liturgical forms probably began to erode in the eighteenth century through the First Great Awakening when a conflict arose over organization of the church and the calling of ministers, leading to opposing factions and eventually to colonial independence from the Amsterdam classis by 1772. At the same time, another medium for ethnic cohesion, the Dutch language, was declining in importance. In the 1760s a dispute arose in New York City about the language to be used in sermons, and this obviously played a role in revising the relation with the Amsterdam classis as well. It was not until 1835 that the last sermon in Dutch was held in Tappan, New York, when the present church building was erected. On significant anniversaries, even into the twentieth century, there was Dutch preaching for sentimental purposes. The Reformed Church in America dropped the word "Dutch" in its name only in 1867.

With religion losing its function as focal point for a weakening ethnical awareness amidst the rising nationalism of Revolutionary and Early National America, Dutch traits retreated from the public into the private sphere, into the realm of the family. Some material aspects, such as the "Dutch" jambless fireplace in New York colonial homes, are evidence of this. Language, again, was important. When a touring party of the Holland Society of New York made a visit to the Netherlands in the late nineteenth century, some were still able to converse in Dutch with their hosts. Theodore Roosevelt on his trip to South Africa exchanged Dutch nursery rhymes with the Afrikaners. Such cultural relics became stilted and were transformed into icons in a gradual process of rediscovery of ethnic origin in the late nineteenth century. Yet they are distinguishable from the reinvented traditions of the nineteenth century, which mistook the seventeenth-century culture of the Dutch Republic for that of New Netherland and used it to depict a Dutch colonial life that never was. While research into architectural and linguistic details of Dutch American culture is in itself worthwhile and yields such nuggets of information as the Dutch origin of words like *stoop, cookies,* or *boss,* it is too often presented as the core of the Dutch contribution to American culture. Such a perspective clouds our view on the larger cultural processes that transformed Dutch American culture over the centuries.

Often these processes are discussed in terms of persistence and waning or Anglicization and "Batavianization." Yet this yields too static an image. It ignores other sources of cultural change that contributed to the dynamism of Dutch American culture. In the roughly hundred years after 1674, the colonial Dutch were defined by the English colonists through its "otherness"—and defined themselves through setting off their "Dutchness" against the "Englishness" of the English. As such, "Dutch identity" may have been more pronounced among the colonial Dutch than among the inhabitants of the Dutch Republic, many of whom were not confronted with an "other" on a daily basis. The continued contacts with the Dutch Republic, especially in the religious sphere, resulted in another source of cultural change. Through religious publications and ministers trained in the Netherlands, the colonial Dutch followed the broad religious developments in the Dutch Republic. Neither were the colonial Dutch immune to cultural changes that encompassed the whole of European culture. Pan-European intellectual movements like eighteenth-century Enlightenment thought and deism also reached and influenced the colonial Dutch.

Yet there is also a fourth source. The relative isolation of the colonial Dutch through its limited contact with the Dutch Republic—immigration having come to a virtual standstill—proved conducive to autonomous cultural developments. Perhaps this aspect is best visible in linguistic changes. Idiomatically, syntactically, and grammatically, the language of the colonial Dutch began to diverge from the slowly standardizing language in the Dutch Republic. This process is not dissimilar from that in South Africa. And there is even a fifth source, shared with other European cultures in America: the very slow adaptation to colonial circumstances, such as differences in climate, the presence of enslaved and indigenous peoples, the abundance of available land, and the scarcity of labor.

With such a wide-ranging array of forces at work, the contribution of American Dutch culture to early America or, even further, to modern American culture, becomes almost elusive. This is exacerbated by a tendency to oversimplify matters by presenting the Dutch contribution in terms of "legacy," "origin" or "birth," the latter an inappropriate metaphor with life, suggesting an unbroken link between past and present. Especially when dealing with such complex issues as tolerance and diversity, claims as to the importance of New Netherland have been exaggerated. New Netherland was diverse in terms of the ethnic origin of its population, but less so in terms of its culture. It was not as tolerant as is often supposed. In the Dutch Republic tolerance was a matter of practice rather than of conviction, dependent upon the interplay between secular and religious authorities, which varied from place to place. The strong bond between ministers and magistrates in New Netherland placed the colony on the repressive side of the spectrum of tolerance within Dutch culture.

Yet in an indirect way, the Dutch presence had a substantial impact. In the same way that the Swedes were allowed to continue their Lutheran worship in public after the conquest of New Sweden, the Dutch were granted "the liberty of their Consciences, in Divine Worship, and Church Discipline" when the English took over New Netherland.[1] More than an imported form of Dutch tolerance, it was the superimposition of an English ruling minority over a largely Dutch population that contributed to extending the existing freedom of conscience in New Netherland into freedom of worship in the colony of New York. A heterogeneity and ethnic diversity developed that made New York into a factious colony. It is even possible that the diversity attracted non-British colonists, such as French Huguenots and Germans. The descendants of New Netherland thus played a role in creating the cultural mosaic that later, through the collective experience of the American Revolution and the creation of a new nation, began to homogenize into the United States of America.

Abbreviations

BDC	Th. G. Evans and T. A. Wright (eds.), *Records of the Reformed Dutch Church in New Amsterdam and New York. Baptisms from 25 December 1639 to 29 December 1800* (Collections of the New York Genealogical and Biographical Society 2) (2 vols., New York 1901–1903, repr. Upper Saddle River, N.J. 1968).
BGE	P. R. Christoph and F. A. Christoph (eds.), *Books of General Entries of the Colony of New York, 1664–1673: Orders, Warrants, Letters, Commissions, Passes and Licenses issued by Governors Richard Nicolls and Francis Lovelace* (New York Historical Manuscripts: English) (Baltimore 1982).
BMGN	*Bijdragen en Mededelingen betreffende de Geschiedenis der Nederlanden*
BMHG	*Bijdragen en Mededelingen van het Historisch Genootschap*
CJVR	A. J. F. van Laer (trans. and ed.), *Correspondence of Jeremias van Rensselaer 1651–1674* (Albany 1932).
CMARS	A. J. F. van Laer (trans. and ed.), *Minutes of the Court of Albany, Rensselaerswijck and Schenectady 1668–1685* (3 vols., Albany 1926–1932).
CM 1655–1656	Ch. T. Gehring (trans. and ed.), *Council Minutes, 1655–1656* (New Netherland Documents Series, vol. 6) (Syracuse 1995).
Corres. 1647–1653	Ch. T. Gehring (trans. and ed.), *Correspondence, 1647–1653* (New Netherland Documents Series, vol. 11) (Syracuse 2000).
Corres. 1654–1658	Ch. T. Gehring (trans. and ed.), *Correspondence, 1654–1658* (New Netherland Documents Series, vol. 12) (Syracuse 2003).
dHM	*de Halve Maen: Magazine of the Dutch Colonial Period in America*
DP	Ch. T. Gehring (trans. and ed.), *Delaware Papers (Dutch Period). A Collection of Documents Pertaining to the Regulation of Affairs on the South River of New Netherland, 1648–1664* (New York Historical Manuscripts: Dutch, vols. 18–19) (Baltimore 1981).
DRCHNY	E. B. O'Callaghan and B. Fernow (trans. and ed.), *Documents Relative to the Colonial History of the State of New York* (15 vols., Albany 1853–1883).

DRNN	A. J. F. van Laer (trans. and ed.), *Documents Relating to New Netherland, 1624–1626, in the Henry E. Huntington Library* (San Marino, Calif. 1924).
DTB	Doop-, trouw- en begraafregisters (vital records)
ERA	J. Pearson and A. J. F. van Laer (trans. and ed.), *Early Records of the City and County of Albany and Colony of Rensselaerswijck* (4 vols., Albany 1869–1919).
ER	E. T. Corwin (trans. and ed.), *Ecclesiastical Records: State of New York* (7 vols., Albany 1901–1916).
FOCM	Ch. T. Gehring (trans. and ed.), *Fort Orange Court Minutes, 1652–1660* (New Netherland Documents Series, vol. 16, part 2) (Syracuse 1990).
FOR 1656–1678	Ch. T. Gehring (trans. and ed.), *Fort Orange Records, 1656–1678* (New Netherland Documents Series) (Syracuse 2000).
GAA	Gemeentearchief Amsterdam
Guide	Gehring, Ch. T. (ed.), *A Guide to Dutch Manuscripts Relating to New Netherland in United States Repositories* (Albany 1978).
Jb CBG	*Jaarboek Centraal Bureau voor Genealogie*
KP	D. Versteeg (trans.), P. R. Christoph, K. Scott, and K. Stryker-Rodda (eds.), *Kingston Papers, 1661–1675* (New York Historical Manuscripts: Dutch) (2 vols., Baltimore 1976).
LCNY	A. J. F. van Laer (trans. and ed.), *The Lutheran Church in New York 1649–1772. Records in the Lutheran Church Archives at Amsterdam, Holland* (New York 1946).
LP	Ch. T. Gehring (trans. and ed.), *Land Papers* (New York Historical Manuscripts: Dutch, vols. GG, HH & II) (Baltimore 1980).
LO	E. B. O'Callaghan (trans.), *Laws and Ordinances of New Netherland, 1636–1674* (Albany 1868).
LWA	Ch. T. Gehring (trans. and ed.), *Laws and Writs of Appeal 1647–1663* (New Netherland Documents Series, vol. 16, part 1) (Syracuse 1991).
MCR	A. J. F. van Laer (trans. and ed.), *Minutes of the Court of Rensselaerswyck 1648–1652* (Albany 1922).
MDC	"Records of the Reformed Dutch Church in the City of New York. Marriages." In: *NYGBR* 6 (1875), 32–39 [1639–1652]; 81–88 [1652–1659]; 141–148 [1659–1667]; 184–191 [1668–1675]; 7 (1876), 27–34 [1675–1681]; 77–84 [1681–1685]; 8 (1877), 33–40 [1685–1688]; 10 (1879), 119–126 [1688–1692]; 11 (1880), 75–82 [1692–1695]; 125–132 [1695–1698]; 172–179 [1698–1702].
MOM	(1) B. Fernow (trans. and ed.), *The Minutes of the Orphanmasters of New Amsterdam, 1655–1663* (New York 1902). (2) B. Fernow (trans. and ed.), *Minutes of the Orphanmasters Court of New Amsterdam, 1655–1663. Minutes of the Executive Boards of the Burgomasters of New Amsterdam and the Records of Walewyn van der Veen, Notary Public 1662–1664* (New York 1907).
NA	Notarial Archives
Nat. Arch.	National Archive, The Hague

NNN	J. F. Jameson (ed.), *Narratives of New Netherland 1609–1664* (New York 1909, 2nd ed. 1967).
NYCM	New York Colonial Manuscripts (in NYSA)
NYGBR	*The New York Genealogical and Biographical Record*
NYH	*New York History. Quarterly Journal of New York State Historical Association*
NYHM	(1) A. J. F. van Laer (trans. and ed.), *Register of the Provincial Secretary, 1638–1642* (New York Historical Manuscripts: Dutch, vol. 1) (Baltimore 1974).
	(2) A. J. F. van Laer (trans. and ed.), *Register of the Provincial Secretary, 1642–1647* (New York Historical Manuscripts: Dutch, vol. 2) (Baltimore 1974).
	(3) A. J. F. van Laer (trans. and ed.), *Register of the Provincial Secretary, 1648–1660* (New York Historical Manuscripts: Dutch, vol. 3) (Baltimore 1974).
	(4) A. J. F. van Laer (trans. and ed.), *Council Minutes, 1638–1649* (New York Historical Manuscripts: Dutch, vol. 4) (Baltimore 1974).(5) Ch. T. Gehring (trans. and ed.), *Council Minutes, 1652–1654* (New York Historical Manuscripts: Dutch, vol. 5) (Baltimore 1983).
NYHS	New-York Historical Society, New York City
NYPL	New York Public Library, New York City
NYSA	New York State Archives, Albany
NYSL	New York State Library, Albany
OFDRCB	A. P. G. J. van der Linde (trans. and ed.), *Old First Dutch Reformed Church of Brooklyn, New York: First Book of Records, 1660–1752* (New York Historical Manuscripts: Dutch) (Baltimore 1983).
OWIC	Archive Old WIC (in Nat. Arch.)
RNA	B. Fernow (ed.), and E. B. O'Callaghan (trans.), *The Records of New Amsterdam from 1653 to 1674 Anno Domini* (7 vols., New York 1897, 2nd ed. Baltimore 1976).
TvG	*Tijdschrift voor Geschiedenis*
VRBM	A. J. F. van Laer (trans. and ed.), *Van Rensselaer Bowier Manuscripts, Being the Letters of Kiliaen van Rensselaer, 1630–1643, and Other Documents Relating to the Colony of Rensselaerswyck* (Albany 1908).
VRMP	Van Rensselaer Manor Papers (in NYSL)
WMQ	*The William and Mary Quarterly: A Magazine of Early American History and Culture*

Notes

Preface

1. Armitage, "Three Concepts of Atlantic History"; Bailyn, "The Idea of Atlantic History"; Emmer and Klooster, "The Dutch Atlantic"; Howe, *American History in an Atlantic Context;* Klooster, "Winds of Change"; Klooster, "The Place of New Netherland"; De Vries, "The Dutch Atlantic Economies;" Games, "Forum: Beyond the Atlantic."
2. *FOCM,* xxxi.

Introduction

Chapter subtitle quoted from Murphy, *Anthology,* 30–31, 68–75.

1. Murphy, *Anthology,* 46–67; Funk, "De literatuur van Nieuw-Nederland," 391; Van Boheemen, "Dutch-American Poets," 122.
2. Van der Donck, *Description,* 2–3. On Van der Donck: Hoffman, "Armory. Van der Donck—Van Bergen," Van Gastel, "Adriaen van der Donck, New Netherland, and America" and Van Gastel, "Adriaen van der Donck als woordvoerder."
3. Van der Donck, *Description,* 3. References in this book are to the nineteenth-century translation by Jeremiah Johnson, republished by O'Donnell in 1968, which has long been regarded as deficient. A new translation by Diederik Willem Goedhuys, entitled *A Description of New Netherland,* will be published by University of Nebraska Press in 2008. It is unfortunate that a modern edition in Dutch is still not available.
4. Van der Donck, *Description,* 5.
5. Ibid. 6, 15.
6. Juet, *Henry Hudson's reize,* LII, LIII; Johnson, *Charting the Sea of Darkness,* 89; Jacobs, "Johannes de Laet en de Nieuwe Wereld"; Zandvliet, *Mapping for Money,* 167 and 291, n. 18.
7. *NNN,* 52.
8. Van der Donck, *Description,* 7, 10; Funk, "De literatuur van Nieuw-Nederland," 385.
9. Van der Donck, *Description,* 10.
10. *NNN,* 45, 102; Hart, *Prehistory,* 18.
11. Van der Donck, *Description,* 8.
12. *NNN,* 103.
13. Van der Donck, *Description,* 12. See also *NNN,* 170.

14. Ibid., 11–12.

15. Ibid., 13.

16. Ibid., 15; Thomas, *Man and the Natural World*, 17.

17. *NNN*, 168.

18. Ibid., 170; Van der Donck, *Description*, 17–18.

19. Van der Donck, *Description*, 17, 36n, 37; *DRNN*, 75–76; Pagden, *European Encounters with the New World*, 17–19; Hine, *Old Mine Road*, 1–16; Abbott, "Colonial Copper Mines," 296.

20. *NNN*, 50, 73; Hart, *Prehistory*, 19; Rink, *Holland on the Hudson*, 30–31; Schmidt, *Innocence Abroad*, 214; Bachman, *Peltries or Plantations*, 56–57.

21. Van der Donck, *Description*, 58–62.

22. Ibid., 58–63; *NNN*, 171.

23. Van der Donck, *Description*, 63–64.

24. Ibid., 64–66.

25. Ibid., 60.

26. Crosby, *Ecological Imperialism*, 11.

27. *NNN*, 168.

28. Van der Donck, *Description*, 19–20; *NNN*, 38.

29. Cronon, *Changes in the Land*; Van der Donck, *Description*, 20; Van Gastel, "Van der Donck's Description," 414.

30. *NNN*, 170; Van der Donck, *Description*, 71, 30–31.

31. Van der Donck, *Description*, 24–25.

32. Ibid., 67–70.

33. Ibid., 25–27; *NNN*, 168–169.

34. Van der Donck, *Description*, 28–29, 33.

35. Ibid., 43–44; *NNN*, 114. De Rasière is ambivalent about the presence of lions and bears.

36. Van der Donck, *Description*, 45.

37. Ibid., 43–47, 57–58; *NNN*, 169–170; Gehring and Starna, *A Journey into Mohawk and Oneida Country*, 6, 35, 37, n. 45, n. 53.

38. Van der Donck, *Description*, 54; *NNN*, 222.

39. *NNN*, 171; Van der Donck, *Description*, 54–56.

40. O'Callaghan, *History of New Netherland* 1: 346.

41. Van der Donck, *Description*, 7, 11.

42. Ibid., 48, 113, 117; Hart, "The City-Colony of New Amstel," II, 8; Rich, "Russia and the Colonial Fur Trade," 312–313; Norton, *Fur Trade*, 104–105.

43. Van der Donck, *Description*, 48–49.

44. *CJVR* 9.

45. Van der Donck, *Description*, 51–54; *NNN*, 114–115, 169.

46. Van der Donck, *Description*, 73; Snow, Gehring, and Starna, *In Mohawk Country*, 107; Elliott, *The Old World and the New*, 41–48; Frederickson, *White Supremacy*, 7–13; Otto, *New Netherland Frontier*.

47. *Corres. 1654–1658*, 84.

48. Richter, *Ordeal of the Longhouse*; Snow, *The Iroquois*; Jennings, *The Ambiguous Iroquois Empire*.

49. Trigger, "The Mohawk-Mahican War"; Starna and Brandão, "From the Mohawk-Mahican War to the Beaver Wars."

50. Van der Donck, *Description*, 91–92; Snow, Gehring, and Starna, *In Mohawk Country*, 118–119; *NNN*, 172; *FOCM*, 150n; Richter, *Ordeal of the Longhouse*, 1–17; Trelease, *Indian Affairs*, 1–24; Trigger, *Handbook of North American Indians*; Schulte Nordholt, "Nederlanders in Nieuw-Nederland," 44; Verbeeck, "Van partner tot horige." See also Merwick, *The Shame and the Sorrow*.

51. Van der Donck, *Description*, 72, 78; Snow, Gehring, and Starna, *In Mohawk Country*, 106, 109–110; *NNN*, 173. De Rasière considered the skin color to be orange, similar to the Brazilians: *NNN*, 105.

52. Megapolensis, *NNN*, 175.

53. Van der Donck, *Description*, 64, 72–73; Snow, Gehring, and Starna, *In Mohawk Country*, 109; Richter, *Ordeal of the Longhouse*, 58–59; Gehring and Grumet, "Observations," 107; Brandão, "*Your Fyre Shall Burn No More*," appendix C. The estimates in Brandão are considerably higher than those of 1994 by Dean Snow, who puts the total for the Iroquois at 9,104 and for the Mohawks at 2,304. Snow, The *Iroquois*, 110.

54. Van der Donck, *Description*, 77; Snow, Gehring, and Starna, *In Mohawk Country*, 109.

55. Van der Donck, *Description*, 77–79, 93; Snow, Gehring, and Starna, *In Mohawk Country*, 109–110, 119; *NNN*, 173, 176; Hamell, "Wampum," 42; Cantwell and Wall, *Unearthing Gotham*, 132–133.

56. *NNN*, 105.

57. Van der Donck, *Description*, 97; Snow, Gehring, and Starna, *In Mohawk Country*, 121; *NNN*, 175.

58. *NNN*, 174; Cronon, *Changes in the Land*, 52.

59. *NNN*, 177.

60. Van der Donck, *Description*, 76; Snow, Gehring, and Starna, *In Mohawk Country*, 108; *NNN*, 107.

61. Van der Donck, *Description*, 79–82; Snow, Gehring, and Starna, *In Mohawk Country*, 110–113; Richter, *Ordeal of the Longhouse*, 18–19.

62. Megapolensis, *NNN*, 179.

63. *NNN*, 103; Van der Donck, *Description*, 98; Snow, Gehring, and Starna, *In Mohawk Country*, 122; *NNN*, 179; *CM 1655–1656*, 86n; Richter, *Ordeal of the Longhouse*, 40, 42–43; Brandão, "*Your Fyre Shall Burn No More*," 28–29.

64. Van der Donck, *Description*, 98; Snow, Gehring, and Starna, *In Mohawk Country*, 122; Richter, *Ordeal of the Longhouse*, 41–43, 46, 56; *NNN*, 179; Jacobs and Shattuck, "Bevers voor drank, land voor wapens," 108; Brandão, "*Your Fyre Shall Burn No More*," 22–25.

65. Eekhof, *Michaëlius*, 121–122, 133; Feister, "Linguistic Communication," 31; Buccini, "Swannekens Ende Wilden," 15–20.

66. *NNN*, 172.

67. Van der Donck, *Description*, 103; Snow, Gehring, and Starna, *In Mohawk Country*, 127; *CM 1655–1656*, 145, 204; Feister, "Linguistic Communication," 33–34; Starna, "Assessing American Indian-Dutch Studies."

68. *NNN*, 177; Van der Donck, *Description*, 102; Snow, Gehring, and Starna, *In Mohawk Country*, 126; Richter, *Ordeal of the Longhouse*, 24.

69. Gehring and Starna, *A Journey into Mohawk and Oneida Country*, 17–18.

70. *NNN*, 174.

71. *Ibid.*, 48.

72. Van der Donck, *Description*, 94; Snow, Gehring, and Starna, *In Mohawk Country*, 120.

73. *NNN*, 105.

74. Van der Donck, *Description*, 72; Snow, Gehring, and Starna, *In Mohawk Country*, 106.

75. *NNN*, 48.

Chapter 1. Reconnaissance and Exploration

1. Van Goor, *De Nederlandse koloniën*; Van den Boogaart, *Overzee*; Boxer, *The Dutch Seaborne Empire*.

2. Klooster, *The Dutch in the Americas*; Den Heijer, *De geschiedenis van de WIC*; Postma and Enthoven, *Riches from Atlantic Commerce*, in which the introduction provides an overview of recent literature on Dutch expansion in the Atlantic.

3. The main source for the voyage is Juet's journal. Hudson's journal has been lost, although some fragments have been saved in quotations by Johannes de Laet. Juet, *Henry Hudson's reize*, 56; Johnson, *Charting the Sea of Darkness*, 115.

4. Juet, *Henry Hudson's reize*, lx–lxi, 58–60, 113; Johnson, *Charting the Sea of Darkness*, 116–117.

5. Juet, *Henry Hudson's reize*, lxi–lxvi, 62–69; Johnson, *Charting the Sea of Darkness*, 118–122.

6. Juet, *Henry Hudson's reize*, 66, 71, 114; Johnson, *Charting the Sea of Darkness*, 121, 123; Bradley, *Before Albany*, 12; Otto, *Dutch-Munsee Encounter*, 37–39.

7. Van der Donck, *Description*, 4; Otto, "Origins of New Netherland," 30–35; Otto, "Common Practices and Mutual Misunderstandings"; Haefeli, "On First Contact." A more elaborate version of the Indians' oral tradition of the first arrival of Europeans is in Heckewelder, "Indian Tradition."

8. Johnson, *Charting the Sea of Darkness*, 127–132, 149–212.

9. Hart, *Prehistory*, 18–22.

10. Ibid., 22–23.

11. In the beginning of the twentieth century, during the construction of the subway on Manhattan, remains were found of a ship, with traces of fire. During the construction of the World Trade Center at the beginning of the 1970s, attempts were made to find additional parts. It has been thought that these remains were of the *Tijger*. Dilliard, *Album of New Netherland*, 27; Solecki, "The 'Tiger'"; Hallowell, "Disappearance of the Historic Ship Tijger"; Cantwell and Wall, *Unearthing Gotham*, 150–153. However, recent research by Gerald de Weerdt, "A Preliminary Assessment," has shown that the remains date from the early eighteenth century.

12. Hart, *Prehistory*, 24–30.

13. Ibid., 30–31; Muller, *De reis van Jan Cornelisz. May*, lii–liii.

14. Hart, *Prehistory*, 32–33; Muller, *Geschiedenis der Noordsche Compagnie*, 67; Hacquebord, Stokman, and Wasseur, "The Directors of the Chambers of the 'Noordse Compagnie'"; *DRCHNY* 1: 5–6, 10–12; Zandvliet, "Een ouderwetse kaart van Nieuw Nederland."

15. Hart, *Prehistory*, 34–35; Rink, *Holland on the Hudson*, 47–48; Jacobs, "The Dutch in the Atlantic, in New Netherland, and in Virginia." A later deposition by Englishman Ananias Banneth, first mate on the ship *Samuel*, reveals that Ruijl died in Virginia, presumably in Jamestown, and was buried there in August 1622. This opens up the possibility that he was already trading there earlier. If so, he may have been the first Dutchman to enter the Chesapeake River. GAA, NA, inv. no. 291, fol. 15 (12 July 1623).

16. *NNN*, 78.

17. Hart, *Prehistory*, 35–36, 52; *DRCHNY* 1: 12; Condon, *New York Beginnings*, 26; GAA, NA, inv. no. 547, fol. 304 (16 October 1620); Jacobs, "Truffle Hunting with an Iron Hog."

18. GAA, NA, inv. no. 645, fol. 36v–37 and 43–43v (9 September 1619).

19. Hart, *Prehistory*, 36–37, 54–55; *DRCHNY* 1: 21; Bachman, *Peltries or Plantations*, 13; *DRNN*, xiii; cf. Rink, *Holland on the Hudson*, 49; GAA, NA, inv. no. 645, fol. 36v–37 and 43–43v (9 September 1619).

20. GAA, NA, inv. no. 200, fol. 625–626v (14 August 1620); *DRCHNY* 1: 24–25.

21. *DRNN*, xii; *DRCHNY* 1: 27, 28; GAA, NA, inv. no. 256, fol. 182v (21 May 1625), inv. no. 441, fol. 155 (30 July 1627); Hart, *Prehistory*, 38, 69.

22. Den Heijer, *De geschiedenis van de WIC*, 13–26; Van den Boogaart, "De Nederlandse expansie in het Atlantische gebied," 113–116; Ligtenberg, *Willem Usselinx*, 45–74; Jameson, *Willem Usselinx*, 22–81; Menkman, *De West-Indische Compagnie*, 30–31, 39–41; Klooster, *The Dutch in the Americas*, 7–8, 17–20.

23. Den Heijer, *De geschiedenis van de WIC*, 26–34; Frijhoff, *Wegen*, 494. Frijhoff's magisterial book is now also available in translation (*Fulfilling God's Mission*). References here are to the Dutch version.

24. Cf. Frijhoff, *Wegen*, 494. That the States General had only one vote does not imply that only one representative was present. In 1638, the whole of the committee of the States General, nine men strong, was present at the meeting of the *Heren XIX*. Nat. Arch., Archive States General, *loketkas* WIC, inv. no. 12564.6 (28 February 1638–1 May 1638).

25. For example, with reference to the discussion on the opening of trade with Brazil in 1638. Nat. Arch., Archive States General, *loketkas* WIC, inv. no. 12564.6 (28 February 1638–1 May 1638).

26. Den Heijer, *De geschiedenis van de WIC*, 31–33, 83; *VRBM*, 86–135.

27. Van Winter, *De Westindische Compagnie ter kamer Stad en Lande*, 12; Israel, *Dutch Primacy*, 156–161; Den Heijer, *De geschiedenis van de WIC*, 33; Gemeentearchief Leiden,

secretariearchief II, inv. no. 6701; Jacobs, "Johannes de Laet en de Nieuwe Wereld," 110; De Laet, *Iaerlyck verhael,* 1: (32); Frijhoff, *Wegen,* 495; Holthuis, *Frontierstad bij het scheiden der markt,* 157–158.

28. *DRNN,* xiii, xv; *NNN,* 75–76; Wieder, *De stichting van New York,* 10; Rink, *Holland on the Hudson,* 70; Sainsbury, *Calendar of State Papers, Colonial Series, 1574–1660,* 36–37.

29. Rink, *Holland on the Hudson,* 69–73; Jacobs, "Hartford Treaty"; *DRNN,* xiv–xvi; *DRCHNY* 1: 27–28, *DRCHNY* 3: 6–8; cf. Schnurmann, *Atlantische Welten,* 83–84.

30. Zabriskie and Kenney, "The Founding of New Amsterdam," 1: 15; Wieder, *De stichting van New York,* 13; Rink, *Holland on the Hudson,* 80.

31. Peters, "Volunteers for the Wilderness"; Zabriskie and Kenney, "The Founding of New Amsterdam," 1: 15, 2: 6; Van Ruymbeke, "The Walloon and Huguenot Elements."

32. Zabriskie and Kenney, "The Founding of New Amsterdam," 2: 5, 6; *DRNN,* 86–89, 132–169; Lyon, "The Transfer of Technology," 337–339. For a possible, though not entirely convincing, identification of Krijn Fredericksz, see Westra, "Lost and Found: Crijn Fredericx."

33. Rink, *Holland on the Hudson,* 83–84, 86–87; Gehring, "Peter Minuit's Purchase of Manhattan Island," 6; *DRCHNY* 1: 37; Zabriskie and Kenney, "The Founding of New Amsterdam," 4: 12, 14, 5: 11–12, 16; Weslager, "Did Minuit Buy Manhattan Island from the Indians?" and *A Man and His Ship,* supports the idea that Verhulst made the purchase.

Chapter 2. Population and Immigration

1. GAA, NA, inv. no. 1031, fol. 914 and 916 (6 February 1659), inv. no. 1580, fol. 13 (7 February 1659). On Steenwijck see also Hallam, "The Portrait of Cornelis Steenwyck."

2. Van den Boogaart, "Servant Migration," gives a total of 6,030 in 1664, which in my opinion and that of other scholars is too low. See, for example, Rink, *Holland on the Hudson,* 158; and Shattuck, "Civil Society," 11. In the estimates made by both Van den Boogaart and Rink, little or no account has been taken of the natural growth of the population (Rink, *Holland on the Hudson,* 165; Van den Boogaart, "The Netherlands and New Netherland," 14: "Natural growth was out of the question.") This is a remarkable statement, as between 1639 and 1665 no fewer than 1,636 children were baptized in New Amsterdam (*BDC* 1: 9). From 1660 to 1664 the average number per year was 91.8. Following the method of Posthumus and using 30 as multiplication factor, the number of baptisms indicates a population size for New Amsterdam of 2,754. As the composition of the population has considerable effect on the number of births and baptisms, I have adjusted the outcome down a bit. See Noordam, "Demografische ontwikkelingen," 43–45, for population estimates of Leiden. For an overview of the population of New York up to the twentieth century, see Rosenwaike, *Population History of New York City.* For Beverwijck, see Venema, *Beverwijck,* 428–429.

3. *DRCHNY* 1: 65; De Boer, "Memorie," 355; Wabeke, *Dutch Emigration,* 14–17; Emmer, "Nederlandse handelaren, kolonisten en planters," 12.

4. Van der Donck, *Description,* 121–122; De Vries and Van der Woude, *Nederland 1500–1815,* 476; Den Heijer, *De geschiedenis van de WIC,* 102; Enthoven, "Dutch Crossings."

5. GAA, NA, inv. no. 944, fol. 463 (11 April 1635); Ernst, "Het Amsterdamse notarieel archief," 148; *DRNN,* 239, 275; *MDC,* 4 June 1644.

6. GAA, NA, inv. no. 2292 III, p. 51 (30 October 1664); Wijnman, "Lieven van Coppenol, schoolmeester-calligraaf," 162–167.

7. NYSA, NYCM 13: 84, p. 5 (16 April 1660), 86 (12 April 1660), 116, p. 15 (25 June 1660); NYSA, NYCM 13: 85 (8 April 1660); *RNA* 3: 427–429; NYSA, NYCM 10–11: 234, 235 and 238 (12 and 16 October 1662); GAA, DTB, inv. no. 48a, p. 133 (1 July 1661) (banns for Boudewijn's marriage to Annetje Aris van Nieuw Amsterdam); Haks, *Huwelijk en gezin in Holland,* 86–87; *BDC* 1: 58 (24 October 1660); GAA, NA, inv. no. 3492, fol. 167 (VII, doc. 6) (3 August 1671), inv. no. 2804, fol. 801 (29 August 1661); Maika, "Commerce and Community," 117–118.

8. Jacobs, "Scheepvaart en handel," 57; *DRCHNY* 1: 114; GAA, NA, inv. no. 2279, III, fol. 73 (25 January 1652); Ernst, "Het Amsterdamse notarieel archief," 148.

9. *DP*, 130; *Corres. 1647–1653*, 54; Bruijn, Gaastra, and Schöffer, *Dutch Asiatic Shipping*, 161–167; GAA, NA, inv. no. 603, fol. 188v (30 March 1648); NYHS, Stuyvesant-Rutherford Papers 2: 6 (*Guide*, no. 461); Frijhoff, *Wegen*, 794–795; Scott, "Voyages"; *VRBM*, 355–389, 580–603; Jacobs, "Scheepvaart en handel," 54–58.

10. Van Alphen, "The Female Side of Dutch Shipping," 125–126; Van Alphen, "Zielverko-pers"; Van Gelder, *Het Oost-Indisch avontuur;* Jacobs, "Soldiers of the Company"; Jacobs, "Soldaten van de Compagnie."

11. GAA, NA, inv. no. 1294, fol. 208 (6 December 1647), fol. 188v (7 November 1647), inv. no. 1341, fol. 75v (6 December 1647). See also *NYHM* 2: 455.

12. GAA, NA, inv. no. 1373, reg. D, not paginated (12 May 1652), inv. no. 1329, fol. 119 (18 December 1657); Ernst, "Het Amsterdamse notarieel archief," 145; NYPL, Bontemantel Collection, New Netherland Papers, box 1, folder "Official list of New Netherland" (undated, ca. 1650; *Guide*, no. 551); NYSA, NYCM 14: 74, pp. 2, 3 (5 September 1662); *DRCHNY* 14: 439.

13. Jacobs, *New Netherland*, 53–54; GAA, NA, inv. no. 1323, fol. 193 (30 June 1646), fol. 196v (5 July 1646), fol. 220 (19 July 1646). Gaastra, *De geschiedenis van de VOC*, 81.

14. *DRCHNY* 1: 38, 139, 155–156, 641, 13: 135, 2: 435, 440; NYPL, Bontemantel Collection, New Netherland Papers, box 1, overview of salaries in New Netherland (undated, late 1650s; *Guide*, no. 596); O'Callaghan, *Documentary History* 3: 56–57; *RNA* 5: 115–116; data on Cape of Good Hope come from personal communication, Ad Biewenga, Free University of Amsterdam.

15. GAA, NA, inv. no. 1330, not paginated (21 April 1660), inv. no. 1303, fol. 124 (10 May 1653), inv. no. 1349, fol. 42v (25 April 1652); Voorhees, "Leisler's pre-1689 Biography"; *VRBM*, 777n, 833–834; *NYHM* 1: 299–300; *NYHM* 4: 132, 315; *BDC* 1: 13–14.

16. GAA, NA, inv. no. 1029, p. 211–212 (10 May 1652); *CM 1655–1656*, 172; *MDC*, 5 November 1656; *Corres. 1647–1653*, 146, 176.

17. *DRCHNY* 13: 205.

18. Jacobs, "Scheepvaart en handel," 61–72; Van Royen, *Zeevarenden*, 13–43.

19. Jacobs, "Scheepvaart en handel"; Ernst, "Het Amsterdamse notarieel archief," 144.

20. Bruijn, *Gelag*, 4–5; Van Royen, *Zeevarenden*, 36–42; Boxer, *Dutch Seaborne Empire*, 57; GAA, NA, inv. no. 1125, fol. 356v (18 June 1658), inv. no. 2287, I, fol. 29 (12 February 1659).

21. *NYHM* 4: 469, 531, 549; *MDC*, 27 April 1647; GAA, NA, inv. no. 1298, fol. 205 (5 September 1650), inv. no. 2030, p. 123–124 (11 September 1650). Cf. Wagman, "Liberty in New Amsterdam," 118. Another example is Govert Loockermans, who originated from Turnhout. He came to the colony as an assistant cook and was later taken into the service of Director Wouter van Twiller as a clerk. He did very well in New Netherland, and ultimately became an important merchant in New Amsterdam and *schepen* (magistrate) in the city government. *DRCHNY* 1: 432.

22. *NYHM* 4: 363, 364; Phelps Stokes, *Iconography* 4: 136.

23. GAA, NA, inv. no. 2290 II (61), p. 30 (3 October 1662); *NYHM* 2: 256–259; *Burghers of New Amsterdam*, 13–14; *RNA* 2: 285; Van de Graaf, "Stadsbestuur van Nieuw-Amsterdam," 135.

24. *NNN*, 181–234; McKew Parr, *The Voyages of David de Vries*. I thank Piet Boon of the Archiefdienst West-Friese Gemeenten for the information on the year of De Vries's death (personal communication, 19 October 2000).

25. NYPL, Bontemantel Collection, New Netherland Papers, box 1, folder "Official list of New Netherland" (ca. 1650, *Guide*, no. 551).

26. *Corres. 1654–1658*, 46.

27. *DRCHNY* 1: 480; *ERA* 1: 29n; NYSA, NYCM 13: 4 (undated, late 1659).

28. *DRCHNY* 14: 436, NYSA, NYCM 9: 564 (28 March 1661); GAA, DTB, inv. no. 478, p. 36 (27 October 1657).

29. *Corres. 1647–1653*, 123; *VRBM*, 157; GAA, NA, inv. no. 1300, fol. 233 (20 November 1651); Plomp, "Nieuw-Nederlanders en hun Europese achtergrond," 145.

30. Boxer, *Dutch Seaborne Empire*, 57; De Vries, "De Van Rensselaer's," 200; Hoffman, "Armory. De Hulter—De Laet—Ebbingh," 343; *Breeden-Raedt*, B 1; Boxer, *Nederlanders in Brazilië*, 202; GAA, NA, inv. no. 1659, fol. 102 (23 July 1641).

31. GAA, NA, inv. no. 1312, fol. 3 (3 January 1639); Kemperink, "Pieter Stuyvesant. Waar en wanneer werd hij geboren?"; Jensma, "Over de jeugd van Pieter Stuyvesant"; Gehring, "Petrus Stuyvesant"; Jacobs, "Like father, like son?"; Jacobs, *"Een pant van ware vrintschap."*

32. *NNN*, 186, 191; *Breeden-Raedt*, B 2v; Zandvliet, *Mapping for Money*, 283, n. 76; Frijhoff, "Neglected Networks."

33. Jacobs, "A Troubled Man."

34. GAA, NA, inv. no. 1333, fol. 81v (29 June 1640), inv. no. 1283, fol. 114, 114v (13 July 1641); *NYHM* 4: 14, 68–69, 142; *LP*, 38, 51, 52, 74.

35. GAA, NA, inv. no. 2956, p. 251 (3 January 1669), where his age is given as 54; *DRCHNY* 1: 431; *NYHM* 3: 28, 29; *NYHM* 4: 119, 185.

36. *Corres. 1647–1653*, 218, 220; Christoph, *Nicolls-Lovelace Papers*, 78–80.

37. Nat. Arch., OWIC, inv. no. 14, fol. 178 (11 September 1636); *NYHM* 4: 1; NYSA, NYCM 8: 148–149, 227–229 (28 September 1656); *DRCHNY* 3: 75; Riker, *Revised History of Harlem*, 785.

38. *Corres. 1647–1653*, 113; *NYHM* 3: 216.

39. *BGE*, 47, 104; GAA, NA, inv. no. 3658, p. 830 (4 April 1668), p. 930 (28 May 1668); *RNA* 6: 256; Verhoog and Koelmans, *De reis van Michiel Adriaanszoon de Ruyter in 1664–1665*, 316–317.

40. Jacobs, "Scheepvaart en handel," 24–26; Rink, *Holland on the Hudson*, 136–137; Matson, *Merchants and Empire*, ch. 1; Maika, "Commerce and Community."

41. *Woordenboek der Nederlandsche Taal*, entry *schots* (1): "representative of a firm on a ship or abroad, *commies*, factor, ledger, Scotchman."

42. Hart, *Geschrift en getal*, 327–328; Rink, *Holland on the Hudson*, 207–209; Gehlen, *Notariële akten*, 141–143; Maika, "Commerce and Community," 83–89.

43. GAA, NA, inv. no. 1295, fol. 41v (16 March 1648), inv. no. 2214, fol. 364 (26 February 1663); *NYHM* 3: 150, 223–224; *NYHM* 4: 531, 537; *LP*, 118, 119; *NYHM* 5: 80–81; *RNA* 7: 151; Nat. Arch., OWIC, inv. no. 14, fol. 176v (8 September 1636).

44. Rau, "Loockermans"; *VRBM*, 360, 597; *NYHM* 2: 1; GAA, NA, inv. no. 1341, fol. 25v (17 April 1647), inv. no. 1346, fol. 20–20v (16 March 1651), inv. no. 1113, fol. 22 (7 April 1655), inv. no. 1359, fol. 83 (12 June 1659), inv. no. 1363, fol. 73v–74 (22 April 1661).

45. Rink, *Holland on the Hudson*, 177ff.; Jansen, "De Wolff," 136; GAA, NA, inv. no. 1595, fol. 424–425 (fol. 185–186v) (27 February 1657), inv. no. 2875, p. 662–663 (30 September 1662), inv. no. 2843, p. 511 (28 October 1666), inv. no. 1081, fol. 201–201v (13 August 1647), inv. no. 1093, fol. 200, 200v (18 February 1650), inv. no. 1140, fol. 365v and 366–367v (29 March 1662), inv. no. 1141, fol. 18–19 and 20–20v (6 and 7 April 1662).

46. NYHS, Stuyvesant-Rutherford Papers 1: 2 (probably 9 May 1647; *Guide*, no. 455); Kooijmans, "De koopman," 71–72; Kooijmans, "Risk and Reputation," 31–32.

47. NYHS, Stuyvesant-Rutherford Papers 3–2 (24 March 1648; *Guide*, no. 464).

48. See Maika, "Commerce and Community."

49. NYHS, Stuyvesant-Rutherford Papers 3: 6 (27 May 1648; *Guide*, no. 468).

50. *NYHM* 4: 564–565, *LO*, 101–102; *RNA* 1: 10.

51. *Corres. 1654–1658*, 5, 25.

52. Ibid., 83; NYSA, NYCM 10–13: 187–189 (13 March 1664), 189–190 (20 March 1664), 191–192 (22 April 1664); *LO*, 462; *RNA* 2: 272–273, 286–287.

53. Rink, *Holland on the Hudson*, 168.

54. Farmers and artisans are difficult to trace in the sources. In a number of cases, a married couple made a will prior to their departure for the colony, but precious few of these describe in what capacity they went to New Netherland. The same problem crops up in the passenger lists drawn up by O'Callaghan, which make little or no mention of passengers' occupations. The lists are based on a WIC account book that recorded the advance of passage money. When someone traveled at his own expense, or when the passage of a contract laborer was paid by his master, they were unlikely to be included in the list. Rink, who made use of O'Callaghan's lists and of details from the notarial archives of Amsterdam, could find only forty-seven farmers among the 1,032 passengers on thirty ships from 1657 to 1664. O'Callaghan, *Documentary History* 3: 52–63; Rink, *Holland on the Hudson*, 166–167.

55. There is some confusion about the origin of Jonas Bronck. Evjen, *Scandinavian Immigrants*, 167–181, is of the opinion that Bronck was the son of a Lutheran minister on the Faeroe Islands. The document registering his banns of marriage in Amsterdam (GAA, DTB, inv. no. 449, fol. 118 (18 June 1638)) lists "Coomstaij" (possibly Kosta near Växjö in Småland in Sweden) as his place of origin, whereas in the contract about the *Brant van Troyen*, "Smolach in Sweden" is named (GAA, NA, inv. no. 1332, fol. 44 (30 April 1639)). Yet a number of Danish books are mentioned in the inventory of his possessions (*NYHM* 2: 121). See also GAA, NA, inv. no. 1555a, p. 583–585 (26 April 1639), p. 591–593 (28 April 1639); *NYHM* 1: 196, 215–216.

56. Van der Donck, *Description,* 129; Folkerts, "Drenthe and New Netherland," 10.

57. *DRCHNY* 1: 379–380.

58. NYPL, Bontemantel Collection, New Netherland Papers, box 1, folder "Extracts from the Register of the West India Company" (9 March and 3 April 1656; *Guide,* nos. 569, 598).

59. *Corres. 1654–1658,* 86–87.

60. *DRCHNY* 14: 444.

61. Cohen, "How Dutch were the Dutch of New Netherland?" Impressive though Cohen's research for 1981 was, his results should be interpreted with caution. Geographical origin should not be equated with culture, for a start. Cohen's dataset was not obtained by random sampling and therefore does not automatically represent the population of New Netherland as a whole. Some of the sources used tend to disregard women and children, like the so-called passenger lists. A bigger problem is that the focus on transatlantic immigrants obscures groups absent in the table above: the English, who immigrated from the surrounding colonies, the native-born New Netherlanders, and the enslaved blacks. The number of English in New Netherland seems to have been considerable, judging on the frequent occurrence of English names in the court records. Some of these may have been itinerant traders, especially in New Amsterdam, but a number of them lived in the predominantly Dutch settlements. In contrast, the English villages on Dutch jurisdiction, such as Newtown, Hempstead, Flushing, Gravesend, and Jamaica (invariably indicated in the Dutch language sources as Middelburgh, Heemstede, Vlissingen, 's-Gravesande, Rustdorp) on Long Island and Westchester (Oostdorp) had very few Dutch inhabitants. Second, the effect of natural increase should not be underestimated. Between 1639 and 1665, 1,636 children were baptized in New Amsterdam alone; even accounting for the high infant mortality rate of the early modern age, this would result in roughly 15 percent of the New Netherland population being locally born by 1664. This is a very rough calculation, using a very high infant mortality rate of 250 and the high estimate of the total New Netherland population of 8,000; it also presumes that the 1,636 baptisms in New Amsterdam represent the total number of children born in the colony, which it obviously did not. All of these factors are weighed to minimize the percentage of locally born New Netherlanders. The actual figure may well be considerably higher.

62. Cohen, "How Dutch were the Dutch of New Netherland?"; NYSA, NYCM 14: 56 (4 February 1662), 20 (9 May 1661).

63. Folkerts, "Drenthe and New Netherland," 9; Folkerts, "Drentse emigratie"; Corwin, *Manual,* 662–663; Wijmer, Folkerts, and Christoph, *Through a Dutch Door.*

64. Kernkamp, "Brieven van Samuel Blommaert," 173 (quotation); Folkerts, "Drenthe and New Netherland," 10.

65. Hart, *Geschrift en getal,* 329; Van den Boogaart, "Servant Migration." Hart mentions 175 contracts of service and 230 people, Van den Boogaart numbers 166 people. I have counted some 218 contracts involving contract laborers. Included are 188 contracts of service from prior to 1665, which involve 251 people in total. The difference from the counts made by Hart and Van den Boogaart can be explained by the period under examination, the continuing indexation activities of the Gemeentearchief Amsterdam, and the criteria applied. Some contracts of service concern merchants who went to the colony as factors. It is possible that Van den Boogaart did not include these contracts in his count. Otherwise, my findings do not differ from those of Hart and Van den Boogaart.

66. GAA, NA, inv. no. 1096, fol. 286–287v (20 March 1651).

67. The origins of fifty-four of these seventy-two contract laborers are listed. Thirty-two came from Garderbroek (1), Voorthuizen (1), Putten (1), Hilversum (4), Naarden (1), Nijkerk (5),

Wekerom (1), Horst (1), Amersfoort (3), Bunschoten (4), De Bilt (1), Maartensdijk (2), West-broek (2), Vreeland (1), Houten (2) and Huizen (2); Rink, "People of New Netherland."

68. GAA, NA, inv. no. 1054, fol. 60–65 (28 March 1639), inv. no. 2279 V, p. 24 (15 May 1652).

69. GAA, NA, inv. no. 1346, fol. 24v–25 (21 March 1651), inv. no. 1352, fol. 53v–54 (1 July 1654), inv. no. 1359, fol. 6 and 24 (6 and 28 January 1659), inv. no. 2279, V, p. 4, 6–7 (2 and 4 May 1652); inv. no. 1343, fol. 7v (8 February 1649), fol. 9 (8 March 1649), fol. 11v (12 March 1649), fol. 24 (11 April 1649), inv. no. 1349, fol. 28 (27 March 1653), inv. no. 1352, fol. 8ov (13 October 1654).

70. *CJVR* 317; GAA, NA, inv. no. 1145, fol. 14–15 (6 April 1663).

71. GAA, NA, inv. no. 1555a, pp. 591–593 (28 April 1639); *NYHM* 4: 52; *NYHM* 1: 194–195.

72. *MCR*, 163–164.

73. *NYHM* 1: 349–351.

74. Lucassen, "Labour and Early Modern Economic Development," 382; Galenson, *White Servitude;* Smith, *Colonists in Bondage; NYHM* 4: 88, 143, 196, 569; *LO*, 24, 32, 104; *LWA*, 5, 20; *Corres. 1647–1653*, 215–216.

75. Galenson, *White Servitude*, 8.

76. GAA, NA, inv. no. 1332, fol. 45 (9 May 1639), inv. no. 1064, fol. 8 (9 June 1642); Phelps Stokes, *Iconography*, 4: 187–188; *LP*, 33; *RNA* 1: 374; *RNA* 3: 83.

77. Frijhoff, *Wegen*, 768–769; Goodfriend, *Before the Melting Pot*, 10; Potter, "Demographic Development," 138; Berlin, "From Creole to African," 268–269; Berlin, *Many Thousands Gone*, 51; Niemeijer, *Calvinisme en koloniale stadscultuur*, 26; personal communication, Ad Biewenga, Free University, Amsterdam.

78. O'Callaghan, *Voyages of the Slavers*, 183–186, 189–191; NYSA, NYCM 10–3: 227–228 (29 May 1664); *CM 1655–1656*, 70; *DRCHNY* 2: 222; Wagman, "Corporate Slavery"; Emmer, "Slavenhandel," 117–118; Goodfriend, "Burghers and Blacks"; Emmer, *De Nederlandse slavenhandel*, 57.

79. Goodfriend, "Burghers and Blacks," 142–143; Narrett, *Inheritance and Family Life*, 187, n. 57; Maika, "Slavery, Race and Culture in Early New York"; *OFDRCB*, 227.

80. Hallema, "Emigratie en tewerkstelling," 206–207; *DRCHNY* 1: 364 (22 February 1650); Johnson, "The Transportation of Vagrant Children," 143–144; Sainsbury, *Calendar of State Papers, Colonial Series, 1574–1660*, 23, 34, 407; GAA, Archive *Burgemeesters*, inv. no. 540 (probably December 1649); Jacobs, "A Hitherto Unknown Letter of Adriaen van der Donck."

81. *Corres. 1647–1653*, 112; GAA, Archive *Vroedschap*, inv. no. 19, fol. 189v–199 (21 November 1651), fol. 210v, 210 (31 January 1652); Van de Pol, *Amsterdams hoerdom*, 205; Engels, *Kinderen van Amsterdam*, 31–33; Groenveld, Dekker, and Willemse, *Wezen en boefjes*, 62–63.

82. GAA, *aalmoezeniers'* archive, inv. no. 437 (undated), inv. no. 39, p. 17 (2 January 1652).

83. *Corres. 1647–1653*, 145–146.

84. Ibid., 15–16, 24; *NYHM* 5: 202; *CM 1655–1656*, 26; *DRCHNY* 1: 556.

85. New York Genealogical and Biographical Society, contract on the upkeep of Hendrick Claesz (6 November 1654; *Guide*, no. 635).

86. *Corres. 1654–1658*, 58, 64–66; *DRCHNY* 14: 434; *DRCHNY* 2: 52; GAA, Archive *Burgemeesters*, inv. no. 56 (2 September 1662); Singleton, *Dutch New York*, 151; Scott, "Orphan Children."

87. NYSA, NYCM 9: 407–408 (9 September 1660), 14: 7 (probably 1659 or 1660).

88. GAA, NA, inv. no. 1205, fol. 45 (1 March 1656), inv. no. 1206, fol. 159–159v (24 November 1657).

89. Peters, "Volunteers for the Wilderness"; Rink, *Holland on the Hudson*, 74–75; Trap, "Een reis die niet doorging."

90. Schulte Nordholt, "Nederlanders in Nieuw-Nederland," 82; O'Callaghan, *Documentary History* 4: 6; *DRCHNY* 1: 181; *NNN*, 272.

91. [Van den Enden], *Kort verhael;* Plockhoy, *Kort en klaer ontwerp*.

92. Van den Enden, *Vrye politijke stellingen,* introduction by W. Klever; Klever, "A New Source of Spinozism."

93. Seguy, *Utopie coopérative et oecuménisme;* Harder and Harder, *Plockhoy from Zurick-zee;* Quack, "Plockhoy's sociale plannen"; Eekhof, *Hervormde kerk,* 2: 60–69.

94. Van Berkum, *De Labadie en de Labadisten;* Saxby, *The Quest for the New Jerusalem;* James and Jameson, *Journal of Jasper Danckaerts;* Scott, *Diary of our Second Trip from Holland to New Netherland.* The originals of these travel journals are in the Brooklyn Historical Society.

95. DRCHNY 13: 205.

Chapter 3. Authority, Government, and Justice

1. NYSA, NYCM 12: 46 (30 December 1656–1 January 1657; *Corres. 1654–1658,* 113–117).

2. De Laet, *Iaerlyck verhael,* 1: (8) (*VRBM,* 91); La Bree, *Rechterlijke organisatie,* 17; Rijpperda Wiersma, *Politie en justitie.*

3. DRCHNY 1: 104, 178, 494; *VRBM,* 91–93, 147; Den Heijer, *De geschiedenis van de WIC,* 31–33, 97–102.

4. Van den Boogaart, "De Nederlandse expansie in het Atlantische gebied," 116; Nat. Arch., OWIC, inv. no. 14, passim; Den Heijer, *De geschiedenis van de WIC,* 31; Jessurun, *Kiliaen van Rensselaer,* appendix 2; DRNN, 129; O'Callaghan, *The Register of New Netherland,* 1–5.

5. DRNN, 2–19; Jessurun, *Kiliaen van Rensselaer,* appendix 2; Rink, *Holland on the Hudson,* 76–79; Bachman, *Peltries or Plantations,* 77–81; Condon, *New York Beginnings,* 77–82.

6. DRNN, 64.

7. Ibid., 79, 82, 89; for instance NYHM 4: 460–461; Jacobs, "Incompetente autocraten?"

8. DRNN, 79.

9. Ibid., 184, 63, 102–105, 176; Jacobs, "Between Repression and Approval," 56; Jacobs, "Incompetente autocraten?"

10. *VRBM,* 91.

11. DRNN, 5, 110–113.

12. Ibid., 40, 51–52.

13. NYSL, SC 16676–89 (2 July 1646; *Guide,* no. 637); LP, 13, 43; LWA, 29–31; Cronon, *Changes in the Land,* 54–81.

14. Barnouw, "The Settlement of New Netherland," 249–250; DRNN, 2, 39; *VRBM,* 136; Frijhoff, *Wegen,* 583; Cau, *Groot placaet-boeck* 1: 625–654; Bruijn and Van Eyck van Heslinga, *Muiterij,* 19–20; La Bree, *Rechterlijke organisatie,* 15; NNN, 339; Bruijn, Gaastra and Schöffer, *Dutch-Asiatic Shipping,* 1: 110.

15. DRNN, 113–114; Wieder, *De stichting van New York,* 17–35; Shattuck, "A Civil Society," 23–29.

16. DRNN, 39.

17. *VRBM,* 148; Schiltkamp, "On Common Ground"; Kunst, *Recht, commercie en kolonialisme,* 57–61.

18. Schiltkamp, *De geschiedenis van het notariaat,* 86–87, 130–133. Besides keeping the minutes of the meetings of director and council, the secretary also acted as notary in the colony. He continued to fulfill this role during the entire existence of the colony, but the importance of his notarial duties began to dwindle from 1650 on, when independent notaries came to the colony.

19. As the local income of the West India Company was derived in part from these rights, the *fiscael* has sometimes been called a fiscal officer. While not incorrect, this description is incomplete. Jacobs, "'To Favor This New and Growing City of New Amsterdam with a Court of Justice.'"

20. DRCHNY 1: 494, 504–509; DRNN, 97; NYHM 2: 187–188; Jacobs, "'To Favor This New and Growing City of New Amsterdam with a Court of Justice.'" In New Netherland historiography, though not in the sources, the term *schout-fiscaal* is often used, both prior to 1653

and after 1660. Only for the years 1653 through 1660, when one man combined the positions of *fiscaal* of the province and *schout* of New Amsterdam, is there any justification for using this term. Even then, the sources do not use the combination but refer to either *schout* or *fiscaal*, according to the capacity in which he was acting.

21. *DRNN*, 64; *DRCHNY* 1: 160–162, 2: 144–145; *NYHM* 5: 129–130. The position of vice commander was in the early years taken on by Jorisz Thienpont, but after his return to *patria* either the secretary or the *fiscael* presumably filled this position. In the reorganization of the New Netherland government in the 1640s, the vice directorate was again made into a separate position, to which Lubbert Dinclagen was appointed. After he was ousted in 1651, the term vice director was only used to indicate representatives of the director general at Fort Orange, the South River, or Curaçao. With the arrival of Nicasius de Sille, the position of someone "second in command" was restored, but the title was changed to "first councilor."

22. *LP*, 2; NYSA, NYCM 8: 782 (26 March 1658); *Corres. 1647–1653*, 123–124; *NYHM* 4: 13; GAA, NA, inv. no. 1283, fol. 114 (13 July 1641).

23. *DRNN*, 187–199.

24. Nat. Arch., OWIC, inv. no. 14, fol. 83v (29 October 1635), inv. no. 50, doc. 32 (20 August 1635); GAA, NA, inv. no. 856, fol. 174 (18 December 1635), inv. no. 917, fol. 309v (1 December 1635), fol. 331–334v (18 December 1635); *VRBM*, 217–218, 320; Jacobs, "A Troubled Man."

25. *NNN*, 187–188; *DRCHNY* 1: 71–81; Nat. Arch., OWIC, inv. no. 50, doc. 32 (20 August 1635), inv. no. 14, fol. 215 (4 December 1636), fol. 216 (8 December 1636); Frijhoff, *Wegen*, 672; Kenney, *Stubborn for Liberty*, 39; *VRBM*, 269, 271; Jacobs, "A Troubled Man."

26. *VRBM*, 235–250.

27. Ibid., 140.

28. Ibid., 148, 476; Fabius, "Het leenstelsel van de West-Indische Compagnie"; Van Grol, *De grondpolitiek in het West-Indisch domein*; Bachman, *Peltries or Plantations*, 97–109; Rink, "Company Management and Private Trade"; Rink, "Before the English," 32–36; Nissenson, *The Patroon's Domain*; Jacobs, "Dutch Proprietary Manors in America"; Jacobs, "Johannes de Laet en de Nieuwe Wereld," 113 and note 29.

29. *VRBM*, 154–158, 164–165, 171–175.

30. De Vries, *Korte Historiael*, 147–148; *VRBM*, 314; Weslager, "Who Survived the Indian Massacre at Swanendael?"

31. *VRBM*, 314–316, 475.

32. Ibid., 201–203, 208–212; Jessurun, *Kiliaen van Rensselaer*, appendix 8.

33. *VRBM*, 250–254, 281, 459; GAA, NA, inv. no. 1054, fol. 90–90v (30 July 1639); *MCR*, 8–11, 16; *CJVR* 5–7; Venema, "7 September 1652;" Van der Wall, "Prophecy and Profit." After he returned to *patria*, Van Slichtenhorst sued the patroon for expenses. See Venema, "The Court Case."

34. Jacobs, "Johannes de Laet en de Nieuwe Wereld," 113–116.

35. *VRBM*, 144–146.

36. *DRCHNY* 1: 87.

37. *DRCHNY* 1: 68–71, 82–83, 87, 91.

38. *VRBM*, 312, 314. Because the conflict between the patroons and the WIC centered around the fur trade, some historians have suggested that the profit from peltries was the patroons' main interest from the beginning. But if that was the intention of the patroons of Swanendael and Pavonia, then it is difficult to understand why they sold their rights back to the WIC. If, merely as a formality, they had fulfilled the required conditions, there would have been good opportunities to carry on an illegal trade in furs, smuggling the pelts back home. The specific instructions from Kiliaen van Rensselaer to his colonists, which explicitly forbade fur trading, make it clear that agriculture was far more important to him, although he viewed the fur trade as a substantial source of additional income. Condon, *New York Beginnings*, 124–125; *DRCHNY* 13: iii; Folkerts, "Kiliaen van Rensselaer," 299.

39. *DRCHNY* 1: 96–100.

40. Ibid., 119–123. There is no evidence that this proposal was ever formally approved by the States General, but from the subsequent course of events it may be concluded that it was. The relinquishment of the monopoly on the fur trade thus took place implicitly; it was simply

not mentioned again in the new version. Cf. Rink, *Holland on the Hudson*, 134–137. *VRBM*, 463–465, 524–527; GAA, NA, inv. no. 1055, fol. 51v–52 (27 October 1639); Klooster, "Failing to Square the Circle."

41. *DRCHNY* 1: 401–405, 528, 638; Faber and De Bruin, "Tegen de vrede"; GAA, NA, inv. no. 1621, *pak* 3, fol. 4 (6 May 1641), inv. no. 1334, fol. 2 (3 July 1640); Kupp and Hart, "The Early Cornelis Melyn"; Huntington Library, San Marino, HM 838, contracts between Van der Capellen and Melijn (25 May and 4 June 1650; *Guide*, no. 5); *Corres. 1647–1653*, 137.

42. *DRCHNY* 1: 470; *NYHM* 2: 170–171; *Corres. 1647–1653*, 137–138, 186–187, 189; *DRCHNY* 14: 382; *Corres. 1654–1658*, 95; GAA, NA, inv. no. 1501, fol. 84 (20 July 1641); O'Callaghan, *History of New Netherland* 2: 286–287, 550–551. Although Van Werckhoven's lands were designated as a patroonship, there are no indications that manorial rights were actually exercised. It is possible that the rights lapsed on Van Werckhoven's death and that his heirs inherited only the ownership of the land.

43. GAA, NA, inv. no. 2614 B, p. 1157–1158 (1 November 1660); *DRCHNY* 13: 121.

44. *MCR*, 30; Gehring, "Petrus Stuyvesant"; Jacobs, "Dutch Proprietary Manors in America"; Venema, *Beverwijck*, 48–53; Venema, "Two More Unpublished Letters"; Venema, "7 September 1652."

45. *NYHM* 5: 2–5; *NYHM* 4: 559, 572–575.

46. Ten years later, when the colony fell into English hands for a second time, the Company's directors declared that the owners of Rensselaerswijck had the right of jurisdiction over Beverwijck. But this declaration was only intended to assist the Van Rensselaers in maintaining their rights under the rule of the English. If the colony were ever to have become Dutch again, the directors' declaration would become invalid. GAA, NA, inv. no. 1096, fol. 366–367 (7 April 1651), inv. no. 3218, fol. 342–342v (2 April 1674), fol. 340 (2 April 1674); *DRCHNY* 2: 558.

47. *DRCHNY* 1: 614; Hart, "The City-Colony of New Amstel"; Hart, "De stadskolonie Nieuwer-Amstel"; Weslager, *Dutch Explorers*.

48. *DP*, 97–100, 112–116, 126–127, 134–145; *DRCHNY* 12: 249; *DRCHNY* 2: 4–8, 68–71.

49. *DRCHNY* 2: 78, 101–102, 165–175.

50. Ibid., 173–175; *DP*, 327–333; Hart, "De stadskolonie Nieuwer-Amstel," 92.

51. This is also pointed out by Rink, *Holland on the Hudson*, 136.

52. *NYHM* 4: 60. On Kieft's War, see also Haefeli, "Kieft's War." The use of the word *contribution*, and not *taxation*, as it has sometimes been translated, is significant. It was not uncommon in the Netherlands that in times of war involuntary levies, called contributions, were imposed on the population of adjoining territories, as a form of protection against the pillage and fire-raising carried out by the other warring party. Groenveld, "Den huijsman wordt er heel verermt," 57–60; Kappelhof, *De belastingheffing in de Meijerij van Den Bosch*, 316–321; Gutmann, *War and Rural Life*, 41–46; Holthuis, *Frontierstad bij het scheiden der markt*, 60–61.

53. *NYHM* 4: 87; *NNN*, 208; *DRCHNY* 1: 150.

54. *NYHM* 4: 117, 124; *DRCHNY* 1: 414.

55. *DRCHNY* 1: 201–203.

56. Both in the way it was set up and in the extent of its rights, the council of Twelve Men, like the two later advisory bodies, the *Acht Man* (Eight Men) and the *Negen Man* (Nine Men), displayed similarities with administrative practice in villages and towns in the eastern part of the Netherlands. However, no evidence exists that they were derived directly therefrom. It is more likely that their somewhat primitive form emanated from the conceptions of both the Company and the colonists on how the relation between the government and the population should be arranged at that crucial moment. Heringa, *Geschiedenis van Drenthe*, 210–214, 398–399; Streng, "Stemme in staat," 95–119; Koenigsberger, *Monarchies, States Generals and Parliaments*, 44, 245, 301.

57. *DRCHNY* 1: 415–416.

58. Ibid., 203.

59. *NYHM* 4: 203.

60. *DRCHNY* 1: 139–140.

61. Ibid., 141–142; Jacobs, "Johannes de Laet en de Nieuwe Wereld," 112; Den Heijer, "Plannen voor samenvoeging van VOC en WIC."

62. *NYHM* 4: 207; *DRCHNY* 1: 140–141, 190–191.

63. *DRCHNY* 1: 210.

64. Ibid., 212.

65. Ibid., 213.

66. Ibid., 148–149; Kunst, *Recht, commercie en kolonialisme*, 77–78.

67. *DRCHNY* 1: 153–154; *VRBM*, 151–153.

68. *DRCHNY* 1: 148, 160–162, 492–494.

69. Ibid., 175–178.

70. *NYHM* 4: 364, 370–377, 394–411, 419–422.

71. *DRCHNY* 1: 160–162; *NYHM* 4: 428–430.

72. *NYHM* 4: 430.

73. *NYHM* 5: 13; *NYHM* 4: 438–441; NYHS, Stuyvesant-Rutherford Papers 2: 7a (21 December 1647; *Guide*, no. 462).

74. *NYHM* 4: 466–467, 482.

75. *NNN*, 349.

76. Ibid., 350.

77. *NYHM* 4: 580–581.

78. *DRCHNY* 1: 258, 262–270.

79. *NNN*, 320, 332.

80. *DRCHNY* 1: 262–270, for example 264.

81. Ibid., 321–324, 348–359.

82. Boxer, *Nederlanders in Brazilië*, 262–265.

83. *DRCHNY* 1: 387–391.

84. Ibid., 391–395.

85. Ibid., 420–421, 444–457.

86. Ibid., 433, 462; Jacobs, "A Hitherto Unknown Letter of Adriaen van der Donck."

87. *Corres. 1647–1653*, 149.

88. *DRCHNY* 1: 463, 471–472, 475; *Corres. 1647–1653*, 166; Jacobs, "'To Favor This New and Growing City of New Amsterdam with a Court of Justice.'"

89. The small benches of justice in New Netherland were: Middelburgh (Newtown, 1642), Heemstede (Hempstead, 1644), Vlissingen (Flushing, 1645), 's-Gravesande (Gravesend, 1645), Breuckelen (Brooklyn, 1646), Beverwijck (Albany, 1652), New Amsterdam (New York, 1653), Amersfoort (Flatlands, 1654), Midwout (Flatbush (1654), Oostdorp (Westchester, 1656), Rustdorp (Jamaica, 1656), Haerlem (Harlem, 1660), Boswijck (Bushwick, 1661), Wiltwijck (Kingston, 1661), Bergen (1661), New Utrecht (1661), Staten Eylandt (Staten Island, 1664). From 1654 Midwout and Amersfoort had a combined court, which was divided in 1661: *LO*, 390–391.

90. *DRCHNY* 1: 161; *CM 1655–1656*, 185–186; Shattuck, "Heemstede," 29–31; McKinley, "English and Dutch Towns," 5.

91. *DRCHNY* 1: 120; Shattuck, "Heemstede," 31.

92. *NYHM* 4: 110; Shattuck, "Heemstede," 30. See also McKinley, "English and Dutch Towns," 15.

93. *NYHM* 4: 321.

94. Schoonmaker, *History of Kingston*, 6; GAA, NA, inv. no. 2279, V, p. 25 (15 May 1652), inv. no. 2281, III (prot. 18), fol. 72 (6 June 1654), inv. no. 2576, p. 75–76, 129–130, 131–132 (28 February, 6 April 1660), DTB, inv. no. 6, p. 408 (1 June 1634); *FOR 1656–1678*, 83–84; Brink, "The Ambition of Roeloff Swartwout,"

95. *DRCHNY* 13: 196–198; *LO*, 395–401.

96. Shattuck, "Heemstede," 34, 35.

97. Ibid., 31, 33.

98. See, for example, NYSA, NYCM 8: 15–16 (26 May 1656) and 16 (3 June 1656) for the approval of director general and council of ordinances of Midwout and Amersfoort.

99. *DRCHNY* 13: 158–160, 199, 201; NYSA, NYCM 9: 622 (27 June 1661).

100. Bontemantel, *De regeeringe van Amsterdam* 1: 78–83.

101. *NYHM* 4: 474–475, 515–516; Shattuck, "Heemstede," 34.

102. *NYHM* 5: 125, 203; *Corres. 1647–1653,* 165; *DRCHNY* 14: 128–130; McKinley, "English and Dutch Towns," 7–8; Shattuck, "Heemstede," 34; Wright, "Local Government and Central Authority."

103. *NYHM* 4: 117, 580, 583.

104. This is a conclusion in sharp contrast to the opinion of some historians, who have pointed to New Netherland's differences from New England, where the democratic town meeting formed the basis of the administration. See, for example, Ritchie, *Duke's Province,* 31: "Institutional life in New Netherland had been weakly rooted." Ritchie bases this on Condon, *New York Beginnings,* 116–172 and on Wright, "Local Government in Colonial New York" and "Local Government and Central Authority in New Netherland."

105. Dapper, *Historische beschryving,* 472–473; Bontemantel, *De regeeringe van Amsterdam,* 91; Fruin, "Bijdrage tot de geschiedenis van het burgemeesterschap van Amsterdam," 310.

106. Phelps Stokes, *Iconography* 4: 133–136; White, "Municipal Government comes to Manhattan"; Jacobs, "'To Favor This New and Growing City of New Amsterdam with a Court of Justice.'"

107. NYSA, NYCM 8: 299 (20 December 1656), 9: 29 (15 January 1660), 9: 33 (15 and 21 January 1660); *RNA* 2: 251–252; *RNA* 3: 110–111, 307; *LO,* 268–269.

108. *RNA* 1: 144.

109. *RNA* 2: 272; Lyon, "The New Amsterdam Weighhouse."

110. *RNA* 1: 21, 33, 69, 92, 264, 300; *RNA* 3: 15–16; *RNA* 7: 191, 194; *CM 1655–1656,* 84; O'Connor, "The Rattle Watch of New Amsterdam"; Van Zwieten, "The Orphan Chamber of New Amsterdam," 322; Van Zwieten, "'A Little Land…To Sow Some Seeds,'" chapter 6.

111. *RNA* 1: 219.

112. When in 1660 both *burgemeesters* were absent for a period, they were deputized for, not by one of the *schepenen* but by former *burgemeester* Oloff Stevensz van Cortlandt. However, this was an exceptional situation.

113. *RNA* 2: 30; *RNA* 3: 155; *RNA* 7: 140, 161.

114. *NYHM* 5: 109–110; *CM 1655–1656,* 182–183.

115. *RNA* 2: 24; *CM 1655–1656,* 212–215.

116. *RNA* 2: 322.

117. *RNA* 2: 323–325; *RNA* 3: 257–260; NYSA, NYCM 8: 717–721 (1 February 1658); Fruin, "Bijdrage tot de geschiedenis van het burgemeesterschap van Amsterdam," 310.

118. *Corres. 1654–1658,* 12.

119. NYSA, NYCM 8: 17–18 (1 June 1656), 18 (7 June 1656), 32–33 (26 June 1656), 9: 332–334 (5 August 1660); *NYHM* 5: 157, 176; *Corres. 1654–1658,* 52; *RNA* 1: 218; *RNA* 2: 109, 121; *DRCHNY* 14: 463–465.

120. *RNA* 1: 92.

121. *RNA* 4: 273.

122. *NYHM* 4: 17; NYSA, NYCM 15: 143 (30 August 1664), 15: 144 (1 September 1664).

123. *BGE,* 1–4; Ritchie, *Duke's Province,* 9–20; Bliss, *Revolution and Empire,* 113–116, 127–129.

124. Ritchie, *Duke's Province,* 20–24.

125. *BGE,* 37, art. 21.

126. Ibid., 35–38, 41–42; Goebel and Naughton, *Law Enforcement in Colonial New York;* Narrett, *Inheritance and Family Life.*

127. *BGE,* 2.

128. Ritchie, *Duke's Province,* 31–32.

129. *BGE,* 79–81; Ritchie, *Duke's Province,* 33.

130. Ritchie, *Duke's Province,* 33–35, Christoph and Christoph, *Records of the Court of Assizes,* xii–xiii.

131. "The Clarendon Papers," 75.

132. Ritchie, *Duke's Province,* 35.

133. Shattuck, "Heemstede"; Ritchie, *Duke's Province,* 35–37; McKinley, "The Transition from Dutch to English Rule," 700–701.

134. *RNA* 5: 248–250; *BGE*, 93–94.

135. NYSA, NYCM 10–13: 251 (8 July 1664); *RNA* 5: 183–185; *BGE*, 74; Ritchie, *Duke's Province*, 41.

136. *CMARS* 1: 7–9; Paltsits, *Minutes of the Executive Council* 2: 548–549 (2 August 1671).

137. *KP* 1: xiii–xiv.

138. NYSL, mss BW 10272 group B, no 2 (17 August 1667 old style).

139. *BGE*, 37; Prud'homme van Reine, *Rechterhand van Nederland*, 129–153.

140. De Waard, *Zeeuwsche expeditie*, 42.

141. In addition to the book by De Waard, an overview of the recapture is given by Shomette and Haslach, *Raid on America*.

142. *DRCHNY* 2: 609–613, 620–622; Den Heijer, *De geschiedenis van de WIC*, 102–108.

Chapter 4. Trade, Agriculture, and Artisans

1. NYPL, Bontemantel Collection, New Netherland papers, box 3 (28 December 1630; *Guide*, no. 544).

2. Kenneth Jackson in Ric Burns' 1999 PBS documentary, entitled *New York: A Documentary Film*. Quoted in Stabile, "The Quintessential City: New York City on Film."

3. *CJVR*, 283–284; Maika, "The Credit System of the Manhattan Merchants."

4. Nettels, *The Money Supply;* Baart, "Ho-de-no-sau-nee en de Nederlanders," 91–92; Wilcoxen, *Seventeenth Century Albany*, 40–44; Bradley, *Evolution of the Onondaga Iroquois*, 178–180; Bradley, *Before Albany*, 76–77; Richter, *Ordeal of the Longhouse*, 32–33; Hamell, "Wampum."

5. *NYHM* 4: 107, 470; *LO*, 433–434; *RNA* 3: 10, 16.

6. *DRCHNY* 14: 470–471.

7. *LWA*, 69–70, 87–89; NYSA, NYCM 8: 580 (15 May 1657); *LO*, 433–434.

8. *Corres. 1647–1653*, 73, 189; *NYHM* 5: 39.

9. *LO*, 433–434; *Corres. 1654–1658*, 173; NYSA, NYCM 9: 464–465 (23 December 1660); *DRCHNY* 14: 487; Scholten, *The Coins of the Dutch Overseas Territories*, 175–176.

10. *DRCHNY* 14: 484.

11. GAA, NA, inv. no. 2578, p. 688–689 (16 November 1662). Seven years later this exchange rate was confirmed by Oloff Stevensz van Cortlandt and Nicolaes de Meijer, who stated that, when New Netherland money was transferred by IOU, four guilders of *sewant* was counted for one guilder in Dutch money: GAA. NA, inv. no. 2956, p. 251 (3 January 1669). Korthals Altes, *Van £ Hollands tot Nederlandse f*, 153–157; McCusker, *Money and Exchange*, 156, n. 8 and 291–296. On the possible effects of the inflation, see Ceci, "First Fiscal Crisis," 847.

12. Van der Donck, *Description*, 110.

13. Ibid., 111; cf. Burke, "New Netherland Fur Trade," 1–2; Burke, *Mohawk Frontier*, 7; "The Clarendon Papers," 20.

14. *DRNN*, 228.

15. *DRCHNY* 1: 37, 39; *NNN*, 83; *DRNN*, 228, 244; De Laet, *Historie ofte Iaerlyck verhael* (1644 version), appendix, p. 29–30; Davies, *A Primer of Dutch Seventeenth Century Overseas Trade*, 140; Emmer, "Nederlandse handelaren, kolonisten en planters," 28; Emmer, "The West India Company," 84; Emmer, "Slavenhandel," 107; Van Dillen, *Van rijkdom en regenten*, 168; Brandão, *"Your Fyre Shall Burn No More,"* 85–91.

16. *DRCHNY* 1: 47; Sainsbury, *Calendar of State Papers, Colonial Series, 1574–1660*, 143–145; *VRBM*, 244, 273, 334; Burke, "New Netherland Fur Trade," 3.

17. *VRBM*, 483; GAA, NA, inv. no. 1073, fol. 221–222 (30 March 1645); NYHS, Stuyvesant-Rutherford Papers, 2: 4 (2 August 1647; *Guide*, no. 459), 2: 5 (12 August 1647; *Guide*, no. 460), 2: 6 (1 November 1647; *Guide*, no. 461), 3: 9 (5 August 1648; *Guide*, no. 471).

18. Rink, *Holland on the Hudson*, 257; Trelease, *Indian Affairs*, 131; *ERA* 1: 244; Burke, "New Netherland Fur Trade," 2; Shattuck, "Civil Society," 247; *DRCHNY* 14: 484; *DRCHNY* 2: 212.

19. Martin, *Keepers of the Game;* Burke, "New Netherland Fur Trade," 2; Norton, *Fur Trade,* 10–11; Matson, "'Damned Scoundrels,'" 395. The traditional view has recently been challenged by the work of José António Brandão, who pointed out that Iroquois warfare was an expression of social and cultural imperatives, among which the need to replace deceased members of the community by captives was prominent. Economic motives, such as the capture of furs from other Indian groups, have led to the labeling of Indian conflicts as the "Beaver Wars," but only in a small percentage of the raids carried out by the Iroquois was the taking of furs the main motive. There is no indication, Brandão contends, that overhunting led to gradual extinction of the beaver or caused the Iroquois to supplement their trade by taking peltries from other Indian groups. Brandão's argument against previous explanations is very persuasive, although he does not provide an alternative explanation for the decline of the fur trade. Brandão, *"Your Fyre Shall Burn No More,"* 31–61, 84–91; Starna and Brandão, "From the Mohawk-Mahican War to the Beaver War."

20. *CJVR* 73.

21. Rich, "Russia and the Colonial Fur Trade," 311; Jacobs, "Scheepvaart en handel," 106.

22. *DRNN,* 10, 67, 196, 214–217; GAA, NA, inv. no. 843, not paginated (7 April 1632).

23. *VRBM,* 144–146; Nat. Arch., OWIC, inv. no. 14, fol. 93 (15 November 1635); *VRBM,* 209, 425; GAA, NA, inv. no. 1054, fol. 68v–69 (1 February 1642), inv. no. 1062, p. 110–111 (7 June 1642).

24. *NYHM* 4: 10; Den Heijer, *De geschiedenis van de WIC,* 45; Bruijn, "Walvisvaart," 22; *DRCHNY* 1: 119–123; Rink, *Holland on the Hudson,* 137.

25. *NYHM* 4: 3–4, 383–386, 390–392, 478, 495, 538; *CJVR* 231–232, 256–257.

26. *NYHM* 4: 524–527; NYSA, NYCM 10–12: 283 (6 September 1663), 10–13: 51 (20 September 1663); GAA, NA, inv. no. 1289, fol. 99v–100 (15 July 1644); Kupp, "Records Depict Fur Smuggling Episode in 1658."

27. Starna and Brandão, "From the Mohawk-Mahican War to the Beaver War."

28. Gehring and Starna, *A Journey into Mohawk and Oneida Country,* 13.

29. Ibid., 15–16.

30. *FOCM,* 388; Richter, *Ordeal of the Longhouse,* 86; Jacobs and Shattuck, "Bevers voor drank, land voor wapens," 100; *LWA,* 72.

31. *FOCM,* 323–325, 328.

32. Gehring and Starna, *A Journey into Mohawk and Oneida Country,* 39–40, n. 69; *NYHM* 4: 42–43, 256–257; Hazard, *Pennsylvania Archives,* 2: 97. I thank Martha Shattuck for this reference.

33. *Corres. 1647–1653,* 55; *NYHM* 5: 116.

34. *Corres. 1647–1653,* 144; *LO,* 236–239, 346; *DP,* 95; *DRCHNY* 2: 48; Puype, *Dutch and other Flintlocks;* Baart, "Ho-de-no-sau-nee en de Nederlanders," 96; Jacobs and Shattuck, "Bevers voor drank, land voor wapens," 109.

35. Jacobs and Shattuck, "Bevers voor drank, land voor wapens," 104–105.

36. *FOCM,* 352.

37. *NYHM* 4: 376–377; *NYHM* 5: 43; *FOCM,* 492; Shattuck, "Civil Society," 256.

38. *FOCM,* 299; Shattuck, "Civil Society," 254–268.

39. *DRCHNY* 13: 175; Shattuck, "Civil Society," 275–280; Sullivan, *The Punishment of Crime,* 148–159; Merwick, *Possessing Albany,* 89, 94.

40. *FOCM,* 502–503, 511–512, 514–515; *LO,* 425–426. The absence of the minutes of the court at Beverwijck for 1661 through 1667 makes it impossible to say whether the dissension between the principal traders and the common traders dragged on.

41. Den Heijer, *De geschiedenis van de WIC,* 81; De Vries and Van der Woude, *Nederland 1500–1815,* 775–776; *DRCHNY* 1: 107, 587, 614.

42. Bachman, *Peltries or Plantations,* 63–73, 157–160.

43. *MUM* 2: 186.

44. *DRCHNY* 2: 244, 526–527.

45. *DRCHNY* 1: 152; *VRBM,* 235; GAA, NA, inv. no. 1307, fol. 64v–65 (10 March 1657); *CJVR* 416; Simmons, *American Colonies,* 132.

46. *Corres. 1654–1658,* 128, 192; De Vries, *Korte Historiael,* 147.

47. *DRNN*, 40, 17.

48. Folkerts, "The Failure of West India Company Farming."

49. NYSL, mss 10643 (1666–1703; *Guide*, no. 173).

50. *MCR*, 44–46; *VRBM*, 605, 824–825; GAA, NA, inv. no. 1060, fol. 89–89v (13 May 1641); Folkerts, "Kiliaen van Rensselaer."

51. Folkerts, "Kiliaen van Rensselaer," 300–301; *VRBM*, 520; *NYHM* 2: 387–389; Van der Donck, *Description*, 21, 129.

52. Folkerts, "The Failure of West India Company Farming"; *NYHM* 1: 179.

53. *Corres. 1654–1658*, 40; De Vries and Van der Woude, *Nederland 1500–1815*, 255.

54. *VRBM*, 505–506.

55. *NYHM* 4: 16, 393, 532; *NYHM* 5: 72; *Corres. 1647–1653*, 49–50, 105, 124; NYSA, NYCM 8: 607 (12 June 1657); *LO*, 445; *RNA* 1: 14, 104–105, 111–112; *VRBM*, 515.

56. *NNN*, 79.

57. GAA, NA, inv. no. 226, fol. 63v–64 (27 May 1625); *NNN*, 79, 82–83; *DRNN*, 89.

58. *VRBM*, 580–603; Van der Donck, *Description*, 40–41.

59. *DRCHNY* 1: 369, 385–387, 369, 419; Folkerts, "Kiliaen van Rensselaer," 302; *VRBM*, 732–740; De Vries and Van der Woude, *Nederland 1500–1815*, 250.

60. *NYHM* 5: 13–14, 156; *RNA* 1: 247.

61. *NYHM* 4: 70–71, 73–74; Williams, "Great Doggs and Mischievous Cattle." This ordinance indicates that the colonists still relied on the Indians for part of their food.

62. *NYHM* 4: 380–381, 488–489; *NYHM* 5: 217–218; *CM 1655–1656*, 91–92; *LWA*, 9, 51; *LO*, 453–454, 462–463; NYSA, NYCM 23: 235 (16 April 1674); *RNA* 7: 22; *RNA* 1: 38–39.

63. Van der Donck, *Description*, 46; *MCR*, 100; *DRCHNY* 14: 129; Beernink, *Arend van Slichtenhorst*, 278; *CMARS* 1: 276–277; *RNA* 7: 24; Herks, *Amersfoortse tabak*, 48–49.

64. NYPL, James Riker Collection vol. 10 (court minutes Haerlem), p. 29–32 (March 1667); *KP* 1: 3–4; *OFDRCB*, 46, 48, 56; *RNA* 3: 137. Other means were also employed. In 1654 the cattle breeders in Beverwijck asked the court permission to close off a section of the public highway with fences to form a "corral" for the cattle. This was agreed to, on condition that a "footstep" was built at each side: *FOCM*, 133.

65. *NYHM* 5: 141–142, 170–171; *LWA*, 46, 53; *Corres. 1654–1658*, 50; *RNA* 1: 32, 44; *RNA* 2: 232–233.

66. *NYHM* 4: 121; *LO*, 364–365; *RNA* 1: 42; *RNA* 7: 215–216.

67. *VRBM*, 176–179, 219, 233, 282–283, 398, 447; Roessingh, *Inlandse tabak*, 108–112, 125–127, 188–189; Herks, *Amersfoortse tabak*, 19, 24, 67; Enthoven, *Zeeland en de opkomst van de Republiek*, 259, 263; Schama, *The Embarrassment of Riches*, 194; Folkerts, "Kiliaen van Rensselaer," 302.

68. GAA, NA, inv. no. 414, fol. 173 (26 August 1636), inv. no. 1497, fol. 100–102 (11 May 1638), inv. no. 1621, not paginated (19 December 1639), inv. no. 696 B, folder 92, p. 118–120 (8 July 1641), inv. no. 1280, fol. 69v–70 (25 May 1639); *VRBM*, 447, 661; Pagan, "Dutch Maritime and Commercial Activity"; Kupp, "Dutch Notarial Acts"; Enthoven, *Zeeland en de opkomst van de Republiek*, 259; De Vries and Van der Woude, *Nederland 1500–1815*, 220; Bailyn, *New England Merchants*, 45; Bijlsma, "Rotterdams Amerika-vaart," 126–137; Ames, *Studies of the Virginia Eastern Shore*, 47–50; Ames, *County Court Records of Accomack-Northampton, Virginia, 1640–1645*, 58, 98–99, 142–145, 148–151, 265, 295–296.

69. Nat. Arch., OWIC, inv. no. 50, doc. 32 (20 August 1635); *NYHM* 1: 34–35, 76, 84, 119–120, 217, 242; *NYHM* 4: 5; Roessingh, *Inlandse tabak*, 121, 146–172; Phelps Stokes, *Iconography*, 4: 184–185; Zandvliet, *Mapping for Money*, 207.

70. *NYHM* 1: 154–155, 334; *DRCHNY* 2: 212; Roessingh, *Inlandse tabak*, 238.

71. *Corres. 1654–1658*, 45.

72. O'Callaghan, *The Register of New Netherland*, 115–116; *NYHM* 4: 19–21; *Corres. 1654–1658*, 45.

73. *LO*, 307–309; NYSA, NYCM 8: 498 (30 March 1657); *LWA*, 81–83; *Corres. 1654–1658*, 148, 155.

74. *DRCHNY* 1: 267–268; *NYHM* 4: 598–599; *Corres. 1654–1658*, 11, 16; *LWA*, 32–33.

75. *RNA* 7: 123; *RNA* 3: 17.

76. Both this estimate and the one for the export of peltries (three hundred to three hundred and fifty thousand guilders) must be treated with caution, as hard evidence is lacking. Even so, it shows that New Netherland was not of particular importance in the total Dutch Atlantic trade, which already in the first twenty years of the seventeenth century had a total value of four to seven and a half million guilders. Enthoven, *Zeeland en de opkomst van de Republiek,* 268; Van den Boogaart, *La expansión holandesa,* 139.

77. Boxer, *Nederlanders in Brazilië,* 16.

78. Both steps in the process of making cloth are mentioned in the two versions of the *Provisional Regulations.* Wieder, in *De stichting van New York (115),* suggests that first weaving was forbidden and that subsequently dyeing was inserted into the stipulation, as dyeing was the step that made unfinished cloth into a trade good. In this way weaving in New Netherland would be restricted to a home industry for use of the colonists only. That such was the intention of the WIC directors is not impossible, but the absence of any spinning wheels or looms in contemporary inventories makes it unlikely. Also, textiles were imported in large numbers. Finally, a stipulation in the *Freedoms and Exemptions* of 1629 contradicts Wieder's suggestion: "The colonists shall not be permitted to make any woolen, linen, or cotton cloth, nor to weave any other fabrics, on pain of being banished and punished for perjury" (*VRBM,* 152). *DRNN,* 13; Shattuck, "Civil Society," 93; De Roever, "Koopmanschappen," 79; GAA, NA, inv. no. 1903, p. 200–201 (2 January 1659), inv. no. 986, pak a, *sub dato* (5 May 1658), inv. no. 2993, p. 212–213 (4 May 1661).

79. GAA, NA, inv. no. 667, fol. 27v (2 August 1632), inv. no. 306, fol. 123v and 119v (24 February 1632), inv. no. 943, not paginated (25 June 1632), fol. 583 (17 July 1632), fol. 656 (3 November 1632), not paginated (6 November 1632); *VRBM,* 298, 406, 410; NYSL, VRMP, box 40 A, folder 7 (16 November 1651; *CJVR* 184, 235; *NNN,* 83, 321.

80. GAA, NA, inv. no. 2280, IV, p. 59–60 (26 July 1653), inv. no. 2140, fol. 92–92v (27 May 1655); *CJVR* 294; *Corres. 1647–1653,* 212.

81. *FOR 1656–1678,* 96; GAA, NA, inv. no. 2860, fol. 200–201v (6 May 1658); *Corres. 1647–1653,* 202–203; Shattuck, "Civil Society," 87; Zantkuyl, "Reconstructie van enkele Nederlandse huizen in Nieuw-Nederland," 171; Venema, *Beverwijck,* 89–91.

82. GAA, NA, inv. no. 1364, fol. 60–60v (28 April 1661); NYSA, NYCM 9: 739 (25 August 1661), 10–11: 15 (15 June 1662), 14: 15 (31 March 1661); *DRCHNY* 14: 507–508, 514, 518–519; *DRCHNY* 2: 221; *DRNN,* 76; Rink, *Holland on the Hudson,* 184–186; Jansen, "De Wolff," 134–136.

83. *FOCM,* 190; *RNA* 2: 410; *Corres. 1654–1658,* 5.

84. *RNA* 7: 258–259; Middleton, "Joris Dopzen's Hog."

85. *MCR,* 28, 35; *CJVR* 303–304, 371; GAA, NA, inv. no. 1359, fol. 6 (6 January 1659), inv. no. 1352, fol. 53v–54 (1 July 1654); NYSA, NYCM 8: 226–227 (27 September 1656). On wheelwrights, see Fabend, "Cosyn Gerritsen van Putten."

86. *MCR,* 132; *NYHM* 4: 496–500; *RNA* 3: 278; *RNA* 1: 5–6, 8; *ER* 1: 236; Eekhof, *Hervormde kerk,* 1: 84; *CMARS* 1: 36; Dapper, *Historische beschryving,* 419.

87. *NYHM* 4: 474; *LWA,* 12, 22, 34; *NYHM* 5: 72; *CM 1655–1656,* 155–156; *FOCM,* 42; *RNA* 4: 264–265.

88. *FOCM,* 39, 68; *RNA* 1: 225, 231, 240, 255, 264.

89. Yntema, "A Capital Industry," 76; *VRBM,* 200; Carr and Walsh, "The Standard of Living in the Colonial Chesapeake," 136; Venema, *Beverwijck,* 292–302.

90. *NYHM* 2: 88–89, 251–252; GAA, NA, inv. no. 1062, p. 110–111 (7 June 1642); *VRBM,* 679; Shattuck, "Civil Society," 92.

91. *LWA,* 52; *CM 1655–1656,* 148, 155.

92. Yntema, "The Welfare of Brewers," 124, 126–127; Yntema, "Beer in Abundance," 95; GAA, NA, inv. no. 2280 III, p. 62–63 (8 May 1653); *NYHM* 5: 205–206; *RNA* 2: 233–241.

93. *LWA,* 22; *RNA* 1: 13–14.

94. *FOCM,* 41, 43, 45–47, 49–50, 211, 213, 219; Jansen, *Jan Steen,* 122; Shattuck, "Civil Society," 207–216.

95. *FOCM,* 219; *LWA,* 22–23, 25–27; *LO,* 360; *RNA* 7: 206; *RNA* 3: 378; *RNA* 1: 43–44.

96. *RNA* 1: 15.

97. *FOCM,* 109–110.

98. Ibid., 199, 415–416; *RNA* 3: 422–423; *RNA* 1: 24–26; NYSA, NYCM 8: 243–244 (10 October 1656), 244–245 (24 October 1656); *LWA,* 73.

99. *RNA* 2: 264.

100. *RNA* 7: 221; *RNA* 1: 46–48; *RNA* 3: 285; *RNA* 3: 389–390; NYSA, NYCM 9: 836 (13 October 1661); for a detailed example, see O'Callaghan, *Register of Solomon Lachaire,* 5–6; *RNA* 3: 262; Middleton, "'How it Came That the Bakers Bake No Bread.'"

101. *NNN,* 106; *DRNN,* 228–230.

102. *VRBM,* 467–468; Baart, "Ho-de-no-sau-nee en de Nederlanders," 96; Baart, "Dutch Material Civilization," 6–10; GAA, NA, inv. no. 2753, fol. 124 (15 April 1660), inv. no. 2992, p. 32–33 (17 January 1661), inv. no. 2486, p. 773 (27 November 1659); *RNA* 3: 61; NYSL, VRMP, box 13, folder 4 (1656–1663); *Corres. 1654–1658,* 41.

103. Eekhof, *Michaëlius,* 124, 135; *NNN,* 130.

104. *CJVR* 40, 287; *DRCHNY* 2: 183–184; GAA, NA, inv. no. 1287, fol. 24 (7 March 1643); *LWA,* 35–36; *NYHM* 5: 110–111; NYSA, NYCM 10–3: 95–96 (17 March 1664), 103–104 (18 March 1664), 8: 580 (15 May 1657); *LO,* 348; *DRCHNY* 1: 215.

105. *Corres. 1654–1658,* 107; *CJVR* 67, 77; GAA, NA, inv. no. 2880, p. 80–82 (17 February 1659); *DRCHNY* 2: 184; Puype, *Dutch and Other Flintlocks;* Baart, "Kammen," 180; Van Dongen, "Inexhaustible Kettle," 136.

106. Wilcoxen, *Dutch Trade and Ceramics;* Wilcoxen, "New Netherland Ceramics"; Baart, "Dutch Material Civilization," 1–6; De Roever, "The Fort Orange 'EB' Pipe Bowls"; Huey, "Archeological Excavations in the Site of Fort Orange," 74.

107. Huey, "Glass Beads from Fort Orange"; Francis, "De kralen waarmee het eiland Manhattan *niet* is betaald"; GAA, NA, inv. no. 524, fol. 28v–29 (29 June 1640), inv. no. 1715, p. 525–526 (9 May 1661), inv. no. 602, fol. 43v–44 (9 July 1643).

108. *Corres. 1654–1658,* 4.

109. *LWA,* 35–36; *NNN,* 323; *DRCHNY* 1: 372–376, 422.

110. *LWA,* 37–38; *NYHM* 5: 110–111, 157–159.

111. NYPL, Bontemantel Collection, New Netherland Papers box 1, folder "Tax list of the Dutch West India Company for taxes received on merchandise conveyed by private parties to New Netherland" (1654–1655; *Guide,* no. 561), folder "Accounts of the West India Company, slave trade etc." (1651–1660; *Guide,* no. 553); *Corres. 1654–1658,* 106, 127.

112. Rink, *Holland on the Hudson,* chapter 7; Maika, "Commerce and Community."

113. *VRBM,* 142; *DRCHNY* 1: 121; Shattuck, "Heemstede," 39; *DRCHNY* 2: 207; *DP,* 330.

114. Jacobs, "Scheepvaart en handel"; Jacobs, "Enkele aspecten."

115. *DRCHNY* 3: 69, 163–164.

116. *DRCHNY* 14: 471.

117. Wilcoxen, "Dutch Trade with New England"; Hatfield, "Dutch Merchants and Colonists in the English Chesapeake."

118. Jacobs, "Scheepvaart en handel," 19–20; GAA, NA, inv. no. 1534, p. 173 (17 February 1651).

119. GAA, NA, inv. no. 1081, fol. 197–198 (9 August 1647), inv. no. 1096, fol. 338–339 (30 March 1651); Jacobs, "Scheepvaart en handel," 65.

120. NYHS, Stuyvesant-Rutherford Papers 3–2 (24 March 1648; *Guide,* no. 464).

Chapter 5. The Reformed Church and the Others

1. *DRNN,* 2–5.

2. Den Heijer, *De geschiedenis van de WIC,* 21–22; Frijhoff, *Wegen,* 495–496; Van Hoboken, "The Dutch West India Company"; Van Dillen, "De West-Indische Compagnie"; Van Hoboken, "Wederwoord"; Groenhuis, *De predikanten,* 35–36; Van Winter, *De Westindische Compagnie ter kamer Stad en Lande,* 13–14; Van Boetzelaer van Dubbeldam, *De gereformeerde kerken,* 17–18; Joosse, *"Scoone dingen sijn swaere dingen,"* 224.

3. Eekhof, *Bastiaen Jansz. Krol*, 8–24; Van Boetzelaer van Dubbeldam, *De gereformeerde kerken*, 19–50; Van Troostenburg de Bruyn, *De hervormde kerk in Nederlandsch Oost-Indië*, 113–121.

4. *ER* 1: 158–161, 277–278; Grothe, *Archief*, 1: 16–18, 31–32; De Jong, *The Dutch Reformed Church*, 1; Eekhof, *Bastiaen Jansz. Krol*, 22–23; Niemeijer, *Calvinisme en koloniale stadscultuur*, 97; Van Boetzelaer, *De gereformeerde kerken*, 72–92.

5. *ER* 1: 89–91, 529–530; *VRBM*, 151; Van Boetzelaer van Dubbeldam, *De gereformeerde kerken*, 93–125; Frijhoff, *Wegen*, 208, 545–546; Groenhuis, *De predikanten*, 22; Roodenburg, *Onder censuur*, 106–107.

6. *ER* 1: 111, 113–114, 116, 186–187; *VRBM*, 169–170; GAA, NA, inv. no. 943, not paginated (17 July 1632); Eekhof, *Bastiaen Jansz. Krol*, 13.

7. *ER* 1: 226, 232; *NYHM* 4: 412, 611–613; *Corres. 1647–1653*, 56–57, 71; Eekhof, *Hervormde kerk* 1: 82–83.

8. Wilhelmus Grasmeer, who went to New Netherland against the wishes of the classis and stayed only a short while, is not included in these numbers. Jacobs, *New Netherland*, appendix 10.

9. *ER* 1: 250–252, 439.

10. Ibid., 422; NYSA, NYCM 13: 18 (13 February 1659); Joosse, "*Scoone dingen sijn swaere dingen*," 461; Niemeijer, *Calvinisme en koloniale stadscultuur*, §§ 14 and 15.

11. Groenhuis, *De predikanten*, chapter 1; Hsia and Van Nierop, *Calvinism and Religious Toleration*; Bergsma, "Church, State and People"; Jacobs, "Between Repression and Approval."

12. Frijhoff, *Wegen*, 358–361.

13. Eekhof, *Michaëlius*; Eekhof, *Hervormde kerk*, chapter 2; Frijhoff, *Wegen*, chapter 17; Frijhoff, "Neglected Networks."

14. Eekhof, *Michaëlius*, 63, 68.

15. Ibid., 63–65, 68–70.

16. Frijhoff, *Wegen*.

17. Jacobs, "A Troubled Man."

18. *NYHM* 4: 291; GAA, archive consistory Amsterdam, inv. no. 7, p. 123 (8 November 1635); *ER* 1: 87–88, 126–127; Nat. Arch., OWIC, inv. no. 50, doc. 32 (20 August 1635), inv. no. 14, fol. 137v (19 May 1636); Roodenburg, *Onder censuur*, 115–116; Jacobs, "A Troubled Man"; Frijhoff, *Wegen*, 664–698; Eekhof, *Hervormde kerk* 1: 55–59.

19. *NYHM* 4: 189–192, 291–297; *Breeden-Raedt*, C 4v; Frijhoff, *Wegen*, 732.

20. Frijhoff, *Wegen*, 749–756.

21. *NYHM* 4: 600.

22. *Corres. 1647–1653*, 82; Eekhof, *Hervormde kerk* 1: 88.

23. *ER* 1: 261–262, 457–458, 515, 607–608, 610–611; Eekhof, *Hervormde kerk*, 1: 87, 182, 177, 205, 263–264; *NNN*, 342–343; Schalkwijk, *The Reformed Church in Dutch Brazil*, 120; Frijhoff, *Wegen*, 701; Groenhuis, *De predikanten*, 26–29.

24. *ER* 1: 308; GAA, NA, inv. no. 1100, fol. 23v, 26 (8 May 1652); *FOCM*, 84–86, 102–103, 106–107.

25. *ER* 1: 301–302; Corwin, *Manual*, 433–435; Jacobs, "Hartford Treaty," 76–77.

26. *DRCHNY* 14: 479; De Jong, *The Dutch Reformed Church*, 41; *OFDRCB*, 30, 226.

27. Eekhof, *Michaëlius*, 103, 111; *NNN*, 130.

28. *ER* 1: 237–239; Eekhof, *Hervormde kerk*, 1: 121; NYPL, Bontemantel Papers, "Official list of New Netherland" (1650; *Guide*, no. 551); *Corres. 1647–1653*, 156; *CM 1655–1656*, 285–286; Groenhuis, *De predikanten*, 133–150; Wouters and Abels, *Nieuw en ongezien*, 1: 506–514; Rooijakkers, *Rituele repertoires*, 128.

29. *DRCHNY* 13: 111; *LWA*, 99; *LO*, 304–307; NYSA, NYCM 8: 789 (26 March 1654); *DRCHNY* 14: 414; *ER* 1: 350; Balmer, *A Perfect Babel of Confusion*, 11–13; Wouters and Abels, *Nieuw en ongezien*, 1: 100–104 and 506–514.

30. *ER* 1: 525–526; Eekhof, *Hervormde kerk*, 1: 203; De Jong, *The Dutch Reformed Church*, chapter 10; Jacobs, "Dutch Protestant Churches," 63.

31. *RNA* 1: 191; *ER* 1: 607–608; Eekhof, *Hervormde kerk*, 1: 177, 182; *FOCM*, 162–164; Venema, *Kinderen van weelde en armoede*, 18; Venema, *Beverwijck*, 442; Nooter, "Between Heaven and Earth," 126; Goodfriend, "Social Dimensions," 257.

32. *FOCM*, 162–164.

33. *OFDRCB*, 36–38, 40–44.

34. Roodenburg, *Onder censuur*, 100, 118; Fabend, *Zion on the Hudson*, chapter 2; Fabend, "Church and State, Hand in Hand."

35. Kingston, Reformed Protestant Dutch Church, Church Records vol. 1, p. 22 (3 July 1661).

36. *CJVR* 131, 230; Roodenburg, *Onder censuur*, 31.

37. Phelps Stokes, *Iconography* 2: 133–135; *RNA* 2: 323; De Waard, *Zeeuwsche expeditie*, 131; Van der Linde, "Selijns," 46.

38. Goodfriend, "Recovering the Religious History of Dutch Reformed Women in Colonial New York," 55; Kloek, *Wie hij zij*, 91; Wouters and Abels, *Nieuw en ongezien*, 1: 261–266; Niemeijer, *Calvinisme en koloniale stadscultuur*, 214; Rothschild, "Sociale afstand," 190–191; Potter, "Demographic Development," 149; *ER* 1: 387; Eekhof, *Hervormde kerk* 2: 16; De Baar, "'Let Your Women Keep Silence in the Churches'"; Goodfriend, "Social Dimensions," 257–258.

39. Eekhof, *Michaëlius*, 117, 130; *NNN*, 124; *Breeden-Raedt*, D 1; *ER* 1: 236, 583, 654; Eekhof, *Hervormde kerk*, 1: 84, 183.

40. *ER* 1: 383, 482–483, 2: 770; Eekhof, *Hervormde kerk* 1: 142, 147–149, 156, 162, 2: 35.

41. *ER* 1: 457, 534; Eekhof, *Hervormde kerk* 1: 234–237, 263–264; *OFDRCB*, 226, 228.

42. Van den Boogaart, "Servant Migration," appendix 1; Shattuck, "Civil Society," 11.

43. Rink, *Holland on the Hudson*, 158; Spaans, *Haarlem na de Reformatie*, 89; Groenveld, *Was de Nederlandse Republiek verzuild?* 6; Kloek, *Wie hij zij*, 91; Wouters and Abels, *Nieuw en ongezien*, 1: 228–246; Venema, *Beverwijck*, 132; Goodfriend, "Social Dimensions," 252. Janny Venema, using the same figures as I do, comes to the conclusion that 40 percent of the adult population of Beverwijck "belonged to the group of people who participated in communion" and thus were members of the Reformed Church. However, the adult-minor ratio that she implicitly applies is unfounded. Extrapolation on the basis of an average family size for the colony is not possible, since as yet no reliable demographic study of New Netherland has been carried out, and applying the average family size of the Netherlands is dangerous, as the specific colonial situation may have resulted in a quite different composition of the population. The New Netherland population may have included fewer old people, as these were less likely to emigrate.

44. *FOCM*, 236–237.

45. *LWA*, 55–56; *CM 1655–1656*, 209–210; *LO*, 211–212, 428–430; *RNA* 1: 20–21.

46. *DRCHNY* 1: 110–111.

47. *FOCM*, 216.

48. *NYHM* 2: 121–125; literature on the Lutherans: Kreider, *The Beginnings of Lutheranism in New York*; Piwonka, "The Lutheran Presence in New Netherland"; Kooiman, *Luthersche gemeenten*; Brandt, "Eenige opmerkingen aangaande de Luthersche kerk in Amerika"; Nicum, "The Beginnings of the Lutheran Church on Manhattan Island"; Lurix, "The Lutheran Struggle for Toleration in New Amsterdam"; Hart and Kreider, *Protocol of the Lutheran Church in New York City*.

49. *LCNY*, 13.

50. Ibid., 13–18.

51. *MDC*, 29 November 1658, 14 October 1656; *LCNY*, 38–40.

52. *ER* 1: 317–318; Eekhof, *Hervormde kerk* 1: 170; 2: 2.

53. *Corres. 1654–1658*, 6.

54. *ER* 1: 320–323.

55. *LCNY*, 18–19.

56. Ibid., 20; *ER* 1: 354–355; GAA, Archive Evangelisch-Lutherse Gemeente, inv. no. 230, p. 1 (14 June 1656); *Corres. 1654–1658*, 93; Olthuis, *De doopspraktijk der gereformeerde kerken*, 151–153, 161–164.

57. *ER* 1: 358–360; Eekhof, *Hervormde kerk* 2: 11; *LCNY*, 20–21.

58. *LCNY*, 22.

59. Ibid., 23.

60. *ER* 1: 386–390; Eekhof, *Hervormde kerk* 2: 16–17; *LCNY*, 24–26, 30–31.

61. *LCNY*, 31–32, 35–36; *ER* 1: 420–423; *Corres. 1654–1658*, 174–175.
62. NYSA, NYCM 13: 18, p. 1 (13 February 1659).
63. *LCNY*, 38–40, 48–49.
64. *ER* 1: 393–400; Eekhof, *Hervormde kerk* 2: 77–78; Warrington, "Speaking Scripture."
65. The events cannot be dated exactly. The incident must have taken place between the arrival of the Quaker ship, on which Hodgson presumably traveled to America, in New Amsterdam in August and 22 October 1657 when Megapolensis and Drisius reported it to the classis.
66. O'Callaghan, *History of New Netherland* 2: 347–350; Brodhead, *History of the State of New York*, 636–637; Zwierlein, *Religion in New Netherland*, 215–219; Eekhof, *Hervormde kerk* 2: 79–81.
67. *ER* 1: 378–381.
68. Ibid., 409–412; Eekhof, *Hervormde kerk* 1: 170; 2; 78–80; *DRCHNY* 14: 369–370.
69. *DRCHNY* 14: 402–403; Harrington, "Speaking Scripture."
70. *DRCHNY* 14: 403–405.
71. Ibid., 405–409; Voorhees, "The Flushing Remonstrance." See also Jackson, "A Colony with a Conscience," written on the occasion of the 350th anniversary of the document in December 2007. The Flushing Remonstrance was not endowed with the honor of being a precursor of the Bill of Rights until after World War II. Its current fame reflects twenty-first century rather than early-modern ideas.
72. *DRCHNY* 14: 489, 491–492; NYSA, NYCM 9: 505 (20 January 1661), 509 (20 January 1661), 537–538 (3 March 1661).
73. NYSA, NYCM 10–11: 213–214 (14 September 1662), 291 (14 December 1662), 10–12: 14 (8 January 1663); *DRCHNY* 14: 526; Kessler and Rachlis, *Peter Stuyvesant and his New York*, 193–196.
74. *ER* 1: 334–336; Eekhof, *Hervormde kerk* 2: 5.
75. *NYHM* 5: 103.
76. *DRCHNY* 14: 369–370; *ER* 1: 393–400; Eekhof, *Hervormde kerk* 2: 56, 58.
77. *ER* 1: 315–316, 432–434, 436–439; Eekhof, *Hervormde kerk*, 2: appendix 6 and 7; Christoph, "The Time and Place of Jan van Loon," I, 8; Thwaites, *Travels and Explorations*, 40: 142–147; GAA, Archive Classis Amsterdam, inv. no. 157, p. 391 (13 January 1659).
78. Schutte, "Bij het schemerlicht van hun tijd"; De Jong, "The Dutch Reformed Church and Negro Slavery in Colonial America"; Boxer, *Nederlanders in Brazilië*, 108; Joosse, "*Scoone dingen sijn swaere dingen.*"
79. Van Deursen, *Mensen van klein vermogen*, 138–139; Van Laer, "Letters of Wouter van Twiller"; GAA, NA, inv. no. 915, fol. 213v (29 September 1633); *NYHM* 1: 69. The date of the arrival of Adam Roelantsz on Manhattan plays an important role in the discussion over the year in which Collegiate School in New York City was founded: Dunshee, *History of the School of the Collegiate Reformed Dutch Church*, 15; Kilpatrick, *The Dutch Schools of New Netherland*, 39–50; Frost, "356 Years of Formal Education in New York City"; Maglione, "The Evidence for the Establishment of Collegiate School in 1628." In my opinion, 1638 is the best defendable year for the formal establishment of an institution of education on Manhattan.
80. On the basis of the information in the marriage register, it is not always possible to ascertain that it concerns blacks. Of twenty-four marriages I am sure, but another three are less clear. I suspect that those are interracial marriages. Goodfriend in "Black Families in New Netherland," 151, gives the number of twenty-six marriages. Christoph in "The Freedmen of New Amsterdam," 168, note 24 gives twenty-seven.
81. The baptismal register (*BDC*) does not always provide sufficient information, and many times the name or the place of origin of the parents must be relied upon. The baptisms of five children from mixed marriages have not been included in the count, and this may be the cause of the discrepancy between my figures and those of Goodfriend, "Black Families in New Netherland" 151, who provides a number of "at least" sixty-one and Christoph, "The Freedmen of New Amsterdam," 160, who counted fifty-eight. Frijhoff, *Wegen*, 772, states that prior to the departure of Bogardus, forty-two black children were baptized.

82. *OFDRCB*, 230.

83. NYSA, NYCM 10–12: 416–417 (6 December 1663); *BDC* 1: 18 (18 February 1645); Elphick and Shell, "Intergroup Relations," 120–121; Gehring and Schiltkamp, *Curacao Papers*, 198–199, 451; *OFDRCB*, 109–114, 226; personal communication, Ad Biewenga, Free University, Amsterdam, who suggested the possible loss of a separate baptismal register.

84. Christoph, "The Freedmen of New Amsterdam," 164; Frijhoff, *Wegen*, 775, 778; Goodfriend, *Before the Melting Pot*, 116. *BDC* 1 (14 April 1647); *MDC*, 27 April 1647. "'t Ledematen boeck,'" first part.

85. Frijhoff, *Wegen*, 766–767. To draw further conclusions on the changing Dutch attitudes toward slavery, comparative research encompassing the whole of the Dutch colonial world, including the pertinent theological discussions in *patria*, is required. Andrea Mosterman of Boston University was working on a dissertation which will cover some of these points as of summer 2008.

86. *DRNN*, 2–5, 36–37; Nat. Arch., Archive States General, Lias West Indië, inv. no. 5755, I C. 539–542, art. 5 (not dated, probably 1638); *ER* 1: 143–145, 203–209; Eekhof, *Hervormde kerk* 2: appendix 3; *VRBM*, 606–608; GAA, NA, inv. no. 1100, fol. 23v, 26 (8 May 1652); Dennis, *Cultivating a Landscape of Peace*, 142; Trelease, *Indian Affairs*, 38–40, 169–172; Rink, "Private Interest and Godly Gain," 252–256; Taylor, *American Colonies*, 252; Rothschild, *Colonial Encounters in a Native American Landscape*, 30.

87. *DRCHNY* 1: 334, 340.

88. Joosse, *"Scoone dingen sijn swaere dingen,"* 465; *ER* 1: 551. On the comparison with Brazil, see Meuwese, "Dutch Calvinism and Native Americans," and Meuwese, "'For the Peace and Well-Being of the Country.'"

89. Eekhof, *Michaëlius*, 120–123, 132–135; *NNN*, 126–129, possibly a reference to Johannes de Laet in his *Nieuwe wereldt*, 89 (*NNN*, 50).

90. *ER* 1: 150–151.

91. *NNN*, 177–178. According to Mohawk scholar Gunther Michelson, Megapolensis"s rendition of what was said to him is garbled. *Tyaten':ro?* is "friend." The second Mohawk term in the statement seems to be *tsyaha':wi?*, "you (plural) are led (to do something)." The third term is *ahsiron':ni*: literally "clothmakers," referring to the Dutch colonists. *Hagiousk* is unidentifiable. Personal communication, 25 June 2004.

92. *ER* 1: 348.

93. Ibid., 326–327, 398–399; Eekhof, *Hervormde kerk* 1: 171.

94. *ER* 1: 398; Eekhof, *Hervormde kerk* 1: 171.

95. Niemeijer, *Calvinisme en koloniale stadscultuur*, 16.

96. Roodenburg, *Onder censuur*; Burke, *Mohawk Frontier*, 151–156.

Chapter 6. Burghers and Status

1. For a more extensive analysis, see Jacobs, *New Netherland*, 328–342.

2. *DRCHNY* 1: 155–156; *NYHM* 4: 13; NYPL, Bontemantel Collection, New Netherland Papers, box 1, folder "Official list of New Netherland" (undated, ca. 1650; *Guide*, no. 551); GAA, Archive *Burgemeesters*, inv. no. 541 (undated, ca. 1657).

3. *NYHM* 4: 14; *DRCHNY* 1: 155–156; NYPL, Bontemantel Collection, New Netherland Papers, box 1, folder "Official list of New Netherland" (undated, ca. 1650; *Guide*, no. 551).

4. GAA, NA, inv. no. 1341, fol. 25v, 26 (17 April 1647), fol. 26, 26v (17 April 1647), inv. no. 1346, fol. 21 (16 March 1651); *RNA* 1: 157; *FOCM*, 237; *VRBM*, 824–825.

5. GAA, NA, inv. no. 1346, fol. 14 (10 March 1651), fol. 14v (10 March 1651), inv. no. 1135, fol. 338–338v (8 December 1660); *MDC*, 4 December 1652; NYSL, VRMP, box 13, folder 32a (1661); *LP*, 76.

6. Groenhuis, *De predikanten*, 66.

7. De Vries and Van der Woude, *Nederland 1500–1815*, 647–651; Schöffer, "La stratification sociale de la République des Provinces Unies au XVIIe siècle"; Van Dillen, *Van rijkdom en regenten*, chapter 14; Frijhoff and Spies, *1650. Bevochten eendracht*, 188–190; Venema, *Kinderen van weelde en armoede*, 18; Venema, "Poverty in Seventeenth-Century Albany."

8. Plomp, "Nieuw-Nederlanders en hun Europese achtergrond," 143, 155–156. Another example is Pieter Claesz Wijckoff: see Wagman, "The Rise of Pieter Claessen Wyckoff."

9. *NYHM* 4: 291.

10. *RNA* 1: 48–49; *RNA* 7: 110–111; De Bruin, *Geheimhouding en verraad*, 25; Pole, *The Gift of Government*.

11. Van Deursen, *Mensen van klein vermogen*, 183–186; Phelps Stokes, *Iconography* 2: 133–135.

12. *RNA* 2: 25.

13. *NYHM* 5: 98.

14. Phelps Stokes, *Iconography* 2: 133–135.

15. Jacobs, *New Netherland*, appendix 6.

16. Ibid.

17. *DRCHNY* 1: 111.

18. *MCR*, 40–41.

19. *NYHM* 5: 130.

20. *RNA* 1: 158.

21. *VRBM*, 204–205, 214.

22. *RNA* 6: 198.

23. *Corres. 1647–1653*, 110.

24. *DRCHNY* 1: 448–449; Valck Lucassen, "Familieaantekeningen Ebbinck en Gerbade," 221; Blackburn and Piwonka, *Remembrance of Patria*, 53; Dilliard, *Album of New Netherland*, 62; *RNA* 2: 183. The windows made for Rutger Jacobsz and Andries Herpertsz are now in the Albany Institute of History and Art.

25. *NNN*, 198, 342; *DRCHNY* 2: 460–469; *NYHM* 2: 406–407; Beernink, *Arend van Slichtenhorst*, 276; *MCR*, 211.

26. *DRCHNY* 13: 198; *FOCM*, 202–203, 246, 444–445.

27. *RNA* 3: 163–164.

28. Ibid., 213–214.

29. NYSA, NYCM 10–3: 215–216 (12 May 1654); Eekhof, *Hervormde kerk*, 2: 142; Broers, "Van Tafel 8 tot Boek 6," 303–304.

30. Knevel, *Burgers in het geweer*, 45–47, 212; Moorman van Kappen, "Iets over ons oud-vaderlandse stadsburgerschap"; De Vries, "Het middeleeuwse burgerschap"; De Monté ver Loren and Spruit, *Hoofdlijnen*, 148–152; Fockema Andreæ, *Het Oud-Nederlandsch burgerlijk recht*, 56–77.

31. *DRCHNY* 1: 415.

32. *NYHM* 4: 58.

33. *NYCM 1655–1656*, 316; O'Callaghan, *History of New Netherland* 2: 176; *MCR*, 173; *DRCHNY* 3: 74–77; *FOCM*, 4–5.

34. *FOCM*, 183.

35. *RNA* 1: 379; *RNA* 2: 98.

36. Maika, "Commerce and Community," 162–237.

37. *RNA* 2: 260–263, 272–273; *Burghers of New Amsterdam* 1885: 3–4.

38. *Burghers of New Amsterdam*, 5–7. I thank Janny Venema of the New Netherland Project, Albany, for the transcription.

39. *LO*, 298–300; *RNA* 2: 286–287; Bontemantel, *De regeeringe van Amsterdam*, 2: 88–90; Moorman van Kappen, *Tot behoef der arme wesen*, 45; Schimmel, *Burgerrecht te Nijmegen*. Cf. Kammen, *Colonial New York*, 36.

40. *RNA* 2: 286–287; *LO*, 298–300; *FOCM*, 300–301, 373–374.

41. *LO*, 301–303; *LWA*, 79–81.

42. *RNA* 7: 154.

43. Ibid., 149–153, 214, NYSA, NYCM 10 111 247 (2 November 1662); *Burghers of New Amsterdam* 16–17; Maika, "Commerce and Community," p. 510; Maika, "Securing the Burgher Right." A certificate for the small burgher right of Lucas Dircksz is in the Pierpont Morgan Library, New York, MA 956, no. 9 (20 December 1659; *Guide*, no. 611).

44. *RNA* 7: 150.

45. Maika, "Commerce and Community," 164; Shattuck, "Women and Trade in New Netherland"; Shattuck, "Women and the Economy in Beverwijck."

46. NYSA, NYCM 10–13: 187–189 (13 March 1664), 189–190 (10 March 1664), 191–192 (22 April 1664); *LO*, 462.

47. NYSA, NYCM 10–13: 245 (3 July 1664); *DRCHNY* 12: 453–454.

48. *DRCHNY* 1: 123.

49. Ibid., 161; *NYHM* 4: 74–75.

50. *NYHM* 4: 520, 580; *DRCHNY* 14: 432; O'Callaghan, *History of New Netherland* 2: 569; NYSA, NYCM 8: 928 (15 July 1658); O'Callaghan, *Calendar*, 199; *RNA* 1: 128–129; *RNA* 3: 17–18; Knevel, *Burgers in het geweer*, 380.

51. *NYHM* 5: 128; NYSA, NYCM 9: 133 (23 March 1660).

52. *DRCHNY* 13: 124–126.

53. *RNA* 1: 65; *RNA* 5: 23; *MOM* 2: 178; *CM 1655–1656*, 76; 153–154; *DRCHNY* 13: 259–260, 268; NYSA, NYCM 10–12: 193–194 (10 July 1663), 195 (10 July 1663), 201 (6 July 1663).

54. *NYHM* 4: 208, 520; *FOCM*, 487; *RNA* 1: 128–129.

55. NYSL, mss 12802, ordinance on the burgher guard of Beverwijck (presumably 1653; *Guide*, no. 164); *FOCM*, 109, 237, 431.

56. *RNA* 1: 265; *RNA* 7: 195–198; *MOM* 2: 76–77; *FOCM*, 451, 470; NYSA, NYCM 9: 551 (10 March 1661).

57. *MOM* 2: 107; *RNA* 1: 302, 314; *RNA* 3: 17; *DRCHNY* 14: 432, 2: 461; *FOCM*, 191.

58. Groenveld, "Natie en nationaal gevoel."

59. *ER* 1: 195, 204; NYPL, Bontemantel Collection, Brazil Dutch West India Papers, no. 1233 (20 April 1649); Van Dillen, "Vreemdelingen te Amsterdam," 22; Teensma, "Resentment in Recife"; Marcus, *The Colonial American Jew*, 1: 69–76.

60. *ER* 1: 335–336; Eekhof, *Hervormde kerk*, 2: 72.

61. *RNA* 1: 240; Marcus, *The Colonial American Jew*, 1: 81, 209–211; Oppenheim, *Early History of the Jews*, 4–5; Israel, "De Republiek der Verenigde Nederlanden tot omstreeks 1750," 110–111.

62. "Powers of Attorney," 175; Oppenheim, *Early History of the Jews*, 9–13; *CM 1655–1656*, 261.

63. *DRCHNY* 14: 315; *Corres. 1654–1658*, 49; Oppenheim, *Early History of the Jews*, 8–9, corrected some of Fernow's errors, but not this one.

64. *Woordenboek der Nederlandsche Taal*, entries *inteekening*, *regard*, and *uitvaren*; Van Hattum and Rooseboom, *Glossarium van oude Nederlandse rechtstermen*, based on Thuys, *Ars Notariatus*. For the meaning of *herideren*, see also VRBM 518; GAA, NA, inv. no. 5129, fol. 121–121v (pp. 143–144) (16 April 1683). In the original Dutch, no reference is made to the "shares" that Fernow cites. It is Fernow's interpretation that the Jews owned shares in the Company. But the major problem originates with his translation of the two words *alsnoch* and *heriderende*. *Alsnoch* is a temporal designation. It may mean either "as yet," or, a little more conditionally, "still," and applies to the present. In his translation, however, Fernow uses the present perfect and leaves *alsnoch* out. The second word, *heriderende*, from the verb "*herideren*," is even more problematic, as it is rather unusual and rarely used in the seventeenth century. It is sometimes rendered as "to invest" but the use of the auxiliary verb makes "to owe" a more likely option. My interpretation is thus at odds with the standard story of the first arrival of Jews in North America. See Swierenga, *The Forerunners*, 37–38; Marcus, *The American Jew*, 14–16; Goodman, *American Overture*, 81; Israel, "The Jews of Dutch America," 344–345; Williams, "An Atlantic Perspective," 377–385.

65. De Boer, "Naamlijsten van bewindhebbers en van hoofdparticipanten der West-Indische Compagnie"; Ebben, *Zilver, brood en kogels*, 182–183; Boxer, *Nederlanders in Brazilië*, 22–23; Van Dillen, "Vreemdelingen te Amsterdam," 16; Swetschinski, "The Portuguese Jewish Merchants of Seventeenth-Century Amsterdam," 199–201. One of them was Joseph da Costa, who in March 1655 was involved in a newly founded trading company arrangement for trade with New Netherland. In collaboration with, among others, Mordechai Abendana (1/4 part)

and David Cardoso Davilar (1/16) the earlier-mentioned merchant family Verbrugge gathered together a total amount of eighteen thousand guilders. Da Costa was to act as the company's factor in New Amsterdam for a period of four years. The Verbrugges had undoubtedly waited with the appointment of Da Costa until the WIC directors had given the Jews permission to remain in New Amsterdam. GAA, NA, inv. no. 1112, fol. 244–244v (22 March 1655), inv. no. 1113, fol. 22 (7 April 1655), inv. no. 1119, fol. 79 (24 October 1656). David Cardoso Davilar acted as intermediary for Duarte Diaz de Paz, who sold his share by the end of 1656: GAA, NA, inv. no. 1116, fol. 134 (18 February 1656), inv. no. 1119, fol. 356 (22 December 1656).

66. I thank Noah Gelfand for this suggestion. Gelfand, "Sugar and God"; Gonsalves de Mello, *Nederlanders in Brazilië*, 258–259, 273; Wiznitzer, *Jews in Colonial Brazil*, 71–73; Baron, *A Social and Religious History of the Jews*, 15: 332. I thank Wim Klooster for this reference.

67. *CM 1655–1656*, 81; *LWA*, 50–51.

68. *CM 1655–1656*, 68, 128, 149–151, 166, 261–262; Swetschinski, "The Portuguese Jewish Merchants of Seventeenth-Century Amsterdam," 11–13.

69. *Corres. 1654–1658*, 93.

70. *CM 1655–1656*, 229, 280; *Corres. 1654–1658*, 83, 93; NYSA, NYCM 8: 531 (21 April 1657); *RNA* 2: 396; *RNA* 7: 154, 258–259, 261; Swetschinski, "The Portuguese Jewish Merchants of Seventeenth-Century Amsterdam," 14; Van Dillen, "Vreemdelingen te Amsterdam," 13; Zwierlein, "New Netherland intolerance."

71. *NYHM* 1: 112–113.

72. *Corres. 1654–1658*, 127; NYSA, NYCM, 10–11: 296 (28 December 1662); Phelps Stokes, *Iconography*, 4: 181; Wagman, "Corporate Slavery," 35; McManus, *Negro Slavery*, 4–6; Higginbotham, *In the Matter of Color*, 103; O'Callaghan, *Voyages of the Slavers*, 12.

73. *NYHM* 4: 354; *NYHM* 5: 123; NYSA, NYCM 8: 894 (14 June 1658), 900 (2 July 1658), 1046 (28 November 1658); *Corres. 1654–1658*, 106; Phelps Stokes, *Iconography* 2: 297–298.

74. NYSA, NYCM 10–11: 168 (8 July 1662); *NYHM* 3: 82–83, 208–210.

75. *NYHM* 4: 212–213; McManus, *Negro Slavery*, 13–14; Higginbotham, *In the Matter of Color*, 105–109; Christoph, "The Freedmen of New Amsterdam," 158–159; Jacobs, "'Te fourneeren nae de loffelijcke costumen der Stadt Amsterdam,'" 374–375.

76. *NYHM* 4: 212–213.

77. *NNN*, 330.

78. *DRCHNY* 1: 335, 343, 425; *NYHM* 4: 342; NYSA, NYCM 10–11: 296 (28 December 1662), 10–12: 429 (8 December 1663), 416–417 (6 December 1663); Goodfriend, "Black Families in New Netherland," 149–151; Jacobs, "'Te fourneeren nae de loffelijcke costumen der Stadt Amsterdam,'" 374–375; Hodges, *Root and Branch*, 12–13.

79. *CJVR* 364–365; Goodfriend, "Black Families in New Netherland," 149.

80. *NYHM* 4: 35, 66; *RNA* 3: 212; *RNA* 7: 207; Christoph, "The Freedmen of New Amsterdam," 157.

81. *RNA* 3: 315; *NYHM* 4: 97–100, 326–328; NYSA, NYCM 10–13: 1 (3 January 1664), 31–32 (4 February 1664), 43 (5 February 1664), 44 (8 February 1664), 45–46 (9 February 1664); Jacobs, "Van Angola naar Manhattan."

82. NYSA, NYCM 8: 831–832 (15 April 1658), 829 (12 April 1658), 9: 780 (8 September 1661); *NYHM* 4: 3–4, 33–34, 37, 100; *MCR*, 12; *RNA* 4: 24; *RNA* 5: 310; Spierenburg, *The Spectacle of Suffering*, chapter 2; Eekhof, *Michaëlius*, 123; *NNN*, 129; *CJVR* 353.

83. Cf. Higginbotham, *In the Matter of Color*, 108.

84. *DRNN*, 140; *DRCHNY* 13: 119–121; *DP*, 111–112; Van Laer, *Correspondence of Maria van Rensselaer*, 44; Dunn, *The Mohicans and their Land*, 141.

85. *NYHM* 4: 566–567; *LWA*, 19–20; *RNA* 1: 11.

86. This section has benefited from extensive discussion with Martha Shattuck.

87. *NYHM* 4: 29–30; *NYHM* 5: 173; *LWA*, 47–48; *LO*, 125–126.

88. *DRCHNY* 13: 218–219.

89. NYSA, NYCM 10–11: 125 (4 May 1662), 134 (11 May 1662), 138 (25 May 1662).

90. *DRCHNY* 12: 295–296. For another incident in 1678, see *CMARS* 2: 324–327; Lustig, *The Imperial Executive*, 88–89.

91. E.g. *FOCM*, 254–255.
92. *NNN*, 174.
93. Ibid., 72, 81, 231; *FOCM*, 454.
94. *VRBM*, 442.
95. *NYHM* 4: 4, 33–34, 43–44, 122; cf. Hauptmann and Knapp, "Dutch-Aboriginal Interaction in New Netherland and Formosa," 172.
96. *NNN*, 340.
97. Wilcoxen, "Arent van Curler's Children"; *CMARS* 2: 86; Burke, *Mohawk Frontier*, 148–149; *RNA* 2: 332.
98. Van Laer, "Documents Relating to Arent van Curler's Death."
99. *DRCHNY* 12: 317; Jennings, "Jacob Young."
100. *NYHM* 4: 480–481; *NYHM* 3: 110–112; NYHS, Stuyvesant-Rutherford Papers 2: 7a (21 December 1647; *Guide*, no. 462), 2: 7b (28 March 1648; *Guide*, 463); *MCR*, 105.
101. Personal communication of Paul Otto, George Fox University, May 2004.
102. *DRCHNY* 1: 210.
103. *Breeden-Raedt* C 3; GAA, NA, inv. no. 1781, p. 166 (1 September 1644); *DRCHNY* 13: 169, 178–179, 304; Gehring and Schiltkamp, *Curacao Papers*, 420.
104. *NYHM* 4: 114.

Chapter 7. Living in a Colony

1. Rhoads, "Franklin D. Roosevelt and Dutch Colonial Architecture"; Voorhees, *The Holland Society*, 80; Freidel, "The Dutchness of the Roosevelts."
2. Reynolds, *Dutch Houses in the Hudson Valley*, v.
3. Cohen, *The Dutch-American Farm*, 48, 51; Hammond, "An Historical Analysis of the Bronck House"; Wagman, "The Rise of Pieter Claessen Wyckoff," 5; Dilliard, *Old Dutch Houses of Brooklyn*, no. 2; Bailey, *Prerevolutionary Dutch Houses*, 88–91, pl. 23.
4. *DRCHNY* 1: 368; Wieder, *De stichting van New York*, 54–55, note 2.
5. *NNN*, 83; Eekhof, *Michaëlius*, 103, 110.
6. Zantkuyl, "Reconstructie van enkele Nederlandse huizen in Nieuw-Nederland"; Zantkuyl, "The Netherlands Town House"; Zantkuyl, "Hollandse huizen, gebouwd in de 17de eeuw in Amerika."
7. *NYHM* 3: 103–104; *NYHM* 5: 215.
8. *LWA*, 5, 12, 19, 90; *CM 1655–1656*, 186; NYSA, NYCM 8: 833 (16 April 1658); *RNA* 2: 419, 424; *RNA* 1: 5; *RNA* 7: 184. For similar measures for the settlement at Fort Zeelandia on Taiwan, see Zandvliet, *Mapping for Money*, 140.
9. Burrows and Wallace, *Gotham*, 241–242, 596–598; Blackburn, "Dutch Domestic Architecture in the Hudson Valley," 163; Dunn and Bennett, *Dutch Architecture near Albany*; Cohen, *The Dutch-American Farm*; Stayton, *Dutch by Design*; Eberlein, *The Manors and Historic Homes of the Hudson Valley*; Embury, *Building the Dutch Colonial House*; Fitchen, *The New World Dutch Barn*; Meeske, *The Hudson Valley Dutch and Their Houses*; Blackburn, *Dutch Colonial Homes in America*; Van den Hurk, "Reconstructie van de architectuur van Nieuw Nederland"; Van den Hurk, "Imagining New Netherland"; Van den Hurk, "The Architecture of New Netherland Revisited"; Van den Hurk, "Origins and Survival of Netherlandic Building Traditions"; Manca, "Erasing the Dutch."
10. Cohen, *The Dutch-American Farm*, chapter 2, in particular p. 38; Cohen, "Dutch-American Farming."
11. These are of the estates of Jonas Bronck (1643), Jan Jansz Damen (1651), and Gijsbert van Imbroch (1665): Bronck: *NYHM* 2: 121–125; Damen: *NYHM* 3: 267–276; *KP* 2: 566–570; Jacobs, "Fortuin in de Nieuwe Wereld."
12. Piwonka, "New York Colonial Inventories," 63, 81; Wilcoxen, "Household Artifacts of New Netherland."
13. An exception is the inventory of merchant Barent van Wely, brother of the *predikant* Everardus Welius who died in New Netherland in 1659, in which his land on the South River

is included. However, Barent van Wely died in Amsterdam, and his inventory was drawn up in that city, so it says little about New Netherland inventories. GAA, NA, inv. no. 3613, p. 237–243 (1 March 1667).

14. *NYHM* 1: 323, 327.

15. *DRNN*, 248; *ERA* 3: 116–117; *CJVR* 231–232, 440; Blackburn and Piwonka, *Remembrance of Patria*, 55, 274–293; Dilliard, *Album of New Netherland*, 63–67; Blackburn, "Dutch Material Culture: Silversmiths." No gold or silversmiths worked in the colony before 1664. Jeuriaen Blanck, who at the baptism of one of his children was described as a "goldsmith," was already in the colony in 1643, but no evidence exists that he actually practiced his craft. His son, also called Jeuriaen, was a silversmith and some of the earliest known silver objects made in New York were from his hand.

16. GAA, NA, inv. no. 1695, unnumbered (28 April 1651), inv. no. 1838, p. 218–219 (9 May 1653), inv. no. 1788, p. 45 (23 January 1651), inv. no. 1839, p. 835 (23 February 1655), inv. no. 2192, p. 421 (5 April 1652), inv. no. 306, fol. 123v/119v (24 February 1632); *CJVR* 238, 266, n. 580. I have only encountered a few furniture makers, among whom the chair maker Frederick Aertsz: GAA, NA, inv. no. 1360, fol. 117v (11 December 1659); *RNA* 3: 147, 363. It is possible that Lodewijck Pos, who is called a *kistemaecker* (chest maker) was also a furniture maker: "Powers of Attorney," 178.

17. Blackburn and Piwonka, *Remembrance of Patria*, 164–167, 174–175, 179–180; Dilliard, *Album of New Netherland*; Blackburn, "Dutch Material Culture: Furniture"; *NYHM* 2: 358–360; Wijsenbeek-Olthuis, *Achter de gevels van Delft*, 189. On the other hand, Van Koolbergen reports of Weesp that every household had at least one table, six chairs, and a few cupboards. Van Koolbergen, "De materiële cultuur van Weesp," 15.

18. *NYHM* 2: 358–360; *RNA* 3: 363; Volk, "The Dutch Kast and the American Kas"; Denton, "The American Kas"; Blackburn and Piwonka, *Remembrance of Patria*, 178–179, 257–271; Kenney, Safford, and Vincent, *American Kasten*.

19. Wijsenbeek-Olthuis, *Achter de gevels van Delft*, 182; *NYHM* 2: 185; *NYHM* 4: 114–115.

20. *CJVR* 17.

21. *NYHM* 4: 113–115; *NYHM* 1: 325.

22. *NYHM* 1: 325; Wilcoxen, "Household Artifacts in New Netherland," 122, 125; Huey, "Archeological Excavations in the Site of Fort Orange," 74; Wilcoxen, *Dutch Trade and Ceramics*; Wijsenbeek-Olthuis, *Achter de gevels van Delft*, 238.

23. *NYHM* 2: 185; *FOR 1656–1678*, 125.

24. Eekhof, *Michaëlius*, 101, 109, 124, 136; *NNN*, 131.

25. *LWA*, 45.

26. *RNA* 2: 296.

27. Burema, *De voeding in Nederland*, 112–116; Jobse-van Putten, *Eenvoudig maar voedzaam*; Groenveld, Dekker, and Willemse, *Wezen en boefjes*, 161–172; Rose, "Proeve van verandering," 204–206; Van der Molen-Willebrands, "De verstandige kock of sorghvuldige huyshoudster"; Rose, *The Sensible Cook*, introduction.

28. *NYHM* 3: 264; *NYHM* 4: 115; *NYHM* 2: 121–122; Edelman, *The Dutch Language Press in America*, 20; Frijhoff, *Wegen*, 596–597.

29. *KP* 2: 566–570.

30. *CJVR* 13, 149, 347; NYSL, VRMP, box 13, folder 12 (1661–1663); *VRBM*, 274; NYHS, Stuyvesant-Rutherford Papers 2: 5 (12 August 1647; *Guide*, no. 460).

31. *DRCHNY* 13: 155.

32. *VRBM*, 208, 418; *CJVR*, 231, 430, 435, 442, 467.

33. *VRBM*, 294, 564; Beernink, *Arend van Slichtenhorst*, 272; *MCR*, 202; *DRCHNY* 2: 54.

34. *RNA* 7: 139. Possible identifications include: *Hollandts placcaet-boeck: begrijpende meest alle de voornaemste placcaten, ordonnantien ende octroyen uytgegeeven by de Edd. Groot-mogende Heeren Staten, van Hollandt ende West-Vrieslandt: sedert den jaere 1580. tot in den loopende jare 1645* (Amsterdam 1645); *Repertorium van de placcaten, octroyen ende ordonnantien ende andere acten ende munimenten, geemaneert ende uytg. by de Hoogh-Mogende Heeren de Staten Generael der Vereenichde Nederlanden, berustende ter griffie vande*

gemelte Heeren Staten Generael, beginnende anno 1584 ende eyndende anno 1642 (Den Haag 1643); *Handvesten, privilegien, octroyen, costumen en willekeuren der stad Amstelredam, door last van de Ed. Groot-achtbare heeren burgermeesteren en regeerders van dien met seer vele stucken en munimenten op nieuws verm.* (Amsterdam 1663); *Consultatien, advyzen en advertissementen, gegeven ende geschreven bij verscheiden treffelijke rechtsgeleerden in Holland* (third ed., Rotterdam 1661–1670); Kornelis van Nieustad and Jacob Kooren, *Hollandse praktijk in rechten: bestaande in vonnissen, observantien van oordeelen en consultatien* (Rotterdam 1655); *"t Boeck der Zee-rechten, inhoudende dat hoochste ende oudste Godtlantsche Water-recht dat de gemeene Cooplieden ende Schippers geordineert ende ghemaeckt hebben tot Wisbuy* (Amsterdam 1664).

35. *CJVR* 432.

36. An example is Sophia van Wijckersloot. In 1652, she married Dirck van Hamel, who several years later was to be appointed secretary of Rensselaerswijck. The couple went to the patroonship together, but in the summer of 1659 Sophia returned alone to the Dutch Republic, where in September 1659 she gave birth to her third child, very likely at the house in Utrecht of her father, Hendrick van Wijckersloot, member of the Utrecht *vroedschap*. In the following spring she returned to the colony, presumably in the company of her infant son Hendrick. Hoffman, "Armory. Van Wijckersloot—Van Hamel—Vosch"; *CJVR* 185–186; GAA, NA, inv. no. 1580, fol. 13 (7 February 1659).

37. *CJVR* 432.

38. *KP* 1: 39–40; *NYHM* 2: 228–229; NYSA, NYCM 10–11: 63 (2 March 1662); *BDC* 1: 64 (5 March 1662); *FOCM*, 71; Gélis, *De boom en de vrucht*, 162–164, 166–167; Dekker, Van den Eerenbeemt, and De Leeuw, *Levensloop, cultuur en mentaliteit*, 23.

39. *CJVR* 326, 328, 380, 394.

40. Ebeling, *Voor- en familienamen in Nederland*, 40–45; Frijhoff, *Wegen*, 134–135; Tebbenhoff, "Tacit Rules and Hidden Family Structures"; Stryker-Rodda, "New Netherland Naming Systems"; Valck Lucassen, "Familieaantekeningen Ebbinck en Gerbade."

41. Rooijakkers, *Rituele repertoires*, 431; Ebeling, *Voor- en familienamen in Nederland*, 42–43; *CJVR* 326; Olthuis, *De doopspraktijk der gereformeerde kerken*, 199–200; De Vries, "De Van Rensselaers," 203–205; GAA, Archive Classis Amsterdam, inv. no. 224, p. 27–34; Knappert, "De eerste honderd jaren der Protestantsche gemeente op Curaçao," 54–55. No register of baptisms is extant for Beverwijck, so it is unknown how this system of substitutes was recorded. Unlike Curaçao, the register of baptisms in New Amsterdam contains no explicit reference to this custom. Occasionally godparents are listed that appear in no other source for the colony and who are likely to have been elsewhere at the time of the baptism. That makes it risky in individual cases to draw any definite conclusions from the registrations of godparents about their stay in New Netherland.

42. Wagenaar, *Galle*, 48; Frijhoff, *Wegen*, 139; *BDC* 1: 23 (13 October 1647), 25 (2 December 1648), 110 (13 August 1673); De Waard, *Zeeuwsche expeditie*, XLV; *CJVR* 367; Dilliard, *Album of New Netherland*, 114; Blackburn and Piwonka, *Remembrance of Patria*, 277.

43. NYSA, NYCM 15: 49 (30 August 1663); Wilcoxen, "Arent van Curler's Children."

44. Of course this quantification entails many problems, such as the identification of the people involved and the fact that the dates in registers of marriages and baptisms are not the exact dates of the marriage and birth but rather of the publication of banns and of baptisms. The number of incidences of premarital conception may therefore be larger than seven. Florence Koorn has carried out a comparable study for Ootmarsum in Overijssel between 1725 and 1729. She traced the first child in 71 out of 143 marriages. In only two cases was the first child born within seven months, which indicates a lower rate of prenuptial intercourse than in New Amsterdam. But Dirk-Jaap Noordam calculated for Maasland between 1670 and 1830 that 27 percent of the brides were pregnant on their wedding days, which is higher than New Amsterdam. Koorn, "Illegitimiteit en eergevoel," 87; Noordam, *Leven in Maasland*, 162.

45. Koorn, "Illegitimiteit en eergevoel," 77–78; Haks, *Huwelijk en gezin in Holland*, 70–73, 75–82, 88; Van der Heijden, *Huwelijk in Holland*. For the case of Geertruijt Wijngaerts and Geleyn Verplanck, see: GAA, NA, inv. no. 2487, p. 297 (31 March 1660) and *RNA* 3: 297, 377, 379; *BDC* 1: 60 (2 March 1661). In Friesland and Zeeland there was no opportunity for

maidservants to file paternity suits, while this was permissible in Holland. Thus in this New Netherland followed the legal customs of Holland, rather than Friesland and Zeeland. Haks, *Huwelijk en gezin in Holland,* 89–90; Heerma van Voss, *Defloratie en onderzoek naar het vaderschap,* 55–60.

46. *KP* 1: 36–37, 39–40, 57–58; Hoes, *Baptismal and Marriage Registers of the Old Dutch Church of Kingston,* 2; Haks, *Huwelijk en gezin in Holland,* 88–93; Van Zwieten, "'[O]n her Woman's troth.'"

47. NYSA, NYCM 8: 87–88 (25 July 1656), 102 (31 July 1656); Eekhof, *Hervormde kerk,* 2: 119. The first announcement of the banns was on 25 March 1656 (*MDC*).

48. *LWA,* 37, 94–95; *LO,* 152–153, 328–329; *NYHM* 5: 108–109, 111–113; NYSA, NYCM 8: 1049 (25 November 1658), 1051–1052 (25 November 1658), 1053 (25 November 1658), 1057 (30 November 1658), 1060–1061 (12 December 1658), 1063 (12 December 1658).

49. *CJVR* 296–297; *MDC,* 27 April 1662; *BDC* 1: 19 (23 July 1645).

50. *CJVR* 46, 300–301; Kooijmans, *Vriendschap,* 149–150.

51. *CJVR* 367.

52. *CJVR* 322.

53. *NNN,* 326; *MCR,* 67–68; NYSA, NYCM 9: 36–37 (23 January 1660); *RNA* 1: 330; *RNA* 7: 242; *RNA* 3: 306; *RNA* 5: 42; *FOCM,* 418; Van Boheemen and Van Haaren, "Ter bruiloft genodigd."

54. De Bruijn and Spies, *Vondel vocaal,* 56–57. The melody was possibly composed by Cornelis Tymensz Padbrué: see Grijp, *Het Nederlandse lied in de Gouden Eeuw,* 32, 303.

55. NYHS, Selijns, volume of poetry, not paginated. I have also used a microfilm in the possession of Jos van der Linde, to whom my thanks are due. Both poems can also be found, with translations, in Murphy, *Anthology,* 132–146, but I have followed the corrected translation in Blom, "Of Wedding and War."

56. Steendam, *Distelvinck,* 1: 62 (wedding of Vincent Adriaensz Roskam and Maria Rodrigo, 24 November 1647); Steendam, *Zeede-sangen voor de Batavische jonckheyt,* 86 (Isaac Bedloo and Elisabeth de Potter, 1653), 88 (Pieter Jacobsz Marius and Maria Pieters, 15 October 1655) and 91 (Lucas Andriesz Sabijn and Eva Louwerens van der Wel, 22 October 1655).

57. NYSA, NYCM 10–12: 21–22 (5 February 1663); Riker, *Revised History of Harlem,* 197–198; Rooijakkers, *Rituele repertoires,* 326–329; Haks, *Huwelijk en gezin in Holland,* 67–68. Also see *RNA* 2: 425 for details on the strewing of palm at a wedding. Van Boheemen and Van Haaren, "Ter bruiloft genodigd," 186. Examples of this tradition in Stuiveling, *Bredero's Groot lied-boeck* 1: 150 and in Jan Steen's painting "*De huwelijksnacht van Tobias en Sara*" (The Wedding Night of Tobias and Sara) (Jansen, *Jan Steen,* 203).

58. *CM 1655–1656,* 68–69.

59. *FOCM,* 217.

60. *MDC,* 23 April 1660; *BDC* 1: 63 (30 December 1661), 72 (1 February 1664), 83 (16 May 1666); *RNA* 5: 148, 206–207, 262–263, 271, 275–276, 282; *RNA* 6: 62, 65, 77, 193; *RNA* 7: 27.

61. Haks, *Huwelijk en gezin in Holland,* chapter 6, in particular p. 176.

62. *CM 1655–1656,* 52; NYSA, NYCM 8: 415 (23 January 1657), 417 (2 January 1657), 419 (8 January 1657), 419 (16 January 1657), 421 (23 January 1656); *RNA* 3: 90; Haks, *Huwelijk en gezin in Holland,* 178–180, 201.

63. *FOCM,* 248–249.

64. *CJVR* 422–423.

65. She was born on 13 January 1660 in Amsterdam, where she was baptized one day later: GAA, DTB, inv. no. 43, p. 428; Valck Lucassen, "Familieaantekeningen Ebbinck en Gerbade," 221. Cf. Jacobs, "Johannes de Laet en de Nieuwe Wereld," 123, where New Amsterdam was mistakenly given as the place of birth.

66. After his study of theology in Utrecht, Samuel Megapolensis studied medicine in Leiden, against the wishes of the classis of Amsterdam, who deemed the combination of doctor and *predikant* undesirable. *ER* 1: 531–532; Du Rieu, *Album studiosorum Academiae Lugduno Batavae,* 494 (14 November 1661).

67. Valck Lucassen, "Familieaantekeningen Ebbinck en Gerbade," 221–222.

68. Groenendijk and Van Lieburg, *Voor edeler staat geschapen;* Valck Lucassen, "Familieaantekeningen Ebbinck en Gerbade," 221.

69. *RNA* 2: 24–25; NYSA, NYCM 10–11: 39–40 (2 February 1662); Eekhof, *Hervormde kerk* 1: 165; Phelps Stokes, *Iconography,* 2: 221–222; Den Boer, "Naar een geschiedenis van de dood," 176.

70. *OFDRCB,* 48, 52–54; *RNA* 5: 253, 313.

71. NYSA, NYCM 23: 296 (4 January 1674), 313 (21 February 1674), 408 (undated, probably February 1674).

72. *MOM* 2: 80.

73. Ibid., 77–78; *RNA* 5: 331; Venema, *Kinderen van weelde en armoede,* 65. In Beverwijck the amount for the pall varied; see Venema, *Deacons' Accounts,* passim. See also NYSL, VRMP, box 49, folder 59 (1670–1689).

74. *RNA* 3: 376; *RNA* 1: 53, 89; Talman, "Death Customs among the Colonial Dutch"; Rose, "Proeve van verandering," 208; Dilliard, *Album of New Netherland,* 114.

75. NYHS, volume of Selijns's poetry, not paginated (Murphy, *Anthology,* 158); Van der Linde, "Selijns," 48.

76. NYSL, VRMP, box 49, folder 59 (17 October 1674).

77. *NNN,* 198–199; Camerata Trajectina, *Pacxken van minnen,* track 13; Boer, "Het lied van Geeraert van Velsen," 280, note 1; Van de Graft, *Middelnederlandse historieliederen,* 50–55; Burgers, "Eer en schande van Floris V," 12–21. I thank Louis Grijp, of the P.J. Meertensinstituut, Amsterdam, for these references.

78. *ERA* 3: 315–317. One of the meanings of *kakadoris* is "quack doctor." The word as used here also has a strong connection with *kak* (shit). So "shit doctor" would also be a good translation.

79. Roodenburg, "Eer en oneer"; Van de Pol, *Amsterdams hoerdom,* 67.

80. *NYHM* 2: 286; *NYHM* 4: 254–255; Roodenburg, "De notaris en de erehandel."

81. Roodenburg, "De notaris en de erehandel," 372, 368; Roodenburg, "Naar een etnografie van de vroegmoderne stad," 224, 241–242; Dorren, "Communities within the Community," 180; Dorren, *Eenheid en verscheidenheid,* 67–92; Bogaers, "Geleund over de onderdeur."

82. *RNA* 6: 40; *MCR,* 35–36, 58, 113, 149 113; *NYHM* 1: 11, 37; Herschkowitz, "The Troublesome Turk," 300; Roodenburg, "De notaris en de erehandel," 376; *RNA* 2: 332, 360.

83. *RNA* 1: 51, 53–54, 58–61, 65, 72, 76; Lyon, "Joost Goderis." This is, as far as is known, the first occurrence of *neuken* (to fuck) in the Dutch language in its sexual meaning. See Sanders, "Neuken." *FOCM,* 176, 179–181. A third incident concerns Anthony Jansz van Salee: *NYHM* 1: 11; Leuker and Roodenburg, "'Die dan hare wyven laten afweyen'"; Van de Pol, *Amsterdams hoerdom,* 75; Roodenburg, "De notaris en de erehandel," 376.

84. *NYHM* 4: 4, 151, 367–368; *LO,* 12, 33, 61–62, 324; *LWA,* 8, 92; *RNA* 1: 2, 34–36.

85. *NYHM* 1: 256; *FOCM,* 5, 331, 334; *RNA* 3: 208; *RNA* 4: 130–131.

86. *MCR,* 94.

87. *FOCM,* 322; Roodenburg, "Eer en oneer," 131; Rooijakkers, *Rituele repertoires,* 401–403.

88. GAA, NA, inv. no. 306, fol. 123v/119v (24 February 1632), fol. 125/120 (24 February 1632).

89. *ERA* 3: 267–269. See also NYSA, NYCM 15: 75 (15 November 1663).

90. De Schepper and Vrolijk, "Vrede en orde door gratie," 109; Van Deursen, *Mensen van klein vermogen,* 134–136; Rooseboom, *Receuil van verscheyde keuren,* 200.

91. *NYHM* 1: 144–145, 151–152, 178–179; *NYHM* 4: 51.

92. Van Deursen, *Een dorp in de polder,* 252.

93. Strubbe and Voet, *De chronologie van de middeleeuwen en de moderne tijden in de Nederlanden,* 46–48, 51–59.

94. *RNA* 1: 223; *FOCM,* 451.

95. *MCR,* 173; *NYHM* 4: 4, 441; NYSA, NYCM 8: 943 (13 August 1658); *DRCHNY* 13: 197; *LO,* 398; O'Callaghan, *History of New Netherland* 2: 434; *FOCM,* 4; *KP* 1: 2; *RNA* 5: 330; *RNA* 1: 90, 274; Shattuck, "Civil Society," 199.

96. *RNA* 2: 169; *RNA* 1: 23; *DRCHNY* 14: 390; *LO*, 249–251; *LWA*, 66–67; Phelps Stokes, *Iconography* 4: 263–264. No information is available about the market days of other places.

97. *DRNN*, 36; Frijhoff, *Wegen*, 303; Stronks, "Het kerkvolk op de zondagen."

98. *RNA* 1: 24–26; *LWA*, 71; *LO*, 259. Prof. J. R. Pole drew my attention to the fact that in *LO*, 259, *balslaen* has been translated as "cricket." This unfortunate and suggestive translation has given rise to the idea that the king of sports was already played in North America in the seventeenth century. While that is not unfeasible, this ordinance is insufficient proof.

99. *FOCM*, 125, 207, 209; NYSA, NYCM 10–11: 241 (16 October 1662).

100. *LO*, 448–449; NYSA, NYCM 10–13: 119 (18 March 1664); *RNA* 4: 301–302; *RNA* 5: 38–39, 60; *RNA* 6: 405–406; Visser, *Geschiedenis van den sabbatstrijd*; Goodfriend, "The Struggle over the Sabbath." It possible that Johannes Megapolensis was the source of inspiration of the new edict. His son Samuel, who in 1664 returned to New Amsterdam, had studied under Voetius in Utrecht.

101. *NYHM* 4: 280–281, 506–510, 579; *CM 1655–1656*, 74–75; *NYHM* 5: 159–160; *DRCHNY* 13: 373–374; *RNA* 1: 342–344; Van Rooden, "Dissenters en bededagen"; Kist, *Neêrlands bededagen en biddagsbrieven*, 1: 208–237.

102. *OFDRCB*, 12–14, 166–184; Kingston, Reformed Protestant Dutch church, Church Records vol. 1; Wouters and Abels, *Nieuw en ongezien*, 1: 204–210; Spaans, *Haarlem na de Reformatie*, 131.

103. *NYHM* 4: 441; *CM 1655–1656*, 173–174; *LWA*, 52–53; *LO*, 205–206; *FOCM*, 474; *RNA* 1: 18–19, 419–421; *RNA* 2: 254; *RNA* 7: 262; *RNA* 3: 431; *MCR*, 105; Gehring and Starna, *A Journey into Mohawk and Oneida Country*, 14; Ter Gouw, *De volksvermaken*, 117–118.

104. *OFDRCB*, 181; Van de Graft, "De duivekater"; Nannings, *Brood- en gebakvormen*, 54–57, 192.

105. *CJVR* 159–160.

106. *CJVR* 48, 231, 370; *MCR*, 50–52.

107. *MCR*, 110; *DRCHNY* 1: 213; *FOCM*, 101; Ter Gouw, *De volksvermaken*, 198.

108. *NYHM* 5: 119; Ter Gouw, *De volksvermaken*, 199; Stuiveling, *Brederode's groot liedboek* 1: 47–49; "Arent Pieter Gysen" on the CD *Muziek uit de Gouden Eeuw* by Camerata Trajectina; Thomas, *Man and the Natural World*, 150–165; Davids, "De zondeval van de dierenbeul," 240–241.

109. *NYHM* 5: 117–118.

110. *RNA* 1: 286; NYSA, NYCM 8: 742 (26 February 1658).

111. *LWA*, 52–53; *LO*, 364–365; *RNA* 1: 36–37, 42; Spaans, *Haarlem na de Reformatie*, 134; Burrows and Wallace, *Gotham*, 392.

112. *FOCM*, 192; Van de Graft and De Haan, *Nederlandse volksgebruiken*, 99; *OFDRCB*, 226, 227.

113. *NYHM* 1: 22; *NYHM* 4: 121; *LO*, 364–365; *RNA* 1: 42; *RNA* 7: 215–216.

114. St. Nicholas Eve is mentioned once, but only as an indication of time, without any reference to celebrations or rituals. *NYHM* 4: 510.

115. *CJVR* 395; Frijhoff, *Wegen*, 828ff.

Epilogue

1. *BGE*, 36. Interestingly, the 1664 version of the capitulation agreement, as translated and published in the *Artykelen van 't Overgaen van Nieuw-Nederlandt*, excluded the words on public worship. The situation after 1664 indicates, however, that public worship was allowed.

Glossary

adelborst	cadet
burgemeester	burgomaster; executive urban magistrate
commies (pl. *commiezen*)	subaltern administrative official
equipagemeester	equipage master
fiscael	high official, charged with upholding the rights of the WIC
gerechtsbode	court usher
Heren XIX	literally: Lords Nineteen; the board of the West India Company
landdag	provincial convention or diet
liefhebbers	literally: devotees; non-members who attended the services of the Reformed Church
morgen (plur.: *morgens*)	measure of land; depending on whether the Amsterdam *morgen* or Rijnland *morgen* is meant (which the sources often do not indicate), it is either 2.069 or 2.103 acres (0.837 or 0.851 hectares)
patria	fatherland, Latin
predikant	minister
sachem	Indian chief
schepel (pl. *schepels*)	dry measure: 0.764 bushel of wheat; 1.29 bushels salt; ca. 28 liters
schepen (pl. *schepenen, schepens*)	member of municipal court of justice
schout	a law enforcement officer, appointed on the overlord's authority, with the combined duties of sheriff and prosecuting attorney
sewant	the southern New England Narragansett Algonquian name for polished shells, threaded like beads; the colonists in New England adopted another Algonquian word, *wampum*.
tienden	tenths
vroedschap	city council
wilden	Indians

Bibliography

Abbott, C. M., "Colonial Copper Mines." In: *WMQ* 3rd ser. 29 (1970), 295–309.

Alphen, M. A. van, "Zielverkopers, transportbrieven en transportkopers." In: J. Krikke, V. Enthoven, and K. Mastenbroek (eds.), *Amsterdam, haven in de 17e en 18e eeuw* (Amsterdam 1990), 22–27.

——, "The Female Side of Dutch Shipping: Financial Bonds of Seamen Ashore in the 17th and 18th Century." In: J. R. Bruijn and W. F. J. Mörzer Bruyns (eds.), *Anglo-Dutch Mercantile Marine Relations, 1700–1850* (Amsterdam, Leiden 1991), 125–132.

Ames, S. M., *Studies of the Virginia Eastern Shore in the Seventeenth Century* (Richmond 1940).

——, *County Court Records of Accomack-Northampton, Virginia, 1640–1645* (Charlottesville 1973).

Archdeacon, Th. J., *New York City 1664–1710: Conquest and Change* (Ithaca, London 1976).

Armitage, D., "Three Concepts of Atlantic History." In: D. Armitage and M. J. Braddick (eds.), *The British Atlantic World, 1500–1800* (Basingstoke 2002), 11–27.

Baar, M. de, "'Let Your Women Keep Silence in the Churches.' How Women in the Dutch Reformed Church Evaded Paul's Admonition." In: *Women in the Church. Papers Read at the 1989 Summer Meeting and the 1990 Winter Meeting of the Ecclesiastical History Society* (Studies in Church History 27) (Oxford 1990), 389–401.

Baart, J., "Ho-de-no-sau-nee en de Nederlanders. De wisselwerking tussen de materiële culturen van autochtonen en allochtonen in 17e-eeuws Nieuw-Nederland." In: Bakker et al. (eds.), *New Netherland Studies*, 89–99.

——, "Dutch Material Civilisation. Daily Life between 1650–1776, Evidence from Archeology." In: Blackburn and Kelley (eds.), *New World Dutch Studies*, 1–11.

——, "Kammen." In: Van Dongen (ed.), *One Man's Trash*, 175–187.

Bachman, V. C., *Peltries or Plantations: The Economic Policies of the Dutch West India Company in New Netherland 1633–1639* (Baltimore 1969).

Bailey, R. F., *Prerevolutionary Dutch Houses and Families in Northern New Jersey and Southern New York* (New York 1936).

Bailyn, B., *The New England Merchants in the Seventeenth Century* (Cambridge, Mass. 1955, 3rd ed. 1982).

——, "The Idea of Atlantic History." In: *Itinerario: European Journal of Overseas History* 20 (1996), 19–44.

Bakker, B., et al. (eds.), *Nieuwnederlandse studiën. Een inventarisatie van recent onderzoek. New Netherland Studies. An Inventory of Current Research and Approaches. Bulletin Koninklijke Nederlandse Oudheidkundige Bond* 84 (1985).

Balmer, R. H., *A Perfect Babel of Confusion: Dutch Religion and English Culture in the Middle Colonies* (New York 1989).

Barnouw, A. J., "The Settlement of New Netherland." In: A. C. Flick (ed.), *History of the State of New York* (10 vols., New York 1933), 1: 215–258.

Baron, S. W., *A Social and Religious History of the Jews. Vol. 15: Resettlement and Exploration* (New York, London, Philadelphia 1973).

Beernink, G., *De geschiedschrijver en rechtsgeleerde Arend van Slichtenhorst en zijn vader Brant van Slichtenhorst, stichter van Albany, hoofdstad van den staat New York* (Arnhem 1916).

Bergsma, W., "Church, State and People." In: K. Davids and J. Lucassen (eds.), *A Miracle Mirrored: The Dutch Republic in European Perspective* (Cambridge 1995), 196–228.

Berkum, H. van, *De Labadie en de Labadisten: eene bladzijde uit de geschiedenis der Nederlandsche Hervormde kerk* (Sneek 1851).

Berlin, I., "From Creole to African: Atlantic Creoles and the Origins of African-American Society in Mainland North America." In: *WMQ* 3rd ser. 53 (1996), 251–288.

——, *Many Thousands Gone: The First Two Centuries of Slavery in North America* (Cambridge, Mass., London 1998).

Biewenga, A., *De Kaap de Goede Hoop. Een Nederlandse vestigingskolonie, 1680–1730* (Amsterdam 1999).

Bijlsma, R., "Rotterdams Amerika-vaart in de eerste helft der zeventiende eeuw." In: *Bijdragen voor Vaderlandse Geschiedenis en Oudheidkunde* 5th ser. 3 (1915), 97–142.

Blackburn, R. H., and N. A. Kelley (eds.), *New World Dutch Studies: Dutch Arts and Culture in Colonial America, 1609–1776. Proceedings of the Symposium Organized by the Albany Institute of History and Art, Albany, August 2–3, 1986, Held in Conjunction with the Exhibition Remembrance of Patria. Dutch Arts and Culture in Colonial America, 1609–1776* (Albany 1987).

Blackburn, R. H., "Dutch Material Culture: Furniture." In: *dHM* 54–1 (1979), 3–5.

——, "Dutch Material Culture: Silversmiths." In: *dHM* 55–3 (1980), 5–11.

——, "Dutch Domestic Architecture in the Hudson Valley." In: Bakker et al. (eds.), *New Netherland Studies*, 151–165.

——, and R. Piwonka, *Remembrance of Patria: Dutch Arts and Culture in Colonial America 1609–1776* (Albany 1988).

——, et al., *Dutch Colonial Homes in America* (New York 2002).

Bliss, R. M., *Revolution and Empire: English Politics and the American Colonies in the Seventeenth Century* (Manchester, New York 1990).

Blom, F. R. E., "Of Wedding and War: Henricus Selyns' Bridal Torch (1663), with an Edition and Translation of the Dutch Poem." Unpublished paper 2006.

Boer, L. P. de, "Naamlijsten van bewindhebbers en van hoofdparticipanten der West-Indische Compagnie." In: *De Navorscher* 63 (1914), 382–388, and 64 (1915), 17–21.

Boer, M. G. de (ed.), "Memorie over den toestand der West-Indische Compagnie in het jaar 1633." In: *BMHG* 21 (1900), 343–362.

Boer, P. den, "Naar een geschiedenis van de dood. Mogelijkheden tot onderzoek naar de houding ten opzichte van de dode en de dood ten tijde van de Republiek." In: *TvG* 89 (1976), 161–201.

Boer, R. C., "Het lied van Geeraert van Velsen." In: *De Gids* 63, no. 2 (1899), 273–308.

Boetzelaer van Dubbeldam, C. W. Th. baron van, *De Gereformeerde kerken in Nederland en de zending in Oost-Indië in de dagen der Oost Indische Compagnie* (Utrecht 1906).

Bogaers, L., "Geleund over de onderdeur. Doorkijkjes in het Utrechtse buurtleven van de vroege Middeleeuwen tot in de zeventiende eeuw." In: *BMGN* 112 (1997), 336–363.

Boheemen, Ch. van, "Dutch-American Poets of the Seventeenth Century." In: R. Kroes and H.-O. Neuschäfer (eds.), *The Dutch in North-America: Their Immigration and Cultural Continuity* (European Contributions to American Studies 20) (Amsterdam 1991).

Boheemen, P. van, and J. van Haaren, "Ter bruiloft genodigd." In: P. van Boheemen et al. (eds.), *Kent, en versint. Eer datje mint. Vrijen en trouwen 1500–1800* (Apeldoorn, Zwolle 1989), 154–187.

Bontemantel, H., *De regeeringe van Amsterdam, soo in 't civiel als crimineel en militaire (1653–1672) ontworpen door Hans Bontemantel* (G. W. Kernkamp [ed.]) (Werken uitgegeven door het Historisch Genootschap, 3rd ser., 7) (2 vols., 's-Gravenhage 1897).

Boogaart, E. van den, "The Archive of the First West India Company." In: *Itinerario: European Journal of Overseas History* 4 (1980), 59–61.

——, et al., *Overzee. Nederlandse koloniale geschiedenis 1590–1975* (Haarlem 1982).

——, "De Nederlandse expansie in het Atlantische gebied 1590–1674." In: E. van den Boogaart et al., *Overzee. Nederlandse koloniale geschiedenis 1590–1975* (Haarlem 1982).

——, "The Netherlands and New Netherland, 1624–1664." In: *The Birth of New York: Nieuw Amsterdam 1624–1664* (Amsterdam, New York 1982, 1983), 9–16.

——, "The Servant Migration to New Netherland, 1624–1664." In: P. C. Emmer (ed.), *Colonialism and Migration: Indentured Labour before and after Slavery* (Dordrecht, Boston, Lancaster 1986), 55–81.

——, et al., *La expansión holandesa en el Atlántico, 1580–1800* (Madrid 1992).

Boxer, Ch. R., *De Nederlanders in Brazilië 1624–1654* (Amsterdam, Antwerpen 1993, 1st ed. 1957).

——, *The Dutch Seaborne Empire, 1600–1800* (London 1965, repr. 1990).

Bradley, J. W., *Evolution of the Onondaga Iroquois: Accommodating Change, 1500–1655* (Syracuse 1987).

——, *Before Albany: An Archaeology of Native-Dutch Relations in the Capital Region, 1600–1664* (Albany 2007).

Brandão, J. A., *"Your Fyre Shall Burn No More": Iroquois Policy toward New France and Its Native Allies to 1701* (Lincoln, London 1997).

Brandt, C. C. E., "Eenige opmerkingen aangaande de Luthersche kerk in Amerika." In: *Een vaste burg is onze God* 14 (1896), 203–213.

Bree, J. la, *De rechterlijke organisatie en rechtsbedeling te Batavia in de 17e eeuw* (Rotterdam 1951).

Breeden-Raedt aende Vereenichde Nederlandsche Provintien: Gelreland, Holland, Zeeland, Utrecht, Vriesland, Over-Yssel, Groeningen, gemaeckt ende gestelt uyt diverse ware en waerachtige memorien door I.A.G.W.C. (Antwerpen 1649).

Brink, A. W., "The Ambition of Roeloff Swartwout, Schout of Esopus." In: *dHM* 67 (1994), 50–61.

Brodhead, J. R., *The Final Report of John Romeyn Brodhead, Agent of the State of New-York, to Procure and Transcribe Documents in Europe, Relative to the Colonial History of said State. Made to the Governor, 12th February, 1845* (Albany 1845).

——, *History of the State of New York* (New York 1871).

Broers, E. J. M. F. C., "Van Tafel 8 tot Boek 6. De belediging in rechtshistorisch perspectief." In: A. Keunen and H. Roodenburg (eds.), *Schimpen en schelden. Eer en belediging in Nederland, ca. 1600–ca. 1850. Volkskundig Bulletin* 18 (1992), 295–313.

Bruijn, J. R., *Het gelag der zeelieden* (Leiden 1978).

——, "De walvisvaart: de ontplooiing van een nieuwe bedrijfstak." In: L. Hacquebord and W. Vroom (eds.), *Walvisvaart in de gouden eeuw. Opgravingen op Spitsbergen* (Amsterdam 1988), 16–24.

Bruijn, J. R., and E. S. van Eyck van Heslinga, *Muiterij. Oproer en berechting op schepen van de VOC* (Haarlem, Bussum 1980).

Bruijn, J. R., F. Gaastra, and I. Schöffer, *Dutch Asiatic Shipping in the 17th and 18th Centuries. Introductory Volume* (Rijks Geschiedkundige Publicatiën, grote serie 165, 's-Gravenhage 1987).

Bruijn, K. de, and M. Spies (eds.), *Vondel vocaal. De liederen van Vondel bijeengebracht en ingeleid* (Haarlem 1988).

Bruin, G. de, *Geheimhouding en verraad. De geheimhouding van staatszaken ten tijde van de Republiek (1600–1750)* ('s-Gravenhage 1991).

Burema, L., *De voeding in Nederland, van de middeleeuwen tot de 20e eeuw* (Assen 1953).

Burgers, J. W. J., "Eer en schande van Floris V. Twee oude twistpunten over de geschiedenis van een Hollandse graaf." In: *Holland, historisch tijdschrift. Tweemaandelijkse uitgave van de historische vereniging Holland* 30 (1998), 1–21.

Burghers of New Amsterdam and the Freemen of New York, 1675–1866 (Collections of the New-York Historical Society 18) (New York 1885).

Burhans, B. C., "Enduring Dutch Nursery Rhyme." In: *dHM* 65 (1992), 61–63.

Burke, P., *Popular Culture in Early Modern Europe* (London 1978, 2nd ed. 1979).

——, *History and Social Theory* (Cambridge 1992).

Burke, Th. E., "The New Netherland Fur Trade, 1657–1661: Response to Crisis." In: *dHM* 59-3 (1986), 1–4, 21.

——, *Mohawk Frontier: The Dutch Community of Schenectady, New York, 1661–1710* (Ithaca, London 1991).

Burrows, E. G., and M. Wallace, *Gotham: A History of New York City to 1898* (New York, Oxford 1999).

Camerata Trajectina, *Muziek uit de Gouden Eeuw. Constantijn Huygens en Gerbrand Adriaensz. Brederode* (compact disc, GLOBE 6013, 1992).

——, *Paxcken van Minnen. Middeleeuwse muziek uit de Nederlanden* (compact disc, GLOBE 6016, 1992).

Cantwell, A.-M., and D. Wall, *Unearthing Gotham: The Archaeology of New York City* (New Haven, London 2001).

Carr, L. G., and L. S. Walsh, "The Standard of Living in the Colonial Chesapeake." In: *WMQ* 3rd ser. 45 (1988), 135–159.

Cau, C. et al., *Groot placaet-boeck, vervattende de placaten, ordonnatien ende edicten vande...Staten Generaal...ende vande...Staten van Hollandt en West-Vrieslandt. Mitsgaders vande...Staten van Zeeland* (9 vols., 's-Gravenhage 1658–1796).

Ceci, L., "The First Fiscal Crisis in New York." In: *Economic Development and Cultural Change* 28 (1980), 839–847.

Christoph, P. R. (ed.), *Administrative Papers of Governors Richard Nicolls and Francis Lovelace, 1664–1673* (New York Historical Manuscripts: English, vol. 22) (Baltimore 1980).

——, and F. A. Christoph (eds.), *Books of General Entries of the Colony of New York, 1664–1673: Orders, Warrants, Letters, Commissions, Passes and Licenses issued by Governors Richard Nicolls and Francis Lovelace* (New York Historical Manuscripts: English) (Baltimore 1982).

——, and F. A. Christoph (eds.), *Records of the Court of Assizes for the Colony of New York, 1665–1682* (New York Historical Manuscripts: English (Baltimore 1983).

——, "The Time and Place of Jan van Loon: Roman Catholic in Colonial Albany." In: *dHM* 60–2 (1987), 8–11; 60–3 (1987), 9–12.

——, "Story of the New Netherland Project." In: *dHM* 61–3 (1988), 5–8.

——, "The Freedmen of New Amsterdam." In: Zeller, *A Beautiful and Fruitful Place,* 157–170.

Christoph, P. R., and F. A. Christoph (eds.), *The Andros Papers, 1674–1676. Files of the Provincial Secretary of New York During the Administration of Governor Sir Edmund Andros 1674–1680* (New York Historical Manuscripts Series, vols. 24–25) (Syracuse 1989).

——, *The Andros Papers, 1679–1680. Files of the Provincial Secretary of New York During the Administration of Governor Sir Edmund Andros 1674–1680* (New York Historical Manuscripts Series, vols. 28–29) (Syracuse 1991).

"The Clarendon Papers." In: *Collections of the New-York Historical Society* 2 (1869), 1–162.

Cohen, D. S., "How Dutch were the Dutch of New Netherland?" In: *NYH* 62 (1981), 43–60.

——, "Dutch-American Farming: Crops, Livestock, and Equipment, 1623–1900." In: Blackburn and Kelley (eds.), *New World Dutch Studies,* 185–200.

——, "Reflections on American Ethnicity." In: *NYH* 72 (1991), 319–336.

——, *The Dutch-American Farm* (New York, London 1992).

Condon, Th. J., *New York Beginnings; The Commercial Origins of New Netherland* (New York, London 1968).

Corwin, E. T., *A Manual of the Reformed Church in America (formerly Ref. Prot. Dutch Church) 1628–1902* (4th ed., New York 1902).

Corwin, E. T., trans. and ed.), *Ecclesiastical Records: State of New York* (7 vols., Albany 1901–1916).

Cronon, W., *Changes in the Land: Indians, Colonists and the Ecology of New England* (New York 1983, 17th ed. 1994).

Crosby, A. W., *Ecological Imperialism: The Biological Expansion of Europe, 900–1900* (Cambridge 1986, repr. 1995).

Damhouder, J. de, *Practycke in civile saeken* ('s-Gravenhage 1626).

——, *Practycke in criminele saecken* (Rotterdam 1628).

Dapper, O., *Historische beschryving der stadt Amsterdam* enz. (Amsterdam 1663, repr. Amsterdam 1975).

Davids, K., "De zondeval van de dierenbeul. Toelaatbaar en ontoelaatbaar gedrag tegenover dieren in Nederland vanaf de late middeleeuwen tot de twintigste eeuw." In: M. Gijswijt-Hofstra (ed.), *Een schijn van verdraagzaamheid. Afwijkingen en tolerantie in Nederland van de zestiende eeuw tot heden* (Hilversum 1989), 237–262.

Davies, D. W., *A Primer of Dutch Seventeenth Century Overseas Trade* ('s-Gravenhage 1961).

Dekker, J. C., H. F. J. M. van den Eerenbeemt, and K. P. C. de Leeuw, *Levensloop, cultuur en mentaliteit. Een geschiedenis van het alledaags bestaan* (Tilburg 1990).

Dennis, M., *Cultivating a Landscape of Peace: Iroquois-European Encounters in Seventeenth-Century America* (Ithaca, London 1993).

Denton, K. A., "The American Kas." In: *dHM* 64 (1991), 13–14.

Deursen, A. Th. van, *Mensen van klein vermogen. Het kopergeld van de Gouden eeuw* (Amsterdam 1991).

——, *Een dorp in de polder. Graft in de zeventiende eeuw* (Amsterdam 1994).

De Vries, J., "The Dutch Atlantic Economies." In: P. A. Coclanis (ed.), *The Atlantic Economy during the Seventeenth and Eighteenth Centuries: Organization, Operation, Practice, Personnel* (Columbia 2005), 1–29.

Dillen, J. G. van, "Vreemdelingen te Amsterdam in de eerste helft van de zeventiende eeuw. De Portugeesche Joden." In: *TvG* 50 (1935), 4–35.

——, "De West-Indische Compagnie, het calvinisme en de politiek." In: *TvG* 74 (1961), 145–171.

——, *Van rijkdom en regenten. Handboek tot de economische en sociale geschiedenis van Nederland tijdens de Republiek* (Den Haag 1970).

Dilliard, M. E., *Old Dutch Houses of Brooklyn* (New York 1945).

——, *An Album of New Netherland: Dutch Colonial Antiques and Architecture* (New York 1963).

Donck, A. van der, *Vertoogh van Nieu Nederlandt* ('s-Gravenhage 1650).

——, *Beschryvinge van Nieuw-Nederlant (gelijck het tegenwoordigh in staet is)* (1st ed. Amsterdam 1655, 2nd ed. Amsterdam 1656).

——, *A Description of the New Netherlands* (J. Johnson (trans.), T. F. O'Donnell (ed.), Syracuse, New York 1968).

——, *A Description of New Netherland*. Ed. Ch. T. Gehring and W. A. Starna, trans. D. W. Goedhuys (Lincoln, NE 2008).

Dongen, A. van (ed.), *One Man's Trash is Another Man's Treasure* (Rotterdam 1995).

——, "The Inexhaustible Kettle. De metamorfose van een Europees gebruiksvoorwerp in de wereld van de Noord-Amerikaanse Indianen." In: Van Dongen (ed.), *One Man's Trash*, 115–173.

Dorren, G., "Communities within the Community: Aspects of Neighbourhood in Seventeenth-Century Haarlem." In: *Urban History* 25 (1998), 173–188.

——, *Eenheid en verscheidenheid. De burgers van Haarlem in de Gouden Eeuw* (Amsterdam 2001).

Dunn, S. W., *The Mohicans and Their Land, 1609–1730* (Fleischmanns 1994).

Dunn, S. W., and A. P. Bennett, *Dutch Architecture near Albany: The Polgreen Photographs* (Fleischmanns 1996).

Dunshee, H. W., *History of the School of the Collegiate Reformed Dutch Church in the City of New York from 1633 to 1883* (2nd ed. New York 1883).

Ebben, M. A., *Zilver, brood en kogels voor de koning. Kredietverlening door Portugese bankiers aan de Spaanse kroon, 1621–1665* (Leidse Historische Studiën 5) (Leiden 1996).

Ebeling, R. A., *Voor- en familienamen in Nederland. Geschiedenis, verspreiding, vorm en gebruik* ('s-Gravenhage 1993).

Eberlein, H. D., *The Manors and Historic Homes of the Hudson Valley* (Philadelphia, London 1924).

Edelman, H., *The Dutch Language Press in America: Two Centuries of Printing, Publishing, and Bookselling* (Nieuwkoop 1986).

Eekhof, A., *Bastiaen Jansz. Krol, krankenbezoeker, kommies en kommandeur van Nieuw Nederland (1595–1645). Nieuwe gegevens voor de kennis van ons kerkelijk en koloniaal gezag in Noord-Amerika* (Den Haag 1910).

——, *De hervormde kerk in Noord-Amerika 1624–1664* (Den Haag 1913).

——, "De 'memorie' van Isaack de Rasière voor Samuel Blommaert. Het oudste Hollandsche bericht betreffende Nieuw-Nederland en New Plymouth, de kolonie der 'Pilgrim Fathers.'" In: *Nederlandsch archief voor kerkgeschiedenis*, N.S. 15 (1919), 245–280.

——, *Jonas Michaëlius: Founder of the Church in New Netherland* (Leiden 1926).

Eggleston, E., *The Transit of Civilization from England to America in the Seventeenth Century* (New York 1901).

Elliott, J. H., *The Old World and the New, 1492–1650* (1st ed. 1970, repr. Cambridge 1992).

Elphick, R., and R. Shell, "Intergroup Relations: Khoikhoi, Settlers, Slaves and Free Blacks, 1652–1795." In: R. Elphick and H. Giliomee (eds.), *The Shaping of South African Society, 1652–1834* (Cape Town 1979, 2nd ed. 1989), 116–169.

Embury, A., *Building the Dutch Colonial House: Its Origin, Design, Modern Plan, and Construction. Illustrated with Photographs of Old Examples and American Adaptations of the Style* (New York 1929).

Emmer, P. C., "De slavenhandel van en naar Nieuw-Nederland." In: *Economisch-Historisch Jaarboek* 35 (1972), 94–148.

——, "The West India Company, 1621–1791: Dutch or Atlantic?" In: L. Blussé and F. Gaastra (eds.), *Companies and Trade. Essays on Overseas Trading Companies during the Ancien Regime* (Comparative Studies in Overseas History 3) (Leiden 1981).

——, "Nederlandse handelaren, kolonisten en planters in de Nieuwe Wereld." In: H. W. van den Doel, P. C. Emmer, and H. Ph. Vogel, *Nederland en de Nieuwe Wereld. Een intrigerende studie van de betrekkingen tussen Nederland en de Amerika's, vanaf de ontdekking van de Nieuwe Wereld tot heden* (Utrecht 1992), 9–80.

Emmer, P. C., *De Nederlandse slavenhandel 1500–1800* (Amsterdam, Antwerpen 2000).

Emmer, P. C., and W. W. Klooster, "The Dutch Atlantic, 1600–1800: Expansion without Empire." In: *Itinerario: European Journal of Overseas History* 23 (1999), 48–69.

[Enden, F. van den], *Kort verhael van Nieuw-Nederlants gelegenheit, deughden, natuerlycke voorrechten en byzondere bequamheidt ter bevolkingh* (n.p. 1662).

Enden, F. van den, *Vrye politijke stellingen. Met een inleiding van dr. W. Klever* (Amsterdam 1992).

Engels, J. Th., *Kinderen van Amsterdam* (n.p. 1989).

Enthoven, V., *Zeeland en de opkomst van de Republiek. Handel en strijd in de Scheldedelta c. 1550–1621* (Leiden 1996).

——, "Dutch Crossings: Migration between the Netherlands and the New World, 1500–1800." In: *Atlantic Studies* 2 (2005), 153–176.

Ernst, H., "Het Amsterdamse notarieel archief als bron voor de geschiedenis van Nieuw-Nederland." In: Bakker et al. (eds.), *New Netherland Studies,* 142–150.

Evans, Th. G. and T. A. Wright (eds.), *Records of the Reformed Dutch Church in New Amsterdam and New York. Baptisms from 25 December 1639 to 29 December 1800* (Collections of the New York Genealogical and Biographical Society 2) (2 vols., New York 1901–1903, repr. Upper Saddle River, N.J. 1968).

Evjen, J. O., *Scandinavian Immigrants in New York, 1630–1674* (Minneapolis 1916).

Fabend, F. H., *Zion on the Hudson: Dutch New York and New Jersey in the Age of Revivals* (New Brunswick, N.J., London 2000).

——, "Church and State, Hand in Hand: Compassionate Calvinism in New Nether-land." In: *dHM* 65 (2002), 3–8.

——, "Cosyn Gerritsen van Putten: New Amsterdam's Wheelwright." In: *dHM* 80 (2007), 23–30.

Faber, D. E. A., and R. E. de Bruin, "Tegen de vrede. De Utrechtse ambassadeur Go-dard van Reede van Nederhorst en de onderhandelingen in Munster." In: J. Dane (ed.), *1648. Vrede van Munster. Feit en verbeelding* (Zwolle 1998), 107–131.

Fabius, G. J., "Het leenstelsel van de West-Indische Compagnie." In: *Bijdragen tot de taal-, land- en volkenkunde van Nederlandsch-Indie* 70 (1915), 555–593.

Feister, L. M., "Linguistic Communication between the Dutch and the Indians in New Netherland 1609–1664." In: *Ethnohistory* 20 (1973), 25–38.

Fernow, B. (ed.), and E. B. O'Callaghan (trans.), *The Records of New Amsterdam from 1653 to 1674 Anno Domini* (7 vols., New York 1897, 2nd ed. Baltimore 1976).

—— (trans. and ed.), *The Minutes of the Orphanmasters of New Amsterdam, 1655–1663* (New York 1902).

—— (trans. and ed.), *Minutes of the Orphanmasters Court of New Amsterdam, 1655–1663. Minutes of the Executive Boards of the Burgomasters of New Amsterdam and the Records of Walewyn van der Veen, Notary Public 1662–1664* (New York 1907).

Fitchen, J., *The New World Dutch Barn. A Study of its Characteristics, Structural System, and Probable Erectional Procedures* (Syracuse 1968).

Fockema Andreæ, S. J., *Het Oud-Nederlandsch burgerlijk recht* (Haarlem 1906).

Folkerts, J., "Drentse emigratie naar Amerika in de zeventiende eeuw." In: *Ons Waardeel* 6 (1986), 73–92.

——, "De Nederlandse archieven in de staat New York en hun bewerkingsgeschiedenis." In: *Nederlands Archievenblad* 93 (1989), 140–153.

——, "Drenthe and New Netherland: Two Outer Provinces at the Time of Emigration." In: *dHM* 62-4 (1989), 8–11.

——, "Kiliaen van Rensselaer and Agricultural Productivity in His Domain: A New Look at the First Patroon and Rensselaerswijck before 1664." In: Zeller, *A Beautiful and Fruitful Place*, 295–308.

——, "The Failure of West India Company Farming on the Island of Manhattan." In: *dHM* 69 (1996), 47–52.

Francis Jr., P., "De kralen waarmee het eiland Manhattan niet is betaald." In: Van Dongen (ed.), *One Man's Trash*, 53–69.

Frederickson, G. M., *White Supremacy: A Comparative Study in American and South African History* (New York, Oxford 1981).

Freidel, F., "The Dutchness of the Roosevelts." In: J. W. Schulte Nordholt and R. Swierenga (eds.), *A Bilateral Bicentennial: A History of Dutch-American Relations, 1782–1982* (Amsterdam 1982), 149–167.

Frijhoff, W., *Wegen van Evert Willemsz. Een Hollands weeskind op zoek naar zichzelf, 1607–1647* (Nijmegen 1995).

——, "Neglected Networks: Director Willem Kieft (1602-1647) and his Dutch Relatives." In: Goodfriend (ed.), *Revisiting New Netherland*, 147–204.

——, *Fulfilling God's Mission: The Two Worlds of Dominie Everardus Bogardus, 1607–1647* (Leiden 2007).

Frijhoff, W., and M. Spies, *1650. Bevochten eendracht* (Den Haag 1999).

Frost, W. L., "356 Years of Formal Education in New York City: the Origins of the First Dutch School in New Amsterdam in the year 1628." In: Zeller, *A Beautiful and Fruitful Place*, 183–186. Also in Ch. T. Gehring and N. A. McClure Zeller (ed.), *Education in New Netherland and the Middle Colonies. Papers of the 7th Rensselaerswyck Seminar of the New Netherland Project* (Albany 1985), 1–4.

Fruin, R., "Bijdrage tot de geschiedenis van het burgemeesterschap van Amsterdam tijdens de Republiek." In: P. J. Blok, P. L. Muller, and S. Muller Fz. (eds.), *Robert Fruin's verspreide geschriften met aantekeningen, toevoegsels en verbeteringen uit des schrijvers nalatenschap* (10 vols., 's-Gravenhage, 1900–1905), 4: 305–337.

Funk, E. P., "De literatuur van Nieuw-Nederland." In: *De Nieuwe Taalgids* 85 (1992), 383–395.

Gaastra, F. S., *De geschiedenis van de VOC* (Zutphen 1991).

Galenson, D. W., *White Servitude in Colonial America* (Cambridge 1981).

Games, A., Ph. J. Stern, P. W. Mapp, and P. A. Coclanis, "Forum: Beyond the Atlantic." In: *WMQ* 3rd series 63 (2006), 675–742.

Gastel, A. van, "Adriaen van der Donck, New Netherland, and America" (Ph.D. Dissertation, Pennsylvania State University 1985).

——, "Van der Donck's Description of the Indians: Additions and Corrections." In: *WMQ* 3rd ser. 47 (1990), 411–421.

——, "Adriaen van der Donck als woordvoerder van de Nieuw-Nederlandse bevolking." In: *Jb CBG* 50 (1996), 89–107.

Gehlen, A. Fl., *Notariële akten uit de 17e en 18e eeuw. Handleiding voor gebruikers* (Zutphen 1986).

Gehring, Ch. T. (ed.), *Delaware Papers (English Period). A Collection of Documents Pertaining to the Regulation of Affairs on Delaware, 1664–1682* (New York Historical Manuscripts: Dutch, vols. 18–19) (Baltimore 1977).

—— (trans. and ed.), *A Guide to Dutch Manuscripts Relating to New Netherland in United States Repositories* (Albany 1978).

——, "Peter Minuit's Purchase of Manhattan Island—New Evidence." In: *dHM* 55-1 (1980), 6–7, 17.

—— (trans. and ed.), *Land Papers* (New York Historical Manuscripts: Dutch, vols. GG, HH & II) (Baltimore 1980).

—— (trans. and ed.), *Delaware Papers (Dutch Period). A Collection of Documents Pertaining to the Regulation of Affairs on the South River of New Netherland, 1648–1664* (New York Historical Manuscripts: Dutch, vols. 18–19) (Baltimore 1981).

—— (trans. and ed.), *Council Minutes, 1652–1654* (New York Historical Manuscripts: Dutch, vol. 5) (Baltimore 1983).

——, "Documentary Sources Relating to New Netherland." In: E. Nooter and P. U. Bonomi (eds.), *Colonial Dutch Studies: An Interdisciplinary Approach* (New York 1988), 33–51.

—— (trans. and ed.), *Fort Orange Court Minutes, 1652–1660* (New Netherland Documents Series, vol. 16, part 2) (Syracuse 1990).

—— (trans. and ed.), *Laws and Writs of Appeal 1647–1663* (New Netherland Documents Series, vol. 16, part 1) (Syracuse 1991).

——, "New Netherland Documentary Projects: New Netherland Project." In: *dHM* 66 (1993), 16.

—— (trans. and ed.), *Council Minutes, 1655–1656* (New Netherland Documents Series, vol. 6) (Syracuse 1995).

——, "Petrus Stuyvesant, directeur-generaal van Nieuw-Nederland." In: *Jb CBG* 50 (1996), 69–87.

—— (trans. and ed.), *Fort Orange Records, 1656–1678* (New Netherland Documents Series) (Syracuse 2000).

—— (trans. and ed.), *Correspondence, 1647–1653* (New Netherland Documents Series, vol. 11) (Syracuse 2000).

—— (trans. and ed.), *Correspondence, 1654–1658* (New Netherland Documents Series, vol. 12) (Syracuse 2003).

——, "A Survey of Documents Relating to the History of New Netherland." In: Goodfriend (ed.), *Revisiting New Netherland,* 287–308.

Gehring, Ch. T., and R. S. Grumet, "Observations of the Indians from Jasper Danckaerts' Journal, 1679–1680." In: *WMQ* 3rd series 44 (1987), 104–120.

Gehring, Ch. T., and J. A. Schiltkamp (trans. and ed.), *Curacao Papers 1640–1665* (New Netherland Documents, vol. 17) (Interlaken, N.Y. 1987).

Gehring, Ch. T., and W. A. Starna (trans. and ed.), *A Journey into Mohawk and Oneida Country, 1634–1635: The Journal of Harmen Meyndertsz van den Bogaert* (Syracuse 1988, repr. 1991).

Gelder, R. van, *Het Oost-Indisch avontuur. Duitsers in dienst van de VOC (1600–1800)* (Nijmegen 1997).

Gelderblom, O., *Zuid-Nederlandse kooplieden en de opkomst van de Amsterdamse stapelmarkt (1578–1630)* (Hilversum 2000).

Gelfand, N., "Sugar and God: Sephardic Commerce and Community in Brazil." Paper presented to the NYU Atlantic Workshop, 4 May 2004.

Gélis, J., *De boom en de vrucht. Zwangerschap en bevalling voor de medicalisering* (Nijmegen 1987).

Goebel Jr., J. and T. R. Naughton, *Law Enforcement in Colonial New York: A Study in Criminal Procedure, 1664–1776* (New York 1944).

Gonsalves de Mello, J. A., *Nederlanders in Brazilië (1624–1654). De invloed van de Hollandse bezetting op het leven en de cultuur in Noord-Brazilië* (Zutphen 2001).

Goodfriend, J. D., "Burghers and Blacks: The Evolution of a Slave Society at New Amsterdam." In: *NYH* 59 (1978), 125–144.

——, "The Historiography of the Dutch in Colonial America." In: E. Nooter and P. U. Bonomi (eds.), *Colonial Dutch Studies: An Interdisciplinary Approach* (New York, London 1988), 6–32.

——, "The Social Dimensions of Congregational Life in Colonial New York City." In: *WMQ* 3rd ser. 46 (1989), 252–278.

——, "Recovering the Religious History of Dutch Reformed Women in Colonial New York." In: *dHM* 64 (1991), 53–59.

——, *Before the Melting Pot: Society and Culture in Colonial New York City, 1664–1730* (Princeton 1991).

——, "Black Families in New Netherland." In: Zeller, *A Beautiful and Fruitful Place*, 147–155.

——, "Amerikaans onderzoek naar Nederlandse kolonisatie: de kinderschoenen ontgroeid." In: *Jb CBG* 50 (1996), 17–29.

——, "Writing/Righting Dutch Colonial History." In: *NYH* 80 (1999), 5–28.

—— (ed.), *Revisiting New Netherland: Perspectives on Early Dutch America* (Leiden 2005).

——, "The Struggle over the Sabbath in Petrus Stuyvesant's New Amsterdam." In: W. Te Brake and W. Klooster (eds.), *Power and the City in the Netherlandic World* (Leiden 2006), 205–224.

Goodfriend, J. D., B. Schmidt, and A. Stott, "Introduction: Holland in America." In: J. D. Goodfriend, B. Schmidt, and A. Stott (eds.), *Going Dutch: The Dutch Presence in America, 1609–2009* (Leiden 2008), 1–23.

Goodman, A. V., *American Overture: Jewish Rights in Colonial Times* (Philadelphia 1947).

Goor, J. van, *De Nederlandse koloniën. Geschiedenis van de Nederlandse expansie 1600–1975* ('s-Gravenhage 1994).

Gouw, J. ter, *De volksvermaken* (1st ed., Haarlem 1871, undated repr.).

Graaf, M. van de, "Het stadsbestuur van Nieuw-Amsterdam 1653–1664" (M.A. Thesis, Rijksuniversiteit Leiden 1996).

Graft, C. C. van de, *Middelnederlandse historieliederen, toegelicht en verklaard* (Epe 1904).

——, "De duivekater." In: *Elsevier's geïllustreerd Maandschrift* 34 (1924), 377–384.

Graft, C. C. van de, and Tj. W. R. de Haan, *Nederlandse volksgebruiken bij hoogtijdagen* (Utrecht 1978).

Grijp, L. P., *Het Nederlandse lied in de Gouden Eeuw. Het mechanisme van de contrafactuur* (Publikaties van het P. J. Meertens-Instituut voor Dialectologie,

Volkskunde en Naamkunde van de Koninklijke Nederlandse Akademie van Wetenschappen 15) (Amsterdam 1991).

Groenendijk, L. F., and F. A. van Lieburg, *Voor edeler staat geschapen. Levens- en sterfbedbeschrijvingen van gereformeerde kinderen en jeugdigen uit de 17e en 18e eeuw* (Leiden 1991).

Groenhuis, G., *De predikanten. De sociale positie van de gereformeerde predikanten in de Republiek der Verenigde Nederlanden voor ± 1700* (Historische Studies uitgegeven vanwege het instituut voor geschiedenis der Rijksuniversiteit te Utrecht 33) (Groningen 1977).

Groenveld, S., "Natie en nationaal gevoel in de zestiende-eeuwse Nederlanden." In: *Scrinium en scriptura. Opstellen betreffende de Nederlandse geschiedenis aangeboden aan prof. dr. J. L. van der Gouw* (Groningen 1980), 372–387.

——, "'Den huijsman wordt er heel verermt.' Gevolgen van de oorlogvoering voor de bevolking van Geertruidenberg en omgeving, ca. 1593." In: A. van Loon, M. Robben, and J. Thijssen (eds.), *Het beleg en de inneming van Geertruidenberg door Prins Maurits in 1593 en de gevolgen van de oorlogvoering voor de bevolking van Geertuidenberg en omgeving* (Geertruidenberg 1993), 54–85.

——, *Was de Nederlandse Republiek verzuild? Over segmentering van de samenleving binnen de Verenigde Nederlanden* (Leiden 1995).

Groenveld, S., J. J. H. Dekker, and Th. R. M. Willemse, *Wezen en boefjes. Zes eeuwen zorg in wees- en kinderhuizen* (Hilversum 1997).

Grol, G. J. van, *De grondpolitiek in het West-Indisch domein der Generaliteit* (1st ed., Den Haag 1934–1947, repr. Amsterdam 1980).

Grothe, J. A., *Archief voor de geschiedenis der oude Hollandsche zending* (6 vols., Utrecht 1884–1891).

Gutmann, M. P., *War and Rural Life in the Early Modern Low Countries* (Assen 1980).

Guy, F. S., *Edmund Bailey O'Callaghan: A Study in American Historiography (1797–1880)* (Studies in American Church History 18) (Washington 1934).

Hacquebord, L., F. N. Stokman, and F. W. Wasseur, "The Directors of the Chambers of the 'Noordse Compagnie,' 1614–1642, and their Networks in the Company." In: C. Lesger and L. Noordegraaf (eds.), *Entrepreneurs and Entrepreneurship in Early Modern Times: Merchants and Industrialists within the Orbit of the Dutch Staple Market* (Den Haag 1995), 245–251.

Haefeli, E, "Kieft's War and the Cultures of Violence in Colonial America." In: M. A. Bellesisle (ed.), *Lethal Imagination: Violence and Brutality in American History* (New York 1999), 17–42.

——, "On First Contact and Apotheosis: Manitou and Men in North America." In: *Ethnohistory* 54 (2007), 407–443.

Haks, D., *Huwelijk en gezin in Holland in de 17e en 18e eeuw. Processtukken en moralisten over aspecten van het laat 17de- en 18de-eeuwse gezinsleven* (Assen 1982).

Hallam, J. S., "The Portrait of Cornelis Steenwyck and Dutch Colonial Experience." In: J. C. Prins, B. Brandt, T. Stevens, and T. F. Shannon (eds.), *The Low Countries and the New World(s): Travel, Discovery, Early Relations* (New York, Oxford 2000), 77–85.

Hallema, A., "Emigratie en tewerkstelling van wezen op de schepen en in het gebied der V.O.C. en W.I.C. gedurende de 17e en 18e eeuw." In: *TvG* 70 (1957), 204–217.

Hallowell, Ch. L., "Disappearance of the Historic Ship Tijger: Part of New York's Heritage Vanished when Bulldozers Dug the Foundation for the World Trade Center." In: *Natural History* 83 (1974), 12–26.

Hamell, G. R., "Wampum: Light, White, and Bright Things are Good to Think." In: Van Dongen (ed.), *One Man's Trash*, 41–52.

Hammond, J. W., "An Historical Analysis of the Bronck House Coxsackie, New York." In: *dHM* 55–2 (1980), 5–8, 17–18.

Harder, L., and M. Harder, *Plockhoy from Zurick-zee. The Study of a Dutch Reformer in Puritan England and Colonial America* (Newton, Kans. 1952).

Harrington, R. W., "Speaking Scripture: The Flushing Remonstrance of 1657." In: *Quaker History* 82–2 (1993), 104–109.

Hart, S., "De stadskolonie Nieuwer-Amstel aan de Delaware-rivier in Noord-Amerika." In: *Maandblad Amstelodamum* 38 (1951), 89–94.

——, *The Prehistory of the New Netherland Company: Amsterdam Notarial Records of the First Dutch Voyages to the Hudson* (Amsterdam 1959).

——, "The City-Colony of New Amstel on the Delaware: II." In: *dHM* 40–1 (1965), 7–8, 13.

——, *Geschrift en getal. Een keuze uit de demografisch-, economisch- en sociaal-historische studiën op grond van Amsterdamse en Zaanse archivalia, 1600–1800* (Dordrecht 1976).

Hart, S., and H. J. Kreider (ed.), *Protocol of the Lutheran Church in New York City, 1702–1750* (New York 1958).

Hartz, L., *The Founding of New Societies: Studies in the History of the United States, Latin America, South Africa, Canada and Australia* (New York 1964).

Hatfield, A., "Dutch Merchants and Colonists in the English Chesapeake: Trade, Migration, and Nationality in 17th-Century Maryland and Virginia." In: R. Vigne and Ch. Littleton (eds.), *From Strangers to Citizens: The Integration of Immigrant Communities in Britain, Ireland, and Colonial America, 1550–1750* (London, Brighton 2001), 296–305.

Hattum, M. van, and H. Rooseboom, *Glossarium van oude Nederlandse rechtstermen* (Amsterdam 1977).

Hauptmann, L. M., and R. G. Knapp, "Dutch-Aboriginal Interaction in New Netherland and Formosa: A Historical Geography of Empire." In: *Proceedings of the American Philosophical Society* 121 (1977), 166–182.

Hazard, S., et al. (ed.), *Pennsylvania Archives* (138 vols., Philadelphia, Harrisburg 1849–1852).

Heckewelder, J., "Indian Tradition of the First Arrival of the Dutch at Manhatan Island, Now New-York." In: *Collections of the New-York Historical Society* 2nd ser., 1 (1841), 69–74.

Heerma van Voss, U. J., *Defloratie en onderzoek naar het vaderschap in het oud-vaderlandsch recht* (Amsterdam 1889).

Heijden, M. van der, *Huwelijk in Holland. Stedelijke rechtspraak en kerkelijke tucht 1550–1700* (Amsterdam, 1998).

Heijer, H. J. den, *De geschiedenis van de WIC* (Zutphen 1994).

——, "Plannen voor samenvoeging van VOC en WIC." In: *Tijdschrift voor Zeegeschiedenis* 13 (1994), 115–130.

Heringa, J., et al. (eds.), *Geschiedenis van Drenthe* (Meppel 1985).

Herks, J. J., *De geschiedenis van de Amersfoortse tabak* ('s-Gravenhage 1967).

Herschkowitz, L., "The Troublesome Turk: An Illustration of Judicial Process in New Amsterdam." In: *NYH* 46 (1965), 299–310.

Higginbotham Jr., A. L., *In the Matter of Color: Race and the American Legal Process: The Colonial Period* (New York 1978).

Hine, C. G., *The Old Mine Road* (1st ed. 1909, repr. New Brunswick, N.J. 1963).

Hoboken, W. J. van, "The Dutch West India Company: The Political Background of Its Rise and Decline." In: J. S. Bromley and E. H. Kossmann (eds.), *Britain and the Netherlands 1: Papers Delivered to the Oxford-Netherlands Historical Conference 1959* (London 1960), 41–62.

——, "Een wederwoord inzake de West-Indische Compagnie." In: *TvG* 75 (1962), 49–56.

Hodges, G. R., *Root and Branch: African Americans in New York and East Jersey, 1613–1863* (Chapel Hill 1999).

Hoes, R. R. (ed.), *Baptismal and Marriage Registers of the Old Dutch Church of Kingston, Ulster County, New York (Formerly Named Wiltwyck, and Often Familiarly Called Esopus or 'Sopus) for One Hundred and Fifty Years from their Commencement in 1660* (2 vols., New York 1891, repr. Baltimore 1980).

Hoffman, W. J., "An Armory of American Families of Dutch Descent: Van Wijckersloot—Van Hamel—Vosch." In: *NYGBR* 65 (1934), 213–224.

——, "An Armory of American Families of Dutch Descent: Van der Donck—Van Bergen." In: *NYGBR* 67 (1936), 229–239.

——, "An Armory of American Families of Dutch Descent: De Hulter—De Laet—Ebbingh." In: *NYGBR* 69 (1938), 339–346; 70 (1939), 55–60.

Hollandtsche Mercurius: behelzende het ghedenckweerdighste in Christenrijck voor-ghevallen, binnen 't gantsche jaer (41 vols., Haarlem 1651–1691).

Holthuis, P., *Frontierstad bij het scheiden der markt. Deventer: militair, demografisch, economisch; 1578–1648* (Houten, Deventer 1993).

Howe, D. W., *American History in an Atlantic Context: An Inaugural Lecture Delivered before the University of Oxford on 3 June 1993* (Oxford 1993).

Hsia, R. Po-Chia, and H. F. K. van Nierop (eds.), *Calvinism and Religious Toleration in the Dutch Golden Age* (Cambridge 2002).

Huey, P., "Glass Beads from Fort Orange (1624–1676), Albany, New York." In: *Proceedings of the 1982 Glass Trade Bead Conference* (Rochester 1983), 83–110.

——, "Archeological Excavations in the Site of Fort Orange, a Dutch West India Company Trading Fort Built in 1624." In: Bakker et al. (eds.), *New Netherland Studies*, 68–79.

Hurk, J. van den, "The Architecture of New Netherland Revisited." In: K. A. Breisch and A. K. Hoagland (eds), *Building Environments: Perspectives in Vernacular Architecture X* (Knoxville 2005), 133–152.

——, "Reconstructie van de architectuur van Nieuw Nederland aan de zand van zeventiende-eeuwse bouwstekken in Noord-Amerika." In: *Erfgoed van Industrie en Techniek* 15: 3 (2006), 90–98.

——, "Origins and Survival of Netherlandic Building Traditions in North America." In: Malcolm Dunkeld et al. (eds.), *Proceedings of the Second International Congress on Construction History*, vol. 3 (Exeter 2006), 3191–3209.

——, "Imagining New Netherland: Origins and Survival of Netherlandic Architecture in Old New York" (Ph.D. dissertation, University of Delaware, 2006)

Israel, J. I., *Dutch Primacy in World Trade, 1585–1740* (Oxford 1989).

——, "De Republiek der Verenigde Nederlanden tot omstreeks 1750—Demografie en economische activiteit." In: J. C. H. Blom et al. (eds.), *Geschiedenis van de Joden in Nederland* (Amsterdam 1995), 97–126.

——, "The Jews of Dutch America." In: P. Bernardini and N. Fiering (eds.), *The Jews and the Expansion of Europe to the West* (2 vols. New York, Oxford 2001), 2: 335–349.

Jackson, K., "A Colony with a Conscience." In: *New York Times,* 27 December 2007.

Jacobs, J. A., "De scheepvaart en handel van de Nederlandse Republiek op Nieuw-Nederland 1609–1675" (M.A. thesis, Rijksuniversiteit Leiden 1989).

——, "The Dutch Protestant Churches in North America during the 17th and 18th Centuries: Some Comments on Historiography and Sources." In: *Documentatie-blad voor de geschiedenis van de Nederlandse zending en overzeese kerken* 1 (1994), 62–79.

——, "The Hartford Treaty: A European Perspective on a New World Conflict." In: *dHM* 68 (1995), 74–79.

——, "Enkele aspecten van de Nederlandse scheepvaart op Nieuw-Nederland" (Paper for the Symposium on Dutch Atlantic Shipping, Institute of the History of European Expansion, Leiden University, 5 June 1996).

——, "Johannes de Laet en de Nieuwe Wereld." In: *Jb CBG* 50 (1996), 109–130.

——, "Between Repression and Approval: Connivance and Tolerance in the Dutch Republic and in New Netherland." In: *dHM* 71 (1998), 51–58.

——, "A Hitherto Unknown Letter of Adriaen van der Donck." In: *dHM* 71 (1998), 1–6.

——, "The Dutch in the Atlantic, in New Netherland, and in Virginia." Guest lecture for the archeologists of Anne Arundel County, Londontown, Maryland, 28 September 1999.

——, *Een zegenrijk gewest. Nieuw-Nederland in de zeventiende eeuw* (Amsterdam, 1999).

——, "Fortuin in de Nieuwe Wereld. Jan Jansz. Damen in Amerika." In: H. Mulder, E. Kloek, and J. Jacobs, *Nederland aan de de Hudson. Utrechters in New York in de 17e eeuw* (Utrecht 2000), 22–36.

——, "Van Angola naar Manhattan. Slavernij in Nieuw-Nederland in de zeventiende eeuw." In: R. Daalder, A. Kieskamp, and D. J. Tang (eds.), *Slaven en schepen. Enkele reis, bestemming onbekend* (Leiden, Amsterdam 2001), 69–75.

——, "'Te fourneeren nae de loffelijcke costumen der Stadt Amsterdam'; Nederlandse regelgeving in Nieuw-Nederland." In: *Pro Memorie. Bijdragen tot de rechtsgeschiedenis der Nederlanden* 5 (2003), 364–377.

——, "'To Favor This New and Growing City of New Amsterdam with a Court of Justice.' Relations between Rulers and Ruled in New Amsterdam." In: *dHM* 76 (2003), 65–72. Also in: H. Krabbendam and G. Harinck (eds.), *Amsterdam-New York: Transatlantic Relations and Urban Identities Since 1653* (Amsterdam 2005), 17–29.

——, "Dutch Sources on Native American History." In: S. W. Dunn (ed.), *Mohican Seminar 1. The Continuance—An Algonquian Peoples Seminar. Selected Research Papers—2000. New York State Museum Bulletin* 501 (2004), 29–37.

——, "A Troubled Man: Director Wouter van Twiller and the Affairs of New Netherland in 1635." In: *NYH* 85 (2004), 213–232.

Jacobs, J. A., "Like Father, like Son? The Early Years of Petrus Stuyvesant." In: Goodfriend (ed.), *Revisiting New Netherland*, 205–242.

——, "Incompetente autocraten? Bestuurlijke verhoudingen in de zeventiende-eeuwse Nederlandse Atlantische Wereld." In: *De zeventiende eeuw. Cultuur in de Nederlanden in interdisciplinair perspectief* 21 (2005), 64–78.

——, *New Netherland: A Dutch Colony in Seventeenth-Century America* (Leiden, Boston, 2005).

——, "Soldaten van de Compagnie: het militair personeel van de West-Indische Compagnie in Nieuw-Nederland." In: M. Ebben and P. Wagenaar (ed.), *De cirkel doorbroken. Met nieuwe ideeën terug naar de bronnen. Opstellen over de Republiek* (Leiden 2006), 131–46.

——, "Soldiers of the Company." In: H. Wellenreuther (ed.), *Proceedings of the 3rd Jacob Leisler Workshop, Centre for the Study of Human Settlement and Historical Change, National University of Ireland, Galway, 25–26 September 2002* (forthcoming).

——, "Dutch Proprietary Manors in America: the Patroonships in New Netherland." In: L. Roper and B. Van Ruymbeke (eds.), *Constructing Early Modern Empires: Proprietary Ventures in the Atlantic World* (Leiden 2007), 301–326.

——, "Truffle Hunting with an Iron Hog: The First Dutch Voyage up the Delaware River." Unpublished paper, 2007.

Jacobs, J. A., and M. D. Shattuck, "Bevers voor drank, land voor wapens. Enkele aspecten van de Nederlands-Indiaanse handel in Nieuw-Nederland." In: Van Dongen (ed.), *One Man's Trash*, 95–113.

James, B. B., and J. F. Jameson (eds.), *Journal of Jasper Danckaerts, 1679–1680* (New York 1913, repr. 1959).

Jameson, J. F., *Willem Usselinx, Founder of the Dutch and Swedish West-India Companies* (New York 1887).

—— (ed.), *Narratives of New Netherland 1609–1664* (New York 1909, 2nd ed. 1967).

Jansen, C. H., "Geschiedenis van de familie de Wolff: sociale en economische facetten van de Republiek der Verenigde Nederlanden in de 17e eeuw." In: *Jaarboek van het genootschap Amstelodamum* 56 (1964), 131–155.

Jansen, G. M. C. (ed.), *Jan Steen. Schilder en verteller* (Amsterdam, Washington 1996).

Jennings, F., "Jacob Young: Indian Trader and Interpreter." In: D. G. Sweet and G. B. Nash (eds.). *Struggle and Survival in Colonial America* (Berkeley, Los Angeles, London 1981), 347–361.

——, *The Ambiguous Iroquois Empire* (New York, London 1984).

Jensma, G., "Over de jeugd van Pieter Stuyvesant." In: *De Vrije Fries, jaarboek uitgegeven door het Fries genootschap van Geschied-, Oudheid- en Taalkunde en de Fryske Akademy* 74 (1994), 21–41.

Jessurun, J. S. C., *Kiliaen van Rensselaer, van 1623 tot 1636* (Den Haag 1917).

Jobse-van Putten, J., *Eenvoudig maar voedzaam. Cultuurgeschiedenis van de dagelijkse maaltijd in Nederland* (Nijmegen 1995).

Johnson, D., *Charting the Sea of Darkness: The Four Voyages of Henry Hudson* (New York, Tokyo, London 1995).

Johnson, R. C., "The Transportation of Vagrant Children from London to Virginia, 1618–1622." In: H. S. Reinmuth Jr. (ed.), *Early Stuart Studies* (Minneapolis 1970).

Jong, G. F. de, "The Dutch Reformed Church and Negro Slavery in Colonial America." In: *Church History* 40 (1971), 423–436.

——, *The Dutch Reformed Church in the American Colonies* (Grand Rapids 1978).

Joosse, L. J., *"Scoone dingen sijn swaere dingen": een onderzoek naar de motieven en activiteiten in de Nederlanden tot verbreiding van de gereformeerde religie gedurende de eerste helft van de zeventiende eeuw* (Leiden 1992).

Juet, R., *Henry Hudson's reize onder Nederlandsche vlag van Amsterdam naar Nova Zembla, Amerika en terug naar Dartmouth in Engeland, 1609* (S. P. L'Honore Naber ed.) (Werken Linschoten-Vereeniging 19) ('s-Gravenhage 1921).

Kammen, M., *Colonial New York: A History* (New York 1975, repr. Oxford 1996).

Kappelhof, A. C. M., *De belastingheffing in de Meijerij van Den Bosch gedurende de Generaliteitsperiode (1648–1730)* (Tilburg 1986).

Kemperink, J. H. P., "Pieter Stuyvesant. Waar en wanneer werd hij geboren?" In: *De Navorscher. Nederlands Archief voor Genealogie en Heraldiek* 98–3 (1959), 49–59.

Kenney, A. P., *Stubborn for Liberty: The Dutch in New York* (Syracuse 1975).

——, F. G. Safford, and G. T. Vincent, *American Kasten: The Dutch-Style Cupboards of New York and New Jersey, 1650–1800* (New York 1991).

Kernkamp, G. W., "Brieven van Samuel Blommaert aan den Zweedschen rijkskanselier Axel Oxenstierna, 1635–1641." In: *BMHG* 29 (1908), 1–196.

Kessler, H. M., and E. Rachlis, *Peter Stuyvesant and His New York: A Biography of a Man and a City* (New York 1959).

Kilpatrick, W. H., *The Dutch Schools of New Netherland and Colonial New York* (Philadelphia 1912).

Kist, N. C., *Neêrlands bededagen en biddagbrieven. Eene bijdrage ter opbouwing der geschiedenis van staat en kerk in Nederland* (2 vols., Leiden 1848–1849).

Klever, W., "A New Source of Spinozism: Franciscus van den Enden." In: *Journal of the History of Philosophy* 29 (1991), 613–631.

Kloek, E., *Wie hij zij, man of wijf. Vrouwengeschiedenis en de vroegmoderne tijd* (Hilversum 1990).

Klooster, W., *The Dutch in the Americas, 1600–1800: A Narrative History with the Catalogue of an Exhibition of Rare Prints, Maps, and Illustrated Books from the John Carter Brown Library* (Providence 1997).

——, "Winds of Change: Colonization, Commerce, and Consolidation in the Seventeenth-Century Atlantic World." In: *dHM* 70 (1997), 53–58.

——, "Failing to Square the Circle: The West India Company's Volte-Face in 1638–1639." In: *dHM* 73 (2000), 3–9.

——, "The Place of New Netherland in the West India Company's Grand Scheme." In: Goodfriend (ed.), *Revisiting New Netherland*, 57–70.

Knappert, L., "De eerste honderd jaren der Protestantsche gemeente op Curaçao." In: *Gedenkboek Nederland-Curaçao* (Amsterdam 1934), 34–56.

Knevel, P., *Burgers in het geweer. De schutterijen in Holland, 1550–1700* (Hollandse Studiën 32) (Hilversum 1994).

Koenigsberger, H. G., *Monarchies, States Generals and Parliaments. The Netherlands in the Fifteenth and Sixteenth Centuries* (Cambridge 2001).

Kooijmans, L., "De koopman." In: H. M. Beliën, A. Th. van Deursen, and G. J. van Setten (eds.), *Gestalten van de gouden eeuw. Een Hollands groepsportet* (Amsterdam 1995), 65–92.

Kooijmans, L., "Risk and Reputation. On the Mentality of Merchants in the Early Modern Period." In: C. Lesger and L. Noordegraaf (eds.), *Entrepreneurs and Entrepreneurship in Early Modern Times: Merchants and Industrialists within the Orbit of the Dutch Staple Market* (Hollandse Historische Reeks 24) (Den Haag 1995), 25–34.

——, *Vriendschap en de kunst van het overleven in de zeventiende en achttiende eeuw* (Amsterdam 1997).

Kooiman, W. J., *De Nederlandsche Luthersche gemeenten in Noord-Amerika, 1649–1772* (Amsterdam 1946).

Koolbergen, H. van, "De materiële cultuur van Weesp en Weesperkarspel in de zeventiende en achttiende eeuw." In: *Volkskundig Bulletin* 9 (1983), 3–52.

Koorn, F., "Illegitimiteit en eergevoel. Ongehuwde moeders in Twente in de achttiende eeuw." In: *Vrouwenlevens 1500–1850. Jaarboek voor vrouwengeschiedenis* 8 (1987), 74–98.

Korthals Altes, W. L., *Van £ Hollands tot Nederlandse ƒ. De geschiedenis van de Nederlandse geldeenheid* (Amsterdam 1996).

Kreider, H. J., *The Beginnings of Lutheranism in New York* (New York 1949).

Kross, J., *The Evolution of an American Town: Newtown, New York, 1642–1775* (Philadelphia 1983).

Kunst, A. J. M., *Recht, commercie en kolonialisme in West-Indië vanaf de zestiende tot in de negentiende eeuw* (Zutphen 1981).

Kupp, J., "Dutch Notarial Acts Relating to the Tobacco Trade of Virginia, 1608–1653." In: *WMQ* 3rd ser. 30 (1973), 653–655.

——, "Records Depict Fur Smuggling Episode in 1658." In: *dHM* 60-1 (1975), 7–8, 14.

Kupp, J., and S. Hart, "The Early Cornelis Melyn and the Illegal Fur Trade." In: *dHM* 60-3 (1975), 7–8, 15.

Kupperman, K. O., "Early American History with the Dutch Put In." In: *Reviews in American History* 21 (1993), 195–201.

Laer, A. J. F. van (trans. and ed.), *Van Rensselaer Bowier Manuscripts, Being the Letters of Kiliaen van Rensselaer, 1630–1643, and Other Documents Relating to the Colony of Rensselaerswyck* (Albany 1908).

—— (trans. and ed.), *Minutes of the Court of Fort Orange and Beverwijck 1652–1660* (2 vols., Albany 1920–1923).

—— (trans. and ed.), *Minutes of the Court of Rensselaerswyck 1648–1652* (Albany 1922).

—— (trans. and ed.), *Documents Relating to New Netherland, 1624–1626, in the Henry E. Huntington Library* (San Marino, Calif. 1924).

—— (trans. and ed.), *Minutes of the Court of Albany, Rensselaerswijck and Schenectady 1668–1685* (3 vols., Albany 1926–1932).

(trans. and ed.), "Documents Relating to Arent van Curler's Death." In: *Dutch Settlers Society of Albany Yearbook* 3 (1927–1928), 30–34.

—— (trans. and ed.), *Correspondence of Jeremias van Rensselaer 1651–1674* (Albany 1932).

—— (trans. and ed.), *Correspondence of Maria van Rensselaer 1669–1689* (Albany 1935).

—— (trans. and ed.), *The Lutheran Church in New York 1649–1772. Records in the Lutheran Church Archives at Amsterdam, Holland* (New York 1946).

—— (trans. and ed.), "Letters of Wouter van Twiller and the Director General and Council of New Netherland to the Amsterdam Chamber of the Dutch West India Company, August 14, 1636." In: *NYH* 50 (1969), supplement.

—— (trans. and ed.), *Register of the Provincial Secretary, 1638–1642* (New York Historical Manuscripts: Dutch, vol. 1) (Baltimore 1974).

—— (trans. and ed.), *Register of the Provincial Secretary, 1642–1647* (New York Historical Manuscripts: Dutch, vol. 2) (Baltimore 1974).

—— (trans. and ed.), *Register of the Provincial Secretary, 1648–1660* (New York Historical Manuscripts: Dutch, vol. 3) (Baltimore 1974).

—— (trans. and ed.), *Council Minutes, 1638–1649* (New York Historical Manuscripts: Dutch, vol. 4) (Baltimore 1974).

Laet, J. de, *Nieuwe wereldt ofte Beschrijvinghe van West-Indien* (Leiden 1625).

——, *Historie ofte iaerlijck verhael van de verrichtinghen der geoctroyeerde West-Indische Compagnie* (Leiden 1644).

——, *Iaerlyck Verhael van de verrichtingen der Geoctroyeerde West-Indische Compagnie (1644)* (Werken Linschoten-Vereeniging 34, 35, 37 and 40) (S. P. L'Honore Naber and J. C. M. Warnsinck eds.) (4 vols., 's-Gravenhage 1931–1937).

"'t Ledematen boeck oft register der ledematen alhier 't sedert de jare 1649' [The Book of Members or Register of the Members Here Since the Year 1649]." In: *NYGBR* 9 (1878), 38–45 [1649–1659]; 72–79 [1660–1666]; 140–147 [1666–1676].

Leuker, M.-T. and H. Roodenburg, "'Die dan hare wyven laten afweyen.' Overspel, eer en schande in de zeventiende eeuw." In: G. Hekma and H. Roodenburg (eds.), *Soete minne en helsche boosheit. Seksuele voorstellingen in Nederland, 1300–1850* (Nijmegen 1988), 61–84.

Ligtenberg, C., *Willem Usselinx* (Utrechtsche bijdragen voor letterkunde en geschiedenis 9) (Utrecht 1914).

Linde, A. P. G. J. van der (trans. and ed.), *Old First Dutch Reformed Church of Brooklyn, New York: First Book of Records, 1660–1752* (New York Historical Manuscripts: Dutch) (Baltimore 1983).

——, "Henricus Selijns (1636–1701), dominee, dichter en historicus in Nieuw Nederland en de Republiek." In: J. F. Heijbroek, A. Lammers, and A. P. G. J. van der Linde (eds.), *Geen Schepsel wordt vergeten. Liber amicorum voor Jan Willem Schulte Nordholt ter gelegenheid van zijn vijfenzestigste verjaardag* (Amsterdam, Zutphen 1985), 37–60.

——, "De 'Remonstrantie van Nieu-Nederlandt' (1649) en haar bijzondere betekenis voor Edmund Bailey O'Callaghan." In: E. F. van de Bilt and H. W. van den Doel (eds.), *Klassiek Amerikaans: opstellen voor A. Lammers* [Leidse Historische Studiën 7] (Leiden 2002), 92–102.

Lucassen, J., "Labour and Early Modern Economic Development." In: K. Davids and J. Lucassen (eds.), *A Miracle Mirrored: The Dutch Republic in European Perspective* (Cambridge 1995), 367–409.

Lurix, K. A., "The Lutheran Struggle for Toleration in New Amsterdam." In: *dHM* 62-1 (1989), 1–7; 62-2 (1989), 1–5.

Lustig, M. L., *The Imperial Executive in America: Sir Edmund Andros (1637–1714)* (Madison, Teaneck 2003).

Lyon, E. K., "Joost Goderis, New Amsterdam Burgher, Weighmaster, and Dutch Master Painter's Son." In: *NYGBR* 123 (1992), 193–202.

Lyon, E. K., "The New Amsterdam Weighhouse." In: *dHM* 69 (1996), 1–10.

——, "The Transfer of Technology from the Dutch Republic to New Netherlands: Forts, Factories and Cities as a Beginning." In: J. Everaert and J. Parmentier (eds.), *International Conference on Shipping, Factories and Colonization (Brussels, 24–26 November 1994)* (Brussels 1996), 333–342.

Maglione, M., "The Evidence for the Establishment of Collegiate School in 1628." In: Zeller (ed.), *A Beautiful and Fruitful Place*, 187–190. Also in Ch. T. Gehring and N. A. McClure Zeller (ed.), *Education in New Netherland and the Middle Colonies: Papers of the 7th Rensselaerswyck Seminar of the New Netherland Project* (Albany 1985), 5–8.

Maika, D. J., "The Credit System of the Manhattan Merchants in the Seventeenth Century." In: *dHM* 63-2 (1990), 1–3; 63-3 (1990), 5–7; 64 (1991), 9–12.

——, "Commerce and Community: Manhattan Merchants in the Seventeenth Century" (Ph.D. dissertation, New York University 1995).

——, "Slavery, Race, and Culture in Early New York." In: *dHM* 73 (2000), 27–33.

——, "Securing the Burgher Right in New Amsterdam: The Struggle for Municipal Citizenship in the Seventeenth-Century Atlantic World." In: Goodfriend (ed.), *Revisiting New Netherland*, 93–128.

Manca, J., "Erasing the Dutch: The Critical Reception of Hudson Valley Dutch Architecture, 1670–1840." In: J. D. Goodfriend, B. Schmidt, and A. Stott (eds.), *Going Dutch: The Dutch Presence in America 1609–2009* (Leiden 2008), 59–84.

Marcus, J. R., *The Colonial American Jew, 1492–1776* (3 vols., Detroit 1970).

——, *The American Jew, 1585–1990* (Brooklyn 1995).

Martin, C., *Keepers of the Game: Indian-Animal Relationships and the Fur Trade* (Berkeley 1978, repr. 1982).

Martinez, J., "New Netherland Documentary Projects: City's Municipal Archives Conservation Work on Brooklyn's Early Records (1645–1821)." In: *dHM* 66 (1993), 15–16.

Matson, C., "'Damned Scoundrels' and 'Libertisme of Trade': Freedom and Regulation in Colonial New York's Fur and Grain Trades." In: *WMQ* 3rd. ser. 51 (1994), 389–418.

——, *Merchants and Empire: Trading in Colonial New York* (Baltimore 1998).

McCusker, J. J., *Money and Exchange in Europe and America, 1600–1775: A Handbook* (Chapel Hill 1978).

McKew Parr, Ch., *The Voyages of David de Vries, Navigator and Adventurer* (New York 1969).

McKinley, A. E., "English and Dutch Towns of New Netherland." In: *American Historical Review* 6 (1900), 1–18.

——, "The Transition from Dutch to English Rule in New York: A Study in Political Imitation." In: *American Historical Review* 6 (1901), 693–724.

McManus, E. J., *A History of Negro Slavery in New York* (Syracuse 1966).

Meeske, H. F., *The Hudson Valley Dutch and Their Houses* (Fleischmanns 1998).

Megapolensis, J., *Een kort ontwerp van de Mahakuase Indianen, haer landt, tale, statuere, dracht, godes-dienst ende magistrature. Aldus beschreven ende nu korte-lijck den 26. Augusti 1644 opgesonden uyt nieuwe Nederlant* (Alkmaar ca. 1644).

——, "Een kort ontwerp van de Mahakuase Indianen, in Nieuw-Nederlandt, haer landt, statuere, dracht, manieren en magistraten, beschreven in 't jaer 1644." In: J. Hartgers, *Beschrijvinghe van Virginia, Nieuw Nederlandt, Nieuw Enge-landt en d'Eylanden Bermudes, Berbados en S. Christtoffel* (Amsterdam 1651).

Meinig, D. W., *The Shaping of America: A Geographical Perspective on 500 Years of History. Vol. 1: Atlantic America, 1492–1800* (New Haven 1986).

Menkman, W. R., *De West-Indische Compagnie* (Patria. Vaderlandse cultuurge-schiedenis in monografieën 42) (Amsterdam 1947).

Merwick, D., *Possessing Albany, 1630–1710: The Dutch and English Experience* (Cambridge 1990).

——, *Death of a Notary: Conquest and Change in Colonial New York* (Ithaca 1999).

——, *The Shame and the Sorrow: Dutch Amerindian Encounters in New Nether-land* (Philadelphia 2006).

Meuwese, M. P., "'For the Peace and Well-Being of the Country': Intercultural Mediators and Dutch-Indian Relations in New Netherland and Dutch Brazil, 1600–1664" (Ph.D. dissertation, University of Notre Dame, 2003).

——, "Dutch Calvinism and Native Americans: A Comparative Study of the Moti-vations for Protestant Conversion among the Tupis in Northeastern Brazil (1630–1654) and the Mohawks in Central New York (1690–1710)." In: J. Muldoon (ed.), *The Spiritual Conversion of the Americas* (Gainesville, 2004), 118–141.

Middleton, S., "'How it Came that the Bakers Bake no Bread': A Struggle for Trade Privileges in Seventeenth-Century New Amsterdam." In: *WMQ* 3rd ser. 58 (2001), 347–372.

——, "Joris Dopzen's Hog and Other Stories: Artisans and the Making of New Amsterdam." In: Goodfriend (ed.), *Revisiting New Netherland,* 129–146.

——, *From Privileges to Rights: Work and Politics in Colonial New York City* (Philadelphia 2006).

Molen-Willebrands, M. E. van der, "De verstandige kock of sorghvuldige huy-shoudster: een burgerlijk of elitair 17e-eeuws kookboek?." In: *Holland, regio-naal-historisch tijdschrift* 28 (1996), 197–213.

Monté ver Loren, J. Ph. de, and J. E. Spruit, *Hoofdlijnen uit de ontwikkeling der rechterlijke organisatie in de Noordelijke Nederlanden tot de Bataafse omwen-teling* (6th ed., Deventer 1982).

Moorman van Kappen, O., *Tot behoef der arme wesen. Hoofdstukken uit de ge-schiedenis van het burgerweeshuis te Harderwijk* (Zutphen 1981).

——, "Iets over ons oud-vaderlandse stadsburgerschap." In: *Gens Nostra* 41 (1986), 180–192.

Muller, S. Fz., *Geschiedenis der Noordsche Compagnie* (Utrecht 1874).

Murphy, H. C., *Anthology of New Netherland or Translations from the Early Dutch Poets of New York with Memoirs of their Lives* (New York 1865, repr. Amsterdam 1966).

Nannings, J. H., *Brood- en gebakvormen en hunne betekenis in de folklore* (Schev-eningen 1932).

Narrett, D. E., *Inheritance and Family Life in Colonial New York City* (Ithaca, London 1992).

Nettels, C., *The Money Supply of the American Colonies before 1720* (Madison 1934).

Nicum, J., "The Beginnings of the Lutheran Church on Manhattan Island." In: *Papers of the American Society of Church History*, 2nd series 2 (1910), 85–101.

Niemeijer, H. E., *Calvinisme en koloniale stadscultuur, Batavia 1619–1725* (Amsterdam 1996).

Nissenson, S. G., *The Patroon's Domain* (New York 1937).

Noordam, D. J., *Leven in Maasland: een hoogontwikkelde plattelandssamenleving in de achttiende en het begin van de negentiende eeuw* (Hollandse Studiën 18) (Hilversum 1986).

——, *Riskante relaties. Vijf eeuwen homoseksualiteit in Nederland, 1233–1733* (Hilversum 1995).

——, "Demografische ontwikkelingen." In: S. Groenveld (ed.), *Leiden. De geschiedenis van een Hollandse stad. Deel 2 1574–1795* (Leiden 2003), 42–53.

Nooter, E., "Between Heaven and Earth: Church and Society in Pre-Revolutionary Flatbush, Long Island" (Ph.D. dissertation, Vrije Universiteit Amsterdam 1994).

Norton, Th. E., *The Fur Trade in Colonial New York, 1686–1776* (Madison 1974).

O'Callaghan, E. B. (ed.), *Documentary History of the State of New York* (4 vols., Albany 1849–1851).

——, *History of New Netherland, or New York under the Dutch* (2 vols., New York 1846–1848, 2nd ed. 1855).

——, and B. Fernow (trans. and ed.), *Documents Relative to the Colonial History of the State of New York* (15 vols., Albany 1856–1883).

——, *The Register of New Netherland 1624-1674* (Albany 1865).

—— (ed.), *Calendar of Historical Manuscripts in the Office of the Secretary of State, Albany, N.Y. Part I. Dutch Manuscripts, 1630–1664* (Albany 1865, repr. Ridgewood 1968).

——, *Voyages of the Slavers St. John and Arms of Amsterdam, 1659, 1663* (Albany 1867).

—— (trans.), *Laws and Ordinances of New Netherland, 1636–1674* (Albany 1868).

O'Callaghan, E. B. (trans.), K. Scott, and K. Stryker-Rodda (eds.), *The Register of Salomon Lachaire, Notary Public of New Amsterdam, 1661–1662. Translated from the Original Dutch Manuscript in the Office of the Clerk of the Common Council of New York* (New York Historical Manuscripts: Dutch) (Baltimore 1978).

——, *Minutes of the Orphanmasters of New Amsterdam, 1663–1668* (Baltimore 1976).

O'Connor, J. E., "The Rattle Watch of New Amsterdam." In: *dHM* 43–1 (1968), 11–12, 14; 43–2 (1968), 9–12; 43–3 (1968) 13–14.

Olthuis, H. J., *De doopspraktijk der gereformeerde kerken in Nederland, 1568–1816* (Utrecht 1908).

Oppenheim, S. *The Early History of the Jews in New York, 1654–1664. Some New Matter on the Subject* (New York 1909).

Otto, P., "The Origins of New Netherland. Interpreting Native American Responses to Henry Hudson's Visit." In: *Itinerario: European Journal of Overseas History* 18 (1994), 22–39.

——, "Common Practices and Mutual Misunderstandings: Henry Hudson, Native Americans, and the Birth of New Netherland." In: *dHM* 72 (1999), 75–83.

——, *The Dutch-Munsee Encounter in America: The Struggle for Sovereignty in the Hudson Valley* (New York 2006).

Pagan, J. R., "Dutch Maritime and Commercial Activity in Mid-Seventeenth Century Virginia." In: *The Virginia Magazine of History and Biography* 90 (1982), 485–501.

Pagden, A., *European Encounters with the New World: From Renaissance to Romanticism* (New Haven and London 1993, 2nd ed. 1994).

Paltsits, V. H. (ed.), *Minutes of the Executive Council of the Province of New York. Administration of Francis Lovelace 1668–1673* (2 vols., Albany 1910).

Pearson, J., and A. J. F. van Laer (trans. and ed.), *Early Records of the City and County of Albany and Colony of Rensselaerswijck* (4 vols., Albany 1869–1919).

Peters, J., "Volunteers for the Wilderness: The Walloon Petitioners of 1621 and the Voyage of the Nieuw Nederlandt to the Hudson River in 1624." In: *Proceedings of the Huguenot Society of London* 24 (1987), 421–433.

Phelps Stokes, I. N., *The Iconography of Manhattan Island, 1498–1909* (6 vols., New York 1915–1928).

Piwonka, R., "The Lutheran Presence in New Netherland." In: *dHM* 60–1 (1987), 1–5.

——, "New York Colonial Inventories: Dutch Interiors as a Measure of Cultural Change." In: Blackburn and Kelley (eds.), *New World Dutch Studies*, 63–81.

Plockhoy, P. C., *Kort en klaer ontwerp, dienende tot een onderling accoort, om den arbeyd, onrust en moeyelyckheyt van alderley handwerckluyden te verlichten door een onderlinge Compagnie ofte Volckplanting aan de Zuyt-revier in Nieuw-Nederland op te rechten* (Amsterdam 1662).

Plomp, N., "Nieuw-Nederlanders en hun Europese achtergrond. De stand van zaken in het genealogisch onderzoek." In: *Jb CBG* 50 (1996), 131–160.

Pol, L. van de, *Het Amsterdams hoerdom. Prostitutie in de zeventiende en achttiende eeuw* (Amsterdam 1996).

Pole, J. R., *The Gift of Government: Political Responsibility from the English Restoration to American Independence* (The Richard B. Russell Lectures 1) (Athens 1983).

Postma, J., and V. Enthoven (eds.), *Riches from Atlantic Commerce: Dutch Trans-atlantic Trade and Shipping, 1585–1817* (Leiden, Boston 2003).

Potter, J., "Demographic Development and Family Structure." In: J. P. Greene and J. R. Pole (eds.), *Colonial British America: Essays in the New History of the Early Modern Era* (Baltimore, London 1984), 123–156.

"Powers of Attorney, Acknowledgments, Indentures of Apprentices, Inventories, etc." In: *Yearbook of the Holland Society of New York* (1900), 169–182.

Prud'homme van Reine, R., *Rechterhand van Nederland. Biografie van Michiel Adriaenszoon de Ruyter* (Open Domein 32) (Amsterdam 1996).

Puype, J. P., *Dutch and Other Flintlocks from Seventeenth Century Iroquois Sites. Proceedings of the 1984 Trade Gun Conference* (Rochester 1985).

Quack, H. P. G., "Plockhoy's sociale plannen." In: *Verslagen en mededelingen der Koninklijke Akademie van Wetenschappen, afdeeling letterkunde* 3rd reeks, 9 (1893), 81–127.

Rau, H., "Govert Loockermans, een Turnhoutenaar in Amsterdam, Nieuw-Amsterdam en New York (1617–1671)." In: *Taxandria*, NR 62 (1990), 5–12.

"Records of the Reformed Dutch Church in the City of New York. Marriages."
In: *NYGBR* 6 (1875) 32–39 [1639–1652]; 81–88 [1652–1659]; 141–148
[1659–1667]; 184–191 [1668–1675]; 7 (1876), 27–34 [1675–1681]; 77–84
[1681–1685]; 8 (1877), 33–40 [1685–1688]; 10 (1879), 119–126 [1688–
1692]; 11 (1880), 75–82 [1692–1695]; 125–132 [1695–1698]; 172–179
[1698–1702].

Resolutiën der Staten-Generaal. Nieuwe reeks, 1610–1670 (Rijks Geschiedkundige
Publicatiën, grote serie) (7 vols., 's-Gravenhage 1971–1994).

Reynolds, H. W., *Dutch Houses in the Hudson Valley before 1776* (New York
1929, repr. 1965).

Rhoads, W. B., "Franklin D. Roosevelt and Dutch Colonial Architecture." In: *NYH*
59 (1978), 430–464.

Rich, E. E., "Russia and the Colonial Fur Trade." In: *The Economic History Review,*
2nd ser. 7 (1955), 307–328.

Richter, D. K., *The Ordeal of the Longhouse: The Peoples of the Iroquois League
in the Era of European Colonization* (Williamsburg 1992).

Rieu, G. du, *Album studiosorum Academiae Lugduno Batavae MDLXXV–
MDCCCLXXV: accedunt nomina curatorum et professorum per eadem secula*
('s-Gravenhage 1875).

Rijpperda Wierdsma, J. V., *Politie en justitie. Een studie over Hollandschen staats-
bouw tijdens de Republiek* (Zwolle 1937).

Riker, J., *Revised History of Harlem (City of New York). Its Origin and Early An-
nals* (New York 1904).

Rink, O. A., "Company Management and Private Trade: The Two Patroonship
Plans for New Netherland." In: *NYH* 59 (1978), 5–26.

——, "The People of New Netherland: Notes on Non-English Immigration to New
York in the Seventeenth Century." In: *NYH* 62 (1981), 5–42.

——, *Holland on the Hudson: An Economic and Social History of Dutch New
York* (Ithaca, London, Cooperstown 1986).

——, "Private Interest and Godly Gain: The West India Company and the Dutch Reformed Church in New Netherland, 1624–1664." In: *NYH* 75 (1994), 245–264.

——, "Before the English (1609–1664)." In: M. M. Klein (ed.), *The Empire State.
A History of New York* (Ithaca, London, Cooperstown 2001), 1–109.

Ritchie, R. C., *The Duke's Province: A Study of New York Politics and Society,
1664–1691* (Chapel Hill 1977).

Roeber, A. G., "'The Origin of Whatever is not English Among Us': The Dutch-
Speaking and German-Speaking Peoples of Colonial British America." In:
B. Bailyn and Ph. D. Morgan (eds.), *Strangers within the Realm: Cultural Margins
of the First British Empire* (Chapel Hill, London 1991).

Roessingh, H. K., *Inlandse tabak. Expansie en contractie van een handelsgewas in
de 17e en 18e eeuw in Nederland* (Wageningen 1976).

Roever, M. de, "The Fort Orange 'EB' Pipe Bowls: an Investigation of the Origin
of American Objects in Dutch Seventeenth-Century Documents." In: Blackburn
and Kelley (eds.), *New World Dutch Studies,* 51–61.

——, "Koopmanschappen voor Nieuw-Nederland. Een blik op de Nederlandse
handelsartikelen voor de inheemse bevolking van Amerika." In: Van Dongen
(ed.), *One Man's Trash,* 71–93.

Rooden, P. van, "Dissenters en bededagen. Civil religion ten tijde van de Republiek." In: *BMGN* 107 (1992), 703–712.

Roodenburg, H., *Onder censuur. De kerkelijke tucht in de gereformeerde gemeente van Amsterdam, 1578–1700* (Hilversum 1990).

——, "De notaris en de erehandel. Beledigingen voor het Amsterdamse notariaat, 1700–1710." In: A. Keunen and H. Roodenburg (eds.), *Schimpen en schelden. Eer en belediging in Nederland, ca. 1600–ca. 1850. Volkskundig Bulletin* 18 (1992), 367–388.

——, "Naar een etnografie van de vroegmoderne stad: de 'gebuyrten' in Leiden en Den Haag." In: P. te Boekhorst, P. Burke, and W. Frijhoff (eds.), *Cultuur en maatschappij in Nederland 1500–1850. Een historisch-antropologisch perspectief* (Heerlen 1992), 219–244.

——, "Eer en oneer ten tijde van de Republiek: een tussenbalans." In: *Volkskundig Bulletin* 22 (1996), 129–147.

Rooijakkers, G., *Rituele repertoires. Volkscultuur in oostelijk Noord-Brabant 1559–1853* (Nijmegen 1994).

Rooseboom, G., *Recueil van verscheyde keuren, en costumen: midtsgaders maniere van procederen binnen de stadt Amsterdam* (2nd ed., Amsterdam 1656).

Rose, P. G., *The Sensible Cook: Dutch Foodways in the Old and New World* (Syracuse 1989).

——, "Proeve van verandering. Nederlandse voedingsgewoonten in de Nieuwe Wereld." In: Van Dongen (ed.), *One Man's Trash,* 203–213.

Rosenwaike, I., *Population History of New York City* (Syracuse 1972).

Rothschild, N. A., "De sociale afstand tussen Nederlandse kolonisten en inheemse Amerikanen." In: Van Dongen (ed.), *One Man's Trash,* 189–201.

——, *Colonial Encounters in a Native American Landscape* (Washington 2003).

Royen, P. C. van, *Zeevarenden op de koopvaardijvloot. Omstreeks 1700* (Hollandse Historische Reeks 8) (Amsterdam, 's-Gravenhage 1987).

Sainsbury, W. N. (ed.), *Calendar of State Papers, Colonial Series, 1574–1660, Preserved in the State Paper Department of Her Majesty's Public Record Office* (London 1860).

Sanders, E., "Neuken." In: *NRC Handelsblad,* 24 June, 1 and 8 July 2002.

Saxby, T. J., *The Quest for the New Jerusalem: Jean de Labadie and the Labadists, 1610–1744* (Dordrecht 1987).

Schalkwijk, F. L., *The Reformed Church in Dutch Brazil (1630–1654)* (Zoetermeer 1998).

Schama, S., *The Embarrassment of Riches: An Interpretation of Dutch Culture in the Golden Age* (London 1987).

"Schepens' Register." In: *Yearbook of the Holland Society of New York* (1900), 158–169.

Schepper, H. de, and M. Vrolijk, "Vrede en orde door gratie. In Holland en Zeeland onder Habsburgers en de Republiek, 1500–1650." In: M. Bruggeman et al. (eds.), *Mensen van de Nieuwe Tijd. Een liber amicorum voor A. Th. van Deursen* (Amsterdam 1996), 98–117.

Schiltkamp, J. A., *De geschiedenis van het notariaat in het octrooigebied van de West-Indische Compagnie (voor Suriname en de Nederlandse Antillen tot het jaar 1964)* ('s-Gravenhage 1964).

——, "On Common Ground: Legislation, Government, Jurisprudence, and Law in the Dutch West Indian Colonies: The Order of Government of 1629." In: *dHM* 70 (1997), 73–80.

Schimmel, J. A., *Burgerrecht te Nijmegen 1592–1810* (Tilburg 1966).

Schmidt, B., *Innocence Abroad: The Dutch Imagination and the New World, 1570–1670* (Cambridge 2001).

Schnurmann, C., *Atlantische Welten. Engländer und Niederländer im amerikanisch-atlantischen Raum 1648–1713* (Köln 1998).

Schöffer, I., "La stratification sociale de la Républicque des Provinces Unies au XVIIe siècle." In: R. Mousnier (ed.), *Problèmes de stratification sociale. Actes du Colloque International (1966)* (Paris, 1968) 121–135.

Scholten, C., *The Coins of the Dutch Overseas Territories, 1601–1948* (Amsterdam 1953).

Schoonmaker, M., *The History of Kingston, New York* (New York 1888).

Schulte Nordholt, J. W., "Nederlanders in Nieuw-Nederland. De oorlog van Kieft met als bijlage het Journael van Nieu-Nederland." In: *BMHG* 80 (1966), 38–94.

Schutte, G. J., "Bij het schemerlicht van hun tijd. Zeventiende-eeuwse gereformeerden en de slavenhandel." In: M. Bruggeman et al. (eds.), *Mensen van de Nieuwe Tijd. Een liber amicorum voor A. Th. van Deursen* (Amsterdam 1996), 193–217.

Scott, K. (trans. and ed.), "Voyages between New Amsterdam and Holland." In: *dHM* 42–4 (1968), 7–8, 10, 15.

—— (trans. and ed.), *Diary of Our Second Trip from Holland to New Netherland, 1683. Dagh teijkeningh van onse tweede reijse uijt Hollant na Nieuw Nederlant, 1683. By Jasper Danckaerts of Wiewerd in Friesland* (Upper Saddle River 1969).

——"Orphan Children Sent to New Netherland." In: *dHM* 49–1 (1974), 5–6.

Seguy, J., *Utopie coopérative et oecuménisme. Pieter Cornelisz Plockhoy van Zurik-Zee, 1620–1700* (Paris 1968).

Shattuck, M. D., "A Civil Society: Court and Community in Beverwijck, New Netherland, 1652–1664" (Ph.D. dissertation, Boston University 1993).

——, "Women and the Economy in Beverwijck, New Netherland." In: *The Dutch Settlers Society of Albany Yearbook* 51 (1989–1993), 21–27.

——, "Heemstede: an English Town under Dutch Rule." In: N. A. Naylor (ed.), *The Roots and Heritage of Hempstead Town* (Interlaken, N.Y. 1994), 28–44.

——, "Women and Trade in New Netherland." In: *Itinerario: European Journal of Overseas History* 18 (1994), 2: 40–49.

Shomette, D. G., and R. D. Haslach, *Raid on America: The Dutch Naval Campaign of 1672–1674* (Columbia 1988).

Sicking, L., and R. Fagel, "In het kielzog van Columbus. De heer van Veere en de Nieuwe Wereld, 1517–1527." In: *BMGN* 114 (1999), 313–327.

Simmons, R. C., *The American Colonies: From Settlement to Independence* (London 1976).

Singleton, E., *Dutch New York* (New York 1909).

Smith, A. E., *Colonists in Bondage: White Servitude and Convict Labor in America, 1607–1776* (Chapel Hill 1947).

Smith, G. L., "Guilders and Godliness: the Dutch Colonial Contribution to American Religious Pluralism." In: *Journal of Presbyterian History* 47 (1969), 1–30.

——, *Religion and Trade in New Netherland: Dutch Origins and American Development* (Ithaca, London 1973).

Snow, D. R., *The Iroquois* (Cambridge, Mass., Oxford 1994, repr. 1996).

Snow, D. R., Ch. T. Gehring, and W. A. Starna (eds.), *In Mohawk Country: Early Narratives about a Native People* (Syracuse 1996).

Solecki, R. S., "The 'Tiger,' an Early Dutch 17th Century Ship, and an Abortive Salvage Attempt." In: *Journal of Field Archeology* 1 (1974), 109–116.

Spaans, J. W., *Haarlem na de Reformatie. Stedelijke cultuur en kerkelijk leven, 1577–1620* (Hollandse historische reeks 11) ('s-Gravenhage 1989).

Spierenburg, P. C., *The Spectacle of Suffering: Executions and Evolution of Repression: From a Preindustrial Metropolis to the European Experience* (Cambridge 1984).

——, "Homoseksualiteit in preïndustrieel Nederland. Twintig jaar onderzoek." In: *TvG* 109 (1996), 485–493.

Spijkerman, H., "The Amsterdam Municipal Archives as a Source for the History of the United States of America." In: *American Archivist* 52 (1989), 88–93.

Stabile, T. "The Quintessential City: New York City on Film." On: www.neh.gov/news/humanities/1999–09/new_york.html (accessed 31 October 2006).

Starna, W. A., "Assessing American Indian-Dutch Studies: Missed and Missing Opportunities." In: *NYH* 84 (2003), 5–31.

——, and J. A. Brandão, "From the Mohawk-Mahican War to the Beaver War: Questioning the Pattern." In: *Ethnohistory* 51, 4 (2004), 725–740.

Stayton, K. L., *Dutch by Design: Tradition and Change in Two Historic Brooklyn Houses: The Schenck Houses at the Brooklyn Museum* (New York 1990).

Steendam, J., *Den distelvinck* enz. (3 vols., Amsterdam 1649–1650).

——, *Zeede-sangen voor de Batavische jonkheyt: behelsende verscheyden bedenkelijke, en stichtelijke stoffen: op bekende, en vermakelijke sang-toonen gepast door Jacob Steendam* (Batavia 1671).

Streng, J. C., *"Stemme in staat." De bestuurlijke elite in de stadsrepubliek Zwolle, 1579–1795* (Hilversum 1997).

Stronks, G. J., "Het kerkvolk op de zondagen. De gereformeerde kerk en de sabbatsontheiliging, ca. 1580–1800." In: *Munire ecclesiam. Opstellen over de "gewone gelovigen" aangeboden aan Prof. dr. W. A. J. Munier ss. cc. bij zijn zeventigste verjaardag* (Maastricht 1990), 139–152.

Strubbe, E. I., and L. Voet, *De chronologie van de middeleeuwen en de moderne tijden in de Nederlanden* (Brussels 1960).

Stryker-Rodda, K., "New Netherland Naming Systems and Customs." In: *NYGBR* 126 (1995), 35–45.

Stuiveling, G., et al. (eds.), *De werken van Gerbrand Adriaensz. Brederode. G. A. Bredero's Boertigh, amoreus, en aendachtigh groot lied-boeck* (3 vols., Leiden 1983).

Sullivan, D., *The Punishment of Crime in Colonial New York: The Dutch Experience in Albany During the Seventeenth Century* (New York 1997).

Swetschinski, D. M., "The Portuguese Jewish Merchants of Seventeenth-Century Amsterdam: A Social Profile" (Ph.D. dissertation, Brandeis University 1979).

Swierenga, R. P., *The Forerunners: Dutch Jewry in the North American Diaspora* (Detroit 1994).

Talman, W. B., "Death Customs among the Colonial Dutch." In: *dHM* 42–4 (1968), 9–10; 43–1 (1968), 13–14.

Taylor, A., *American Colonies: The Settling of North America* (New York, London 2001, repr. 2002).

Tebbenhoff, E. H., "Tacit Rules and Hidden Family Structures: Naming Practices and Godparentage in Schenectady, New York 1680–1800." In: *Journal of Social History* 18 (1985), 567–585.

Teensma, B. N. "Resentment in Recife: Jews and Public Opinion in 17th-century Brazil." In: J. Lechner (ed.), *Essays on Cultural Identity in Colonial Latin-America* (Leiden 1988), 63–78.

Thomas, K., *Man and the Natural World: Changing Attitudes in England, 1500– 1800* (London 1983, repr. Oxford 1996).

Thuys, J., *Ars notariatus, dat is: konste en stijl van notarischap* (Amsterdam 1628).

Thwaites, R. G. (ed.), *Travels and Explorations of the Jesuit Missionaries in New France, 1610–1791. The Original French, Latin and Italian texts, with English Translation and Notes* (73 vols., Cleveland 1896–1901).

Trap, H. J., "Een reis die niet doorging." In: *Leids Jaarboekje* 90 (1998), 54–57.

Trelease, A. W., *Indian Affairs in Colonial New York: The Seventeenth Century* (Ithaca 1960).

Trigger, B. G., "The Mohawk-Mahican War (1624–28): The Establishment of a Pattern." In: *Canadian Historical Review* 52 (1971), 276–286.

——, *Handbook of North American Indians*, vol. 15 (Northeast) (Washington 1978).

Trompetter, C., "De migratie van Twente naar Amsterdam in de zeventiende en achttiende eeuw. Ontwikkeling en lokale verschillen." In: *Tijdschrift voor Sociale geschiedenis* 21 (1995), 145–165.

Troostenburg de Bruyn, C. A. L. van, *De hervormde kerk in Nederlandsch Oost-Indië onder de Oost-Indische Compagnie (1602–1795)* (Arnhem 1884).

Turner, F. J., "The Significance of the Frontier in American History." In: G. T. Taylor (ed.), *The Turner Thesis: Concerning the Role of the Frontier in American History* (Lexington 1972), 3–27.

Valck Lucassen, Th. R., "Familieaantekeningen Ebbinck en Gerbade." In: *De Nederlandsche Leeuw* 36 (1918), 221–225.

Van Ruymbeke, Bertrand, "The Walloon and Huguenot Elements in New Netherland and Seventeenth-Century New York: Identity, History, and Memory." In: Goodfriend (ed.), *Revisiting New Netherland*, 41–56.

Venema, J., "Poverty in Seventeenth-Century Albany." In: *dHM* 64–1 (1991), 1–8.

——, *Kinderen van weelde en armoede. Armoede en liefdadigheid in Beverwijck/ Albany* (Zeven Provinciën Reeks 6) (Hilversum 1993).

—— (trans. and ed.), *Deacons' Accounts, 1652–1674. Dutch Reformed Church, Beverwijck/Albany, New York* (The Historical Series of the Reformed Church in America 28) (Rockport 1998).

——, "The Court Case of Brant Aertsz van Slichtenhorst against Jan van Rensselaer." In: *dHM* 74 (2001), 3–8.

——, "7 September 1652: A Letter by Jan Baptist van Rensselaer." In: *dHM* 75 (2002), 9–13.

——, *Beverwijck: A Dutch Village on the American Frontier, 1652–1664* (Hilversum 2003).

——, "Two More Unpublished Letters by Jan Baptist van Rensselaer: 1652, 1655." In: *dHM* 79-4 (2006), 69–74.

Verbeeck, L., "Van partner tot horige: de relatie tussen Indianen en Nederlanders in Nieuw Nederland, 1609–1673." In: P. Mason (ed.), *Indianen en Nederlanders, 1492–1992* (Leiden 1992), 103–128.

Verhoog, P., and L. Koelmans (eds.), *De reis van Michiel Adriaanszoon de Ruyter in 1664–1665* (Werken Linschoten-Vereeniging 62) ('s-Gravenhage 1961).

Verney, J., O'*Callaghan: The Making and Unmaking of a Rebel* (Ottowa 1994).

Versteeg, D. (trans.), P. R. Christoph, K. Scott, and K. Stryker-Rodda (eds.), *Kingston Papers, 1661–1675* (New York Historical Manuscripts: Dutch) (2 vols., Baltimore 1976).

Visser, H. B., *Geschiedenis van den sabbatstrijd onder de gereformeerden in de zeventiende eeuw* (Utrecht 1939).

Volk, J. G., "The Dutch Kast and the American Kas: A Structural/Historical Analysis." In: Blackburn and Kelley (eds.), *New World Dutch Studies,* 107–117.

Voorhees, D. W., *The Holland Society: A Centennial History 1885–1985* (New York 1985).

——, "Leisler's Pre-1689 Biography and Family Background." In: *dHM* 62-4 (1989), 1–7.

——, "The 'Fervent Zeale' of Jacob Leisler." In: *WMQ* 3d ser. 51 (1994), 447–472.

——, "Tying the Loose Ends Together: Putting New Netherland Studies on a Par with the Study of Other Regions." In: Goodfriend (ed.), *Revisiting New Netherland,* 309–328.

——, "The 1657 Flushing Remonstrance in Historical Perspective." In: *dHM* 81-1 (2008), 11–14.

Vries, D. P. de, *Korte Historiael ende Journaels Aenteykeninge van verscheyden voyagiens in de vier delen des werelts-ronde, als Europa, Africa, Asia ende America gedaen* (H. T. Colenbrander ed.) (Werken Linschoten-Vereeniging 3) ('s-Gravenhage 1911).

Vries, J. de, and A. van der Woude, *Nederland 1500–1815. De eerste ronde van moderne economische groei* (Amsterdam 1995).

Vries, K. de., "Het middeleeuwse burgerschap: condities en consequenties." In: *TvG* 74 (1961), 220–225.

Vries, W. de, "De Van Rensselaer's in Nederland." In: *De Nederlandsche Leeuw* 66 (1949), 150–172, 194–211.

Waard, C. de (ed.), *De Zeeuwsche expeditie naar de West onder Cornelis Evertsen den Jonge 1672–1674. Nieuw Nederland een jaar onder Nederlandsch bestuur* (Werken Linschoten-Vereeniging 30) ('s-Gravenhage 1928).

Wabeke, B. H., *Dutch Emigration to North America, 1624–1860* (New York 1944).

Wagenaar, F. P., "'Dat de regeringe niet en bestaet bij het corpus van de magistraet van Den Hage alleen.' De Societeit van 's-Gravenhage (1587–1802). Een onderzoek naar bureaucratisering" (Ph.D. Dissertation, Rijksuniversiteit Leiden 1997).

Wagenaar, L. J., *Galle. VOC-vestiging in Ceylon. Beschrijving van een koloniale samenleving aan de vooravond van de Singalese opstand tegen het Nederlandse gezag, 1760* (Amsterdam, 1994).

Wagman, M., "The Rise of Pieter Claessen Wyckoff: Social Mobility on the Colonial Frontier." In: *NYH* 52 (1972), 5–24.

——, "Corporate Slavery in New Netherland." In: *Journal of Negro History* 65 (1980), 34–42.

——, "Liberty in New Amsterdam: A Sailor's Life in Early New York." In: *NYH* 64 (1983), 101–119.

Wall, E. G. E. van der, "Prophecy and Profit: Nicolaes van Rensselaer, Charles II and the Conversion of the Jews." In: C. Augustijn et al. (eds.), *Kerkhistorische opstellen aangeboden aan (Essays on Church History Presented to) Prof. dr. J. van den Berg* (Kampen 1987), 75–87.

Wassenaer, N. van, *Historisch verhael alder gedenck-weerdigste geschiedenissen die van den beginne des jaeres 1621 ... tot 1632 voorgevallen sijn* (21 vols., Amsterdam 1622–1635).

Weerdt, G. A. de, "A Preliminary Assessment and Identification of the Shipwreck Remains Uncovered in 1916 at the World Trade Center Site in New York City." In: *Northeast Historical Archaeology* 34 (2005), 89–94.

Weslager, C. A., *Dutch Explorers, Traders, and Settlers in the Delaware Valley, 1609–1664* (Philadelphia 1961).

——, "Who Survived the Indian Massacre at Swanendael?" In: *dHM* 40-3 (1965), 9–10, 15–16.

——, "Did Minuit Buy Manhattan Island from the Indians?" In: *dHM* 43-3 (1968), 5–6.

——, *A Man and His Ship: Pieter Minuit and the Kalmar Nyckel* (Wilmington, Del. 1990).

Westra, F., "Lost and Found: Crijn Fredericx—A New York Founder." In: *dHM* 71 (1998), 7–16.

White, Ph. L., "Municipal Government Comes to Manhattan." In: *New-York Historical Society Quarterly* 37 (1953), 146–157.

Wieder, F. C., *De stichting van New York in juli 1625. Reconstructies en nieuwe gegevens ontleend aan de Van Rappard-documenten* (Werken Linschoten-Vereeniging 26) ('s-Gravenhage 1925).

Wijmer, D. J., J. Folkerts, and P. R. Christoph, *Through a Dutch Door: 17th-Century Origins of the Van Voorhees Family* (Baltimore 1992).

Wijnman, H. F., "Lieven van Coppenol, schoolmeester-calligraaf." In: *Jaarboek van het Genootschap Amstelodamum* 30 (1933), 93–188.

Wijsenbeek-Olthuis, Th., *Achter de gevels van Delft. Bezit en bestaan van rijk en arm in een periode van achteruitgang (1700–1800)* (Hilversum 1987).

Wilcoxen, Ch., "Arent van Curler's Children." In: *NYGBR* 110 (1979), 82–84.

——, *Seventeenth-Century Albany: A Dutch Profile* (Albany 1981).

——, "Household Artifacts of New Netherland, from its Archaeological and Documentary Records." In: Bakker et al. (eds.), *New Netherland Studies,* 120–129.

——, *Dutch Trade and Ceramics in America in the Seventeenth Century* (Albany 1987).

——, "New Netherland Ceramics: Evidence from Excavations of Fort Orange, 1624–1676." In: Blackburn and Kelley (eds.), *New World Dutch Studies,* 37–42.

——, "Dutch Trade with New England." In: Zeller, *A Beautiful and Fruitful Place,* 235–241.

Williams, J. H., "Great Doggs and Mischievous Cattle: Domesticated Animals and Indian-European Relations in New Netherland and New York." In: *NYH* 76 (1995), 244–264.

——, "An Atlantic Perspective on the Jewish Struggle for Rights and Opportunities in Brazil, New Netherland, and New York." In: P. Bernardini and N. Fiering
(eds.), *The Jews and the Expansion of Europe to the West* (2 vols., New York,
Oxford 2001), 2: 369–393.

Winter, P. J. van, *De Westindische Compagnie ter kamer en Stad en Lande* (Werken
uitgegeven door de Vereeniging Het Nederlandsch Economisch-Historisch
Archief 15) ('s-Gravenhage 1978).

Wiznitzer, A., *Jews in Colonial Brazil* (New York 1960).

Woordenboek der Nederlandsche taal (43 vols., 's-Gravenhage 1882–1998).

Wouters, A. Ph. F., and P. H. A. M. Abels, *Nieuw en ongezien. Kerk en samenleving in de classis Delft en Delfland 1572–1621* (Werken van de Vereniging voor
Nederlandse Kerkgeschiedenis 1 and 2) (2 vols., Delft 1994).

Wright, L. G., "Local Government and Central Authority in New Netherland." In:
New-York Historical Society Quarterly 42 (1973), 7–29.

——, "Local Government in Colonial New York, 1640–1710" (Ph.D. dissertation,
Cornell University 1974).

Yntema, R., "A Capital Industry: Brewing in Holland, 1500–1800." In:
R. E. Kistemaker and V. T. van Vilsteren (eds.), *Beer! The Story of Holland's
Favourite Drink* (n.p. 1994), 72–81.

——, "Beer in Abundance: Distribution and Consumption in Early Modern Holland." In: R. E. Kistemaker and V. T. van Vilsteren (eds.), *Beer! The Story of
Holland's Favourite Drink* (n.p. 1994), 82–95.

——, "The Welfare of the Brewers: Guilds and Confraternities in the Brewing
Industry." In: R. E. Kistemaker and V. T. van Vilsteren (eds.), *Beer! The Story of
Holland's Favourite Drink* (n.p. 1994), 118–131.

Zabriskie, G. O., and A. P. Kenney, "The Founding of New Amsterdam: Fact and
Fiction." In: *dHM* 50-4 (1976), 5–6, 15–16; 51-1 (1976), 5–6, 13–14; 51-2
(1976), 5–6, 13–14; 51-3 (1976), 11–14; 51-4 (1977), 11–12, 15–16.

Zandt, C. Van, "The Dutch Connection: Isaac Allerton and the Dynamics of English Cultural Anxiety in the Gouden Eeuw." In: R. Hoefte and J. C. Kardux
(eds.), *Connecting Cultures: The Netherlands in Five Centuries of Transatlantic
Exchange* (Amsterdam 1994), 51–76.

Zandvliet, C. J., "Een ouderwetse kaart van Nieuw Nederland door Cornelis
Doetsz. en Willem Jansz. Blaeu." In: *Caert-Thresoor* 1 (1982), 57–60.

——, *Mapping for Money: Maps, Plans, and Topographic Paintings and their Role
in Dutch Overseas Expansion during the 16th and 17th Centuries* (Amsterdam
1998).

Zantkuyl, H. J., "Reconstructie van enkele Nederlandse huizen in Nieuw-
Nederland uit de zeventiende eeuw." In: Bakker et al. (eds.), *New Netherland
Studies*, 166–179.

——, "Hollandse huizen, gebouwd in de 17de eeuw in Amerika." In: *Amsterdamse
Monumenten* (1987), 47–76.

——, "The Netherlands Town House: How and Why it Works." In: Blackburn and
Kelley (eds.), *New World Dutch Studies*, 143–160.

Zeller, N. A. McClure (ed.), *A Beautiful and Fruitful Place. Selected Rensselaerswijck Seminar Papers* (n.p. 1991),

Zwierlein, F. J., *Religion in New Netherland: A History of the Development of the
Religious Conditions in the Province of New Netherland, 1623–1664* (Rochester
1910).

——, "New Netherland Intolerance." In: *The Catholic Historical Review* 4 (1918), 186–216.

Zwieten, A. E. van, "The Orphan Chamber of New Amsterdam." In: *WMQ* 3rd ser. 53 (1996), 319–340.

——, "'[O]n Her Woman's Troth': Tolerance, Custom, and the Women of New Netherland." In: *dHM* 72 (1999), 3–14.

——, "'A Little Land…To Sow Some Seeds': Real Property, Custom, and Law in the Community of New Amsterdam" (Ph.D. dissertation, Temple University, 2001).

Index

www.ingramcontent.com/pod-product-compliance
Ingram Content Group UK Ltd.
Pitfield, Milton Keynes, MK11 3LW, UK
UKHW041009050325
455862UK00004B/247